J. Munsensmith.
LEEDs.
Dec 1969.

' Review Copy from
Church Quarterly '

THE SOCIOLOGY OF RELIGION

INTERNATIONAL LIBRARY OF SOCIOLOGY

AND SOCIAL RECONSTRUCTION

Founded by Karl Mannheim

Editor W. J. H. Sprott

A catalogue of books available in the INTERNATIONAL LIBRARY OF SOCIOLOGY AND SOCIAL RECONSTRUCTION and new books in preparation for the Library will be found at the end of this volume

The Sociology of Religion

A study of Christendom

WERNER STARK

Professor of Sociology Fordham University

VOLUME FOUR

Types of Religious Man

London

ROUTLEDGE AND KEGAN PAUL

First published 1969
by Routledge and Kegan Paul Ltd
Broadway House, 68–74 Carter Lane
London, E.C.4
Printed in Great Britain by
Cox and Wyman Ltd
London, Fakenham and Reading
SBN 7100 6640 6

THE MICROSOCIOLOGY OF RELIGION

In two volumes

I. TYPES OF RELIGIOUS MAN

II. TYPES OF RELIGIOUS CULTURE

Contents

Preface

The first three volumes of the present work were concerned with the external relationships of religious communities, i.e. their relationships to the inclusive societies which surround and contain them. With this fourth volume, our investigation enters a new field, and we have formally marked the fact that we are crossing a borderline by prefixing to our text a new and appropriate motto. It indicates the problem area with which we shall have to deal now: it is the *inner* life of religious communities, or, speaking more professionally, the specific roles which in their interplay constitute these communities and provide the forms within which their vital processes can unfold, continue and develop towards greater maturity.

It is one of the disadvantages of a work like the present which comprises several volumes and appears over a number of years that the reader has sometimes to wait a while for the discussion of a topic which particularly interests him. A review of our first volume, for instance, complained bitterly that (besides a host of other subjects) 'the authority structure within religious institutions' was an issue 'scarcely raised'. It was not, in fact, 'scarcely raised', it was not raised at all; nor should it have been. To a systematic scholar, there is a proper place and time for everything. The authority structure (to retain an ugly term) in and of those religious organizations which we normally describe as churches belongs to their constituent internal, not to their limiting external, realities. It should not have been touched before; it is thoroughly investigated here.

Even this volume will not yet present all the considerations which are usually thought to belong to the specialty known as the sociology of religion. If the reviewer whom we have just mentioned found it 'odd' that there was 'no discussion of the secularization of the universal church' in volume III, he will miss it also in volume IV; but he will get it in volume V, right at the end of our analysis, and there it will be where it ought to be, for logic demands that we should first speak of the rise, and of the emergent characteristics, of the social embodiments of the Christian religion before we discuss the difficulties which relatively recent developments have created for them.

In the preface to volume I, I expressed the conviction that my text would arouse a good deal of hostile criticism due to divergencies of religious opinion, and this expectation was to some extent borne out by subsequent reactions. Yet only to some extent. The welcome which my books received in such publications as the Anglican journal, *Theology*, the *Baptist Times* and the *Methodist Recorder*, not to speak of others, is reassuring proof of the fact that fruitful and irenic discussions are possible among men of good will, whatever their personal backgrounds and commitments. So far as the present volume is concerned, religious prejudice is in all probability going to be less in evidence than before, for we have found the truly dominant churches to be comparable, if not similar, in structure; all the more likely is it that anti-religious prejudice will raise its head. Both classical protagonists of the sociology of religion, Emile Durkheim and Max Weber, were confirmed unbelievers, and Weber in particular has started a tradition which – highly successful because of its compatibility with deep-seated intellectualist conceptions and convictions – has led to a rather negative assessment of the whole phenomenon of religiosity. The sacraments, for instance, are to Weber merely evidence for the survival of magical ideas and practices, bits of savagery left over in our civilized world. It is hardly possible that such a hostile attitude should lead to a due appreciation of the life of faith, personal or collective; it is almost unavoidable that it should lead to its undue depreciation. When, not so long ago, a certain university discussed the establishment of a department of social anthropology, an old professor was heard to mutter: 'Why do they study those nasty customs? Why don't they simply wait until they die out?' That man would assuredly not have made a good social anthropologist. If my respectful attitude to the phenomena of religion should draw fire from certain circles, this is as it ought to be. Their bullets will neither hurt nor wound.

The friends who have been with me on my earlier journeys of exploration are with me still, as I am happy to record. Dr. Madeline H. Engel has continued to look after my English; Fathers Edwin A.

Quain, S.J., and Robert J. McNamara, S.J., have once again read my manuscript and given me their reactions to it; and, of course, my wife has stood by me all through my recent labours. I have had an enlightening correspondence on some points of the Scottish tradition with Dr. John Highet, the Rev. Mr. Johnston R. McKay and the Rev. Mr. Andrew Herron. I want to assure all of them that I appreciate their kindness. Part of the preliminary research on volume IV was done in the University Library at Freiburg i. Breisgau; a grant from the Philosophical Society of Philadelphia enabled me to work there. For this material support, too, I am duly grateful.

New York,   W . STARK
December 1968.

Acknowledgments

As in volumes I to III, we list here, with thanks, the publishers who have been good enough to permit us to quote from books under their imprint. The authors' names are given in brackets.

Baker Book House (Moe, C.); Beacon Press (Weber, M., *The Sociology of Religion*); Cambridge University Press (Brooke, R. B.); The Clarendon Press (Rostovtzeff, M.); Doubleday & Company, Inc. (Kipling, R.); Fortress Press (Wingren, G.); Franciscan Herald Press (Thomas of Celano); Harper & Row (Pauck, W.); Holt, Rinehart & Winston (Macchioro, V. D., Young, K.); P. J. Kenedy & Sons (Lynskey, E.); John Knox Press (Goodykoontz, H. G.); The Macmillan Company (Weber, M., *The Theory of Social and Economic Organization*); William Morrow and Company, Inc. (Aron, R.); John Murray (Salmon, G.); Newman Press (Sheppard, L. C.); Oxford University Press (Scholes, P.); Random House (Newman, E.); Sheed & Ward (Butler, B. C., Dawson, C.); Simon & Schuster (Wallace, I.); Thames & Hudson (James, E. O.); Viking Press (Werfel, F.); A. P. Watt & Son and Mrs. George Bambridge (Kipling, R.).

'The Fathers of the Church have sometimes considered her as a unity and sometimes as a multiplicity. But even when they emphasized one of these two aspects, both of which are in fact present, they did not forget about the other. A multiplicity which is not reduced to unity is a confusion; a unity which is not dependent on multiplicity is a tyranny. It is an error to exclude either the one or the other, as the Curialists do, who overlook multiplicity, or the Huguenots, who overlook unity.'

Pascal, *Thoughts on the Truth of the Christian Religion*

Introduction

Many religious communities in all parts of the world are known by the names of their founders: thus the followers of the Buddha are called Buddhists, those of Mohammed, Mohammedans, those of Christ, Christians. Even where admiration or derision have succeeded in fixing a different sobriquet on a group, the founder's name provides as a rule a much-used alternative. The Puritans are at times also described as the English Calvinists and the freewill wing of the Methodist movement as the Wesleyans. This well-established and widespread linguistic usage alone can to some extent explain the origin and the prevalence of the approach to the study of religion and its social aspects which we find classically developed in Max Weber. Weber starts with, and builds on, the concept of 'charisma': and the term 'charisma', as he uses it, is applied to *a certain quality of an individual personality* by virtue of which he is set apart from ordinary men and treated as endowed with supernatural, superhuman, or at least specifically exceptional powers or qualities'.[1] Everything begins with the appearance of such a charismatic man, and, in a sense, everything ends with him, for the personal charisma which is the core-phenomenon of religion is, in Weber's view, ephemeral: it dies with its carrier, even though it leaves behind an ever-cooling, ever-decaying, ever-ossifying body of adherents. A characteristically and consistently individualistic sociology of religion is thus initiated.

But, needless to say, Weber's individualism has a much deeper root. It springs in the last analysis from the great tradition of idealistic philosophy which informed German thinking (and not only German thinking) for nearly five hundred years and provided a pervasive intellectual atmosphere which every student inhaled without knowing it and made his own. This world-view, which was propagated, not only by philosophers like Fichte, but also by

[1] *The Theory of Social and Economic Organization*, transl. Henderson, A. M., and Talcott Parsons, ed. New York 1947, p. 358. Our emphasis.

I

poets like Goethe, operated with two key-conceptions: nature and man; society counted for little. Even God was, to such a style of speculation, 'not a being outside of us . . . but rather Pure Reason, *the* ego in our empirical egos',[1] in Johannine language, often used to wrap a Christian cloak around this creed, 'the light which en-lighteneth every man that cometh into this world'. One great representative of this spirit, Johannes Scheffler, better known as 'the Messenger from Silesia' or Angelus Silesius, could go so far as to write:

> I know that without me God cannot live a day.
> If I am brought to nought, he too must fade away.[2]

Man therefore confronts the mystery of being, the depth of being, and the divine ground of being, in himself: he cannot perceive it, or Him, anywhere else. It is easy to see that Weber's concept of charisma, defined as it is as a certain quality of an *individual* personality, is one of the end products of this philosophico-religious system. Charisma, the capacity to arouse, to captivate, to compel, cannot be rationally explained: it is a mysterious endowment found here and there in some outstanding founder-figure. He certainly draws followers after him—but they are fascinated by they know not what. As religious experience and power are *höchstpersönlich*,[3] they are not fully communicable; and so the group which has formed can only survive by a kind of inertia, as a coral reef continues even after the life within it has become extinct. Churches are precisely such coral reefs – burnt-out shells of a once burning personal religiosity.

It was not in this way that other societies thought of charisma. The so-called primitives connected it, not with the individual – and least of all with the isolated individual who appeared to them as something unnatural, something marked with the sign of mis-fortune and therefore unpleasant and menacing[4] – but with a

[1] Aster, E. von, 'Geschichte der neueren Philosophie', in Dessoir, M., *Lehrbuch der Philosophie*, vol. *Die Geschichte der Philosophie*, Berlin 1925, p. 495.
[2] *Sämtliche Poetische Werke*, ed. Held, H. L., ed. München 1924, vol. III, p. 12. My translation.
[3] This German word, as used in the present context, means more than 'highly personal'; it means 'exclusively personal'.
[4] A good deal of this attitude which makes the isolated man a repellent rather than an attractive figure, still survives in such underdeveloped areas as the Italian province of Lucania. Cf. Carlo Levi, *Christ Stopped at Eboli*, ed. New York 1947, pp. 88 and 89.

group, for instance the clan or the sib; they worked with the conviction that in certain descent lines mysterious qualities are inborn and ever reborn; in other words, they entertained a collective concept of charisma.[1] They produced no Fichte or Goethe or Angelus Silesius; they left no sophisticated literature; but they had their philosophy and we can read it in their actions as clearly as in any book. When those Heruli who, in the course of the great migrations, had settled in Byzantine territory, needed a new king, they did not choose the strongest – the most charismatic – personality in their midst. They sent a mission to 'the island of Thule', their original home, to fetch a 'man of royal blood'. Their agents, once arrived, selected the individual whom they liked best, and to that extent personal qualities were indeed co-decisive; but clearly they were only of secondary importance. The main thing was that the new king should be of kingly lineage, for it was that lineage which, in their eyes, possessed and carried the mysterious endowment. The sequel proves it. When the chosen man died on the journey, the ambassadors immediately returned once more to Thule; and when Justinian, with the help of a faction, provided the tribe with a king of his choosing, one Suartuas who was indeed a Herul but not of the royal house, they suffered him only temporarily. As soon as the finally selected scion of the charismatic sib, Todasius, approached, they all joined him, for *he* was the right man; *he* held the occult power which a ruler needs. Rather than accept Suartuas at the behest of the Emperor, the Heruli defected from the Empire, merging their fate and fortune with that of the Gepidae.[2] [3]

[1] *Cf.* Nitschke, A., *Heilige in dieser Welt*, Stuttgart 1962, p. 60; Amira, K. von, *Grundriss des Germanischen Rechts*, Strassburg 1913, p. 128.

[2] Procopius, *The Gothic War*, II, 15; Prokop, *Gothenkrieg*, transl. Coste, D., Leipzig n.d., p. 125.

[3] Hereditary charisma or the charismatic family are indeed mentioned by Weber, but where he does so, he uses – and, in view of his individualistic base definition, he must use – the crucial term in a transferred and even denaturalized meaning. Hereditary and familial charisma are 'non-genuine'. First of all, the charisma is merely transferred: if it is 'transmitted by heredity', it is simply 'participated in by the kinsmen of the bearer'. But the main point is that it is contaminated. When charisma is 'traditionalized . . . the following are the principal motives underlying this transformation: (*a*) the ideal and also the material interests of the followers in the continuation . . . of the community, (*b*) the still stronger ideal and also stronger material interests of the members of the administrative staff, the disciples or other followers of

This attitude survived for a very long time. Seven hundred years after Procopius, around 1250, Petrus de Prece, while extolling the personal charisma of the Emperor Frederick II, yet ascribes the seat of excellence to his line, and not only to him. It is the 'heavenly house of the Augusti', he says, 'which shines unendingly in its stars'. In exactly the same spirit the contemporary Nicolaus de Bari asserts that in Frederick of Hohenstaufen not only one superman, but the imperial seed (*imperiale semen*) has, so to speak, descended from heaven. It is characteristic that later the mysteriousness, the vaunted immortality, of the House of Hohenstaufen is replaced by the far less rational legend of the mysteriousness, the supposed immortality, of one scion of that House – the charismatic Frederick II (for whom, finally, in an unimportant variation, his grandfather Frederick I, called Barbarossa, is substituted). He is supposed to lie asleep in the Kyffhäuser mountain, ready to re-emerge when the time is ripe. Clearly it was easier for a later, more individualistic age, to think in terms of personal immortality rather than in terms of collective supernaturality.[1] But it was precisely that belief in a collective supernaturality which constituted the parent reality from which the later legend was derived, and in relation to which it was merely a secondary development.

Still further illustrations could be given, but they will hardly be needed in this work. For we have shown in the first volume of our *Sociology of Religion* that the indwelling power to cure scrofula with which the English and the French kings were credited, was considered to be a mystery of the blood royal, and not a capacity of the individual personalities.[2] Weber himself regarded the ascription of miracles to a man as a prime sign of his charisma;[3] but the great feats of preternatural healing which Charles II of England or Louis XIII of France were supposed to have performed were

[1] Cf. Kantorowicz, E., 'Zu den Rechtsgrundlagen der Kaisersage', *Deutsches Archiv für Erforschung des Mittelalters*, vol. 1957, pp. 115 et seq., especially pp. 130–3 and 149.
[2] Cf. vol. I, especially p. 64.   [3] Loc. cit., p. 359.

the charismatic leader in continuing their relationship'. Cf. loc. cit., pp. 366, 365, 364.

Where the term 'charismatic' is applied by Weber to a collectivity, e.g. a *gens* (gentile charisma), as in *Ancient Judaism* (transl. Gerth, H. H., and Martindale, D., New York 1952 – cf. p. 465 and the references given there), it means no more than prestige, with the implication, moreover, which we have just stressed, that this prestige is merely transferred.

attributed to their families rather than to themselves. Even at this late date, the Germanic idea of a specific holiness of selected lineages was still alive, and the Weberian conviction that only individuals could be charismatic had not yet been born.

As is usual in such cases, the difference in ideas which we have just studied stems from a dissimilarity in the underlying axiological systems. To Weber and men like him the human personality was the apex of all values; it is the seat of all virtues, while the masses are mean and low. In a more collectivistic age, it is the other way round: the community is the apex of all values; the individual is valuable only if and in so far as he embodies the communal excellencies. We have ranked the collectivistic and individualistic conceptions of charisma as earlier and later, and so they were, if we fix our attention on the degree of their ascendancy. Yet from another point of view, the point of view of the sociology of knowledge, they appear in a different light – not as modes of thought of which the one superseded the other, but as eternal alternatives, like 'community' and 'association' as conceptualized by Ferdinand Tönnies, of which they are indeed aspects or implications, collective charisma being co-ordinate with community and individual with association. The 'primitive' idea of holiness as an attribute of a stream of life rather than of an odd personality is far from dead. Not long before Weber, Cardinal Newman, for instance, restated it with all desirable clarity. To him, the individual is essentially the seat of weakness and even wickedness, the community, on the other hand, is the focus of strength and sanctity.[1] And, in reformulating this conception, he merely restated what is a common and basic Catholic conviction. 'O Lord Jesus Christ,' the celebrant prays in every Mass, 'look not upon my sins, but upon the faith of Thy Church . . .' True, Catholicism has produced many, many charismatic personalities in Weber's sense of the word; but they themselves, and precisely they, would have been the first to insist that sanctity is collective and not personal. For the saint knows that he is a son – the son of a holy mother, the Church, in which an original charisma, that of her Founder, is mysteriously present and transmitted, in the way that among the Heruli, or among the medieval French and English, it was thought to dwell and find perpetuation in a royal clan.

[1] Cf. Stark, W., *Social Theory and Christian Thought*, London 1959, pp. 106 et seq., especially p. 132.

If the facts of history are considered without prejudice, it is easily and convincingly seen that there is not only the case on which Weber bases his sociology of religion – individual charisma founding and forming a collectivity, a church – but also the correspondingly opposite case to which he is totally blind – a collectivity, a church, fostering and forming an individual charisma. In the old, homely phrase, he knows that the egg comes before the hen, but he forgets that you need a hen before you can have an egg. It is obvious that such one-sidedness cannot lead to a balanced, and that is to say, to a truly scientific, sociology of religion. And it is even more obvious that those religious communities which have arisen in an older, more collectivistic age and still carry its spirit within themselves, will and must appear to men of Weber's philosophy in a totally misleading light. Roman Catholicism is but one example of many which could be adduced.

A few illustrations will show what results an overly individualistic approach to the study of socio-religious phenomena may easily produce. There is, for instance, the long chapter of supposed forgeries which, on closer inspection, turn out to be far less fraudulent than they are assumed to be. The Council of Sardica passed a decree which permitted appeals from provincial judgments to the papal see and was thus a milestone on the road to that pontifical primacy and supremacy which later generations were further to perfect. But in the next, the fifth century, this decree is described by Pope Zosimus, not as Sardican, but as Nicaean, and as that Council had more prestige than the Sardican, the authority of the canon concerned was correspondingly enhanced. George Salmon, in his lectures on *The Infallibility of the Church*, is not far from accusing Zosimus, or at least 'some too zealous subordinate' at his court, of a definite lie; he speaks of a 'false quotation' of the Sardican canons and of an 'attempt to pass off the decrees of that council as Nicene'.[1] But this concept of falsification presupposes a mentality which makes a sharp distinction between one council and another, between the year 325 when the prelates assembled at Nicaea and the year 343 when they met at Sardica (our Sofia). The modern mind makes such distinctions for it is inherently nominalistic: only the individual person or event is real, categories are not. But the fifth century thought in different terms. Quite apart from the fact that eighteen years meant very little in that slow-moving period,

[1] Abridged ed., ed. H. F. Woodhouse, London 1952, pp. 193, 196, 197.

6

categories were as real then as individual persons or events; indeed, more so. The succeeding councils flowed into each other, so to speak; there was *one* council which met, now here, now there, now somewhere else; and as Nicaea was the most resplendent link in the chain, it became 'The Council' to which all conciliar canons were carelessly ascribed.[1] Human nature being what it is, we need not deny that self-interest may have had a hand in the confusion. But it is a great deal fairer to presume that the supposed misquotation was merely the effect of a generalizing tendency of the mind deeply engrained in all societies in which the whole is valued more highly than the part, the clan, for instance, more than the individual, or the Mother of Saints more than the saints themselves.[2]

Incidentally – our argument can as readily be applied to the defence of Protestant leaders as to the exoneration of a Catholic pope. Both Wyclif and Hus were accused of 'wholesale plagiarism' from Gratian's *Decretum*, but H. B. Workman, who 'exposed' this fact in his *Letters of Hus*, finds it necessary to add in his later work, *The Evolution of the Monastic Ideal*: 'Plagiarism in medieval times was in the air, and did not mean what it means to the modern.'[3] The fact is that plagiarism is not the right word to use at all. In an age in which authors are notoriously vain, it may be difficult to understand that the written word was, in other cultures, regarded as a common opinion and a common possession of which anybody might make use without infringing another man's rights. Yet this was undoubtedly the case. How many medieval painters found it necessary to affix their names to their canvases? Only very few.

As we have touched on the papal prerogative already, we may as well use it for a further illustration of the blindnesses with which an overly individualistic sociology of religion is certain to be afflicted. Salmon indignantly quotes from *Keenan's Catechism*, an instructional book much used in contemporary Catholic Ireland: 'Must not Catholics believe the Pope himself to be infallible?' No, 'this is a Protestant invention; it is no article of Catholic faith'.[4]

---

[1] Cf. Harnack, A., *Grundriss der Dogmengeschichte*, Freiburg i. Br. 1889, p. 122.
[2] For another case which should be similarly handled, cf. Workman, H. B., *The Evolution of the Monastic Ideal*, ed. Boston 1962, p. 172, footnote. Different monasteries were as much seen as *one* institution as succeeding church assemblies were as *one* council.
[3] Loc. cit., p. 135, note 4.　　　　[4] Salmon, loc. cit., p. 9.

No article of the Catholic faith! Has not the Vatican Council declared it to be precisely that? Individualist that he is, scion of a tradition similar to that behind Max Weber, Salmon assumes as a matter of course that the dogma of papal infallibility attributes infallibility to the pope as an individual, to 'the pope in himself'. He refers over and over again to 'the *personal* infallibility of the Pope',[1] as if there could be no other. This is where the crux of the difficulty lies; this is the root from which the discussion springs. According to Salmon's unconscious metaphysics, every man is an island; according to that of Catholicism, no man is. The framework of the dogma concerned, as it was clarified at Trent and defined in Rome, is, of course, the definition of the Church as the Body of Christ, the mystical body in which all men are members. In a body, however, be it mystical or physical, there can be no isolated men or members, for all are *one* life. The doctrines on faith and morals which it is the pope's prerogative authoritatively to enunciate, and which thereafter bind every Catholic, are products of that *one* life. They are the precipitate of the thought of a collective person, not the pronunciamentos of an individual, however highly placed; in Hegel's terminology, they stem from an 'Objective Spirit'. It would therefore be better to speak of an 'impersonal' or 'objective' infallibility of the pope than to speak of a personal and subjective one; and it would perhaps be best to say that his authority is collective. The pope is an organ of the Body of Christ; more specifically he is its voice, the organ of speech which finds words for the thoughts which the Body has brought to fruition. In the context of a philosophy of this kind, the very idea of a personal, i.e. exclusive, inspiration, can have no place; indeed, it is absurd. 'Any spirit which professes to come to us alone, and not to others,' says Newman in a remarkable passage, 'is not of God.'[2]

But even if we concede that an overly individualistic social philosophy must generate many specific errors, even if we admit beyond that that there lies in it a general source of erroneousness – the tendency to restrict the sociology of religion to religious associations, and either to deny that there are, properly speaking,

---

[1] Ibid., p. 4 and *passim*. Our emphasis. Weber, who knew very little about Catholicism, is under exactly the same misapprehension as Salmon. Cf. Weber, M., *The Sociology of Religion*, transl. Fischoff, E., Boston 1963, p. 74.
[2] *Sermons Bearing on Subjects of the Day*, London, Oxford, Cambridge 1869, p. 130.

religious communities, or to devalue the churches which claim to be such – the question remains whether Weber was not correct in at least one of his basic assertions, namely that every religious grouping starts with an individual founder, an eponymous hero similar to the presumed first father of a primitive clan. It seems hard to reject this proposition; it is certainly true of Christianity, for where would Christianity be without Christ? We ourselves shall open our investigation, after some necessary preliminaries are put out of the way, with a discussion of the founder-figure or figures. And yet, even this simple and prima facie commonsensical assertion must not be absolutized. We shall only be justified in beginning our analysis with the study of a charismatic individual (the Christian must say: the archetype of all charismatic individuals) because we are writing a book on Christendom. But before Christianity there was Judaism, and Judaism had no personal originator. It stands before us as a formation of the anonymous forces of history, and even Jesus Christ Himself (as He Himself was clearly aware and as clearly admitted) had His place within that living stream of Hebrew religion whose sources are lost to sight and appear as mysterious as any remote beginning. Nor did He arrest that stream or even deflect it from its course. On the contrary, He broadened its bed and speeded it on its way. If He was the first of the saints, He was also the last of the prophets. In saying all this, we have no less an authority than St. Augustine on our side. 'What is now called religion existed among the ancients,' he writes. 'It was not missing between the origin of the human race and the time when Christ came in the flesh. Since then, the true religion, which was already in being, began to be called Christian.'[1] In the final analysis, religion – all religion – emerges, as folkways do, from the collective life of human kind. Its existential ground lies in the community. The God-related individual may well mark its heights, its perfections, but its depths, its origins, are not in the self-enclosed soul. They rest in the search by all of us for ultimate reality.

What we are up against here is not *a* problem of sociology, but rather *the* problem of sociology – the relationship between man and society – which meets us, and must meet us, in every corner of the field. To Weber, and other typical moderns like him, music, for

[1] *Retractationes*, I, XIII, 3. *Patrologia Latina*, ed. Migne, J. P., vol. XXXII, Paris 1877, col. 603.

instance, is the gift of some exceptional individuals to their fellows – a gift which they draw from the treasury of their own selves and which cannot be traced further back, for they dispense what they have not received. Differently expressed, the individual is the ultimate source, the true creator, of aesthetic, as he is of religious, values. Beauty as well as holiness springs ready-made from his head, as Minerva did from the head of Zeus. Yet this opinion is at best half of the truth as the unprejudiced expert well understands. 'It is self-evident that the germ of all music lies in folk music,' writes the authoritative Percy Scholes in his *Oxford Companion to Music*. And he adds: 'Music existed for thousands of years before the coming of the professional . . . composer, and has continued to develop since, quite apart from his activities. Every form of vocal and instrumental music we possess has developed out of folk-song or dance, and it is not more possible to make a balanced or comprehensive study of the history of music without an examination of the treasures of folk-tunes than it is to make a similar study of literature without an examination of folk-poems and folk-tales.'[1]

But even this statement, which is as applicable to the development of religion as it is to that of song or symphony, does not yet convey the truth in its entirety, for it puts the emphasis too much on the early periods and too little on the continuing importance of the anonymous sources of beauty-in-sound. The twentieth century is not as different, in this respect, from, say, the first, as might be assumed. Heítor Villa-Lobos sometimes uses mechanistic methods which seem to be miles apart from peasant music-making: for instance, 'he traces the contours of a picture on graph paper, and then plots the melody, a semitone to a square of the graph in the vertical direction, and an eighth-note to a horizontal unit. Thus an ascending curve in the picture results in a melody going up, and a descending line produces a falling musical phrase'.[2] But in spite of these typical rationalist-intellectualist procedures, Scholes is of the considered opinion that the new thing that Villa-Lobos has brought to the concert hall is the riches of his country and nation never fully tapped and transmitted before. Almost all Villa-Lobos has ever written is 'strongly influenced by the melody and rhythms of Brazilian folk-tune'.[3] Even the twelve-tone-scale which to most

[1] Ed. Oxford 1950, p. 330.
[2] Cf. Slonimsky, N., *Music in Latin America*, 1945, cit. Scholes, p. 1159.
[3] Scholes, loc. cit., p. 1158.

hearers is the perfection of modernity, belongs in truth to the ancient treasury of peasant art. When Béla Bartók started to collect Magyar, Slovak and Rumanian folk-music, he found that 'few of the melodies were in the conventional major and minor scales . . . Ancient scales, though abandoned in serious composition, were . . . still alive and Bartók resolved to use them. Naturally, in doing so, he found himself bringing into existence new harmonies, and this, in time, led to his gradual abandonment of the diatonic system and of the chromatic system based upon it, and to the gradual taking up of a new style in which the twelve notes of the chromatic scale were considered as independent entities, ready to submit to all sorts of unheard-of combinations'.[1] When Zoltán Kodály visited America in 1946 and was interviewed by Olin Downes, he asserted that *all* music comes from popular sources and that total decay must ensue if contact with these popular sources is lost.[2] Well might the student of religious life see in these sentiments a wider truth which applies to his field as well as to others. A purely intellectualist approach to the mystery of being may indeed produce interesting philosophies, but it will never engender a living faith. Yet we are still caught in understatement. The dependence of even the highest achievements on the lowest, i.e. deepest, realities of collective existence is not only a wider truth, it is a universal one. What are all the glories of Rimbaud or Rilke in comparison to the great miracles, wrought by primitive and nameless men, which we call the modern languages, French and German? What are all the clevernesses of an Ulpian or a Gajus, or of their modern counterparts, in comparison to that legal folk-lore which gave us the principle *in dubio, pro reo* or *qui tacit, consentit*? Indeed, what is the atomic bomb in comparison to the wheel, the mill and the boat, without which we could not live, although we could well live without the atomic bomb.

Religion, then, must be seen both in its collective roots and results, and in its individual and individualistic incarnations. We have to remember this as we approach the substantive study of the microsociology of religion, i.e. the study of the social relationships which obtain in, and constitute, religious communities and associations. As we envisage it, the microsociology of religion has four major foci of interest. There is, firstly, the description of the basic

[1] Ibid., p. 79.
[2] Cf. *The New York Times*, 7 March 1967 and 3 November 1946.

human types or roles which constitute the particular societies concerned. The charismatic man in the narrower sense of the word is only one of them. The priest, for instance, is another, and we must not, and will not, begin by depressing him to the position of a perverter: scholarship demands objectivity as Weber always said but did not always remember. When the salient human types or roles are identified, the operative inter-human relationships or modes of interaction can come in for scrutiny. This is the next, the second, task. The circle of disciples around a founder during his life and the brotherhood of disciples after his death have to be described, and then (again without prejudice) the lasting forms of church life which evolve from these beginnings. We shall find Tönnies's terms 'community' and 'association' helpful; we shall see that Catholicism illustrates the former, Protestantism rather the latter type of social organization (though Lutheranism and Calvinism, at any rate, as they have historically developed, are not fully associational). The confrontation and comparison of these differing variants of Christianity will give us a third area of analysis. Fourthly and finally, community and association have not only to be considered as concrete forms of social life, but also as fostering soils of specific cultural systems. In other words, the sociology of knowledge has to be called in to complete the work of the sociology of religion in the narrower sense of the word. This final effort will be reserved for the fifth (and concluding) volume of the present work; the other three problem areas will be surveyed in this volume.

1 · THE FOUNDER AND THE SECOND[1]

In a recent rearrangement of the Louvre, it so happened that two of the finest of all medieval paintings, Giotto's *Stigmatization of St. Francis* and Fra Beato Angelico's *Coronation of the Virgin*, came to hang opposite each other. Both depict on their predellas the same story: a pope, complete with his tiara, is asleep; he dreams that a house is falling down; but that dread event is arrested in mid-passage because a young man stems the walls back and holds them up – a symbolic representation of the Church's weakness and a prophetic adumbration of the strength which would presently reinvigorate and rescue her. The only difference between the two pictures is that in the one St. Francis is the friend-in-need, the saviour of the structure, in the other it is St. Dominic. The modern nominalistic and individualistic mind will immediately theorize that the Dominicans were jealous of the glory of St. Francis (for it is of him that the legend is first related, and Giotto lived a hundred years before Fra Beato), and that they simply annexed it, in a *pia fraus*, for their own founder. But this deduction presupposes an implied metaphysic which makes a sharp distinction between saint and saint, or rather man and man, and neither Angelico nor Giotto, neither Dominicans nor Franciscans, made this distinction as we do in the twentieth century. For them, Francis was in a sense Dominic and vice versa, as, for the author of the Apocalypse, Domitian was Nero, and Nero, Caligula, and Caligula, Nabuchodonosor.[2] We have a truly magnificent witness here who can testify to the truth of our interpretation: Dante. Where he begins to extol the two great Mendicants, raised up by Providence to succour the Church, he writes:

> I will speak but of one; he who gives praise
> To one of them, in truth of either speaks,
> For to one end the deeds of both were ordered.[3]

---

[1] This has been suggested as a technical term to describe the disciple who becomes a founder's immediate successor in leadership. Cf. Honigsheim, P., 'Religionssoziologie', in Eisermann, G., *Die Lehre von der Gesellschaft*, Stuttgart 1958, p. 127. Cf. also below, pp. 75 et seq.

[2] Cf. our vol. III, p. 5.   [3] *Paradiso*, canto XI, verses 40–2. My translation.

Not that he is blind to the difference between his heroes. 'The one was all seraphic in his ardour,' he writes, 'the other by his wisdom shed his light.'[1] The contrast between the more emotional Francis and the more rational Dominic is thus well apprehended and expressed. Yet, in spite of this, Dante regards them as *one* hand, for theirs was *one* role and, indeed, *one* sanctity.

One role and one sanctity: the collectivistic, philosophically speaking, 'realistic' mentality,[2] which makes Dante bracket two highly profiled charismatic personalities together as if they were but one, is, of course, capable of much wider, indeed, universal, application. All saints are in a sense One Saint, for all Saints 'are' Christ. Perhaps it is the metaphysic of the greatest of all 'realistic' metaphysicians, Plato, which can help us to achieve the clearest verbal formulation of this basic conviction. Everything is what it is, not by dint of its own inherent individual characteristics, but by dint of its inherence in an archetype which stands primarily for a species and ultimately for the divine idea of that species. A rose is a rose because it participates in rosehood or rather in the divine idea of what a rose is and is meant to be; a man is a man because he participates in mankind or rather because he reflects the divine idea of manhood; and a saint is a saint because he participates in sanctity or rather in Christ Who is the Divine Idea of Sanctity, which is Sonship, incarnate – Who is the unique figure in Whom a divine idea has been revealed and made, so to speak, tangible in the flesh. 'All personal holiness,' writes Humbert Bouëssé,[3] is, by virtue of the communion of saints, a common possession of the Church as such; on the profound and invisible mystical plane, it has a social bearing: it edifies the Body of the Church.' To edify does not mean here merely 'to heighten the tone of' (though it means that as well): it means 'to build up', 'to make an edifice of' – and an edifice is *one* like an organism, for the stones in it have coalesced for ever. In the same spirit, Karl Adam has expressed himself as follows: 'It was a conviction inbred in the consciousness of the primitive Church, and again and again confessed in the line Paul – Ignatius – Cyprian – Augustine, that the Spirit works in us through the

---

[1] Ibid., verses 37 and 38.

[2] In opposition to philosophical nominalism which considers general terms, such as society or church, as merely names (nomina), philosophical realism ascribes to them true, if metaphysical, reality.

[3] Bouëssé, H., *Le Sacerdoce Chrétien*, Bruges 1957, p. 138.

Community, and that the Community is the true organ of the Spirit. Not the "I", but the "We" is the carrier of the Spirit.'[1]

Sociologically speaking, this conviction has made Catholicism what it is. 'It is because Catholics retain this ancient belief in the Church as the one communion of believers,' says a recent writer,[2] 'that [their] approach to all problems . . . is necessarily different from Salmon's' and all Protestants – and different also, we may add, from Weber's and all individualists. 'The Catholic faith is not just the aggregate of the religious opinions of the members of the Church,' we read in another context.[3] 'It is a corporate faith, something more or other than such an aggregate. It is primarily the faith of a society, and only secondarily that of its members taken individually.' And again:[4] 'Christianity presents us with an association [the sociologist would rather say: a community] based upon a shared faith – not the chance coincidence of a number of individual opinions, but a faith which is primordially corporate, essentially the faith of the society, in which faith the members of the society participate; their faith is their own, and yet it is not their own, because it comes to them from, and remains always essentially the faith of, the society.'

So basic is the point and so widespread the conviction that literally hundreds of passages could be quoted in support of it. Here only two more can be appended, to drive home the fact without a proper understanding of which a sociology of religion is about as impossible as a psychology without a concept of the subconscious. 'The Church is not a voluntary religious association formed by the coming together of individual believers,' writes Christopher Dawson, 'but a supernatural divine organism which transmits the gift of eternal life to mankind.'[5] And Karl Adam: 'The Church prays, not in the name of any individual, nor as the mere sum of all individuals, but as a fellowship.'[6]

This collectivism is found, not only in Roman Catholicism, but

---

[1] Adam, K., *Glaube und Glaubenswissenschaft im Katholizismus*, Rottenburg 1920, p. 17. Adequate documentation concerning patristic literature is out of the question, but for a sample cf. Lawson, J., *The Biblical Theology of St. Irenaeus*, London 1948, p. 92.

[2] Butler, B. C., *The Church and Infallibility*, New York 1954, p. 124.

[3] Ibid., p. 211.   [4] Ibid., pp. 122 and 123.

[5] *The Formation of Christendom*, New York 1967, p. 287.

[6] *The Spirit of Catholicism*, ed. New York 1937, p. 147. (All later references are to this work.)

in all faiths, or variants of faiths, which are anxious not to lose contact with the inceptions and traditions of Christianity. The Anglican Dr. Sparrow Simpson, for instance, writes with a pen which might well have been wielded at Rome: 'It is the corporate institution which is redeemed . . . Both the individual and the institution are the objects of Christ's love. But the greater includes the less.'[1]

If we look for the last sociological roots of all this, we do not have far to seek. They lie in the spirit of community (in Tönnies's sense of the word) or rather in the life of community (as the sociologist of knowledge might prefer to say). Sometimes they stand out very clearly in a stray passage. Thus Arnold Rademacher says in *Die Kirche als Gemeinschaft und Gesellschaft*:[2] 'The individual represents the divine image, in which man was made, but imperfectly; it is reflected in its perfection only in the religious community.' Goethe who, in spite of his pantheism and individualism, had a heart wide enough to encompass even Catholicism (witness the end of Faust, part II), said in the same vein that 'only all men together are the true man'.[3]

But protests against this interpretation might well be raised. What about mysticism, it might be said? Is not the mystic on a lonely search, and does he not receive a personal reward? Is he, at least, not to be understood in terms of an individualistic psychology, and his relation to God in terms of an I-and-Thou relationship? And is he not the finest flower of Catholic spirituality? Friedrich Heiler, who knew Catholicism better than any other Protestant before him ever did, answered this last question with a very decided *yes*. Yet even he, in a chapter entitled 'The Fourth Gospel and Catholic Mysticism', penned the following passage which confirms rather than contradicts our over-all assessment. 'It is true that this union of the confessors of Christ with their Saviour remains – like the union of the Son with the Father – within the confines of a personal mysticism; this *unio* is not an absorption of the soul in the infinite like the *enosis* of the mysticism of Plotinus; even in the most intimate communion with Christ, the soul continues to be a self.' Yet he goes on to say, and this is

---

[1] *A New Commentary on Holy Scripture*, ed. Gore, Ch., ed. London 1929, p. 394.
[2] Augsburg 1931, p. 51.
[3] *Wilhelm Meisters Lehrjahre*, pt. II, bk. VIII, ch. 5. *Goethes Sämtliche Werke, Jubiläumsausgabe*, Stuttgart und Berlin n.d. [1902–7], vol. XVIII, p. 326.

decisive in our context: 'It is not the isolated individual soul which achieves union with the Lord, but the whole community of disciples as a unitary religious organism.'[1]

But we need not rely on a secondary source, however authoritative, for support of our thesis; we can call up a historical event which will be even more convincing. The individualism and nominalism which, in the fullness of time, was to produce the Protestant faith, and in the aftermath figures like George Salmon and Max Weber, raised its head for the first time in the great wonder of the Schools, Peter Abelard. The sole reason why God appeared in the flesh, this doctor taught, was to instruct us by His words and example, and the sole reason why He suffered and died was to commend His charity towards us. There appears to be very little wrong with a statement of this kind, for who would deny that Christ is, *inter alia*, also a teacher to His flock? Nevertheless, the champions of orthodoxy were clear-sighted enough to see, in Abelard's formulation, the breakthrough of a revolutionary, and in the last analysis destructive, idea. Christ was to them more than merely an educator; and if He was essentially an educator and no more, then a gulf was opened up between the Son of Man and the sons of men, for teacher and pupil are ever two different, nay contrasted, personalities. Technically expressed, Abelard had embraced nominalism – we might almost say, introduced nominalism into the Church's social philosophy. Against him, St. Bernard of Clairvaux stands forth as the most resplendent defender of traditional and basic realism. With a sure touch, he builds his counterattack around the two most decisive passages in the Pauline canon – I Corinthians XV, 22, and Romans V, 18. 'As in Adam all die, so also in Christ all shall be made alive,' reads the one passage, and the other: 'As by the offence of one, unto all men to condemnation, so also by the justice of one, unto all men to justification of life.' Adam's deed was perpetuated by generation, Bernard urges, not merely by bad example, Christ's by regeneration, not only by providing a good and uplifting model to follow. Adam's children and Christ's brethren *immediately* participate in the guilt of their first father and in the merit of their divine brother; they cannot be divided and divorced, for they are one body and one life.[2]

[1] *Der Katholizismus*, München 1923, p. 69.
[2] Cf. Luddy, A. J., *The Life and Teaching of St. Bernard*, Dublin 1927, especially pp. 438 and 439.

In this clash of the giants, the Catholic position stands out in all its essential qualities. But what we are more immediately concerned with is the fact that the man who entered the lists as upholder of philosophical realism and religious community was a mystic, an ecstatic, who sought and found the beatific vision by his own personal striving for, and straining after, God. He is not like Bunyan's pilgrim Christian who sets out for the Celestial City alone, or like Christian's wife Christina, who follows because she has her own beckoning vision; he is conscious that in him all men are seeking and finding the divine countenance. 'Nobody must live for himself,' Bernard preaches in his most inspiring work, the *Sermons on the Song of Songs*, 'but all must live for all.'[1]

Out of this confrontation between Abelard and Bernard there developed, after many permutations and transmutations, the conflict between Protestantism, the more individualistic variant of Christianity, and Catholicism, the consistently collectivistic type of it. But it would be wrong simply to equate Protestantism with the largely coinciding positions of individualism, nominalism and association. To be in accord with the facts, we must make a decisive distinction here between the Radical Reformation, represented by the Anabaptists in the sixteenth century, and by the Quakers in the seventeenth, and the Reformation of those who are usually called the Reformers – Luther and Calvin. For the sociologist, the Anabaptists and the Quakers are indeed the perfect antitype to the sharply profiled life and thought – to the integrated body – of Catholicism; Luther and Calvin are far less so. We must think of these men and their followers as somewhere along a continuum between the one pole, consistent ecclesiastical 'realism' or community, and the other pole, consistent ecclesiastical 'nominalism' or association, approaching indeed the latter, but by no means coinciding with it.

The Quakers call themselves a 'Society of Friends' and the label was truly well chosen. In order to interpret it correctly, we must, however, put the emphasis on 'friends' and not on 'society', for many of the salient characteristics of the social bond, as the world understands it, were absent from this informal circle. The Quakers, for instance, rejected the very principle of the division of labour. The inner light, the recognition of which is religion, 'enlighteneth

[1] XLI, 6; cf. *Patrologia Latina*, as quoted, vol. CLXXXIII, Paris 1879, col. 987.

every man that cometh into this world'. The faith of the Friends is fully democratic. As in a democracy everyone is, in principle and ideally, endowed with the same rights as a citizen, so in this religion everyone is endowed with the same charisma, the same source of holiness, and hence as a believer on a par with all his neighbours. There is nothing to divide here. But where there is no division of labour, there will also be no defined roles and functions. There will, of course, be no appointed teachers and preachers, for everybody may teach and preach when the spirit moves him, and nobody when the heart is silent. Again, where there are no roles and functions, in other words, where there is no social structure, there can also be no norms, and in so far as sociologists nowadays define social life as a system of norm-suffused actions, the Quaker family can qualify as a social formation only by a special extension of the usual definition. As for 'ideologies' or dogmas which, in societies properly so called, constitute the mental parallels, the superstructure, to the norms of action, the substructure, they are simply unthinkable in the Quaker orbit. The Friends insist that the wind must be allowed to blow wherever it listeth. In one word, we have here the social minimum, as in the Catholic Church we have the social, or rather integrational, maximum.

The phrase 'the Quaker Church' – if anybody were unrealistic enough to use it – would hardly be more than a contradiction in terms. And for this reason, the Society of Friends is only of marginal interest to the microsociology of religion in the proper sense of the word – however central in importance it may be in other contexts, e.g. in the macrosociology of religion or in the study of mysticism or of personal piety. But not only is this loose-textured, and even untextured, group marginal to the microsociology of religion, it is marginal, and that for identical reasons, to the study of Christendom also. Fox regarded himself as another Christ, and he conceded Christhood to all his fellow-finders of the light within.[1] Christ therefore did not die for others, at least not in the sense in which Christians of the mainstream, be they Catholic or Protestant, understand it: He died for Himself. This idea had been clearly expressed already by the Anabaptists and had been one of the causes of the enmity which they had soon encountered. Denk, for instance, had led Abelard's conception of the merely exemplary character of Jesus to its logical conclusion. To make more of Him than a

[1] Cf. our vol. II, pp. 94, 95, 106, 107, 108, 153, 277.

model, he declared, was to make an idol of Him. This was a settled doctrine among the Anabaptists.[1] The Quakers followed in their footsteps. It was in their conviction not the Christ who died in Jerusalem who lifted men up towards the Father, it was the Christ alive here and now, the Christ within.[2] This may well be true religiosity, but it is not true Christianity. One outer indication that the Friends can be acknowledged as Christians only if the meaning of the word is greatly stretched, or even strained, as they can be acknowledged as a society only if the same is done to the word society, is the fact that the British Quakers – the most highly profiled part of the Quaker International – were excluded, or excluded themselves, from the World Council of Churches when that great union was initiated in 1948.

What we have now put before our reader is a scheme which might well be called a typology of charisma. Catholicism and Radical Protestantism are the opposite poles or extremes on a line along which socio-religious formations can be ranged according to their nearness to, or distance from, the one end or the other, the conviction that charisma is the attribute of a church or the conviction that it is the characteristic of a person as a person. The parallelism between this continuum and that of Tönnies – from community to association – is obvious. The question which we must now put is this: where do the Reformers usually so called, Luther and Calvin, and their respective groupings, fit into the scheme? Obviously, they are not too far removed from the individualistic border-line of the spectrum. But this is and can be only a preliminary answer. To make it more satisfactory, we must introduce two vital distinctions: that between the Wittenberger and the Genevan; and – even more importantly – that between either of them when young, and either of them when no longer quite so young. The fact is that life led both back in the direction of that Catholicism which, in their first ferment, they had abandoned and condemned.

The young Luther's ecclesiology was essentially a meditation on one decisive Gospel passage – Matthew XVIII, 20: 'Where there are two or three gathered together in my name, there am I in the midst of them.' Taken in isolation, this logion would appear to

[1] Cf. Bohatec, J., *Calvins Lehre von Staat und Kirche*, Breslau 1937, pp. 315, 316, 321.
[2] Cf. Braithwaite, W. C., *The Beginnings of Quakerism*, ed. Cambridge 1955, p. 97.

have negative implications, so far as ecclesiasticism is concerned: priests are not necessary for proper worship, nor special buildings, nor other traditional *paraphernalia*. Indeed, these *paraphernalia* appear almost as *impedimenta*. Luther's doctrine of the 'priesthood of all believers' sought to provide a positive formulation of this sociological negativism. 'All Christians are truly of the priestly class,' we read in *An den Christlichen Adel deutscher Nation* (1520), 'and among them there is no distinction.'[1] This is the radical egalitarianism of Anabaptists and Quakers which, in logic, would seem *a limine* to exclude all social structuring, all organization properly so called. Nor should the difference between Luther's 'priesthood of all believers', and Denk's or Fox's 'Christhood of all believers' be exaggerated. Some of his writings, e.g. *De Instituendis Ministris Ecclesiæ* (1523), explain in so many words that Christians are priests because of their *conformitas* with Christ.[2]

Yet Luther takes back with his right hand, what he has granted with his left. All baptized persons are indeed priests and may act as priests, but all baptized persons must not act as priests; all are not allowed to do so. To be entitled to do so, a call, nay an appointment, is needed. And who can issue the call or effect the appointment? On this point, Luther is vague beyond words. And here is where the great shift occurs. In *De Captivitate Babylonica Ecclesiae Praeludium* (1520), he says in one paragraph that priests are *ex nobis electi*, and in the next paragraph that they are *per Ecclesiam vocati*.[3] But there is a great – if hidden – difference between the two positions. If priests are *electi*, the multitude, a heap (Hauffen)[4] of Christians, is first, the *pastores* second; if priests are *vocati*, there is first an institution and this then gives itself, as a secondary development, *pastores*. Before, say, 1523, the split between the two principles is as yet unrecognizable. But later, and especially after the shocking experiences of the Peasants' War, Luther increasingly chooses between the alternatives and, in a profound fear of all anarchy, decides in favour of an ever-advancing ecclesiasticism.

[1] *D. Martin Luthers Werke*, vol. VI, Weimar 1888, p. 407. (Quotations in this section from Luther and Calvin are given in our own translation, unless otherwise stated.)

[2] Ibid., vol. XII, as quoted, 1891, pp. 178 et seq. For the nearness of the young Luther to the Anabaptists, cf. Bohatec, loc. cit., p. 336.

[3] Ibid., vol. VI, as quoted, p. 564.

[4] Cf. ibid., p. 407. The term is characteristic of nominalism. A heap (e.g. of sand) is not structured.

'The outer things (*Stück*) should and must necessarily be there first, and the inner [can only develop] afterwards; they come from the outer,' he writes on one occasion.[1] But this is precisely the ontological principle of organicism, of community: the whole is before the parts, the church of the believers before the believers themselves.

One tell-tale detail of *De Instituendis Ministris Ecclesiae* is Luther's insistence that the ordinary Christian, although in principle priest, may not distribute holy communion;[2] he advises the Bohemian Utraquists that, unless and until they have proper office-bearers, i.e. unless and until they are properly organized, they must forgo this sacrament. This, however, is the thin end of the wedge. As A. W. Dieckhoff has shown,[3] Luther's mind produces about this time a distinction which becomes decisive – the distinction between public and private religious life. Holy communion is public, therefore only publicly instituted ministers may celebrate it; informal prayer is private, therefore anybody can lead in it, e.g. the 'housefather' of whom Luther expects so much. The ultimate division between public pastor and private 'priest' is that the former is called to teach (in the pulpit), and to rule, the latter to instruct (in the family), pray and lead a life of sacrifice.[4] This is precisely the Roman Catholic division of functions between clergy and laity but for one detail (which, of course, is important, but not with regard to the problem in hand) – the disappearance of the sacrament of ordination. Luther has, to all intents and purposes, un-priested his universal priesthood; at the same time, he has created a special priesthood, semi-secular in nature, a priesthood which is not granted the distinguishing mark of a *character indelebilis*. In a matter mystical, he has indeed moved away from Catholicism, but in matters sociological he has returned to it.

Perhaps it is not too harsh to say that what emerges is a distinction between the mass of believers on the one hand and a church bureaucracy on the other. There are two reasons why we are justified in using this apparently pungent mode of expression. One is Luther's conception that the call to a pastor lies parallel to other calls to public office;[5] the other is the historical fact of his accept-

---

[1] Ibid., vol. XVIII, 1908, p. 136. [2] Cf. loc. cit., vol. XII, pp. 171 et seq.
[3] *Luthers Lehre von der kirchlichen Gewalt*, Berlin 1865. The book is still important.
[4] Cf. ibid., especially p. 157.
[5] Cf. Brunotte, W., *Das geistliche Amt bei Luther*, Berlin 1959, especially p. 47.

ance of caesaropapism which was bound further to increase the similarities between service in the Church and service in the State, both of which he saw increasingly as subordinate to one authority, the ruler. But however the development is described, it comes in any case to a far-reaching, almost total abandonment of the un-ecclesiastical egalitarianism and informality which characterized the Radical Reformation, and towards which the man from Eisleben had made some – albeit faltering – steps in his youth.

In order to show *how* widely Luther wandered, in the course of his life, from his early ecclesiological position, all we have to do is to adduce a few quotations from his later works. 'The Holy Spirit,' he writes for instance, 'carries on His work without ceasing until the last day, and to this end He has instituted a community on earth by means of which He speaks and does everything.'[1] The word 'everything' is certainly revealing here. More particularly, it is the Church which leads to God and saves, not the individual conscious-ness or conscience. 'He who wishes to find Christ, must first find the Church ... Outside the Christian Church, there is no truth ... The Christian Church [it is], the assembly of all believers on earth, in which alone you can find Christ ... It is ordained that outside the Christian Church, there is no God, no grace, no blessedness.'[2] How far was the man who could pen these passages from the principle of the medieval Church, *extra ecclesiam nulla salus*, which is so often held reproachfully against modern Catholicism, but which is unavoidably implied in the collective concept of charisma?

But even more Catholicizing elements are to be found in the later Luther. There is, *inter alia*, the idea that the Church administers a divine *depositum*, a fund of grace, out of which individuals draw their substance and sustenance. (It makes little difference that the word of God takes the place of the sacraments left by God.) 'If we have the Gospel in its pure form, then we have the treasure which God gives to His Church so that we should not be lacking in anything.'[3] Sometimes the word 'treasure' is used more generally to describe the redemption achieved by Christ, and then the differ-ence from Catholic conceptions becomes very small indeed. But even the most characteristic Catholic expression, the word of our Holy Mother the Church, makes its appearance in Luther's thought

[1] Werke, as quoted, 1910, vol. XXX/1, p. 191.
[2] Ibid., vol. X, 1/1, 1910, pp. 140, 711, 72, and vol. XXII, 1929, p. 310.
[3] Ibid., vol. XXII, as quoted, p. 309.

and Lutheran literature. The Holy Spirit, Luther writes in one important statement, 'has a concrete community in the world who is the mother that engenders and sustains every Christian by the word of God which He reveals and spreads . . . so that they can grasp it, accept it, stick to it, and remain with it'.[1] The term 'concrete community' (*sonderliche gemeyne*) shows that the meaning of such passages must not and cannot be weakened by the assertion that the Church of which the Reformer is speaking is merely the unknown, spiritual, 'ghostly' communion of saints. No, it is the incarnate and organized Church, the hard and fast ecclesiastical institution, which he holds up as the individual believer's genetrix, she who brings him to life and is therefore ontologically before and above him. Sometimes this becomes clear beyond the shadow of a doubt even in earlier writings: 'We must give honour, and be obedient unto, our spiritual mother, the Holy Christian Church, the ecclesiastical authority, what it will prescribe, proscribe, assert, ordain, prohibit [or] admit, so that we take our direction from it. As we respect, fear and love our bodily parents, so also our spiritual governors. We must defer to them (*lassen sie recht habenn*) in all things which are not contrary to the first three commandments.'[2] Luther was not entirely blind to the fact that such sentiments largely coincide with the Romanist position.[3]

In its outlines, the case of Calvin runs parallel to that of Luther. He, too, travelled from a more individualistic to a more institutional religiosity. Yet there are differences of detail which are significant and must not be missed. There is not only a progressive shift to the right, there is also in Calvin's thought a systemic co-existence of the two antagonistic principles of personal and collective charisma which proves how difficult it is for the Christian completely to foresake the principle of community or community-primacy.

Calvin's rivenness is interestingly reflected in the literature about him. To Emile Doumergue (*Jean Calvin, Les Hommes et les Choses de son Temps*, 1899 et seq.), he is, in spite of everything, an organismic thinker; to Karl Ricker (*Grundsätze der reformierten Kirchenverfassung*, 1899) and Matthias Schneckenberger (*Vergleichende Darstellung des lutherischen und reformierten Lehrbegriffs*, 1855) he is not. Ernst Troeltsch, in his great work, *The Social Teaching of the Christian*

[1] Ibid., vol. XXX/1, 1910, p. 188.   [2] Ibid., vol. VI, 1888, p. 255.
[3] Ibid., vol. XXXIII, 1907, p. 455.

Churches, sides with the latter two;[1] but Josef Bohatec in his massive tome, comprising 754 pages, *Calvins Lehre von Staat und Kirche mit besonderer Berücksichtigung des Organismusgedankens*,[2] does not. According to him, *corpus mysticum* is the key concept of Calvinist, as it is of Catholic, religious sociology. Where is the truth? We shall try to depict it, as best we can.

The basis of the whole Calvinic system is the double concept of total corruption and partial election. 'In Adam's fall, we sinnèd all', as an old New England hymn has it; therefore we are all in justice fore-ordained to eternal shame and punishment. Yet God, out of His own free will and mercy, in compassion plucks a few burning sticks out of the fire. Some are separated out of the mass of perdition and predestined to everlasting glory and blessedness, in spite of their sinfulness; nobody, however, knows who they are. Already this truly fundamental theology shows that the great Genevan was deeply committed to an individualistic ecclesiology. The elect are scattered over all periods of history as well as across all the broad acres of the globe; they do not know each other; they cannot know each other; consequently they appear as a disconnected congeries of men, a random collection, anything but an organized body, at least to start with. There is not a herd of sheep and a herd of goats; all animals look alike; but they are not, any more than Cain is like Abel, or Judas is like John.

In building his specific religious sociology, Calvin then uses the thought-form which, above all others, is characteristic of individualism and nominalism – the figure of a social contract. Reviving in this area, as he does in all others, characteristic Old Testament conceptions, he teaches that God invites those whom he has predestined to blessed association with Himself into a covenantal relationship. 'I will take you to myself for my people,' YHWH said to the Israelites in the desert (Exodus VI, 7). 'I will be your God.' But what He said once, He says for evermore, for He is not caught in the coils of time and space. The church that arises from this call to a covenant and the acceptance of it, is clearly the result of a meeting of wills. It is therefore contractual in nature. The primacy is with the contracting parties; the emergent society is merely secondary. As can be seen, it was not so far as one might

---

[1] First published in 1911; English paperback ed., New York 1960, pp. 579 et seq.

[2] Cf. note 1 on p. 20. Reference: *passim*.

assume from Calvin to his fellow-citizen Rousseau. If the latter is famous because he upheld the doctrine of a *contrat social*, so ought to be the former. They were brothers under the skin.

But we have not told the whole story of Calvin yet. He certainly gives to the covenant conception a central place within his doctrinal system. We can see this clearly from passages such as the following which is taken from the Reformer's main work, the *Institutes of the Christian Religion*:[1] 'The Lord always covenanted with His servants thus: "I will be your God, and you shall be my people." The prophets also commonly explained that life and salvation and the whole sum of blessedness are embraced in these words.' This is pure and consistent contractualism.[2] Yet at the next stage of the argument, there occurs a radical volte-face which proves that even a contractualist, if he is a Christian, cannot do without the organo-logical simile. Those whom He has separated out from the mass of perdition, Calvin now asserts, God implants in an organism of which Christ is the head: they become members of His body. We are back in the New Testament, back with Bernard and Aquinas. 'Implantation' – *insitio in corpus Christi* – is a technical term in the Calvinic dictionary, a term which proves that he embraces the collectivistic-realistic alternative as fully as the individualistic-nominalistic alternative, whatever the difficulties which such a mixing of metaphors, or rather of metaphysics, may bring with it.

Once he has crossed this Rubicon, Calvin continues on his journey towards Rome. Like Luther, for instance, he makes use, on a fairly large scale, of the concept of the Church as a 'holy mother'. Yet there remains a difference. He hardly ever uses this simile without indicating that to him it *is* a simile, a comparison, rather than the expression of a philosophical truth. This is what Bohatec has not sufficiently appreciated. Even in his organicism, the Reformer remains a semi-contractualist; if the Church is *un corps*, she is also *une alliance*. Thus we read: 'The Elect of God . . . grow together into one body, as it were (*velut corpus*).' Or: 'All the elect are, by the bond of faith, conjoined in one church or society and in one people of God of which, as of a body (*comme*

---

[1] II, X, 8. Cf. *The Library of Christian Classics*, vol. XX, Philadelphia n.d., pp. 434 and 435. The biblical quotation is from Leviticus, XXVI, 12.
[2] For a list of passages from Calvin in which this concept of a *mutuus contractus* or *alliance éternelle* is elaborated, cf. Bohatec, op. cit., p. 334, note 111.

d'un corps), Christ our Lord is the guide and prince and chief.' Or: 'The whole body of the faithful is nothing unless it is something like one man (*comme un homme*).'[1] Indeed, even where there is an apparent rejection of the metaphorical character of the body-metaphor, there remains a last reserve. 'There is not merely a similarity to the human body: but the Son of God is in truth our chief.'[2] The word here used, *nostre chef*, has at least as much reference to the ruler of a multitude as to the head of an organism.[3] Yet what must be most decisive is surely the handling of the mother-metaphor itself. Is the church our mother in the sense that she gives us birth, that she is ontologically before us? Calvin at times says that, too, but he is apt to mix in an entirely different image – that of the mother who collects her little ones in her lap. The very beginning of the fourth book of the *Institutes*, the book in which, more than in any other, Calvin develops his sociological opinions, is characteristic: 'I shall start with the church into whose bosom God is pleased to gather His sons . . .'[4] Something that is collected is at first dispersed, and even when the collecting is over, there is juxtaposition rather than fusion. Calvin, as can be seen, never becomes a true organicist.

To this extent, then, Troeltsch is right and Bohatec wrong. Yet there is one more aspect, and it is important. Why does God, our father, collect us in the Church, our mother? We are being brought together, Calvin replies, so that 'we may be nourished by her help and ministry so long as we are infants and children, but also may be guided . . . until we are mature and at least reach the goal of faith'.[5] (Even here, incidentally, the organic simile breaks down; we never really grow up: 'Our weakness does not allow us to be dismissed from school, until we have been pupils all our lives.')[6] The Church, in other words, has in the first place and fundamentally a pedagogic function. She wields the dominie's – the school-master's – rod, to use a Scotticism. But this conception, and it is one of Calvin's firmest, brings her close to the side of those other two educational agencies, the family and the school in the secular

[1] *Corpus Reformatorum*, vol. XXIX, Braunschweig 1863 (*Calvini Opera*, vol. I), col. 72; vol. L, 1880 (*Calvini Opera*, vol. XXII), col. 57; and vol. LXXIX, 1895 (*Calvini Opera*, vol. LI), col. 523.
[2] Ibid., vol. LIV (*Calvini Opera*, vol. XXVI), Braunschweig 1883, col. 70.
[3] Cf. Bohatec, loc. cit., p. 271.
[4] IV, I, 1. *The Library of Christian Classics*, as quoted, vol. XXI, p. 1012.
[5] Ibid.   [6] IV, I, 4. Loc. cit., p. 1016.

sense of the word.[1] These, however, are logically before the individual: he is made by them, not they by him, and therefore we
have here a truly, if somewhat remotely, organic element in
Calvin's ecclesiology. He was not the full organicist Bohatec
depicts, but he was an organicist of sorts all the same.

After thus setting the record straight, we can return to the
parallel between Calvin and Luther. Calvin, too, shifted more and
more from an individualistic to an institutional conception of
Christianity. He begins to preach that the invisible church of the
elect is 'somehow' (*aliquatenus*)[2] made manifest in the visible
church. Bohatec asserts – and we are inclined to believe him – that
the year 1539 marks a turning point in this respect.[3] By that time,
the lesson of the anarchic experiment of the Anabaptists in Münster
from 1534 to 1536 had sunk deeply into the Genevan's soul. It
had seared in, so to speak. The *fanatici* become to him an object of
disgust almost as repellent as the *Papistae*. It is increasingly his
wish, not to be like them. And as they are failures as church-
builders – they can at best erect a pig-pen (*porcorum haram struunt*),[4]
he says contemptuously, but not a church – he wants to succeed in
this very task. What the Peasants' War had done to Luther, the
Münsterites obviously did to Calvin: they drove him back towards
the Middle Ages, and, if the truth be told, even towards the Church
of Rome. But already the *Institutes* of 1536 are well on the way.[5]

Setting his face against 'fanatical men' and 'fanatical beasts',
Calvin insists, in these *Institutes*, that there is no lonely road to God.
'Many are led either by pride, dislike, or rivalry to the conviction
that they can profit enough from private reading and meditation:
hence they despise public assemblies and deem preaching super-
fluous. But, since they do their utmost to sever or break the sacred
bond of unity, no one escapes the just penalty of this unholy

---

[1] Bohatec, loc. cit., p. 377. Cf. also pp. 358 and 359. The point should have
been more strongly developed and stressed.

[2] *Corpus Reformatorum*, vol. XXIV, as quoted, col. 543.

[3] Cf. p. 276 and the literature quoted there. Cf. also pp. 300 et seq. and the
important p. 357.

[4] *Corpus Reformatorum*, vol. LXV (*Calvini Opera*, vol. XXXVII), 1888, col.
277.

[5] Cf. Bohatec, loc. cit., p. 347. That later Calvinists, especially in England,
Holland and America (e.g. John à Lasco) return to more individualistic
attitudes (i.e. build up Calvinistic sects) need not concern us here. Cf.
Bohatec, pp. 368 et seq., 375.

separation without bewitching himself with pestilent errors and foulest delusions.'[1] No, Calvin insists, almost in so many words, there is no salvation outside the visible, tangible, empirical church. 'There is no way to enter into life unless this mother conceive us in her womb . . . Away from her bosom one cannot hope for any forgiveness of sins or any salvation, as Isaiah and Joel testify. Ezekiel agrees with them when he declares that those whom God rejects from heavenly life will not be enrolled among God's people. On the other hand, those who turn to the cultivation of true godliness are said to inscribe their names among the citizens of Jerusalem . . . By these words God's fatherly favour and the especial witness of spiritual life are limited to his flock, so that it is always disastrous to leave the church.'[2]

From this insistence on the necessity of a social form of religion, it is but a small step to the insistence on the necessity of an authoritarian clergy, and Calvin finds the step an easy one to take. God promised 'that he would give what ought to suffice for all: that they should never be destitute of prophets. But as he did not entrust the ancient folk to angels but raised up teachers from the earth truly to perform the angelic office, so also today it is his will to teach us through human means. As he was of old not content with the law alone, but added priests as interpreters from whose lips the people might ask its true meaning, so today he not only desires us to be attentive to its reading, but also appoints instructors to help us by their effort.'[3] These instructors are inspired, however difficult it may be at times to believe it. Who would not hear echoes of Catholicism in the following words? 'Those who think the authority of the Word is dragged down by the baseness of the men called to teach it disclose their own ungratefulness. For, among the many excellent gifts with which God has adorned the human race, it is a singular privilege that he deigns to consecrate to himself the mouths and tongues of men in order that his voice may resound in them. In every age the prophets and godly teachers have had a difficult struggle with the ungodly, who in their stubbornness can never submit to the yoke of being taught by human word and

[1] IV, I, 5. Loc. cit., p. 1018.
[2] IV, I, 4. Ibid., p. 1016. The biblical references are to Isaiah XXXVII, 32, Joel II, 32, and Ezekiel XIII, 9.
[3] Ibid., I, IV, 5; pp. 1017 and 1018. Cf. Deuteronomy XVIII, 15, and Malachias II, 7.

ministry. This is like blotting out the face of God which shines upon us in teaching.'[1] Calvin's ecclesiasticism reaches its climax in the following passage which is about as Catholic as it can be. 'God Himself appears in our midst, and . . . would have men recognize him as present in His institution.'[2] In view of all this, it is but fair that he should have admitted agreement with the Papists in one point – the conviction that those who separate themselves from the Church, fall away from Christ.[3]

The one important, and all-important, insight which emerges from this discussion is the recognition that Christianity – apart from a few marginal groups which are as loosely connected with it as their members are with each other – has ever held fast to, and, after deviation, been forced back towards, the belief in a collective charisma, in a holy community and communion. We must see in this concept one of the core-convictions of the faith.

THE DISTINGUISHING MARK OF RELIGIOUS CHARISMA

What has gone before should be amply sufficient to lay the basis for a fundamental proposition which we have to formulate now: the original Christian Church and the continuing Catholic Church can sociologically be best understood if they are seen as parallel to the clan, the social constitution under which so much of humanity lived for so very long. All MacDonalds are one because they are incarnations of the life of their primal progenitor, Donald; all O'Malleys are one because they are incarnations of the life of their primal progenitor, Malley; all men are one because they are incarnations of the life of their primal progenitor, Adam; but they are one also in so far as they are members of the sub-clan founded by Jesus Christ. The clan of Adam was, by his folly, involved in a collective guilt; *all* guilt is collective according to a clansman's thinking.[4] But if one member of the lineage can bring down all its members, then, by the same token, one member of the lineage can raise them all up, for just as guilt is collective, so also is merit. The raising up – the redemption – of our lineage is precisely what our brother, Christ, did for us. His act of reconciliation (longed

---

[1] Ibid., p. 1018.   [2] Ibid., p. 1017.   [3] Bohatec, loc. cit., p. 380.
[4] Cf. Stark, W., 'The Sociology of Knowledge and the Problem of Ethics', in *Transactions of the Fourth World Congress of Sociology*, vol. IV, Louvain 1959, pp. 85 et seq.

for, hoped for, prayed for by generations of saintly men intermixed with generations of sinners) has blotted out Adam's deed of defiance, the cause of the Fall. Jesus, of course, wished to save all, but not all were willing to accept His call to a new life; some have remained outside His fold and have yet to be brought in; 'but as many as received Him, He gave them power to be made the sons of God, to them that believe in His name' (St. John's Gospel I, 12). If we are Adam's family by generation, we are Christ's by regeneration; if we are descended from, and yet linked to, Adam in the flesh, we are derived from, and committed to, Jesus in the spirit. The Church is the lineage of Christ. It is filled by His continuing Self because He was its Founder, as other founder-fathers have started their respective lineages on their courses and remained present within them.

Seen in this light, the Founder of Christianity appears as the leader of a secession movement, the secession being from a soiled into a cleansed clan, from the darkness of sin into the light of grace. What was it that enabled Him to collect followers around Him, to form a Church? Since Weber we say: it was His charisma. Yet this is at best half an answer; it certainly is not a full one.

All that mattered for Weber was the sheer fact *that* there was a following: at this point he proved himself a thorough positivist. And he thought this was sufficient. Any further step, he felt, might lead to an unfortunate fall from the high standards of scholarly objectivity; any attempt, for instance, to build up a typology of charismatic leaders would induce scholars to divide them into morally good and morally bad ones, but this cannot be done without ceasing to be value-free, i.e. ceasing to be scholarly. Hence we have no choice and must bracket together St. Francis and Napoleon, Jesus and Hitler.[1] They all belong in the same category because they all have the decisive quality of charisma: a personal magnetism which attracts men as the lodestone attracts iron particles.

In an important paper, 'Political Leadership and the Problem of the Charismatic Power', Carl J. Friedrich has recently discussed this issue and come to the conclusion that a category so wide as to include Moses and Mussolini, Jesus and Hitler, is not useful in political analysis.[2] This, it would appear to us, is merely the voice of common sense; and common sense can also tell us that Weber's

[1] Weber, *The Theory of Social and Economic Organization*, as quoted, p. 359.
[2] *Journal of Politics*, 1961, pp. 3 et seq., especially pp. 15 and 16.

omnium gatherum is as useless in socio-religious as it is in political analysis. What is needed, in both academic divisions, are obviously narrower, more close-fitting definitions.

This brings us up against a truly decisive question: what is the distinguishing mark of religious charisma in contrast, especially, to the leadership qualities of the superman of politics? In trying to answer it, we must, of course, eschew the simple and cheap device of saying that the one is good and saintly, the other bad and wicked. The dividing line between the two must be drawn factually; Weber is right; nothing else is scholarly. The facts are at our disposal. We must use them to distil from them ideal types.

Weber himself gives us (though in an entirely different context) the touchstone which we need, for he distinguishes *Gesinnungsethik* and *Erfolgsethik*, the ethics of Jesus and the ethics of Machiavelli.[1] Even Machiavelli wished to be a servant of good, but he was prepared to use *any* means to achieve his end. This marks the parting of the ways. Jesus, as Weber sees Him, was *not* prepared to use any means but only such as would not contaminate the end, only such as would be in harmony with the end. What separates the two positions is really the question of the legitimacy of the use of power. Machiavelli accepted it, Jesus rejected it. If it is permitted to profile this contrast sharply, we should say that Machiavelli was actuated by the love of power and Jesus by the power of love. But this sets the political and the religious charisma unequivocally off from each other. The charismatic figure in politics uses this-worldly methods, the charismatic figure in religion other-worldly ones. Of course, this is only ideal-typically true. In religious life, as history shows it as an ingredient in the secular scene, there were many leaders who used this-worldly means – there are only too many examples of this. But what we have to say of them is simply that *in so far as* they used political means, their charisma was not archetypally religious, and their total charisma – their over-all power to fascinate, to attract, to compel – was mixed. 'He was a saint, even though he was involved in wars,' St. Peter Damian said of Pope Leo X; but he added: 'It was not because he was involved in wars that we can

---

[1] Cf. Weber's lecture 'Politik als Beruf'. For an English version, cf. *Politics as a Vocation*, transl. Gerth, H. H., and Mills, C. Wright, Philadelphia 1965. Cf. further, Stark, W., 'The Agony of Righteousness: Max Weber's Moral Philosophy', published in *Thought*, 1968, pp. 380 et seq.

call him a saint.'[1] Perhaps there has never been in this world any charismatic personality in this pure sense which we are trying to give to the term, except Jesus Christ. But His light shone through others as well, even though it was somewhat dimmed by the impurity of the medium through which it had to pass. Grey is not white, but it has white in it, and that white, when envisaged in purity, is symbolic of the religious charisma in the proper – the ideal–typical – meaning of the word.

We do not have to copy passages from the Gospels here in order to illustrate Jesus' rejection of power. It comes out most movingly in His confrontation with Pilate, but it looks through many other contexts as well. All we would say in passing to our next point is that He was much more consistent in this regard than a cursory reading of the sources might indicate. Eduard Meyer, in his magisterial *Ursprung und Anfänge des Christentums*,[2] has strongly emphasized this aspect of Christ's public ministry. 'He does not wish to seek conflict and catastrophe' – for even this would be co-operation with the men of power. 'He travels through Galilee hidden and unrecognized, [and] as He keeps out of the way of Herod, so He forbids His disciples after Peter's confession to speak of His messiahship and avoids, even at Jerusalem, an open declaration, as long as it is possible.'[3] Much has been written, especially by German scholars, about Christ's *Messiasgeheimnis*, or messianic secret, His unwillingness to reveal His messianic consciousness. Meyer has given us as good an explanation as any. Christ rejected publicity because He rejected power – both positively and negatively, both the possession of it and the application of it by others.

But we have an even more telling point to make. The Scriptures not only present Jesus to us as the archetype of a man shorn of power, they also present Him to us as the antitype of the man endowed with power. The contrast on which we are trying to base our definition of religious charisma in the narrower and only proper sense of the word is present, but thinly hidden, in the Gospels and other contemporary accounts.

We have, on an earlier occasion, quoted from Virgil's Fourth Eclogue,[4] the remarkable poem in which the coming of a saviour

---

[1] Cf. *Patrologia Latina*, as quoted, vol. CXLIV, Paris 1853, col. 316.
[2] 3 vols., latest ed. Darmstadt 1962.
[3] Ibid., vol. II, pp. 449 and 450. Cf. Mark VIII, 30, and IX, 9.
[4] Vol. I, pp. 106 and 107.

is foretold. We emphasized that two interpretations were put upon the passage concerned: some thought it was referring to an emperor who was about to be born, a saviour by the fist; others that it was promising an emissary from heaven who was presently to take upon himself human flesh, a saviour by the spirit. The great either/or – King Jesus or King James?, as Andrew Melville expressed it some fifteen hundred years later[1] – is thus formulated even before the birth of Christ, His appearing in lowliness and humility. But the theme is not stilled by His choice of a stable for a birthplace and all the other evidences of His desire to be associated with the poor. The shining image of a saving sword-swinging superman, of a royal redeemer *à la* Alexander or Augustus, remained and acted as a seduction to which even Christ Himself was exposed, and from which His disciples found it very difficult to wean themselves.

Oscar Cullmann has drawn attention to the fact that the hard words, *Apage, Satanas*, are ascribed to Jesus twice in the Gospel according to St. Matthew, and he is inclined to see a connection between the two occasions.[2] 'The Devil took Him up into a very high mountain and shewed him all the kingdoms of the world and the glory of them, and said to Him: All these will I give thee, if falling down thou wilt adore me. Then Jesus saith to him: Begone, Satan! . . . [and] the Devil left Him' (IV, 8–11). Later on, the Evangelist records how Peter had understood Christ's messiahship and revealed his understanding on the way to Cesarea Philippi, and how Jesus thereupon began to tell His disciples how He would be subjected to suffering and put to death. 'And Peter taking Him, began to rebuke Him, saying, Lord . . . this shall not be unto thee. Who turning said to Peter: Go behind me, Satan, thou art a scandal unto me, because thou savourest not the things that are of God, but the things that are of men' (XVI, 21–3). Peter obviously found it difficult to accept a saviour who would not resist his enemies, as we can also infer from his conduct in the moment of crisis, when he brought a weapon to the Mount of Olives (John XVIII, 10); but it was precisely such a saviour that Jesus desired to be. We see clearly, wherein the linkage between the two passages lies: the one is more symbolical (some would say, mythological), the other more historical. But they both agree in the rejection, on Jesus' part, of

[1] Cf. our vol. III, p. 116.
[2] Cf. *Petrus: Jünger, Apostel, Märtyrer*, 2nd rev. ed. Zürich 1960, pp. 206, 207, 208, 213.

power as this world wants it and wields it, for His kingdom was not of this world.

Cullmann is not treating us here to a specious but spurious interpretation. His argument is convincing: Peter is addressed as Satan because he makes himself the mouthpiece of the satanic seduction attempted once before in the desert. The historical kernel of the story of the three temptations, and especially of the third temptation of which we have spoken here, is Jesus' resolve not to seek power, for it is in His opinion an unacceptable tool in the pursuit of religious, redemptive ends. The mocking inscription above the cross: Jesus of Nazareth, king of the Jews, reveals Christ, if we understand the matter properly, as precisely what He wanted to be: a king without power, a prince of peace, the very antitype of a king or prince as a godless humanity has always conceived them.

Should all this be deemed still insufficient to point up the contrast between religious and political charisma, the thirteenth chapter of *The Apocalypse* should clinch the matter. For there 'the Beast' (Domitian) is dramatically opposed to 'the Lamb of God' (Jesus) – the beast equipped with all the teeth and claws of leopard, bear, lion and dragon, well able to slay the lamb, defenceless, poor and meek. It has often been doubted that the Book of Revelation really fits into the New Testament, and it must be admitted that there are difficulties. But we see before us one reason why this document, too, can legitimately find its place within the Sacred Scriptures. It preaches in its own fashion one of the truths which Jesus propagated – that force can have no attraction for the truly religious man. The fathers of Nicaea who closed the canon but took the Apocalypse in, may well have been alive to this fact.

In more recent times, it was above all Henryk Ibsen who, in his great and deep drama *Brand*,[1] returned to this basic Christian theme. The hero is determined to serve God and good, and he tries his best to drag all others along with him. His intention is fine, but he lacks that element of love without which true religiosity cannot unfold and cannot exist. It is his fatal error to try to do by compulsion what no compulsion can ever accomplish. Disappointed and defeated, at long last face to face with death, he cries to heaven in despair:

[1] 1866. We shall quote the closing words in our own translation.

> Ere I die, reveal to me,
> Does not suffice for victory,
> Manly will, will *quantum satis*?

But a voice answers him from across the great divide:

> He is *Deus Caritatis*.

CHARISMATIC CALL AND CHARISMATIC RESPONSE

The appeal of the saint, and above all of the Saint of Saints, Jesus Christ, rests, as we have just seen, on his radical otherness, his archetypal distinction from the common run of men. We can describe it both sociologically and theologically, and if we do so, we get two different definitions which, however – as we hasten to add, and have to underline – are complementary rather than contradictory. Sociologically speaking, i.e. remaining strictly within the realm of observable facts, we must say that the charismatic call finds its appropriate echo because it is revolutionary, though not in the sense in which the word is used in politics. Selfhood and sin are rejected, along with such special manifestations of them as the craving for power and the application of it to other men; a total change of human nature – a change of the heart – is demanded. It is this radicalism of the charismatic man which commands and compels respect and response. While the emphasis is, in a factual analysis, unavoidably negative, it is replaced, in a fideist view, by a positive counterpart. The negation of the world as we know it stems from the acceptance of a world which we do not know (in the scientific sense), but the existence of which we may assume and assert (in faith), if and in so far as we are religious. The charismatic man refuses to enter into a life determined by hate and sin, but he is also the harbinger of a higher life dominated by sanctity and love. This double character of his, this facing two-ways, has in history led large masses of followers to his feet.

To a race sunk in distress and despair, but at the same time filled with longing and hope, the charismatic call must ever be a *fascinosum*. But it would be wrong to ascribe the formation of groups of disciples, which in the end generate churches, merely to the power of the call, as if the charismatic man alone was active and did everything, and the masses were passive and did nothing except run after him. It is one of the errors of Max Weber's super-individualism that he is inclined to this view, just as it is the corresponding opposite error of a Marxist like Max Maurenbrecher to maintain that the masses make a man into a leader, and not the leader the masses into a coherent group.[1] The truth, surely, lies in the middle. We must see the charismatic call *and* the charismatic response, for only together can they lead to the appearance of a charismatic whole. There is, as always, a living interplay between the individual and society. Normally the call is the cause which produces the church as its effect. But it can sometimes happen, as Joachim Wach has rightly emphasized, that 'the effect produces the cause . . . It is the problem of Björnson's drama, *Beyond Human Power*, in which the hero is forced into the career of a miracle man by his admirers'.[2] Even Jesus waited for Peter's free confession of faith in Him before He ever pronounced the word 'church' (Matthew XVI, 13–18).

Basically, the charismatic response is laid on in what, with André Malraux, we may call the human condition. Nobody in this century has dealt more incisively with it than Franz Kafka in his two existentialist novels, *Das Schloss* and *Der Prozess*.[3] In *Das Schloss*, a man named K. – and this is not only Kafka, but every one of us – arrives in a village, believing that he has a meaningful task to fulfil there. But he can never find out for sure what his task is, and whether it is really meaningful. There is a castle on the hill where the rulers live, and they know the answer. But K. can never establish contact with them. The closer he approaches to it, the farther away it seems to be. *Der Prozess* is, if possible, even more torturing. K. is accused of something, he knows not what, and while he is surprised that his guilt is asserted, if not indeed presumed, he yet cannot bring himself to feel innocent and safe. And just as K. in *Das Schloss* fails to find an answer to the question which possesses and obsesses him, so does K. in *Der Prozess*. Why are we here? And why are we not at least carefree like flowers and the beasts? Who knows? We may and must ask, but there is no reply.

It is easy to see that the two novels deal with man's place in creation and in society – in creation where we appear, not only as beings who must die, not only as beings who know that they must die, but also as beings who would find out why they must live;

[1] Cf. his book *Von Nazareth nach Golgatha*, Berlin–Schöneberg 1909, especially p. 48.
[2] Wach, J., *Sociology of Religion*, London 1947, p. 344.
[3] *The Castle* and *The Trial*, originally published in 1926 and 1925 respectively.

and in society where we enter into relationships with others like us, relationships which, even when they are at their best, are over-laid by the shadow of our inescapable self-preference, so that we can never be quite happy about them. Out of this deep double source flows our need of salvation, our need to know and to love, which we ourselves seem unable to still. The human race has ever slaked this thirst by the intuition of a deity, and this intimation has, among the most advanced cultures, been significantly twofold: among the Greeks, the twin concept of an unmoved mover (the god who worked in the beginning) and of a co-ordinator of dis-cordant elements (the god who is still at work); among Christians, YHWH, the Father, and Jesus Christ, the Son, two persons Who are yet only one as They are One Spirit. It makes little difference if theism is demoted to the status of an 'idea' as it is by Kant and the Kantians, or even to that of an 'ideology' as it is by Marx and the Marxists. The problem lies at the borderline between the knowable and the unknown, and grappling with it means, and must mean, a foray into the latter realm.

The need is real, for it is doubtful whether a creature constituted as man is, man who possesses a mind craving for meaning and a heart dreaming of love, can ever live happily without some re-assurance on the two aspects of ultimate mystery which obtrude on us. Yet it is not like body-hunger which has to be assuaged at any price; it is merely a mind-hunger which can be held in abeyance and sidestepped, at least to some degree. There have been, and there are, classes and societies which have suspended the search for the ultimate, and it is this fact which makes the response to the charis-matic call so deeply problematical, both on the level of theory and on that of action.

An example of a class which has at best a muted interest in metaphysic-religious issues is the bureaucracy.[1] The bureaucrat's life and work is set in a paper world artificially created inside the real world, and there everything runs off according to knowable, rational rules and regulations. In so far as there are problems in-herent in such a setting, they are amenable to solution by means of

---

[1] On this point Weber has made valuable contributions. Cf. *Wirtschaft und Gesellschaft*, ed. Tübingen 1947, pt. II, chap. IV, par. 7, or *The Sociology of Religion*, transl. Fishoff, as quoted, pp. 80 et seq. For a critical appraisal of the discussion concerned, cf. Stark, W., 'Max Weber's Sociology of Religious Belief', in *Sociological Analysis*, 1964, pp. 41 et seq.

pure logic, paper logic as Cardinal Newman called it. Disturbing facts and features from outside, such as unpredictable catastrophes or irrational passions, appear only on the far horizon and can be rationalized into marginal phenomena of no real importance. The bureaucrat is not like the captain on the bridge who looks out on to an uncharted sea and has to know about depth and distance; he is rather like a passenger who has gone down below and battened the hatches so that he can be undisturbed in his narrow cabin. A grand proof that this characterization of the bureaucratic mentality is correct, is the existence, and the nature, of Confucianism, as Weber has well explained.[1] This is a pseudo-religion rather than a religion. If it has a concept of the creator-god at all, it is one in which mystery is truly minimized; and its recommendations about human conduct concern courteous behaviour, not love. We often speak of the bureaucracy as a machine and the metaphor is justified; but a machine is not mysterious because men have made it, nor does it suggest, even from afar, the possibility of loving relationships as they are presaged, in however crude a form, in the animal realm, in the mutual relations of males and females or of parents and their young.

But the bureaucrat is not the only man who lives in a pan-mechanistic world. The industrial worker does so, too, and he also is not, by his life experience, or at least by his work experience, led to concern himself with ultimate mystery. In so far as modern society is industrial, it is apt to produce at most low-tension religiosity.[2]

This brings us from contained class to inclusive society, and the step is short.[3] It is common knowledge that large cities are less given to religiosity than village communities, and this is easy to explain as the bulk of their population is made up of the industrial proletariat. Towns are, according to Tönnies's analysis, essentially associational; but association links with a mechanical mode of social coherence, and this in turn leads to a mentality which models itself on rational mechanics and thereby excludes mystery almost totally from purview. If tragedy breaks into such a society, for instance illness or bereavement, it is held at arm's length, as it were. There is the assumption that science will somehow deal with decay and death at some future date, as it will with all disturbing things,

[1] Cf. Fishoff, loc. cit., p. 90.   [2] Cf. ibid., pp. 100 and 101.
[3] Cf. Stark, loc. cit., pp. 49 et seq.

and in the meantime there are such techniques as the tranquillizer pill which will help to overcome the momentary crises, not to speak of the shaving, painting and perfuming of corpses which is meant to leave to the departed at least the outer aspect of presence and contentment. Associational society, of which town life is but one example and all modernity another, is therefore antecedently unlikely to generate a deep concern with ultimate questions. We might as well expect love or charity on the stock exchange.

Two final remarks are needed on this wider issue. The readiness, or rather a lack of readiness, to respond to the charismatic call is, partially at least, dependent on the degree of activism which characterizes a society. The Gospel story of Mary and Martha (Luke X, 38–42) is revealing in this respect. Martha was preoccupied with many things, therefore she had no time for the one thing which Jesus thought necessary. Without a measure of contemplation, a religious quest cannot possibly appear, let alone succeed. Even social work, undertaken in the best spirit of charity, can lead to an ultimate involution of the life of faith, if it is allowed so to proliferate as to cover up the religious source from which it originally sprang.[1]

This is one of our final remarks; the other concerns the strain of consistency which, as the sociologist constantly discovers, runs through every society. Once a culture's compass is set, be it in the direction of a comparatively religious or of a comparatively irreligious world-view, it will continue in the same direction and tend to evolve a maximally closed system. Logical positivism, the ideological growth of modern urbanized society and its mechanistic-rationalistic mentality, a philosophy which could hardly have developed in the pre-capitalist world, is a good illustration here. Not that it is simply to be identified with the atheist position. Many of its protagonists, while asserting that the existence of a deity cannot be rationally proved, are perfectly prepared to concede that it cannot be rationally disproved either. But they are in effect doing much more than the professed atheists: they maintain that we cannot even sensibly *speak* about God, or about the Supernatural or the Absolute, as we have no verifiable sense-experiences corresponding to it and hence are without the most primitive

[1] This must be held against such writers as Harvey Cox and his book, *The Secular City*, New York 1965.

precondition of meaningful discourse in this field.[1] Differently
expressed, they do not return a negative answer to the twin
question which is at the root of all religion, they claim that it
cannot even be raised. Thus mystery is radically cut out of the
scheme of things. The passenger down below behind the battened
hatches is told that he may not even think of the wider world
around his boat.

But we should be less concerned with the disappearance of a
charismatic response to the charismatic call than with its original
appearance. What is it that explains the success of Christianity in
the first centuries? For, clearly, a success it was. The words which
Theodoret, in his *History of the Church*,[2] puts into the mouth of the
dying Emperor Julian (the Apostate) – 'Thou hast conquered, O
Galilean!' – indicate a great historical truth. In order to explain
this victory of Christ over Caesar (and the victory of the weak
over the strong always demands an explanation), we have to offer
an analysis of the contemporary facts.

At the time when the world was getting ready to abandon the
religion of Julian and to take up that of Jesus, the human race was
passing through the second of the great metaphysical crises which
it has had to face and to endure on its way through history. We
call these crises metaphysical because they involved the last things
– birth and life, death and destiny, sin and salvation. Of the first
of these crises we know, so far as the factual detail is concerned,
next to nothing. And yet it is obvious that there must have been
such a crisis, namely when the awakening intellect had matured
enough to envisage the discouraging aspects of the human situation – the uncertainty of all things, including nature, the fateful
concatenation between birth and death, evolution and deperition,
and the certainty of a personal decease as the terminus of all
human endeavours. Doubt must have been rampant and despair
not far under the surface. But the mental difficulties were overcome,
for the collective consciousness of the species developed, as an
acceptable and satisfying, if not satisfactory, answer to the nagging
questions which had been raised, the first religions, including that
of YHWH among the Jews and the great creation myths of the

---

[1] Cf., e.g., Ferré, F., *Language, Logic and God*, New York 1961, especially ch. 3,
'The "Elimination" of Theological Discourse'.
[2] III, 20. Cf. *Patrologia Graeca*, ed. Migne, J. P., vol. LXXXII, Paris 1859,
cols. 1119 and 1120.

cultures around the Jews. The modern intellectual, looking back on these intuitions or imaginings, is apt to decry them as tissues of absurdities. But if he sees them in this light, he misses the whole point. An exclusively rational solution to the existential problems of man is not possible, in *any* generation. All that can happen, in *any* period of history, is the development of a sentiment of security, the formation of an atmosphere or aura of protectedness in which anxiety cannot raise its head and men may feel sheltered against the deathly winds of a hostile material universe. Such a sentiment was generously provided by all the religions of the early days. Without them, or, to be more precise, without their discourage-ment-dispelling, confidence-creating effects, the human race would not have survived, let alone advanced.

The religions of the early days show us man turned towards nature rather than towards his fellow-men. Of course, this is only true if we add: relatively speaking. There has never been a time when human relations were unproblematical. The stories of Cain and Abel or Romulus and Remus are records of the dawn rather than of the arrived day, and their symbolism shows us, not only that even brothers can hate each other, but also that primitive man was fully conscious of the ever-threatening danger of fratricidal conflict and mutual destruction. Yet the clan was closely knit; it was not there that the mortal menace lay. And it was not from there that the blessing of reassurance could come. Menace lay in nature with her dark, disturbing and destructive forces; reassur-ance also came from nature with her mysterious but mighty and ever-reasserted power of renewal. John Barleycorn had to die in the fall, yet he reappeared after the spring rains, and so life was always victorious, and its victory enveloped also that brittle creature, man. The rites of the pre-Christian religions are clearly geared to the calendar; it was by living with nature, by so to speak inserting himself in nature, that man felt he could conquer death. And if there remained a last lingering doubt about the reliability of the cosmic laws, a doubt that the spring rains *would* come to re-awaken John Barleycorn, it was removed by the rituals them-selves in their second function, as it were. They were an acting-out, and thereby a dissipation, of the remaining anxieties, *rites de passage*, we might say, if we be permitted to give a new meaning to an old term, which would help nature herself to advance from winter into a new spring.

It was the great and basic error of the Myth-and-Ritual School which we have encountered twice before[1] to assert that Christianity, too, was a calendric religion, a new form of an old thing. In his book, *The Nature and Function of Priesthood*, E. O. James allows that 'it was unquestionably the historic Jesus who in the first instance produced the conviction of his Messiahship among his initial followers'. But he says on the very same page concerning the symbolization of Christ as 'the lamb slain from the foundation of the world', that 'behind this imagery lay a complex mythology derived from Babylonian, Egyptian, Iranian and possibly Mandean sources'. As for the Jewish tradition, he makes much of the Pesach Feast which in date coincides so closely with the Christian Easter: 'As part of the New Year Festival in the spring (Nisan), it may have been originally a ritual offering on behalf of the divine king: the firstborn having been slain as a substitute for the royal victim.' The Pesach of the flocks is then joined by the Pesach of the fields, the Massoth or Feast of Unleavened Bread 'which belongs essentially to the agricultural tradition as an offering of the first-fruits'. Both feasts centre on fertility rites: 'The purpose of the Pesach was the offering of the firstborn to promote the annual increase of the flocks and herds on which the pastoral people depended for their subsistence. Similarly, the Massoth had as its chief aim the fertility of the crops for the ensuing season.' The thrust of James's argument can easily be detected: his tendency is to push Jesus back into the dark dawn, into the murky regions of primitive peasant religiosity. He calls Him 'a historical Figure not altogether unfamiliar in the conception of the Man-god in the myth and ritual of the Graeco–Roman world'. Nothing much therefore happened with the formation of Christianity: 'The tradition so deeply laid in the theocracies and their priesthoods in the Ancient East lived on, renewed, reinvigorated and re-enforced . . .'[2] We are invited to believe that the coming of Christ is epoch-making only for the annalist who formally distinguishes B.C. and A.D., but not for anybody else.

However, James and those who think like him are simply wrong. If the facts are considered without prejudice, one is surprised by Christianity's detachment from nature rather than by its involvement in nature. And this is something which the sociologist will

[1] Cf. vol. I, pp. 32 et seq., and vol. III, pp. 29, 40, 41.
[2] Loc. cit., London 1955, pp. 144, 157, 158, 159, 238, 276. Cf. also pp. 148 and 170.

not find difficult to understand. Christianity is a child of town-life and not of the countryside. 'Early Christianity . . . found its chief opportunity in the towns', writes Herbert Workman.[1] 'The bishop was from the first almost wholly a city officer; only slowly did the Church acquire influence over the countryside pagans, and then chiefly by missions worked from the cities. In the fourth century Christianity was practically still a matter of the towns.' This fact shows itself clearly in the ritual where the basic preoccupations of a religious community are bound to be reflected. The Rogation Days, when the fruit of the fields are blessed, are the palest of all holy days, and the Pontificale Romanum entrusts these benedictions to simple *lectores*, i.e. officers beneath the rank of priest.[2] Even where an agricultural rite, the procession of the Blessed Sacrament across the fields, has evoked a supreme expression of Catholic spirituality, as it has in César Franck's sublime *Dieu s'avance à travers les Champs*, this has nothing whatever to do with nature as such. This song is – like the same composer's equally sublime hymn *Panis Angelicus* – an echo of Thomist mysticism, a meditation on a deep tenet of religious philosophy. It is true that Easter and Christmas are fixed to calendric dates which suggest the older calendric religions. But so far as Easter is concerned, this simply reflects the Jewish Pesach-Feast during which the masses were out and about and any public excitement was apt to come to a head. This date was set for Christianity, not by Christianity. As for Christmas, it is only since comparatively recent times that the main emphasis has fallen on the solstice day. It was the calendrically un-important Epiphany which carried, for centuries, the main emphasis; and even now it bears the deeper meaning, for it is Christ's manifestation to mankind that is theologically decisive, not the sheer fact of His physical birth. In any event, such continuity as there is between the new religion of Christianity and the old religion incarnated in the Pesach is largely external. The *meaning* of the 'lamb slain' is entirely different. Lenin resided in the very same houses in which the Tsars had dwelt before – the Winter Palace and the Kremlin. Are we to say that for this reason little happened when he replaced Nicholas II?

There is, rightly considered, a sharp dividing line between the older religions by which the Myth-and-Ritual School sets so much

[1] Loc. cit., p. 30.
[2] Cf. Lécuyer, J., *Prêtres du Christ*, Paris 1957, p. 77.

store, and the newer religion of Christianity which is really very different in character; it is only that the truth is obscured by certain verbal veilings, especially the habit of using metaphors taken from nature, like the simile of the fig-tree, or, for that matter, the simile of the lamb. The cosmic processes were the pattern in which the old religions immersed the religious life of their devotees; they were the be-all and end-all of these religions; they were far less to Jesus and St. Paul, to whom they were merely a store-house of symbols which were convenient for use as they were sure to be understood in a world which had long lived under the traditional myths and rituals. The question which Christianity posed was not: how can man be free from physical evil, e.g. hunger, but how can he be justified, i.e. free from moral evil? Death was not simply a dissolution of the body, but a foundering of the soul in sin, and resurrection was not merely a return to life, but a rebirth unto righteousness. In other words, there is a far heavier ethical element in Christianity than in any of the earlier dispensations. And this in turn reveals the problematic in response to which the new revelation was received. The anxieties which plagued men at the end of Antiquity and the beginning of the Middle Ages were not centred on a possible failure of nature to continue steadily into the future, they were concerned with a progressive loosening and threatening breakdown of the social order which had encompassed men since time immemorial in the past.

Rudolf Bultmann puts his finger on the essential fact when he says, in his discussion of the great crisis with which we are here concerned, that 'the self can no longer conceive of himself as an exemplification of a general category; he can no longer find his quietude by deflecting his eyes from the individual to the community'. The social whole appears now, in the age of Caesarism, as an enemy of man; it does violence to him – it does not protect him. 'But this means that the understanding of reality has . . . undergone a total transformation.'[1] The last words are, as Bultmann himself proves in another part of his fine book,[2] something of a mis-statement. It was not that one explanation had given way to another; that would not have brought on the great soul-shaking and God-searching in the context and consequence of which Christ's

---

[1] *Das Urchristentum im Rahmen der antiken Religionen*, Zürich 1949, p. 186. Our translation.
[2] Pp. 179 and 180.

charismatic call was received and accepted. No, what happened was that both cosmos and society had assumed the mask of incomprehensibility. 'Man's relation to the world had become problematical ... He knows himself to be exposed to the vagaries of good and evil – to be without power over the good and without protection against evil.' Earlier on, man had relied upon *nomos* and *logos*, reasonable and therefore understandable order in society, and reasonable, at least quasi-rational, and therefore understandable, order in the universe. Both had disappeared, as the sun, on an evil day, may become hidden behind rain-clouds. The sociologist may be permitted to believe that the disappearance of trust in *logos* was a consequence of the disappearance of trust in the *nomos* or *nomoi*. He will look for a key in the social history of mankind.

Possibly, indeed probably, it was not the failure but the success of primitive society and its associated religiosity which brought on the great unsettlement which lasted roughly eleven hundred years, from the bursting out of the Macedonians from their homeland and their bid for world conquest to the turning back of the Mohammedans on the threshold of France after their career of aggression had run its course. Over-population started to plague many tribes, and over-population is a sign of victory, not of defeat, in the struggle for survival. But over-population destroyed, and had to destroy, the tribal pattern of life within which mankind had found, for centuries, an acceptable existence and a satisfying world-interpretation. The basic belief that all tribesmen or clansmen were the offspring of a primal ancestor who, for his part, had been an incarnation of the beneficent powers of nature, had generated, both a feeling of kinship inside society, and a feeling of kinship with the outer world. But this feeling, the very pivot of primitive man's life assertion and assurance, could last only so long as his embeddedness in nature lasted. And this could not last when the given framework of existence became too confining and had to be burst. First, there came the development of towns; in the Platonic and Aristotelian polis we have still an afterglow of the old order and religiosity, but we can never forget that their work was a defence, and a losing one, against the practice and theory of social dissolution;[1] then there came the great migrations; both urbanization and migration alienated men from their traditional folkways and folk-beliefs. A new pattern of pacification and a new system

[1] Ibid., pp. 164 et seq.

46

of steadying thought were needed. Many attempts were made to provide them. There was the cult of the Great Mother; there was the religion of Mithras; there was the worship of Isis and Serapis; there were others still. But it was Christianity, with its double call for a brotherhood of man and common sonship under God, which most deeply responded to the needs of the hour: and therefore it was also responded to.

The old religions could not still the new hunger for peace and a peace-providing philosophy. They were not made for the purpose. They dealt with man's place in nature, and more especially with the fertility of the fields and the flocks, but not so much with the problems of human existence and co-existence. Yet two new shoots appeared on the tree of the old religiosity. They demand the attention of the sociologist of religion and the student of Christianity.

One of these half-old, half-new beliefs was the cult of the sacred ruler. It was he who, like no one else, incarnated, since time immemorial, the life of the tribe and guaranteed its harmonious integration in the cosmos, as well as the ordered, law-informed integration of the fellow-tribesmen in the society. When large-scale empires arose which were politically unified but religiously multiform, it was only natural that there should be a tendency to complete political unification by religious, and this could best be done by encircling the Emperor's head with a crown and a halo. Alexander the Great had pushed in this direction, and Augustus and the Augusti took him for their model. Between them there stands, as a connecting link, the Egypt of the Ptolomaei. The association of Caesar and Antony with Cleopatra was not only based on that lady's personal attractions (nor yet on the fact that her country could provide Rome with bread-corn); it also had the desired effect of shedding the mysterious glow of Eastern kingship over the Western power-seekers. From Caligula onward, all Roman emperors were *divi* and other religiously suffused titles were soon added, such as *soter*, *epiphanes*, *kyrios*, and so on. When it looked, for a moment, as if Augustus would give the world peace, this ruler-deification gained substance, so to speak. The promise of the *pax Augustea* was a bright star of hope, but it soon lost its lustre. Not only did the pacification and political integration of the *orbis terrarum* remain incomplete, but the mystique of the ruler proved, because of its inherent character, insufficiently intense, one might almost say, insufficiently authentic, to still the general religious hunger, especially among the lower classes. For in addition to the old religiousness which was doubtlessly present in it, it contained two semi-rationalistic and therefore only semi-religious ingredients: the cult of the hero and the cult of the sage. And this was enough to deprive the concept of a god-king of its ultimate attractiveness. A hero and a sage could not redeem; at least so thought the masses of the poor: he was but human, all too human. Sociologically speaking, the cult of the sacred ruler was an upper-class religion, something official and academic, and therefore remote. It had little to give to those who were beyond the narrow circle of the contemporary establishment.[1] As for parallel developments among the subject nations, they ended in the same disappointment. The enchantment of the Jews with the Macchabees lasted but a day, as had the belief of Aggeus and Zacharias in the messianic quality of Zorobabel.[2]

In order to be truly compelling, the appeal had to come from below, not from above.[3] If the imperial cult left the hearts of the masses cold, the mystery religions which sprang up everywhere gave them warmth. Here was true religiosity: 'The deepest reason for their power to attract can be found in their claim to be able to give to the individual a liberating answer to his existential question what his fate in the beyond was going to be. They set out to show him how he could, by giving his life in this world a moral content, secure salvation for the life hereafter.'[4] In one sense, even these religions had philosophical antecedents. Socrates, with his call of 'Know Thyself', had redirected attention away from nature towards man and the implications, positive and negative, of man's social existence: Plato and Aristotle were preoccupied with the polis.[5] But soon development was to lead far away from an intellectualism which would, once again, have pleased only the educated. Out of the growing realization of the deep problematic of all social ordering, which, needless to say, arose from the contemplation of the sufferings of the poor, Orphism developed something akin to the biblical concept of the Fall. 'From the murder com-

---

[1] Cf. Baus, K., *Von der Urgemeinde zur frühchristlichen Grosskirche*, Freiburg–Basel–Wien 1963, pp. 103, 106, 107.
[2] Cf. Bultmann, loc. cit., p. 89.
[3] Cf. especially Meyer, as quoted, vol. III, pp. 326 and 328.
[4] Baus, loc. cit., pp. 107 and 108. Our translation.
[5] Cf. especially Bultmann, loc. cit., pp. 135 and 137.

mitted by the Titans,' from whose ashes they arose according to the Zagreus myth, so a prime student of the subject has summed up the basic Orphic belief, 'the whole of mankind inherits a sort of original sin from which each soul must be purged. The soul is a prisoner ... in the body and can escape and rejoin the original divine essence only by death. It is possible, however, to anticipate this reunion, without being obliged to await death, by virtue of the mystery, which temporarily delivers the soul from its bodily prison and brings it into touch with the divine essence'.[1] This sounds already like the coming Christian system of belief, and near-Christian is also the conviction that a communion with the divine *can* be established, and that, not by means of thought, but only by means of experience, a rite, an opening of the heart within a cultic frame so that the divine love and life can flow into it, comforting, healing and saving.

Nevertheless, even these mystery religions (of which Greek Orphism was only one) could not, by themselves, provide the new world faith that was wanted. They possessed indeed what emperor worship lacked: a depth dimension, a capacity to allay anxiety and to satisfy the heart. But they lacked on their part what emperor worship possessed: a world-wide focus, the figure of a divine king common to all men. Such a Kyrios-Soter came to them only in Jesus Christ. He was indeed the Lord, more powerful than the most powerful; but He was also the Lord of lowliness, more humble than the most humble. In Him, the dialectical contrast of the two types of religious movement, which between them represented and showed forth the salvation-hunger of humanity, was totally overcome.

We can sum up the analysis which we have just completed in slightly different language and in doing so demonstrate how well it tallies with the total character and construction of the present work. The decay of the old nature religions and the longing for a new social religion produced on the one hand a state church (such as we have studied in vol. I) and on the other hand a multitude of kindred sects (such as we have studied in vol. II). But both established and dissenting religiosity are deeply involved in the secular world, the one by love, the other by hate; both have therefore qua religions narrow limitations. A truly liberating religious faith can only spring up when and where these limitations are lifted. There

[1] Macchioro, V. D., *From Orpheus to Paul*, New York 1930, p. 101; cf. also pp. 118, 193, 194.

must be two concomitant breakthroughs out into the open, one from the narrow ideological confines of an upper set, the other from the closed-in conventicle-mentality of a lower class. Christianity achieved both, and, humanly speaking, i.e. leaving aside (as we must in a purely sociological treatise) the supernatural character of the Founder, His being in the Christian view divine love incarnate in a man, it could achieve both because it was formed in an atmosphere of internationalism and at least relative social openness. We have seen in vol. III (especially on pp. 11–22) that, in religion, universalism means freedom from national exclusiveness and class dividedness. Such universalism was given to an exceptional degree in the parent world of Jesus Christ and Roman Catholicism; and in so far as it was not given, it was created by Him and His disciples in the early days.

It was a widespread conviction among the Fathers that the coming, and the success, of the Roman Empire were providential, for the Empire created an integrated world in which the Gospel could spread without let or hindrance. 'God . . . brought it about that the Roman Emperor had the rulership over the whole world,' writes Origines in *Contra Celsum* (II, 30). Thereby He 'prepared the peoples for His doctrine . . . Had the peoples been compelled to carry on wars and defend their fatherland . . . how then could this peaceful doctrine, which does not even allow revenge against enemies, have made its way? . . . There were not to be several kingdoms. Otherwise the peoples would be strangers one to another'.[1] Nothing that has happened since these words were written has done anything to controvert or even diminish their truth-content. All the modern observer has to urge is that they are too narrow, and that in two respects: the political integration of the world not only helped the Gospel to spread, it also helped it to arise; and the political integration of the world was not only the work of the Romans but the effect of a far wider process which spanned centuries as it spanned the contemporary world.

Eduard Meyer, one of the greatest historians of antiquity since antiquity, has asserted that it was the erection of the Persian Empire by Cyrus (*ca.* 550 B.C.) which started humanity on its career towards unification and thereby prepared the universal charismatic response to Christ's universal charismatic call which we are endeavouring to elucidate here. He speaks of a 'decisive turning point for the

[1] Cit. Moe, O., *The Apostle Paul*, Minneapolis 1950, p. 185.

whole history of religion in general', and justifies his judgment as follows: 'The national form of political life is definitely buried so far as the world west of the Iranian plateau is concerned; its place is taken by the universal empire and alien domination. Thereby religion is divorced from government and the powers that be; it becomes an independent force,' into which the deepest collective insights and aspirations of the old and yet still vital folk-cultures can enter. It shapes into an autonomous focal area at and in which past and future meet: the godward traditions of the past and the salvational hopes for the future join and fuse here. Religion thus becomes more meaningful than it had ever been before. When the empire of Cyrus crumbles, that of Alexander takes its place; and if Alexander's world-domination was formally of short duration, it was really much more important than might be concluded from the outer course of political events. Alexander was the creator not only of an ephemeral world state but also of an enduring world culture – Hellenism. Greek now becomes the universal tongue, and Jews like St. Paul use it no less than Philo in the south or Marcus Aurelius in the west. And political integration is not lost either. The Hellenistic *oikumene* turns into the Roman *orbis terrarum*. It is not dissolved and destroyed, but merely embraced and reorganized. Even the Hebrews are drawn into this development, with incisive consequences, also, and especially, in the religious field. Meyer finely remarks and demonstrates how the name of God changes in the successive portions of the Bible: first, He is YHWH, a tribal god; but with Daniel who knew the East, and with the Macchabees who fought Rome, it changes to Heaven, a universal concept and symbol, taken from a physical reality which comprises all.[1]

This is not to say that Jewish nationalism faded painlessly away. Far from it; the Jews clung almost desperately to it, and the religious Jews clung to it even more than the rest of them. The Pharisees' over-anxious observance of all the *minutiae* of the Law, for instance, was inspired by their resolve not to lose their identity as a separate people: he who eats no pork is different from him who does.[2] But there was one crucial factor which did make the Jews more inclined than other nations to accept the call of Jesus when it came:

[1] Loc. cit., vol. II, pp. 17–21; for the quotation cf. p. 18.
[2] Cf. the remarkable Aristeas letter quoted in Moe, loc. cit., p. 65. Cf. also Cerfaux, L., *The Church in the Theology of St. Paul*, transl. Webb, G., and Walker, A., ed. New York 1959, pp. 9 et seq.

their unwillingness, almost their inability, to think in terms of a sacred king in and of this world. On 30 October (or 24 Tishri) 445, the Jewish people, led by their priests and levites, had solemnly accepted the charter brought to them by Ezra from Babylon, and in it they forswore for ever independent statehood, including a monarchy of their own. Henceforth 'King' meant for them, in so far as they were religious, 'God', and only God. The Pharisees in particular embraced this conviction. Any earthly king would be a competitor to the Heavenly King; to want an earthly king was therefore deeply wrong, almost a blasphemy. Politically, the group favoured an aristocracy: no one ruler, no competitor to the True Ruler.[1] Thus Israel was free of the tendency towards ruler-deification which beset others, and could more readily enter into the spirit of the Gospel message. Of course, there were Jews who still dreamt of a restoration of the Kingdom of Israel. Even the Gospels bear witness to their existence.[2] But their relative soberness was hardly more realistic than the highly strung utopianism of the eschatologically inclined majority who believed, or knew, that only the end of the world could give them a king, their King. In any case, they belonged almost exclusively to the upper classes, and hence not to the strata who easily and eagerly responded to Jesus' charismatic call.

Inside the fold of Judaism, there were some who were exceptionally inclined towards internationalist modes of thinking and feeling, and among them the people of Galilee and the people of the diaspora stand out as most significant. From the former originated the first disciples, from the latter the founders of the world church. The traditional adage that nothing good was apt to come out of Galilee was due to the fact that there was a fairly heavy intermixture of non-Jews with Jews in this particular district. At one time Assyrian colonists had been brought in, and they had not been entirely assimilated, even after the Macchabees had started to press for greater conformity with the Jewry of Palestine. Greek-given names, too, seem to have been far from unknown here, as historical research can show.[3] Of the crucial importance of the Jews from the diaspora it is almost unnecessary to speak. The acriby of Mauren-

---

[1] Cf. Meyer, loc. cit., pp. 1, 305, 314.

[2] Cf., e.g., Matthew XX, 20 and 21. Cf. also Acts I, 6.

[3] Cf. especially Maurenbrecher, M., *Von Jerusalem nach Rom*, Berlin–Schöneberg 1910, pp. 19 et seq.

brecher has made it likely that of the twenty-two members of the oldest Christian community at Jerusalem which we know by name, eighteen were from the diaspora.[1] We cannot and need not discuss them all, nor yet all or any disciples outside the city, for the case of Paul of Tarsus is typical. 'Tarsus was located on the borderline between two worlds, viz. the oriental and the occidental, and thus combined in its life two kinds of people and two kinds of cultures, Greek and oriental. The main part of the population was presumably . . . Syrian, with a very large addition of Jews.'[2] These were Jews with a difference. Not only were they, as townsfolk, out of the matrix of nature,[3] as we have already emphasized, but they were also, as emigrants, out of the matrix of the nation. Moe, in discussing Paul's missionary work, describes it as the fulfilment of an old prophecy: 'May Japhet dwell in the tents of Sem!' (Genesis IX, 27).[4] We must not, however, forget that Sem had first gone to dwell in the tents of Japhet, and that he had learned there to think in truly internationalist, instead of narrowly nationalist, terms.

But in saying all these things, we are not really saying enough yet. In addition to the various concrete mutual adjustments which the societies of late antiquity in fact achieved, there are also the general integrative tendencies which pervaded them, and although they are less tangible, they are equally real and perhaps more important. When men or societies enter into constructive contact, so von Wiese has explained,[5] they can and regularly do run through a gamut of relationships, which range from 'approach' at the lower or weaker end of the scale to 'fusion' at the higher and stronger end – at the terminal point, as it were. The nations of antiquity never reached fusion; they approached it only from afar. In real, so to speak, substructural, life, the barriers remained, even if they were lowered. But what was not possible in the substructure, was possible in the superstructure, what was not possible in the real sphere, was possible in the ideal sphere, in thought and especially in religion. The Church which ultimately emerged from the

[1] Ibid., p. 37.　　　　　　　　　[2] Moe, loc. cit., p. 26.
[3] Cf. ibid., p. 31, on the city character of Paul's language, especially his similes. Cf. also pp. 156, 191, 328.
[4] Ibid., p. 161.
[5] *System der allgemeinen Soziologie*, ed. München und Leipzig 1933, pp. 240 et seq., especially pp. 250-6.

integrative tendencies of the epoch, the *Catholica*, represents a total synthesis of all the religious tendencies of the *oikumene*, of the *orbis terrarum*, in so far as they were assimilable to her core-structure, the figure and doctrine of Jesus Christ.

Two great Protestant writers have acknowledged this fact – Friedrich Heiler and Adolf Harnack. 'All the religious ideas and sentiments, all the forms of cult and piety which have in the past been alive within humanity, can be found in Catholicism,' writes the former.[1] And the latter expresses himself as follows: 'How rich and how manifold are the ramifications of the Christian religion as it steps at the very outset on to pagan soil! . . . Christianity showed itself to be synchretistic. But it revealed to the world a special kind of synchretism, namely the synchretism of a universal religion. Every force, every relationship in its environment was mastered by it and made to serve its own ends . . . Unconsciously it learned and borrowed from many quarters: indeed, it would be impossible to imagine it existing amid all the wealth and vigour of [its contemporary] religions, had it not drawn pith and flavour even from them. These religions fertilized the ground for it, and the new grain and seed which fell upon that soil sent down its roots and grew to be a mighty tree. Here is a religion which embraces everything. And yet it can always be expressed with absolute simplicity: one name, the name of Jesus Christ, still sums up everything.'[2]

The fact that the Catholic Church represents a synthesis of all earlier religious ideas and sentiments in so far as they are capable of combination with the Gospel did not, however, have to wait nearly two thousand years for recognition. The chief apostles, Peter and Paul, saw very clearly that the community which was forming under their hands would not be like a lake, with circumscribed banks, but rather like the open sea into whose waters all rivers must ultimately flow. The tenth chapter of *Acts* tells us of an interesting dream which Peter had: he was hungry and saw a vessel descending from heaven in which there were various foods, including some forbidden by the Mosaic dietary laws, and he heard

---

[1] Loc. cit., p. 161.

[2] Harnack, A., *The Mission and Expansion of Christianity in the First Three Centuries*, trans. Moffatt, J., ed. New York and London 1908, vol. I, pp. 312 and 313. Cf. also chap. III (pp. 24–35), especially p. 35. Cf. further the excellent exposition in Dawson, Chr., *The Formation of Christendom*, New York 1967, pp. 148 et seq.

himself bidden to eat of them. But, as a Jew, he demurred: 'I never did eat any thing that is common and unclean.' Yet 'the voice spoke to him again the second time: that which God hath cleansed do not thou call common'.[1] 'That vessel signified the Church,' St. Augustine says in a sermon,[2] and so, surely, was the vision interpreted by all. Indeed, *Acts* themselves interpret it in this vein. 'You know how abominable it is for a man that is a Jew to keep company or to come unto one of another nation,' Peter is reported as saying to those around him as he takes up contact with the Roman centurion Cornelius. 'But God hath shewed to me to call no man common or unclean.'[3] From Paul we get the same idea in a much more direct form. He not only writes, in I Corinthians XII, 6: 'There are diversities of operations, but the same God who worketh all in all,' he writes even more unambiguously in Romans I, 14: 'To the Greeks and to the barbarians . . . I am a debtor.' It would be quite wrong to interpret such passages in a restrictive spirit. Peter and Paul wished to teach all, but they were also prepared to be taught. Giving they received.

There is no quarrel about the facts. Heiler himself draws (if in another context) attention to the passages which we have quoted.[4] But he is not happy about the development he is reporting; nor is Harnack. Was the purity of the Gospel preserved in the process? Was there not, already in the apostolic age, a necessity for the call uttered later (perhaps too late) by Luther: back to the Word? The answer must of course depend on the question whether or not unassimilable elements streamed in through the open door, bringing contamination and falsification. But this is really an issue of valuation with which the scholar has no concern. Our task in this section was simply to explain the world-wide acceptance of the Christian message, and in our effort to do this, we have – not surprisingly – been led to the conclusion that the echo was universal because the call it re-echoed was universal too.

In the Gospel according to St. Matthew, there are one or two passages which seem difficult to reconcile with the internationalism of the Christian message which we have just asserted and which otherwise shines so strongly through the pages of the New Testament.

---

[1] *Acts* X, 9 et seq.
[2] Sermon CIL, 5. Cf. *Patrologia Latina*, as quoted, vol. XXXVIII, Paris 1865, col. 802.
[3] *Acts* X, 28.   [4] Loc. cit., pp. 47, 50, 51.

As Jesus sends the Twelve on their first missionary journey, He is reported as saying: 'Go ye not into the way of the Gentiles, and into the city of the Samaritans enter ye not. But go ye rather to the lost sheep of the house of Israel' (X, 5 and 6). This sentiment is later repeated and reinforced: 'I was not sent but to the sheep that are lost of the house of Israel' (XV, 24). We shall soon see how this difficulty can and must be removed;[1] here we wish to use the two quotations to push our argument on. The message is meant for those who can be compared to lost sheep, in other words, for those who have no shepherd. These are the people covered by the Hebrew word *anawim* which means the poor in contradistinction to the rich, the humble in contradistinction to the proud, and the hearts heavy with longing in contradistinction to the smug. It was from them that Jesus expected a living response to His call of love, and it was from them that most of the early disciples were in fact recruited. His most essential teaching was addressed to them: the Sermon on the Mount. 'Seeing the multitudes, He went up into a mountain . . . and opening His mouth, He taught them saying: Blessed are the poor in spirit, for theirs is the kingdom of heaven. Blessed are the meek, for they shall possess the land . . . Blessed are they that hunger and thirst after justice, for they shall have their fill' (Matthew V, 1–6). Here, then, we have *the* charismatic group which corresponds to, and responds to, the charismatic call. It was of them that Jesus thought when He said: 'I am the good shepherd, and I know mine and mine know me' (John X, 14).

The good shepherd and the lost sheep: there is but one image, one simile, here, and its unity symbolizes the unity of Christ and His people in one body, or, more generally, the unity of the charismatic leader with his devoted flock. But why were the sheep lost and in need of searching and collecting, of holding and hedging by an encompassing love?

The situation in Palestine around the time of Christ's public ministry is usually described in political terms, and the political aspect was in fact the most obtrusive. It impressed both His contemporaries and later historians before and above all others. There were three major parties: the Sadducees who were the Hellenizers, men who called themselves Alcimus instead of Eljakim or Menelaus instead of Menahem; the Pharisees who resisted Hellenization,

[1] Cf. below, p. 83.

and who defended Jewish identity and integrity by withdrawing into the shell of inherited custom and law; and finally the Zealots who hated foreigners, especially the Romans, so much that they were prepared to fight them physically, if possible in open war, if not by irredenta and terrorism. This alone shows that there were some who fitted in nowhere: for, clearly, there was also the alternative of disregarding the whole political issue and/or reacting to alien domination in terms of non-violence.

But a purely political description will not do in a sociology of religion. We have to attend to the social and the religious circumstances, and, of course, particularly to the interrelation between the two. The Sadducees were a kind of aristocracy: they were the priestly nobility with which the officers and officials of the Hasmonaean dynasty (priestly or noble by descent) were closely allied. The Pharisees were a kind of bourgeoisie: St. Luke describes them as covetous and mammonistic (XVI, 14), and all that we hear of them confirms that they were men of means. There surely is something in Maurenbrecher's remark that only the well-to-do could bear the rigours of the style of life which they demanded. The Zealots were largely recruited from the lower classes and for this reason Jesus has often been connected with them.[1] The Marxists, particularly, are apt to see Him in these terms.[2] But this is a mistake. The apostle St. Simon, sometimes also described as Simon Zelotes, seems to have been a convert from militancy rather than a link with it. In any case, a revolutionary class is apt to split into those who will use force and those who will not. The former were the Zealots of the day, the latter the *anawim*.[3] In one respect the Zealots were obviously more radical than the *anawim*: he who is prepared to attack, to maim, to kill, goes further than he who will do none of those things. But in another and more decisive respect, Jesus of Nazareth was more radical than, say, John of Giscala. For while

[1] Cf. Brandon, S. G. F., *Jesus and the Zealots*, Manchester 1967.
[2] Cf. especially Kautsky, K., *Der Ursprung des Christentums*, Stuttgart 1908. For the historical sources on which the above test is based, cf. Wellhausen, J., *Sketch of the History of Israel and Judah*, ed. London and Edinburgh 1891, especially pp. 158, 160, 174; Maurenbrecher, M., *Von Nazareth nach Golgatha*, as quoted, p. 183; Moe, loc. cit., p. 64.
[3] At an earlier period the word had been used to describe those 'united by an all-inclusive hatred against ungodly Jews and pagans' (cf. Cerfaux, loc. cit., p. 123), but the prophetic intervention and the preaching of Jesus worked like a catalyst in separating the peaceful from the warlike.

John rejected only Roman power, Jesus rejected all power, power as such. If there was a radical revolutionary, it was He.

The religious style of the two upper-class groups was in line with their total character. For the Sadducees religion reduced itself to the cult. They were ceremonialists. For the Pharisees religion reduced itself to the law. They were formalists. As the sociologist of knowledge knows, this is precisely what is apt to happen, and what has, throughout history, usually happened, to noble and bourgeois strata. No wonder that Jesus set little hope on them, so far as the generality of them was concerned, and that He could only win odd individuals of their kind over to His side. As for the proletariat, the hunger and thirst 'after justice' which may evoke true religiosity and lead to a genuinely charismatic response to the charismatic call, was indeed rampant among them. But such a need can be satisfied in two ways: by hate and by love. The followers of John of Giscala chose the former path, the disciples of Jesus of Nazareth the latter. That is why there were at first so few disciples of Jesus. But this is also why they could and did become the living stones of Christ's church.

The contents of the last paragraph can also be formulated by saying that for the nobles, the rich, and the insurrectionist poor, the religious quest was inhibited by certain foreground preoccupations – status and ceremony, wealth and attention to formality, hate and fighting forays. Max Scheler was surely right when he urged that only those can envisage the Highest Good whose eyes are not blinded and whose view is not blocked by some inferior value.[1] In a sense, *all* men are poor for all are born naked, all face a life beset with difficulty and interspersed with pain and sorrow, and all travel towards the grave. The religious call is therefore in principle addressed to them all. But few are in practice like Nicodemus, who came to Jesus although he was a Pharisee, a rich man and a ruler. The *anawim* were not simply the poor, i.e. the poor in earthly goods; they were 'the poor in spirit', i.e. those who were innocent in mind, those who had built no barriers between the Gospel and their hearts. The poor in earthly goods and 'the poor in spirit' no doubt largely coincided. But the poor in earthly goods could also be Zealots, and the rich in earthly goods could in some instances also become 'poor in spirit'. Perhaps we come closest to

[1] Scheler, M., *On the Eternal in Man*, transl. Noble, B., New York 1960, especially p. 251.

the truth when we say, using a formula of Max Weber's,[1] that there was an elective affinity between material indigence and spiritual openness, though no close, and certainly no necessary or mechanical, concatenation.

However that may be, it is a sober historical fact that the sheepfold which Christ erected was filled by those who had been lost, those whom the Sadducees, the Pharisees and the Zealots disregarded, the *amme ha' ares* (a term very near to *anawim*) or simple souls. And it was with the help of such simple souls that the Church spread across the globe and renewed herself throughout the centuries. We can give only a few indications here; the subject is too large to be adequately discussed in the framework of a more general investigation; but our comments will be on strategic points and thus, it is hoped, carry conviction.

What was it in the first place that enabled Christianity to break out of the narrow circle of Jewish lower-class life and to spill over into other areas, especially the area of Hellenistic city society? It was the existence there of strata parallel to the Hebrew *amme ha' ares* or *anawim*. 'As to the composition of the individual congregation,' Moe says with regard to St. Paul's foundations, 'it is quite certain that the membership came mostly from the lower classes ... Slaves, the liberated, tradesmen and women manifestly brought the largest contribution to the Pauline congregation ... Even at the close of the second century, Celsus and Caecilius throw into the face of the Church that it is composed mainly of insignificant people.'[2] The author, it is true, then goes on to mention a few converts who belonged to the upper ranks – Sergius Paulus, proconsul of Cyprus, Erastus, city treasurer of Corinth, and one or two others. And why should Paul not have encountered, and won over, a handful that was kindred to Nicodemus, a rich man who realized that he was in the last resort as poor as all others? Exceptions confirm, but do not controvert, the rule. Moreover, most of the wealthy whom we can identify and enumerate, were women, and women were an underprivileged group. Lydia, Phoebe, Priscilla, they were like the royal ladies, Elizabeth of Hungary, Agnes of Bohemia, and so on, who came to embrace Franciscanism more than a millennium later. In II Corinthians VIII, 2, Paul speaks of the 'very deep poverty' of the Macedonian congregations; it was

[1] Cf. Stark, W., *The Sociology of Knowledge*, London 1958, pp. 256 et seq.
[2] Moe, loc. cit., p. 571.

only in 'the riches of their simplicity' that they abounded. At two points in his epistles (I Thessalonians IV, 11, and Ephesians IV, 28) we can see that those he was addressing in Salonica and Ephesus were manual workers. Most famous is, of course, the passage from I Corinthians I, 26–30: 'See your vocation, brethren, that [among you] there are not many wise according to the flesh, not many mighty, not many noble. But the foolish things of the world hath God chosen, that He may confound the wise; and the weak things of the world and the things that are contemptible hath God chosen . . . that no flesh should glory in His sight. But of Him are you in Christ Jesus . . .' Albert Kalthoff has made it seem probable that the Roman congregation, too, was rather similar in social composition to the Corinthian or Ephesian.[1]

Thus, in the south of Europe as in Asia Minor, the carriers of the Gospel were the poor and lowly. It was no different in the north of Europe. Among the missionaries there, St. Martin of Tours stands out by more than a head's height. He is sometimes numbered among the apostles, and rightly so as he spread the good news all over France. Workman calls him 'the Great-heart of Gaul'. Nearly four thousand churches and over four hundred towns, hamlets and villages bear his name (not reckoning those in Germany or otherwise abroad). To whom did this great preacher of Christ address himself? We get the answer through the biography of the Saint from the pen of Sulpicius Severus. 'The reader who shall take up this work and ask the secret of his influence,' i.e. the secret of the influence of St. Martin which it reflects and records, Workman writes, 'will not have far to go . . . The book lifts life into a higher level; it brings before us the heights of Christian power and peace accessible . . . not to the wise and wealthy, not to priests and bishops, but to the poorest and meanest of the laity.'[2]

That Franciscanism was an appeal to – or perhaps we should say, was a return to – the very same strata is too well known to need documentation here. We have spoken of the Franciscans and other renewal movements, such as the Passionists and the Redemptorists, in vol. III,[3] and need not reopen the subject. Suffice it to say that the proper charismatic response to Christ (in contradistinction to

---

[1] Cf. especially *Die Entstehung des Christentums*, Leipzig 1904, especially. pp. 26 et seq. and 79 et seq.

[2] Workman, loc. cit., pp. 109 and 102. Cf. also p. 110.

[3] Cf. especially pp. 280 et seq. Cf. also Workman, loc. cit., pp. 285 et seq.

cool, conventional adherence) has always come from those whom He addressed in the Sermon on the Mount.

However: if it is true that Christianity was, especially in its formative period, focused on, and centred in, the poorer classes, if it was indeed, what Celsus sneeringly called it, 'a faith fit only for fullers and bakers',[1] how then is it that it did not develop into a confined sect, but broadened out into a universal church? There can be few more important questions, and we shall discuss it in the next section. Up to the catastrophe of Calvary, the half-formed body of believers certainly had in it several possibilities which might equally well have come to fruition – at least the two which we have just brought up, proletarian sect and universal church. It was the next period, the apostolic age, that made its decision in favour of the latter alternative and thereby initiated the evolution of that well-nigh unique phenomenon, the Catholic Church, which we have described, in its international and inter-class inclusiveness, in vol. III. But before we approach this subject, we have still one aspect of the problem of charismatic response to consider and to elucidate – a negative aspect, the relative, indeed far-reaching, absence of intellectuals from the responsive group. The Gospel often links the Pharisees with the Scribes, i.e. the men learned in holy philology and sacred law, and this is so because most Scribes were Pharisees. But the personal coincidence of the two strata does not imply a functional one. A bourgeoisie is one thing, an intelligentsia is another. Why its coolness towards the new religion which was spreading across the world?

Of course, the simple fact that many early disciples, for instance eleven of the twelve apostles,[2] were from the *amme ha'ares* militated against a large-scale conversion of scribes and other educated people to incipient Christianity. Literally, *am ha'ares* means something like 'son of the soil' or 'person connected with the land', but it is painfully obvious that the term had, by the first century, contracted a definitely pejorative meaning. Perhaps 'country bumpkin' or 'village yokel' comes rather close to it. This coloration of the word tells us not only something about those whom it describes, namely that they were not academically trained, but also something about the people who used it, namely that they had a very good

[1] Cit. Workman, p. 99.
[2] All but Matthew (originally Levi) who was a tax-gatherer. Cf. *Acts* IV, 13, where St. Peter and St. John are called 'illiterate and ignorant men'.

opinion of themselves, that they nurtured a superiority complex in relation to their more natural and naïve neighbours which was by no means kept out of religious life. 'No ignorant man hates sin, no *am ha'ares* is pious,' said so great a sage as Rabbi Hillel.[1] The crowds which beset the first Christians echoed the same sentiment: 'This multitude that knoweth not the law, are accursed' (John VII, 49). The opinion of Jesus was very different: 'At that time, Jesus answered and said: I confess to thee, O Father, Lord of heaven and earth, because thou hast hid these things from the wise and prudent and hast revealed them to little ones. Yea, Father: for so hath it seemed good in thy sight' (Matthew XI, 25 and 26).

The educational contrast between a sophisticated intelligentsia and an unsophisticated lower stratum is not, however, a peremptory bar to their co-operation. In the Marxist camp, for instance, or in the British Labour Party, the two have joined forces, and though it is an open secret that the intellectuals there have at times tended to look down on their allies while the latter cordially repaid their dislike in kind, the unity of the movements was not jeopardized. There must be something much more fundamental involved, so far as Christianity is concerned. In order to find out what it is, we have only to look at Eduard Meyer's deep-digging analysis.

Commenting on Matthew XI, 25–30, the text from which we have just quoted, Meyer asserts that this passage 'contains so striking a characterization of Christianity, and of the revolution which it brought into the world, as hardly any other logion. In the place of the dominion of the intellect and of the schooled perception of reason which found its most perfect expression in the philosophical systems [of heathen antiquity], but is also sought by Judaism and by Sirach in the striving for . . . godly wisdom and in the interpretation of the law, are put the forces of emotional life, the longing for salvation and peace, for immediate contact with the supernatural world of God. These forces find their satisfaction in a divining grasp of the Godhead and the mystical, intuitive insight achieved through it; in spite of, or rather because of, its darkness, it can give interior certitude, conquer doubt and soothe reason. Therefore the Mediator between God and man, the Son, calls the simple-minded to Himself to whom He reveals His knowledge

[1] Pirke Aboth II, 5, cit. Moe, p. 64. Cf. also p. 52.

which they willingly accept and effortlessly carry'.[1] 'It is a transfer of the leading position from the educated to the uneducated, from the higher strata whose creative power is exhausted, to the lower masses, which progressively takes place in the first centuries of the Christian era. . . . In this movement there unfold from below special forces which no longer root in reason, in logical thought, but in the inchoate, yet for all that all the more powerful strivings of emotional life. However much they may carry with them that is absurd and befogging, they yet contain a sound and vivifying kernel. They assert themselves above all in the field of ethics and in the formation of social life . . .'[2] The last, almost laudatory, words are important and should be remembered, especially as Meyer is inclined to speak of a 'tremendous decline in culture'.[3]

In another context, Meyer returns once more to this subject, and his second analysis is, if possible, even clearer and more enlightening. In Christianity, he says,[4] 'the decisive element is not the intellect and man's own power, but divine grace, and for that reason the preachers address in principle all humanity and in the first place the middle and lower strata of the world of culture, the uneducated and simple-minded who have neither an inclination towards, nor yet the schooling for, logical judgment and philosophical knowledge, but follow the dark lead of their sentiments and are therefore open to the *pneuma*. They offer to these circles what neither the philosopher nor the . . . moralist can offer them, a strong support in life and thought. This support is won by faith, i.e. by total acceptance of the revelation preached to them, even if its content appears strange and irrational to the educated, and by willing subordination to divine authority which has mercy on them. This is nothing less than the rejection of all that constitutes the innermost essence of philosophical thought and its spiritual freedom. For philosophy the ideal is the sage who depends on himself alone, for Christianity the believer who finds his refuge in God. We have here touched on the truly decisive factor,' Meyer goes on to say. 'Philosophy is a movement from above downward, sprung from enlightenment, from the emancipation of the mind from the traditional concepts of custom and religion, and therefore in essence unbelieving . . . Christianity, on the other hand, and all kindred phenomena, are a movement from below upward, grown from

[1] Loc. cit., vol. I, p. 289.   [2] Ibid., pp. 290 and 291.
[3] Ibid., p. 290.   [4] Vol. III, pp. 325 and 326.

religion and from the imagery of mythopoeic thought stubbornly preserved by the masses . . . and therefore by its very nature irrational and willing to follow authoritarian leads.' It is interesting to see that, while our earlier quotation ended on a positive note (Christianity helped to stabilize man and to moralize society), here the final impression with which we are left is negative (Christianity is superstition). Meyer's former presentation tells us where an 'understanding interpretation' has to be sought; the latter reflects more the intellectualist prejudice which Meyer shared with his fellow-professors, and indeed with his fellow-academics of all ages.[1]

That the academics of all ages were indeed a class which, taken in the lump, refused that charismatic response which the fishermen of Galilee and their likes in all countries and periods so willingly returned, can be seen most dramatically in the contrasting receptions which St. Paul received in Athens and in Corinth. Ernest Renan has described the Athens of Paul's day as 'a university city, a sort of Oxford',[2] and the label is correct, in spite of its anachronism. It was full of intellectuals, nay full of representatives of enlightenment, and when the Apostle preached to them, their reaction was highly characteristic of such men: 'Some . . . mocked. But others said: we will hear thee again concerning this matter' (Acts XVII, 32). Intellectuals have always fallen into two categories: some with a naked superiority complex, and others of more refined manners who clothe and cloak that complex in good behaviour. Paul was a hit with neither of them; and his assertion that all mankind is descended from one ancestor, that consequently the Athenians have the same progenitor as the Barbarians (ib. 26), did not please them either. Paul felt crushed. According to his own report, he travelled from Athens to Corinth 'in weakness and in fear and in much trembling' (I Corinthians II, 3).

In Corinth, however, he found a much more fruitful field, for this was not a university city, but a humming and booming commercial town. Rebuilt by Caesar after about a century of desolation, it was peopled mainly by ex-soldiers and ex-slaves, typical proletarians, and could hardly have been more different from Athens

---

[1] On the positive side, cf. also pp. 265 and 266, on the negative side pp. 336–8 and 529–30.
[2] *Histoire des Origines du Christianisme*, vol. III (*Saint Paul*), Paris 1869, p. 185. Cf. also Moe, loc. cit., pp. 280, 290, 292.

than it was. If Athens was an Oxford, then Corinth was a Birmingham or Manchester. Not that it was without its intellectuals; but Paul had learnt his lesson and gave them a wide berth. 'The Apostle did not allow himself to be disturbed by the fact that his preaching did not win many of the cultured and well-to-do classes, but mainly the people of lesser pretensions.' Among the latter, he was a success indeed. Together with Ephesus, Corinth became the 'classically Pauline congregation'. True, it was to him 'a child of pain' as well as 'a child of joy'. Yet Moe emphasizes, in saying this, that 'as time passed, Paul came increasingly to embrace this congregation . . . with unique fatherly love'.[1] The reason for the rewarding nature of his work in this city, and for the consequent affection which he felt for it, was clearly sociological – the presence of a class or classes antecedently sympathetic to the Gospel message. We gather as much from Paul's own reminiscing words: 'When I came to you . . . my speech and my preaching was not in the persuasive words of human wisdom [i.e. philosophy], but in shewing of the Spirit and power . . . We speak the wisdom of God in a mystery . . . which none of the princes of this world knew . . . What man knoweth the things of a man, but the spirit of a man that is in him? So the things also that are of God, no man knoweth but the Spirit of God' (I Corinthians II, 1–11).

It is by no means fanciful to discover in the last versicle an echo of the Platonic concept of the necessary correspondence of *noesis* and *noema*, knower and thing known, in which we have to recognize one of the remoter starting points of the sociology of knowledge. Only those who are somehow god-like can see God, Plato thought and taught; yet in his case the implications were decidedly aristocratic.[2] In Paul they are not so. Following Christ, he is convinced that the veil which divides the world of the senses from the world of the Spirit is only rolled back when the Gospel is preached to the poor (Matthew XI, 5). To them it was that Paul now desired to preach it. The poor of Corinth are the poor of the Spirit. They can and do receive the knowledge of the spiritual things, the mysteries, which are 'foolishness', i.e. unknowable, to the wise of 'the world'.

This brings us finally up against the last, and, in a sense, the most intriguing problem which has to be considered under the rubric 'Charismatic Call and Charismatic Response': why did the meeting

[1] Moe, loc. cit., pp. 314 and 317; cf. also pp. 297, 298, 299, 365.
[2] Cf. Stark, *The Sociology of Knowledge*, as quoted, p. 42.

of Christianity and the intellectuals, as in Athens, trigger a negative reaction? Why did it reveal the very opposite of an elective affinity? The obvious answer, namely, that Christianity is too irrational, is at best half the truth. Intellectuals have at all times entertained similarly irrational beliefs. Pareto has left us in no doubt on this score. Our analysis should be more searching; it should be more philosophical. It should and will lead us to a realization of the deeply problematic character of the relationship between reason and life.

It is the intellectual's fate – or, as most of them would say or feel, it is the intellectual's glory – to live by means of his rationality. Reason is the capital with which he trades. In saying this, we are not using unduly metaphorical language; we are much rather stating a sober fact. According to Marx's formal definition, the intellectual is indeed a proletarian for he has nothing to sell but his labour power; but, as Nassau Senior, for instance, pointed out, thus coming much closer to hard reality, that labour power is in fact a true capital because it represents a kind of accumulation carried out during the years of learning and is, both because of the natural rarity of mental talents and because of the restrictedness of educational opportunities, a quasi-monopoly (a quasi-oligopoly, as a purist with a knowledge of economic jargon would say). No wonder, then, that the typical intellectual thinks highly of reason. It is for him something standing over against life, something that is at least commensurable with life, if not indeed superior to life; it is certainly, in his conviction, not something contained in life, let alone something inferior to it. Hence there arises a specific intellectualist ideology, and its most characteristic (truth-resisting, if not truth-destroying) feature is the playing-down and arguing-away of the element of mystery within reality. Mystery is an *abhorrendum*, not a *fascinosum* to him. But it is an *abhorrendum* not only because he cannot handle it; it is an *abhorrendum* also, and even more, because it disturbs the feeling of security, of enclosedness, in an ultimately stable and reliable, scientifically understandable and technologically manageable universe of predictable laws on which his whole freedom from anxiety, his whole personal happiness depends. The fact that most intellectuals have secure and sufficient incomes helps greatly in the development and continuation of this world-view. There remain, of course, the pains and problems and catastrophes unavoidably connected with human life – disease and death and heartbreaks of all kinds. They are pushed to the outer perimeter of the intellectualist consciousness; when they strike, they are, in the case of strong personalities, accepted with stoic fortitude; in the case of weaker vessels, they are confronted with a feeling of helplessness. Here is ultimately – pragmatically – the weakest point of intellectualism. In the face of bereavement, simple people have often borne up better than the sophisticated.

But it is with the last things, the mysteries of life's meaning, the joyousness of birth and the horror of decease, that the religious consciousness is concerned. The man of faith confronts, not the predictable and controllable, but the unpredictable and uncontrollable, part of reality. He does not exclude the primal anxiety from his purview, he rises above it in the certainties (such as they are) of his creed. He is not the partial man who operates within a well-defined area and refuses to look beyond it, but rather the total man who knows that a mechanical model is not a true representation of reality but merely a miserable, reduced replica of it, comparable to what the tragedy of Hamlet would be like if the Prince of Denmark were left out of it. All men who want to be full men, who wish to come face to face with the human condition as it really is, are called to develop a truly comprehensive philosophy of life, but many refuse to do so, and among the refusers the common run of intellectuals is very prominent. Yet there are strata who are so circumstanced that they cannot easily refuse: their existence is so sorrow-laden, or merely insecure, that they must move forward into faith, especially as the sop of reason is unavailable to them. These precisely are the 'poor in spirit', the *anawim*, the *amme ha'ares*, who received the divine call of mercy when it came, even though it remained shrouded in the continuing mystery of suffering. They are but small people when measured by the yardstick of reason, but great when judged in terms of life and love.

Lest the confrontation of reason on the one hand, life and love on the other, which we have just presented, be thought imaginative or artificial, let us quickly show that it is derived from a sober analysis of intellectualist and religious mentality. The most instructive *objectum demonstrationis* is the definition of truth. The rationalist restricts himself to propositions; only they can be correct or otherwise. The religious man, on the other hand, knows another and wider truth, a truth which may even be loaded with mystery.

We might call it experiential or existential. If it is inferior in theoretical certitude, it is superior in practical application. It does not only help us to think, but it helps us to *live*. 'Truth is not something that one [verbally] asserts or denies, that one comprehends or knows,' writes Karl Hermann Schelkle,[1] 'that is the Greek and occidental concept of truth; it is something that exists or happens.' Greek and occidental means 'rationalistic' here – sophistic or at most Aristotelian. For we find the same confrontation of a propositional and an experiential concept of truth in Greece itself, and all through the occident. E. O. James brings this out very well: 'Neither the Orphics nor the Pythagoreans shared the detached curiosity of the Ionians since they were primarily concerned with the problem of right living and the purification of the soul rather than with the pursuit of knowledge [scientific knowledge] for its own sake . . . For the Milesians *philosophia* meant intellectual 'curiosity', while for Pythagoreanism and Orphism it represented a way of life in which union with, and likeness to, God was to be sought through [religious] knowledge . . . Thus knowledge was regarded as an essential element in the quest of salvation through sanctification in a world in which good and evil were in fundamental opposition.'[2]

We can see here once again how close Orphism came to Christianity, and why the two could meet and merge. But it was Christianity, or rather Christ, who presented the existential definition of truth in its purest and most powerful form. 'I am the way and the truth and the life,' He said according to St. John (XIV, 6). I *am* the truth, not I *know* the truth. Truth is not an objectified, or even objectifiable, proposition or set of such; it is part and parcel of life, not something abstracted from it. It is implemented in action, not by proof. This idea of it is supremely important precisely in the context of this chapter of our study of the sociology of religion – supremely important for the understanding of the formation of a circle of believers and finally of the Church. 'Every one that is of the truth heareth my voice,' Jesus said to Pilate (John XVIII, 37). Truth is in religion not a string of words, however reasonable and realistic, as it undoubtedly was to Pontius, a philosopher as well as a proconsul, it is a stream of life and love

---

[1] *Jüngerschaft und Apostelamt*, Freiburg, Basel, Wien 1961, p. 61. Our translation.

[2] James, loc. cit., p. 235.

which encompasses the master and the disciple. One can see here most clearly what we mean when we speak, in our title of this section, of a *charismatic* call and a *charismatic* response. When John Henry Newman was raised to the cardinalate, he chose for his device the four words: *cor ad cor loquitur* – the heart speaks unto the heart. This must surely be a key concept for any sociology of religion that does not exhaust itself in the enumeration of externals.

Of course, it would be wrong to assert that Christianity alone possesses, and operates with, the existential conception of truth. The Jews had it before the first Christian was ever born. 'Truth is, for the thinking of the Old Testament, not primarily the correctness of a sentence, [incorporating] a perception, but that which is valid, that which compels acceptance, that which can be relied on,' says Bultmann.[1] In his remarkable book, *Tristes Tropiques*, Claude Levi-Strauss ascribes it to two great philosophies of life which are otherwise worlds apart. He calls Buddhism a *religion du non-savoir* but immediately goes on to deny that it is based on a belief in the infirmity of our understanding. No, Buddhism teaches, 'we do discover the truth', but we discover it 'in the form of a mutual exclusion of being and knowing'. Audaciously it has, 'alone with Marxism, reduced the metaphysical problem to the problem of human conduct'.[2] The parallel between Marxism and Christianity which is suggested to us (though not to him) by Levi-Strauss's words, is certainly valid. Already the agreement on the basic question as to what class is most likely to perceive the truth is really striking: both Marxism and Christianity ascribe to the lowest, last and least an especially favourable position in the quest for truth. But there is more. According to a Marxist philosopher like Georg Lukács (as many pages of his *Geschichte und Klassenbewusstsein* attest) we do not get into contact with the truth if we formulate theoretical propositions (which always imply an alienation between thought and life); we get into contact with it if we give ourselves to revolutionary practice, i.e. immerse ourselves in the stream of history and press on in the direction which it pursues. History is here 'the truth': the truth is existential. You can be *in*

---

[1] Loc. cit., p. 22. But cf. above all the same author's article 'Untersuchungen zum Johannesevangelium', *Zeitschrift für Neutestamentliche Wissenschaft*, 1928, pp. 113 et seq.

[2] Paperback ed., Paris 1955, p. 372.

the truth rather than grasp it by standing over against it. Surprisingly, Levi-Strauss asserts that *only* Marxism and Buddhism represent this solution to man's quest for ultimate certainty. This proves that he knows far too little of that Christianity in whose matrix he has spent most of his life. Christianity incarnates the philosophy which he lauds to a higher degree and in greater purity than either Buddhism or Marxism. Buddhism has a finally unacceptable concept of conduct since the conduct it recommends is negative – escape. Marxism has a finally unacceptable concept of supreme reality since the reality which it sets up as supreme, namely history, is clearly nothing of the kind. To be in the truth and to be of the truth means, and must logically mean, to be in contact with the *Supreme* Good, or God, and to be one with Him in love, for love is (in the eyes of faith) the Spirit which informs His essence, His very being. 'God's Gospel is not a philosophical wisdom for the use of an intellectual *élite*,' a recent writer has well written. 'It does not appeal in the first place to the intellect; it aims at men's hearts, in order to enkindle there the love of God and neighbour.'[1]

Turned towards Logical Positivism or linguistic analysis, the doctrine in which the modern rationalist's negative attitude to Christianity is now pre-eminently anchored, Willem Zuurdeeg has recently stated the issue very clearly and we can use his fine analysis to conclude our attempt to explain the failure of the charismatic call to appeal to the non-charismatic group of intellectuals. In *An Analytical Philosophy of Religion*,[2] he distinguishes three possible uses of language: the indicative (conveying references to the empirical world), the analytical (relating definitions to one another), and the convictional (a term which is perhaps self-explanatory). Convictional language, too, he points out, refers to reality, but it is the medium of conduct, not of science, it belongs to practical, not to theoretical reason, as Kant might have worded it. So far as formal verification is concerned, convictional language may be inferior to indicative and analytical; when we act, we take many things for granted, and have to, even in the pursuit of an inferior good. But so far as personal meaning is concerned, convictional language is superior. Indicative and analytical statements are something which we possess and use; they are ours, but they have become separated from us, like tools which we have made and now handle. Convictional language on the other hand *is* the person who

[1] Bouëssé, loc cit., p. 155.   [2] Nashville 1958.

speaks it or thinks it. It is identical with our selves. Religious language, Zuurdeeg asserts, is convictional language, and therefore it is incomprehensible, nay meaningless, for those who know only indicative and analytical, i.e. scientific and logical, language.[1] St. Paul would have agreed with Wittgenstein and Ayer that the latter kinds of language cannot encompass religious truths. But, he said, 'the kingdom of God is not in speech, but in power' (I Corinthians IV, 20).

Of course, in speaking, in the foregoing paragraphs, of intellectuals, we have not meant all of them, but only many of them – those who absolutize a *relativum*, namely reason, which is commensurate to the problems of science and technology, but not commensurate to those of life and super- or after-life. We have, in other words, used an ideal type which does not comprise all members of the class but only the most characteristic ones. There have at all times been intellectuals and even rationalists who were conscious of the limitations of intellect and reason, who knew, in St. Bernard's excellent formulation, that nothing can be more contrary to reason than to endeavour to transcend reason by means of reason.[2] Such was St. Augustine; such was St. Thomas Aquinas; such was above all Blaise Pascal, to mention only the most resplendent of them.[3] Some of them were even mystics and, in Evelyn Underhill's words, belonged to 'the great and strong spirits who do not seek to *know*, but are driven to *be*'.[4] There is nothing ultimately irreconcilable about philosophy and faith. Plato and Plotinus were philosophers, yet they were also men 'homesick for heaven', as Heiler has expressed it, who brackets St. Paul with them.[5] The ideal man has once again been described most strikingly by Dante who calls for a *luce intellettual piena d'amore* – 'light intellectual brim-ful of love'.[6] There have been men who have conformed to this model, and they were jewels of the Church no less than the poor to whom St. Lawrence first gave that name; but there have always been very few of them.

The contrast between the stance of rationalism and the attitude of faith, i.e. a negative and a positive response to the charismatic

[1] Cf. op. cit., especially chapter 1.   [2] Luddy, loc. cit., p. 428.
[3] On St. Augustine, cf. the apposite remarks of E. O. James (loc. cit., p. 239); on St. Thomas, Dawson (loc. cit., p. 231); the reference to Pascal's *Pensées* must be *passim*.
[4] *Mysticism*, London 1911, p. 456.   [5] Heiler, loc. cit., p. 58.
[6] *Paradiso* XXX, 40.

call, is paralleled by, if not indeed reflected in, the conflict between intellectualism and art. The intellect, Sir Herbert Read has asserted in *Art and Society*,[1] is the foe of creativity. Defending up-to-date anti-rationalism in art, he writes: 'It is possible to maintain that from one point of view the modern taste is essentially right. For it involves a rejection of those purely intellectual standards . . . which . . . have always been inimical to the very existence of art.' There is a close connection between this judgment and our subject in hand. The truths of religion can be much more easily and much less inadequately expressed in artistic than in linguistic terms – or better, in the language of art than in the language of science. St. Thomas Aquinas's hymns are much more convincing, so far as live faith is concerned, than even his best arguments. Speaking of Mozart's *The Magic Flute*, Ernest Newman has finely said that 'something in the very depths of him was calling, as it did also in the *Requiem*, for realization in music – a sense of the seriousness of life and the gravity of death'.[2] Thus is the artistic genius brought up against the last things for the apprehension of which the common run of rationalists has no organ. Max Weber coined a more remarkable phrase than he knew when he called himself on one occasion 'religiously deaf'. But those who can hear will find, for instance, in Anton Bruckner's *Te Deum* a statement of faith which is not only supremely moving but also experientially satisfying and convincing. The rationalistic demotion of art to something 'merely sentimental' is not the least disservice which the discursive intellect has done to religion, and, indeed, to all humanity. The fact is and remains that the rationalist as such has no ear for the divine call.

We have started this long section with a reference to Kafka's two great novels, *Das Schloss* and *Der Prozess*. We want to close it by pitting against them two other great novels, *Barbara oder die Frömmigkeit* (translated by a perceptive interpreter[3] *The Pure of Heart*) and *Der veruntreute Himmel* by Kafka's compatriot, Franz Werfel. In either book Werfel presents us with the picture of a simple serving-woman who is strong in the faith (though Teta in *Embezzled Heaven* has yet some way to go before she reaches the perfection of Barbara). These simple souls – these *amme ha'ares* – know very little, but what they know, they know well; they have

[1] Cf. paperback ed., New York 1966, p. 113.
[2] *Great Operas*, paperback ed., New York 1958, vol. II, p. 117.
[3] Geoffrey Dunlop.

few opinions, but they have deep convictions; and these convictions concern the last things. When, in the household in which Teta Linek is serving, death strikes down the only son, the highly educated master of the house is confronted with the incomprehensible. 'Do you know why we men of the modern age are such God-forsaken, miserable creatures?' he exclaims. 'We are on excellent terms with life, on loathsomely excellent terms . . . With its opposite in that room upstairs we don't know how to get on at all . . . none of us, not one. . . .' But he has forgotten the cook. 'The only person far and near who was "on good terms with death" was Teta. For her alone had death a meaning in the ordered universe. We of the modern age were confused, uncertain, passive, demoralized, afraid in the face of that which was the pivot of all earthly happenings. Who displayed the more spiritual attitude towards the greatest question of all – we, the so-called intellectuals, who looked upon death as decay, or this simple serving-woman for whom it was the most significant stage in a clear and radiant cosmic system? We thought her notions of this luminous architecture child-like and primitive, but *we* possessed no notions at all. There was within us only a spiritual vacuum, as in the minds of animals.'

What was it that gave Teta Linek her luminous certitude, her steadfastness, her security? 'For sixty years she had hardly missed a single early morning mass. These sixty years of her life had been sixty complete years of the Church cycle. The cycle of the ecclesiastical year mirrors on a divine plane the cycle of the earthly year. Just as the latter contains its seasons of blossoming trees, cutting of the corn, gathering of the vine, and fall of the snow, so does the former its succession of feast-days in constant recapitulation. And as the man who lives close to nature shares with his body and soul in the seasonal course of the earthly year, the pious believer participates in the eternally unchanging round of the ecclesiastical year. They bloom and ripen and fade in accordance with the varying phases of the earthly and divine suns.

'Though Teta did not grasp the deep significance of the mass, its externals had become during those sixty faithful years flesh of her flesh and blood of her blood, and she could not have absorbed the externals as she had done without at the same time absorbing a great deal of the essence. In the same way a peasant understands the mystery of growth without ever having learned anything of the laws of biology. Teta knew, for instance, that the first Sunday after

Easter was called 'White Sunday', and that it was dedicated to the martyr St. Pancras. She did not have to look towards the high altar to be aware that the priests were garbed in snow-white vestments, and that white would remain the prevailing colour until Ascension Day, when it would be replaced by the burning red of the spirit of love on the eve of Whitsuntide. Every year she looked forward to this colourful red, her favourite hue, which imbued the summery atmosphere of the church with a delightful disquieting fiery tinge. Sixty years of experience had familiarized her with every slightest modulation of the liturgy, and she could have repeated every Latin phrase, syllable by syllable, even though she did not understand its meaning. She knew which portions of the gospels or epistles were to be read each day, and greeted the various sections of the way of salvation with proud and friendly recognition, just as she had greeted the century-old limes at Grafenegg every year when they put forth their blossoms in spring or decked themselves in the motley colouring of autumn. All this, so to speak, was her higher life – her art, her literature, her beauty, her lasting festive joy, and her comforting feeling that she was being well taken care of.'[1]

These lines, surely, contain the answer to Kafka's questions. It is an answer given by a life, the life of faith, not by an intellect, a formal ratio. And thereby hangs the whole secret of religious sociality. The unities which it establishes are only themselves if they are communities or communions, for only in them can there be engendered the depths of feeling which will still the anxious searchings of the poor man's soul and link him vitally and lovingly to the Founder of his faith and to the brothers and sisters with whom he shares it.

THE PROBLEM OF SUCCESSION AND THE ROLE OF THE SECOND

Our investigation has now reached the point where the study of the social formations comprising (and dividing) Christendom can properly start, and our task will be to look first of all at the circle of disciples which collected around Jesus Christ during His life-time on earth. Yet one more 'outstanding' single and solitary figure has

[1] *Embezzled Heaven*, transl. Firth, M., New York 1940, pp. 117, 122, 264, 265, 266; cf. also pp. 300 and 327.

to be considered before we can finally turn to the social embodiments of the faith – the person whom Paul Honigsheim has called 'the Second'.[1] No founder is immortal, so far as his earthly sojourn is concerned. When he dies, his followers are like orphaned children. Who will look after them? Who will lead them? Into the void steps the Second, a highly problematical person, if ever there was one.

We call him problematical because he is really in an impossible position. He is succeeding to one who can have no successor. The charismatic man is in a manner unique – each of them, not only Jesus Christ. We are incapable of imagining a second St. Francis, a second St. Teresa, a second Jean-Baptiste Vianney. Yet somebody has to carry on the work. The mantle *falls* on somebody; he does not assume it. It is truly excellent to call him the second, because he is not only later in time, but also – let us repeat it, in a manner – second best.

The second has always had a very bad press. Who can stand comparison with a charismatic man? Above all, who can stand comparison with Jesus Christ? What people have always felt about the second is strikingly expressed in Rudyard Kipling's poem 'The Disciple'.[2]

> He that hath a Gospel,
>   To loose upon Mankind,
> Though he serve it utterly—
>   Body, soul, and mind—
> Though he go to Calvary
>   Daily for its gain—
> It is His Disciple
>   Shall make his labour vain.
>
> It is His Disciple
>   (Ere Those Bones are dust)
> Who shall change the Charter
>   Who shall split the Trust—
> Amplify distinctions,
>   Rationalize the Claim,
> Preaching that the Master
>   Would have done the same.

[1] Cf. above, p. 13, note 1.
[2] *Limits and Renewals*, ed. London 1949, pp. 115 and 116. We are quoting the first, third and fifth stanzas.

> He that hath a Gospel
>   Whereby Heaven is won
> (Carpenter or Cameleer,
>   Or Maya's dreaming son),
> Many swords shall pierce Him,
>   Mingling blood with gall;
> But His Own Disciple
>   Shall wound Him worst of all!

The sentiment expressed in these lines is widespread.[1] Max Weber certainly shared it. He would never have expressed himself as sharply as Kipling did; he realized that, in order to be chosen by the master, the disciple would have to possess certain high qualities (which on one occasion he even describes as charismatic),[2] i.e. he would have to be at least worthy of love (charismatic in a passive sense, so to speak); yet as Weber believed that 'in its pure form, charismatic authority may be said to exist only in the process of originating', he *had* to regard the second as the onset of a downward plunge. Indeed, there is one passage in which he comes rather close to Kipling's opinion: 'The problem of succession . . . is crucial because through it occurs the routinization of the charismatic focus of the structure. In it, the character of the leader himself and of his claim to legitimacy is altered.'[3] These words, which reflect something rather deep down in Weber's mind, entitle us to bracket him with the poet. We are now approaching the discussion of his key concept of the 'routinization of charisma', and this sombre process here casts its shadow before it, so to speak. The second cannot give the love which the founder gave, so we are told, nor therefore can he receive it. With his appearance, the religious phenomenon as a whole descends to a lower, less vital level. It was fire, it now turns to ashes; at the very least, there is a loss of light and heat.

This theory contains, no doubt, a good deal of truth. But the critical question is, how much truth it contains, and we must try to discuss and to answer it in a spirit of calmness and objectivity. Even minor men have a right to justice. Kipling – and Weber –

---

[1] Cf., e.g. Santayana, G., *The Life of Reason*, [vol. II], Reason in Society, ed. New York 1927, p. 122.

[2] *The Sociology of Religion*, transl. Fischoff, as quoted, p. 60.

[3] *The Theory of Social and Economic Organization*, as quoted, pp. 360, 361, 364, 371.

have loaded the dice against the second, and that is not fair play.

We can best bring a proper scholarly attitude into this value-occupied, not to say prejudice-overrun, area by calling the fundamental concepts of functionalism to our aid. A comparison between the founder and the second is permissible, if and in so far as they have the same function to fulfil; otherwise the common denominator is missing which allows the comparison in the first place. But, almost by definition, the functions are different, even though the life both figures subserve is the same. The founder has to found; the second has to preserve. The one has to strike out into some new line; he is revolutionary; the other has to garner and to treasure up what has been offered; he is conservative. Consequently there is no sound basis to the bitter Kipling–Weber judgment. One might as well blame a physician for not being a lawyer, or a woman for not being a man.

But, it may be said, this counter-criticism assumes that charisma can be continued, and this is not so. The world-history of charismatic personalities is, as it were, a series of one-act plays. Weber saw matters in this light, but this only goes to prove how excessively individualistic he was. Certainly, the chain of charismata which we can observe in reality has its discontinuity, but the disconnected appearances of it still form a chain. St. Joseph of Cupertino lived nearly four hundred and fifty years after St. Francis of Assisi – he died in 1663, Francis in 1226 – but how close they are to each other in spirit and in type! Two blood brothers could not be more similar. Even discontinuity and continuity are not mutually exclusive phenomena in this world of ours which is so replete with incarnate and vitally tough self-contradictions. To speak once more in terms of a common metaphor, the flame of charisma may burn very low after a charismatic man has been removed by death, but it may be fanned again into its pristine vigour when a new saint appears whose breath has the required strength.

We are arguing, then, that charismata form families, so to speak, and that there is a large Christian family which contains smaller sub-families, the Franciscan, the Benedictine, the Dominican, the Jesuit, the Passionist, and others. Not all members of a family are alike. Some are less vital than the rest. Some are merely links between others, like that Abraham Mendelssohn who is reported to have said: Woe is me! I never was myself. First I was my father's

(Moses Mendelssohn's) son; now I am my son's (Felix Mendelssohn's) father. There would never have been the sublimely gifted Felix without the very ordinary Abraham; and in the same way there would never have been the sublimely saintly Cupertino without some father-in-God who engendered him in the spirit as Abraham did Felix Mendelssohn in the flesh.

But the counter-critic may yet persist. He may argue that filiation in the spirit is not like filiation in the flesh. The body of a physical son is derived from the body of his physical father, but the mind of a saint is not in the same sense derived from the minds of those who went before him. It is highly probable that St. Joseph of Cupertino had never met a saint before he became one himself. His educators, his novice-master for instance, must be presumed to have been ordinary people, and he must therefore have gone against them, in the direction of the original charisma of the Founder, and not forward, towards a final routinization. This argument would bring us back to Weber's basic assertion, namely that every charismatic man is a radical new beginning, and that his appearance is an impenetrable mystery – the mystery of a personality.

We would agree that any and every charismatic man is a revolutionary, but we would deny that his appearance is an impenetrable mystery. For, clearly, the charisma has to be evoked; the charismatic man has to be called before he can call others. The call can come to him in many different ways, but inherently the most likely, and historically the most frequent, way is through the agency of an ordinary, non-charismatic or half-charismatic man. St. Joseph of Cupertino may not have met a saint in the flesh before he became one himself; it is even likely that he did not; but he heard the Gospels read out in church and the *Vitae* and *Fioretti* of St. Francis in the novices' refectory, and it was then that the lightning struck in his soul and caused the conflagration there. It mattered very little what the reader's personal character was; even if he was a worldling, he yet mediated between one charismatic person and another. So does the dead telephone wire carry living messages from man to man and even from heart to heart. Certainly, the Apostles were in a special position in that they could be with Jesus while He was in the flesh; but it is perfectly possible at any time to meet Him in the spirit. The strongest insistence on this fact and truth came possibly from Martin Luther with his emphasis on 'the word'; the 'word of God', he felt and repeated, is not simply words, it is the continuing incarnation of the Word, of the Holy Trinity's Second Person. Catholics have not spelled this out with equal concern nor reiterated it with equal persistence, but they have, of course, taken the point for granted all along.

Even assuming, then, that the second and his successors (for *he* can have successors) were non-charismatic men, they would yet have a great function to fulfil in the economy of salvation; they would have to keep the memory of the genuine charisma whose human carrier had departed alive and smouldering, if not burning, so that it can be fanned into a full flame again. We shall have to return to this issue.[1] Here we would only say, in a brief formula, that the second is not a perverter but a preserver. He or his likes may have no personal charisma, but they have the collective charisma of their predecessors, including the Founder, whose legacy they administrate and whose servants they are – unworthy servants perhaps, but yet servants, and servants who can be highly effective even if they are in a sense characterized by unworthiness.

In what we have just said we have, however, made an undue – a grossly undue – concession to the idea that charisma is discontinuous, and we must take at least part of it back. Peter or Paul or whoever the Second was in the case of Christianity (we shall presently investigate it), was not his Master's equal, but he was a charismatic personality all the same. Would he ever have emerged as the orphaned disciples' leader if he had not evinced the Master's spirit? Abu Bekr was no Mohammed and Sariputta no Gautama, but that does not mean that they were ordinary, let alone that they were irreligious, people. In theory, using 'ideal types', it is easy contrapuntally to contrast genuine and official charisma; in reality, where we have to consider concrete personalities, it is wrong to use such concepts whose extremity and absoluteness makes them unfit for the descriptive study of the tangible, the historical, and the real. (Max Weber would not have denied this.) We are not gainsaying that there is a diametrical opposition between black and white; what we are insisting on is the fact that between white and black there are all the colours of the spectrum, and that you do not sink from the one directly down into the other. Routinization is a danger laid on from the beginning in any religious grouping; if no renewal of charisma, no new outbreak of sanctity, occurs, it will dull and deaden the love that brought the community into being

[1] Cf. below, p. 173.

79

and may ultimately turn the church concerned into a mechanism which automatically repeats the motions that once were full of meaning, love and grace. Perhaps it is even true to say that a church – every church – is something of a machine from the hour of its birth; every organization is; but, if so, the church – so long as it continues to deserve its name – is essentially a machine for the production of holiness.

SOME HISTORICAL EXAMPLES

Jesus and St. Peter

In the history of Christianity, it has frequently been Paul of Tarsus who has been cast for the role of the second, and that has regularly meant, the role of the villain. In 1823, for instance, Jeremy Bentham published, under the pseudonym of Gamaliel Smith, a volume with the highly revealing title, *Not Paul, But Jesus*. Since then, the question as to whether, or to what extent, Paul was a routinizer, has been discussed with much acrimony and even some passion. Many details have been thrown into the battle, Paul's insistence on some petty custom like the veiling of women (I Corinthians XI, 2–16) on the one side, his final defence of free prophesying on the other (ib. XII, 3; XIV, 39; I Thessalonians V, 19 and 20). A point-for-point investigation of this matter is neither possible nor necessary here. Sohm raised the discussion to a higher level by asking whether Paul was inherently a routinizer, and he answered it, on the whole, in the affirmative: 'We must assume that St. Paul, the Roman citizen, was influenced by the imperial ideal which aimed at the establishment of a uniform civilization for the whole world,' writes Sohm's American interpreter, Walter Lowrie. 'The prevalent notion that matters of external order and organization were foreign to St. Paul's interest, rests upon . . . assumptions which hardly will endure to be candidly stated. The apostle's great and predominant interest in the fundamental questions of religion and morality does not raise the least presumption that he was indifferent to matters of external order . . . Still less does his contention for Christian freedom in face of the exactions of the Mosaic law afford the least suggestion that the Apostle was disposed to ignore the practical advantages of uniform order and organization.' Even the often-to-be-found attempt to rescue Paul from the reproach of routinization by denying that the so-called Pastoral Epistles (or even Ephesians) are his, is rejected by Sohm and Lowrie: 'If the Pastoral Epistles are not genuine, they witness at least to the belief that St. Paul was the great organizer of the Church.' In any case, 'the early [unsuspect] epistles . . . are sufficient to prove St. Paul's keen interest in the regulation of the external order of the Church'. Moreover, 'the epistles furnish hints of only a small minority of the ordinances which the Apostle must have established among the churches of his foundation. The general regulation of Christian life and worship belonged of course to the period of his sojourn in the community; it was only with the unforeseen emergencies he dealt in his epistles, and even in such cases he preferred to postpone the regulation of details till such time as he might revisit the congregation – I Corinthians XI, 34'.[1]

Paul, then, did push the Church, or the churches, in the direction of legalization, in spite of everything that can be adduced in defence of him. However reluctant a disciplinarian he may have been, the informal group of disciples held together by love becomes under his hands more of an ordered congregation of stable members controlled by norms. But Sohm and Lowrie are fair enough to show us the circumstances that determined the Apostle – that *forced* him forward on the road. (They should only have emphasized this compulsion to organize a good deal more.) Chaos was a real and imminent threat. Regulation was therefore essentially a defensive move. 'St. Paul's denunciation of the disorder at Corinth reveals, not a disorderly supper preceding the Eucharist, but a drunken and gluttonous Eucharist.'[2] No wonder that he implored and commanded his followers: 'Let all things be done decently and according to order' (I Corinthians XIV, 40).

But it is not a consideration of details, however careful and comprehensive, that will help us to elucidate the developments of the fourth and fifth decades of the first century. A typological investigation like the present will be much better served by a review of the whole situation as it took shape after the execution of Jesus

Lowrie, W., *The Church and its Organization: An Interpretation of Rudolph Sohm's Kirchenrecht*, New York, London and Bombay 1904, pp. 178 and 177. Cf. also pp. 167–9, 170–6, 196–8, 199–201. Cf. also Heiler, loc. cit., pp. 52 and 53; Campenhausen, H. von, *Kirchliches Amt und geistliche Vollmacht in den ersten drei Jahrhunderten*, Tübingen 1953, pp. 39 and 52.
Lowrie, loc. cit., p. 281.

and the conversion of Paul. When we set about it, we find at the first step that there is not one 'Second' who even outwardly and formally replaces the Master, but rather three protagonists, each with his own specific function to fulfil; and we find at the last step that the concept of the 'routinization of charisma' is far too simple and narrow to encompass the complexities of real life.

The three protagonists of whom we have just spoken were St James,[1] St. Peter and St. Paul. So far as the Christians of the city of Jerusalem were concerned, it was without a doubt St. James who around A.D. 48, was the Second. Sources of the patristic age evince a tendency to say that he occupied the See of Jerusalem, and although this is manifestly an anachronism, it is one that is not totally wrong if rightly, i.e. restrictively, interpreted. *Acts* (chapter XV) show us that between him and Paul there arose a conflict which was focused on the treatment of the Gentile converts to the Christian faith. Should they become Jews first before they were allowed to become Christians? James or those around him thought yes; Paul judged, no. The so-called Council of Jerusalem (another anachronism) elaborated a compromise, with incisive consequences

Ostensibly the difference had to do with the treatment (one might even say: the physical treatment) of the individual convert: should he be circumcised or not, that was the question. 'Some, coming down from Judaea, taught the brethren . . . except you are circumcised after the manner of Moses, you cannot be saved . . . Paul and Barnabas had no small contest with them . . .' In the ensuing discussions, Peter took the side of Paul: 'God . . . put no difference between us and them, purifying their hearts by faith.' James also agreed in the end 'that they who from among the Gentiles are converted to God are not to be disquieted'. He merely suggested that, in deference to the Mosaic law, 'they refrain from the pollutions of idols and from fornication and from things strangled and from blood (*Acts* XV, 1, 2, 8, 9, 19, 20). This compromise was found generally acceptable. The converts therefore did not have to submit to the surgery that had been demanded of them. But what was involved was not a small ritual operation, it was much rather a large socio-political decision. Those who wanted to insist on circumcision were

---

[1] We are not concerned with the question as to who this was. Protestants like to describe him as 'the Lord's brother', Catholics tend to identify him with the Apostle St. James the Less. As historical sources are lacking, the discussion is pointless.

typical sectarians. They envisaged the future of Christianity in the form of a small sect, a holy fraction within a no longer holy nation. It is in such still semi-Pharisaic circles that we must look for the origin of the sentiments expressed in Matthew X, 5: 'These twelve Jesus sent, commanding them, saying, "Go ye not into the way of the Gentiles and into the city of the Samaritans enter ye not".'[1] So far as Jesus Himself is concerned, this passage (hardly a genuine logion) is totally blotted out, and obviously so, by His parable of the Good Samaritan (Luke X, 30–7). Indeed, this parable must have done much to set the nationalistic Jews against Him. But nationalism survived even among His followers, and sectarian tendencies reduced the circle of the sympathies of some of them still further. Thus there arose in certain minds the scheme of a restricted Christian conventicle, a wheel as it were within a wheel. Those who pulled the other way, Peter and Paul, had an entirely different vision. They saw the religion of Jesus and the Church around Him at least as a spreading faith, and they may even have had before their minds' eye the shining image of the Catholica, the universal Church, the mother of all. Their victory was the beginning of a world-wide apostolate and therefore an implicit repudiation of both sectarianism and religious nationalism, the fractional forms of Christendom which we have studied in our volumes I and II.

Paul was the chief agent of that apostolate. He had spread the Gospel through the Gentile world already before the Council of Jerusalem; he was to do so with even more vigour after it. Indeed, to bring the message to such people as the inhabitants of Colossae was to him to 'fulfil the word of God' (Colossian I, 25).[2] His character and his intervention in history are therefore totally misunderstood if he is described as a routinizer. The whole question of routinization is, so far as Paul is concerned, merely a secondary issue. Of course, he was a disciplinarian where discipline was needed. He asked that prophets should do their prophesying one after the other, not all at the same time. Who would not have done the same? It is good that new wine should ferment, but who would let the bottle burst? Not that he organized and ordered the churches is Paul's enduring achievement, positive or negative, but that he initiated them; not that he cut back Christianity, but that he invigorated it and made it grow and gain. St. Paul has therefore

[1] Cf. above, p. 56.
[2] Cf. also ibid. III, 11; Galatians III, 28; I Corinthians XII, 13.

something of a founder about him.[1] Certainly, he cannot be compared to Christ *the* Founder, but above the corner-stone and beneath the coping-stone there are others who also carry and constitute the building. In order to describe Paul of Tarsus correctly, we need some such concept as that of a *minor founder*.[2] In Paul, we behold an archetype which was to be re-incarnated many times in the history of the Church. Behind him, there appear such figures as Benedict, Francis, Dominic, Bernard, Ignatius, Alphonso, and many others. They all were minor founders, revolutionaries and reformers and even reactionaries (goers back to the original) rolled into one, and certainly not routinizers in the sense of Kipling and Weber.

Our conclusion is, then, that Paul was not the Second according to Honigsheim's definition of the term. But what about Peter? The answer cannot be simple, but it can be clear. In so far as he was like Paul, a spreader of the Gospel,[3] he, too, was a minor founder. In so far as he was what James must be assumed to have been, a preserver of the Gospel, the *praeses* of a concrete and organized circle of believers, of an ongoing church, he was a second. And if he was indeed the head of the world-wide community of Christians rapidly forming in his day, as every indication attests that he was, then he was not only *a* second, but *the* Second in the full sense which Honigsheim has given the word. 'If anyone should say, why then was it James who received the See of Jerusalem?' writes St. Chrysostom, 'I should reply that Jesus made Peter the teacher, not of that See, but of the world.'[4]

In Paul's Epistle to the Galatians we get a glimpse of a conflict which arose between the two Princes of the Apostles, and the passage concerned sheds much light on the part which Peter played

[1] Cf. the beautiful words of Campenhausen, loc. cit., pp. 48 and 49.

[2] Weber comes fairly close to the formulation of such a concept; cf. *The Sociology of Religion*, as quoted, p. 46.

[3] Cf. Campenhausen, loc. cit., p. 20.

[4] Cit. Chapman, J., *Studies in the Early Papacy*, New York, Cincinnati, Chicago n.d., p. 81. Cullmann (a Protestant) has shown, in chapters 2 and 3 of his scholarly work, that according to all probability Peter was first the head of the community at Jerusalem so that James was his successor there; that he afterwards shifted to, and ruled over, Antioch, which, with half a million inhabitants, was something like a capital of the East, and that he ended his labours in Rome, the true hub and heart of the empire, where he was directly the spiritual leader of the local Christians and thereby indirectly the leader of all Christians everywhere.

in the crucial years. 'When Cephas was come to Antioch,' Paul records, 'I withstood him to the face, because he was to be blamed. For before that some came from James, he did eat with the Gentiles: but when they were come, he withdrew and separated himself, fearing them who were of the circumcision' (Galatians II, 11 and 12). What have we to conclude from this account – that Peter was a weak, vacillating man? By no means. For the sociologist at any rate, the facts as related are more revealing about the *role* of Peter than about his personality. He was confronted with a potential schism; in this situation, which can be described as a conflict between a sectarian and a universalist conception of Christianity (between a Christian Hinayana and a Christian Mahayana, so to speak), Peter took his stand openly and unambiguously in the universalist camp. We have seen this already.[1] Why then did he act against his confessed conviction and have to be criticized by Paul? The answer is plain: because to him the unity and integrity of the Church was more important than his own opinion, however firmly held. His temporary withdrawal from the Gentile circle in Antioch was a gesture of goodwill towards the Pharisaic believers in Jerusalem who had not yet risen to the heights of a vision of a universal church; it was an attempt to mediate between the parties, better perhaps: to postpone the decision of the issue so that tempers might cool and prejudices get worn and weakened. Peter's action shows less a personal state of indecision on his part than a common and indeed typical attitude on the part of a formal head, president or pope.[2] However hot he may, in his heart, feel on the subject, he must not, because of his position, play the partisan: his chief duty is to keep the whole from bursting asunder. In other words, he is a preserver, a shepherd who must not lose or scatter his sheep. It was indeed as the Good Shepherd's successor that the early Church conceptualized Peter, the Second.[3] Jesus' words to him, recorded in the last chapter of St. John's Gospel – 'Feed my lambs, feed my sheep' (XXI, 15–17) – are a moving testimony to this sacred charge, this imposition of a duty, this entrustment with a role. To have the primacy, says St. Chrysostom, means to care for and truly to love the flock. It was by caring for and loving the flock that Peter was to show his devotion to his Divine Lord.[4] Out of this fund of ideas

---

[1] Cf. above, pp. 55 and 82.
[2] Cf. Cullmann, loc. cit., pp. 57 and 58; Dawson, loc. cit., p. 131.
[3] Cf. Heiler, loc. cit., pp. 285 and 286.   [4] Cit. Chapman, p. 82.

arose the title of Peter's successors. They called themselves, not *servi Dei*, but rather *servi servorum Dei* – not only God's servants, but above all servants of God's servants, shepherds of those whom He had shepherded.

The second's essential function is thus clearly delineated: it is conservation. We have shown it in its august, truly religious aspect. We must now, in conclusion, also show it in its workaday, more mundane implications. The second is plainly an officer of administration (in this Weber is correct), though he may be, and often is, much more than merely that. In Peter's case, four administrative actions are recorded which prove that he was – *inter alia!* – a technical administrator: (1) he arranged the election of an additional apostle to replace Judas Iscariot and presided over the proceedings; (2) he acted as speaker of the group; (3) he acted as defender of the group; and (4) he exercised disciplinary authority, as in the trials of Ananias, Saphira and Simon Magus.[1] Sohm is inclined to date the appearance of canon law, and hence the legalization of the Church, from Pope Clement's Epistle to the Corinthians;[2] he might as well have dated it from before Pentecost Day. The trouble with him and Weber, his disciple, was that they had lodged in their minds a firm antithesis between law and love. What they did not understand was that both may well be evidence of the same spirit and the same life.

St. Francis and Frate Elia

We cannot, unfortunately, consider the complex case of St. Benedict here. If he is seen in relation to his predecessors, e.g. St. Anthony of the Desert, he is indeed a second, an organizer; but if he is seen in relation to his successors, his own sons, he is certainly a founder, a minor founder, to be exact. His own life, too, is split into two periods: Monte Subiaco and Monte Cassino. At Subiaco, he is the hermit who lives outside of settled society, the total revolutionary, at Cassino, the abbot who creates a lasting form of social life. He appears therefore as his own second, the preserver of his own otherness and revolutionary attitude. This goes to show how difficult it is to apply ideal-typical definitions, however

---

[1] *Acts* I, 15 et seq.; II, 14 et seq.; IV, 8 et seq. and V, 29 et seq.; V, 1 et seq. and VIII, 18 et seq. Cf. also Cullmann, loc. cit., pp. 35 et seq.
[2] Campenhausen, loc. cit., p. 93; Lowrie, loc. cit., pp. 14 et seq.

reasonable in themselves, to historical reality. One thing, above all, is clear: the tempered asceticism which emerges in the Holy Rule is a religiosity which constantly re-incarnates itself and therefore lasts. Perhaps one can call this routinization; but only he can give the term a pejorative undertone in speaking of Benedict and Benedictinism who prefers one ascetic to many or a brief self-surrender to one that spans centuries.

Instead of going more deeply into the case of St. Benedict, however, we propose to use St. Francis and Frate Elia as our second illustration. The shadow that has fallen across St. Paul because he did not measure up to the stature of his master (as if anyone could), lies much more deeply still over the little friar from Cortona whose fortune and misfortune it was to step for a while into the shoes of the Poverello. Ed. Lempp's book, *Frère Elie de Cortone* (1901), depicts him as the Judas of St. Francis, and he does not fare much better at the hands of Paul Sabatier.[1] In view of this denigration of the man, it is imperative to go back to the very first original sources, and in doing so we find a rather different picture. Thomas of Celano's earlier *Life of St. Francis* of 1229 shows us that Francis was fond of Elias. Not only did he appoint him Provincial Minister of Syria; that might be written off as merely betokening confidence in his administrative ability; but Francis also gave him his special blessing and showed him the stigmata, including the wound in his side – an act that reveals real closeness and affection. There is also a letter of St. Clare to Blessed Agnes of Bohemia which proves how highly Elias was respected by those who constituted the inner-most circle of the Franciscan founding family.[2]

But already the second *Life of St. Francis* by Thomas of Celano (1246) presents to us, at least if we look behind the words used, an unfavourable image of Elia. 'He is seldom mentioned and never by name. Such references as there are . . . are guarded, cold and evasive. While it is tacitly admitted that he received a special blessing, the significance of this is as far as possible minimized.'[3] Lempp's contempt has thus a long pre-history. Facts are adduced which seem to justify it. Elia is said to have liked good food and fine horses.[4] That was not at all St. Francis's way. But a little charity

---

[1] Cf. our vol. III, p. 289.
[2] Cf. Brooke, R. B., *Early Franciscan Government*, Cambridge 1959, pp. 8 et seq.
[3] Ibid., p. 15.   [4] Ibid., pp. 48 and 49.

must make a lot of difference here. It is highly probable that Elia was not a healthy man.[1] He may well have needed special food; he may well have been unable to walk far on foot. Evil tongues will not find it difficult to transmute light food into fine food and riding from necessity into riding for luxury's sake. But all these considerations are really merely secondary. We must try to cut through the jungle of the discussion to the kernel of the truth. Why did Elia come to the top? Why was he needed? What was his role and function?

The central fact is very simple. Elia got to the top because St. Francis wanted to have him there. He felt that an able administrator was needed, and he knew that he himself was no administrator, good, bad, or indifferent. Indeed, Francis realized that some routinization was needed, at least in the sense of reducing chaos to order. We can investigate this with the help of a very revealing historical source, a source as simple and as moving as any and every document concerning the life and sufferings of the Saint of Assisi. 'While the tree of his order was everywhere spreading by a multiplying of its members and was stretching its branches laden wonderfully with fruits to the ends of the earth,' Thomas of Celano's longer *Vita* reports, St. Francis 'began to meditate alone more often how that new plant might be preserved and how it might increase, bound together by the bonds of unity. He then saw many raging savagely against his little flock, like wolves . . . He foresaw that even among his own sons certain things contrary to holy peace and unity would occur. . . .'[2] Francis may have been a dreamer, but he was not totally devoid of knowledge of the world.

Now what happens to a man who is thus deeply preoccupied? He will have uneasy, disturbed nights. 'While the man of God revolved these and similar things in his mind, one night, while he was asleep, he saw this vision. He saw a little black hen, much like a tame dove, whose legs and feet were covered with feathers. She had innumerable chicks which pressed close around her, but they could not all get under her wings. The man of God . . . became his own interpreter of this vision. "The hen," he said, "is I, small as I am in stature and naturally dark . . . The chicks are my brothers,

[1] Ibid., pp. 151, 152, 170.
[2] Transl. Hermann, P., *St. Francis of Assisi: First and Second Life of St. Francis by Thomas of Celano*, Chicago 1963, p. 96.

multiplied in number and in grace, whom Francis's strength does not suffice to defend from the disturbances of men . . ." What was to be done? Francis had no doubt whatever. "I will go and will commend them to the holy Roman Church, by the rod of whose power those of ill-will will be struck down and the children of God will enjoy full freedom . . . Under her protection, no evil will befall the order . . .' 'This,' Thomas of Celano adds,[1] 'was the whole intention of the holy man of God in commending himself to the Church; these were the most holy testimonies to the foresight of the man of God in commending himself against the time to come.' The next chapter then relates Francis' journey to the Curia, his reception by Honorius III, and the appointment of the Cardinal-Bishop of Ostia, Hugo, later Gregory IX, as Protector, whose 'protection and rule' Francis told the pope he was craving.

It was Francis himself, then, who initiated the 'routinization' of his movement, its transmutation into something like the older, and that meant, the fully organized, orders. But a religious order of the traditional kind needs an administrative head, and Francis picked Peter Catanii for the job. When he died, almost immediately, in 1221, Francis appointed Elia in his stead. While the others described him merely as Vicar, Francis called him Minister General. He wanted Elia to be more than his own lieutenant; he wanted him to be a true superior.[2] Thomas of Celano's shorter *Vita* describes Frate Elia as one 'whom Francis had chosen to take the place of a mother in his own regard and to take the place of a father for the rest of the brothers'.[3] These words betray nothing of the common prejudice of the later years; on the contrary, they breathe the family spirit of the early, non-routinized days.

Writers like Sabatier and Lempp stand aghast at Elia's appointment. It scandalizes them, and they find it incomprehensible. If, however, the facts are studied without preconceived ideas, we see that the choice of the man from Cortona was not altogether irrational. In our terminology, he was not a second in the pejorative sense of the word, even though, as a person, he had painful shortcomings. What, according to some critics, especially from the Protestant side of the fence, 'ruined' the Friars Minor, was the introduction of a distinction between lay brothers and priests; but this move was resisted by Elia, and it was not Elia but his successor

[1] Ibid.   [2] Cf. Brooke, loc. cit., pp. 106 et seq.
[3] Hermann, loc. cit., p. 52. Cf. also, p. 83.

Parenti against whom the lay brothers remonstrated and demonstrated. It is also said that the securing of inordinate papal privileges harmed and, so to speak, denaturalized the Order; but Elia 'did not accelerate the progress away from St. Francis's ideal by obtaining many additional privileges'. Again, such blame as there is should go to Parenti.[1]

But we are not really saying enough, if we point out that Elia was not quite a typical routinizer. He actively resisted routinization, and he fell precisely because he did so. His bad reputation simply added insult to injury. Among his arch-enemies, Salimbene de Adam is one of the fiercest, and he, writes Miss Brooke, 'criticized Elias, not because he failed to follow St. Francis, but because he failed to transform the Order into a clerical militia organized upon the traditional lines'. 'His transgressions against the Rule,' she says in another part of her learned book, 'were less instrumental in provoking determined resistance against his authority than were his "reactionary" tendencies. It was not the *zelanti* who successfully combined against him, but the learned.' Still later, summing up, Miss Brooke asserts that, not a body of outraged mendicants faithful to the Franciscan ideal, but on the contrary 'an *élite* of intellectuals and administrators . . . succeeded in drawing from Gregory IX the reluctant admission that Elias was unfit to rule the Friars Minor'.[2]

Before saying a word about Giovanni Parenti who was St. Francis's second if anyone was, one of the chief reasons for Elia's removal in 1227 and again in 1239 must still be mentioned: his 'inordinate' visitations of individual houses. Jordan of Giano makes this point. So does Thomas of Eccleston. 'In 1237,' for instance, 'Wygerius . . . was sent to England by Elias to conduct a visitation. The proceedings he instituted provoked consternation throughout the province.' Elia's incentive in this matter was in all probability the wish to counteract centrifugal tendencies. Can the objective observer blame him for that wish? But it was not only the ordinary brethren whom Elia incensed, it was even more the big-wigs. Writing of the Provincial Ministers, Miss Brooke reports: 'He did not allow them to build up a body of supporters in a given locality, but before they had had time to establish themselves anywhere he moved them to other provinces as distant from the

[1] Brooke, loc. cit., pp. 161, 166, 167.
[2] Ibid., pp. 55, 161, 181.

first as he could arrange.'[1] This can, of course, be interpreted as a Machiavellian move on the Minister General's part for the defence of his personal power. But is it not at least as justifiable to assume that what Elia really wanted was to keep the Franciscan family together, even though it was scattered over the face of the earth?

The reader should not think, however, that we are anxious to whitewash Frate Elia. We are not concerned with his personal weaknesses at all: they were many. What we are concerned with is his historical role, and that was hardly that of a routinizer. Indeed, he was removed, he *had* to be removed, because he did *not* routinize enough: he was as little a hen under whose wings all the chicks could be collected as Francis had been; more soberly expressed, he did not succeed in establishing a degree of order and coherence sufficient to ensure the survival and development of the Franciscan movement. That movement was from its first hour exposed to the danger of degeneration and dissolution. St. Francis's aim, a group of propertyless, wayfaring Gospel-singers, lacked the stiffening which had provided the backbone of the Benedictine communities: inclusion of, emphasis on, the duty to work. There is but a thin dividing line between a beggar for God's sake and a beggar pure and simple, and as time went on, the latter class infiltrated into, and all but swamped, the former. Something had to be done to keep the ideal untarnished, and it was done, but not by Elia. It was Parenti who called a halt to the nefarious processes which were going on. Those who, like Weber, loudly complain about routinization, would have complained even more loudly (and then with more justification) if the 'routinizer' Parenti had not appeared on the scene and done his work.[2]

Giovanni Parenti was trained to be a lawyer. 'The impression is . . . of a strict disciplinarian in whom legal training had imbedded a firm respect for the letter of the law.'[3] This is clearly what the Order needed. Other steps which Parenti took were also largely inspired by the need for discipline. He secured, for instance, for the Friars complete exemption from episcopal power. Clearly this was a *conditio sine qua non* for the firming up of the Franciscan family. It had to have its own controllers and controls: the episcopal régime

---

[1] Ibid., pp. 162, 163, 193, 155–56.
[2] Cf. the case of the Minimi, strikingly similar to that of the Friars Minor, in our vol. III, p. 180. Cf. also ibid., p. 296.
[3] Brooke, loc. cit., p. 126.

was too loose and too remote. The gaining of the privileging bulls *Nimis iniqua* and *Nimis parva* shows, Miss Brooke tells us, an 'inability to persevere wholeheartedly in the path of humility'. The judgment is unfair. Not a betrayal of Franciscan humility was involved, but a conquest of Franciscan waywardness. Be this as it may, Miss Brooke's final conclusion is that 'from a purely practical standpoint', Parenti's 'attitude was justified and reasonable'.[1]

Parenti was in charge from 1227 to 1232. In the latter year, the rank and file put Elia back into power, but for once history repeated itself. By 1239, Elia's half-routinization or half-government had again led to untenable conditions, and after a brief interregnum by Albert of Pisa, Haymo of Faversham became head of the Order. He was exactly the same sort of man as Parenti had been. 'The thread was taken up,' says our mentor in this matter, 'where it had been left by John Parenti . . . Haymo . . . was a priest and a theologian before he was a friar and neither was a profession he could renounce on becoming a Minor. Both fundamentally conditioned his outlook and his approach to the Franciscan way of life. He would have made an ideal Dominican.'[2] The last words mean in effect that Haymo, like Giovanni Parenti, was something of a legalist. The Dominicans were the great constitution-makers of the Mendicants, and Haymo took precisely this feature of their activity and development for his model.

Two facts clearly emerge from the foregoing analysis. The first is that it is life, vital necessity, which forces an organizer on a religious movement, even if the movement itself is loath to accept organization. Elia tried to get away with a modicum, a minimum, of ordering; it proved impossible; without the intervention of men like Parenti and Haymo, there would have been more than disorder: there would have been dissolution and disappearance. *Sal volatile* simply evaporates if it is not enclosed in a bottle. The second fact is implied in the first, and we have just stated it: Elia was not the second in the true sense of the word. He was a kind of stand-in man between Francis the founder and the true seconds, Parenti and Haymo. History and historians, both heartbreakingly unfair, have made a scapegoat of him. The Judas of St. Francis? Certainly not.

In the long catalogue of Elia's sins, real and supposed, one item is the building of the great basilica at Assisi where the ashes of the

[1] Ibid., p. 133; cf. also pp. 129 et seq.   [2] Ibid., pp. 177, 202, 203.

Poverello now repose. 'Sabatier and Lempp . . . contend that Elias began his preparations for a magnificent church in Francis's honour immediately after his death and thus offended all who valued primitive ideals, and who felt that the saint's wish to be buried humbly at the Portiuncula should have been respected.' Technically, Elia became guilty in this matter. 'By exacting money from the provinces, [he] both broke the Rule himself and forced the brethren to break it, and his levies were regarded as a legitimate grievance.'[1] Admitting this, was Elia, we must ask, guilty in a higher sense as well, was he morally and religiously guilty? Not all will return the same answer to this query,[2] and honest disagreement is certainly possible here. But *if* the role of a senior son is to keep the memory of his father alive and to show his glory to all the world, then Elia cannot be blamed. The grand Basilica di San Francesco in Assisi Superiore and the even grander church of Santa Maria degli Angeli at Assisi Inferiore are indeed rich, nay overflowing with riches. But it is not riches that is extolled there, it is poverty – the poor remains of the Saint up above on the hill, the humble wayside chapel of the Portiuncula down below in the valley.[3] Riches kneel, if we may so express it, in adoration before poverty. Is this a betrayal of the Franciscan, or of the Christian, spirit? Surely not. It is its preservation and propagation. Even the stones of Assisi proclaim the charisma of Francesco Bernardone. If it is still alive today, instead of being spent and lost, this is the work of Elia, Giovanni Parenti and Haymo of Faversham, and indeed of that great lover of the brethren and organizer of the brotherhood, St. Bonaventure, who came after them and was like them in many respects, as he was like St. Francis himself in many others.

Joseph Smith and Brigham Young

In order to show that the problem of succession, or the problem of the second, is world-wide, we want to append here a brief word on a case which unrolled, not in the Middle East of the Mediterranean, but in the Middle West of America – the succession of

[1] Ibid., pp. 121, 150. [2] Cf. our vol. III, p. 302.
[3] The Portiuncula chapel which the Saint loved, and where he liked to assemble the brothers, and the spot of the *transito*, or passing away, of St. Francis are both enclosed in the giant structure of Santa Maria degli Angeli.

Brigham Young, a fairly typical second, to Joseph Smith, a fairly typical founder. Other examples from the Protestant area might also have been selected, for instance the relationship of William Booth to George Railton in the history of the Salvation Army. Booth was a man of great personal power, and it was not difficult for him to make disciples, but the decisive organizational idea which gave outline and permanence to his life's work came, not from him, but from his right-hand man, Railton. When Booth called himself 'General' before Railton joined him, this was simply short for 'General Superintendent of the Christian Mission'. Railton saw in this sobriquet a practical possibility which a nothing but pious person might never have discovered – the use of the Queen's army as the model of a 'Salvation Army'. It was he who started to use the title 'Lieutenant' in its more usual connotation and thereby introduced into, and forced upon, a religious movement as yet formless a definite form which enabled it to last and to grow.[1]

The founder of the Mormon Church, Joseph Smith, was murdered by an enraged mob on 27 June 1844 at Carthage, Illinois. Although the social foundations of the movement which he headed were broad and firm, there was a life-and-death crisis which might not have been overcome, if the group had not had at its disposal an organizing genius of the purest water, Brigham Young. This is not the place to survey his administrative achievements in depth and detail, but it is possible to say that they included three major feats which, in lesser men, would have demanded three separate personalities and three different types of talent: he organized the great westward trek of his people to the vastnesses of Utah; he organized the territory occupied in these vastnesses which he liked to call Deseret – in itself a double task which included the ordering of the State as well as the Church: he was both State governor and Church president; and, finally, he made himself entrepreneur-in-chief in the economic field. In this area, too, his activities were manifold: agriculture, transportation and industry (with the only exception of mining), all benefited greatly from his imagination, know-how and drive.[2] Irving Wallace is surely right

[1] Cf. Sandall, R., *The History of the Salvation Army*, vol. I, London and Edinburgh 1947, pp. 146 et seq.
[2] Young, K., *Isn't one Wife Enough?* New York 1954, pp. 87, 88, 322, 329, 339, 340; also 158, 159, 163, 288.

when he calls Young 'one of the greatest organizers in American history'.[1]

Of course, what Young is best known for in the wider world is the system of polygamy which he built up. It was started by Joseph Smith, but only faltering steps were ventured at first, and it took the safety of a self-contained settlement well away from civilization and the ruthlessness of a man of Brigham Young's calibre to realize the idea of plural marriage to the full.[2] The causes of this phenomenon are many and complex. The shout of 'lechery!' contributes little to its understanding, even if historical proof is adduced that both the prophet and his successor were uncommonly fond of woman-flesh. Here we are mainly interested in Young's administrative ability, and even polygamy bears in a manner witness to its magnitude. The Mormons, like all sects, seem to have had more female followers than male:[3] allotting several wives to each believer was therefore a good way of nipping a police-problem in the bud (and unattached, footloose spinsters would soon have been such a problem). 'President Young advised the menfolks to marry available young women so they would have a home and protector if the soldiers were quartered in our midst,' wrote one biographer.[4] Though the words refer to a special occasion, the dispatch, in 1857, of federal troops to the territory, they uncover a much more general motive. Moreover, the Utah of those days was severely underpopulated. What better way of filling it up than to set all the believing females a-breeding? It was the understandable desire to move the population figure from minimum to optimum which the Mormons, and certainly not without justification, used to defend

[1] *The Twenty-seventh Wife*, New York 1961, p. 60. Cf. also O'Dea, T. F., *The Mormons*, Chicago 1957, pp. 77, 79.

[2] Wallace, loc. cit., p. 80.

[3] Cf. our vol. II, p. 41. Statistical figures of any reliability are hard to come by, and the excess of women has been doubted. Yet though the surplus may not have been large, it did in all probability exist. And there was the likelihood which an open-eyed man like Brigham Young would not miss that Female influx would far exceed male once conditions became more settled. K. Young (pp. 124, 125) quotes a contemporary source: 'Utah in those days was full of girls and women who had come from European countries and from the Eastern states. Brigham Young used to say to the men: Marry these girls and give them a home and provide for and protect them. Let them be wives and mothers, so all men who could looked upon it as a duty.'

[4] Young, loc. cit., p. 107. Cf. also pp. 124 and 125, 367. (Similar conditions had led to similar arrangements in another 'city of saints' – Münster, 1534-5.)

their singular marital arrangements. 'I have a good many wives and lots of young mustards that are growing,' said Heber C. Kimball in a sermon against birth-control. 'The Lord told me to get them. What for? . . . Not to have women to commit whoredom with, to gratify the lusts of the flesh, but to raise up children.'[1]

Yet a third factor was conceivably involved, though if it was, it was less conscious than the other two. Mormons, like all other Americans, and as sectarians even more than all other Americans, believed in equality, but in a vigorous and expanding economy there are strong tendencies towards, and only half-suppressed desires for, visible inequality.[2] The system of plural marriage met these desires: wives were objects of conspicuous waste as well as helpmates and investments. Their number was an index of social superiority, a status symbol.

Measured by this last yardstick, Brigham Young, with twenty-nine mates and fifty-six offspring, was certainly a success in life. But other indicators tell a similar story. Though some of the estimates of his wealth are clearly exaggerated – one, by a defaulting, divorce-seeking wife, ran as high as a monthly income of at least $40.000[3] – there is good, indeed legal, proof of his substantial enrichment. His last will and testament established a trust fund of two million dollars for the family[4] – not bad for a man who had started at zero point.

In view of this his preoccupation with material things, some observers, especially with European and Catholic backgrounds, have felt reluctant to acknowledge that Brigham Young was a religious leader in the proper sense of the word. But we must remember that his ambit was American and even near-Puritan. We cannot introduce here, by way of an excursion, an essay on 'the Mormon ethic and the spirit of capitalism', but we can express the conviction that even among these in several respects anti-Calvinist people, the acquisition of worldly goods was definitely considered as a sign of divine favour. Young's wealth therefore, growing as it did, especially in and through the railway boom, was a help rather than a hindrance to his leadership position. Yet that position was in large measure independent of its outer trappings, power, money and all. It rested in the last analysis on the man's singular personality.

[1] Ibid., p. 176. Cf. also pp. 114 and 115, 241 and 242.
[2] Cf. Young, loc. cit., pp. 210 and 211.
[3] Wallace, loc. cit., p. 308.   [4] Ibid., p. 371.

Successor to a figure whom Max Weber himself – if with some reservations – acknowledged to be charismatic,[1] he also had a share in that mysterious quality which makes men willing to follow and to obey and indeed to extol and to worship a fellow human being. 'His words went through me like electricity,' wrote one who had heard him.[2] And if he (Orson Hyde) was a believer, others from without the fold were similarly affected. 'He assumes no airs of extra sanctimoniousness', reported the Englishman Richard Burton, yet 'he impresses a stranger with a certain sense of power. His followers are wholly fascinated by his superior strength of brain.'[3] Ann Eliza Webb, later the twenty-seventh Mrs. Brigham Young, and finally his most determined foe, came originally under his spell as so many others had done. 'I felt his power . . . I began to understand a little how it was that he compelled . . . people to do his will . . .'[4] 'Of Brigham's power there was no doubt,' writes Thomas O'Dea, who knows all the evidence, in his close study of *The Mormons*. 'He was a man who could both demand and receive unquestioning obedience.'[5] Thus Young was possessed of practically all the qualities which go to make a specifically religious leader. He stands before us, not as a perverter, but as the preserver and perfecter of a prophet's mission.

---

[1] Cf. *The Theory of Social and Economic Organization*, as quoted, p. 359; *The Sociology of Religion*, as quoted, p. 54; *From Max Weber: Essays in Sociology*, eds. Gerth, H. H., and Mills, C. Wright, ed. New York 1958, p. 246.
[2] Wallace, loc. cit., p. 61.   [3] Ibid., p. 93.
[4] Ibid., p. 157.   [5] O'Dea, loc. cit., pp. 123 and 79.

The concept of charisma which is at the basis of the present investigation, and which should have slowly built up in the reader's mind as he was working through the first chapter of this volume, is not, like that of Max Weber, individualistic, but essentially sociological. The term is applied to a certain quality of a collective circle rather than to 'a certain quality of an individual personality'. It describes the presence of requited love in that circle rather than a one-sided, if compelling, magnetism. Of course, the charismatic relationship must not be regarded as synallagmatic. The love returned is not necessarily, or even often, or even ever, an equivalent of the love offered and given in the first place. Our difference from Weber is therefore not absolute, but only relative; yet it is a difference radical enough to produce dissimilar, and well-nigh contrasting, pictures of the sociology of religion in the end. In a typical family, descending love is said to be stronger than ascending love, love of the parents for the children more intense than that of the children for the parents. Nobody would, because of this lack of symmetry, conceive of the family in other than terms of mutual emotional involvement. And so it is also with the family of faith. It is true that Jesus *called* His apostles. 'You have not chosen me,' He said to them according to the Fourth Gospel, 'but I have chosen you' (St. John XV, 16). Yet why did He call and choose them? Only because He knew that they would be able, however imperfectly, to reciprocate His love. 'It is not the most exalted, the most moral or the most efficient which He elects,' writes Joachim Wach, 'it is those to whom His heart inclines in a deep inward affinity.'[1] The charismatic call is, in spite of all disparity, a call of like to like.

The formation of charismatic circles around great religious founder-figures is a simple empirical fact which the sociologist as such may well take for proven and granted. A wider and deeper analysis, however, would have to enter into a searching investigation of what is generally called the religious act. That act – the taking up of contact with the deity, the 'beatific vision', as the mystics are wont to call it – is curiously ambiguous, so far as the involve-

[1] Wach, J., *Meister und Jünger*, Leipzig 1925, p. 32. Our translation.

ment of third parties is concerned. On the one hand, the religious experience is incommunicable; on the other hand, however, those who have undergone it, have always shown an irrepressible desire to communicate it. The explanation of this fact may have to be sought in the nature of the religious experience itself. Sometimes God is seen and known as Supreme Love, sometimes as Supreme Power. In the first case (substantially the case of Catholicism), the search for disciples follows as a matter of course. Love is longing for companionship. The sharing of values is of its essence. 'The spirit of faith is never an isolated or an isolating thing, but always a spirit that presses towards fellowship because it is derived from the Spirit of God, the spirit of union and love,' an outstanding Catholic theologian has written in a great book.[1] Where God is experienced primarily as Power (substantially the case of Calvinism), the formation of religious associations is prefigured to a lesser extent in and by the religious act, and this is one of the reasons why the principle of sociality is less fully developed in this tradition than in the other. Yet two secondary factors are active and effective. If God is Supreme Power, then honour must be given to Him, and it has to be given to Him by obedience to His commandments. These, however, prescribe social control and collective worship. Furthermore, the concept of power alone does not yield a satisfactory theology. It is easy to explain creation if God is seen as Love: God, even though perfect in Himself, is then a Being longing for an *Alter Ego*, to share His perfection and return His Love, and this leads to the idea of Sonship, first the sonship of One, and then the sonship of many. It is not equally easy to explain creation if God is seen as Power: 'the strong one is most powerful alone', says the poet.[2] Hence even where the majesty of God is stressed before and above all else, His condescension towards the creatures is given some place in the picture. Calvinism has for this reason taught that some at least, the elect, have been called into a holy fellowship, and thereby the principle of sociality has been asserted here too, if in a somewhat muted manner.

Still more interesting in our context than either Christian case is, however, the case of Buddhism, for its whole nature would seem to prefigure a lonely search for salvation, and yet it has produced the religious community or communities like all other religions. Gautama pioneered what Max Scheler liked to call a soul-technique,

[1] Adam, K., op. cit., p. 150.   [2] Friedrich Schiller, *Wilhelm Tell*, I, 3.

a technique of release from the evils of existence, and when he reached his goal of blissful detachment, he might have come to rest in his achievement. This is what Mara (the Devil) suggested to him, and this, in the Buddhist tradition, ranks as 'the Great Temptation'. Gautama rose superior to it. The fruit of the tree is not for the tree; it is for those that hunger. 'The last great tempta-tion – to speak in the language of Buddhist Dogma – is to remain a *Pratyekabuddha*, a saviour of oneself, and to reject the immense task of becoming a *Samasambuddha*, a saviour of all.'[1] As especially the Mahayana tradition has emphasized, Gautama was 'he who cares for others'. Even here, therefore, the principle of fellowship won out in the end.

The sources of sociality, as can be seen, run deep in religious life. Love, alas, has had some ups and downs in the course of its history, but if it had ever died, or if it were ever to die completely, this would simply be the end of the whole phenomenon of religiosity. It will be one of our tasks to show its survival – in our usual meta-phor, the glow beneath the embers and ashes – even in those periods of ebbing warmth which Weber comprised under his concept of the routinization of charisma. First, however, we have to speak of the charismatic community in its fullest realization which is known to Christians as the apostolic circle, the earliest and closest disciples around the still living Lord.

THE BEGINNING: THE CIRCLE AROUND THE FOUNDER

The deep conviction which we have just summarized, namely that the charismatic community is anchored in the very ground of being, formed part and parcel of the teachings of Jesus Christ. When He prayed for His disciples, He said to the Father: 'As thou hast sent me into the world, I also have sent them into the world' (John XVII, 18). There is thus an unbroken chain between the Godhead and the apostles. And later the apostles were directly assured of this by their Master and Lord. The same Gospel reports the risen Christ as saying to the eleven faithful ones: 'Peace be to you. As the Father hath sent me, I also send you' (XX, 21). The circle of disciples is in this way – through this belief in a connection with the divine – not an ordinary society as everyday life produces them in large number. It is the archetypal society which most closely –

[1] Wach, J., *Meister und Jünger*, as quoted, p. 23. Our translation.

though, because of the human character of its members, not fully – approaches the divine idea of what a society ought to be. And this is merely another way of saying that it was filled, to the extent that it is humanly possible, by *charisma* and *caritas*.

In this first circle, which constituted the *fons et origo* of the later Church, there are two social relationships which demand study: the relation of the Master to His disciples, and the relations of the disciples to each other. The character of the former has been splendidly elucidated by Joachim Wach in his brief but deep essay *Meister und Jünger*, and we can do no better than to follow his lead. In order to show the specific difference between the charismatic nexus between master and disciple and outwardly comparable formations of secular life, Wach compares it, point for point, with the relation of teacher and pupil. We have summarized his findings in the form of a table:

Master–disciple	*Teacher–pupil*
1. The relationship is purely personal	The relationship is tied up with an object (the imparting of knowledge or skill)
2. The relationship is an end in itself	The relationship has an (exterior) purpose
3. Both master and disciple are irreplaceable	Both teacher and pupil are replaceable
4. There is on both sides free election and free following (a call and its response)	There is formal enrolment (a scholastic enterprise and job structure in the background)
5. The master gives of himself	The teacher gives of his knowledge
6. The disciple understands the master	The pupil understands the teacher's instruction
7. The relationship is total	The relationship is partial
8. True contact occurs in a moment of grace (*kairos*)	Instruction can always take place

What Wach has to tell us here, illustrates not only the contrast between Jesus and the apostles on the one hand and a secular teacher, for instance, a technological instructor, and his students, on the other, but also the profound difference between the apostolic circle and the contemporary rabbinical schools.[1] So far as higher

[1] Cf. the excellent analysis in Schelkle, op. cit., pp. 17 et seq.

religious education among the Jews was concerned, it was fully understood that the novice had his choice among several possible mentors, and that the whole relationship would be temporary, finding termination when the pupil transferred to another teacher or set up as a teacher himself. The follower of Jesus has no such choice for He is unique, nor is his discipleship for time only for He is the final reality: those who follow Him enter into the Kingdom of God (Luke IX, 62; Mark X, 23). Not only are Christ's disciples called by Him, but they are called out of a sentiment of love. 'And Jesus, looking on him, loved him and said to him . . . Come, follow me' (Mark X, 21). But, as a love-relationship, the tie between Master and Disciple, between Jesus and St. John, for instance, is simply, and at the same time supremely, personal: 'Blessed are ye when they shall revile you and persecute you and speak all that is evil against you, untruly, *for my sake*: be glad and rejoice, for your reward is very great in heaven' (Matthew V, 11 and 12).

In case it be said that the above picture is unfair in so far as it gives an all too sober, predominantly utilitarian, description of the teacher–pupil relationship, let us assume that this relationship, too, is filled by love. Plato's idea of higher education, for instance, aimed at this condition, as against the more down-to-earth attitude of Aristotle. There are, however, as Anders Nygren has so splendidly shown,[1] two forms of love which must be distinguished, especially in a context such as our own: *eros* and *agape*. Where *eros* holds sway, the lover intends to lift the loved one up to his own level. It is not so in the case of *agape*. *Agape* demands that the lover come down to the level of the loved one, to accept his or her poverty and lowliness, for instance.[2] It is difficult to see how the teacher–pupil relationship can be other than erotic in the given (non-sexual) sense. The religiously charismatic master–disciple relationship on the other hand tends, to say the least, towards a meeting of the partners which involves self-humiliation on the part of the superior for the sake of the inferior whom he loves. This, clearly, is the case

---

[1] Cf. *Agape and Eros*, transl. Watson, P. S., ed. London 1953; first (Swedish) ed., part I, Stockholm 1930, part II, ibid., 1936.

[2] In the case of a person more lowly placed, love is *agape* and not merely *eros*, if he or she is indifferent to the raising up he is to receive, or at least to the outer advantages it may have to offer, and loves simply for love's sake. This is the case of the Magdalen of the Gospels, immediately to be considered.

of Christianity, the religion of the God who took upon Himself human nature and became like us, a mortal being, in everything except sin. Thus even if and where a teacher–pupil relationship is filled by love, it will not compare with the master–disciple relationship in the religious sphere.

It is extremely instructive at the juncture which we have reached to cast a glance at Judas Iscariot, the disciple who failed. An incident in the house of Simon the Leper reveals his weaknesses well before the final betrayal. As the company sat at table, the Magdalen entered and started to anoint Jesus with precious ointment – an action which, in terms of contemporary culture, betokened the deepest devotion. Judas was ill-pleased: why was the precious ointment not sold and the proceeds given to the poor? why was it wasted? But Jesus rebuked him. The Magdalen had done right.[1] And why had she done right? Because her deed had been love pure and simple, the genuine expression of the highest sentiment of which a human being is capable. Judas (if we set aside, as we charitably may, the suspicion that he wished to appropriate the money to himself)[2] allowed a prudential, even calculating, consideration to enter into his thinking. He looked for an extraneous use, for an ulterior purpose; he did not understand that deeds of love are highest and finest when such considerations (however laudable in the context of secular life) are totally absent. Love is only itself when it is love for love's sake. Our own activistic age may find this difficult to understand, but perhaps the fault lies with our age and its activism which is all too closely tied to consequences and causes, as if no value could be valuable in itself. Perhaps we can best explain what we mean with the help of a distinction used by that great explorer of love, St. Bernard of Clairvaux. He contrasts effective and affective love and calls the former inferior, the latter superior.[3] Of course, effective love *is* love, even as *eros* is; but it is not the highest love, not love in all its purity. In the narrowest circle of disciples, in the archetypal society in the religious meaning of the term, which must be held together by the bond of perfection, nothing will do but the best. Matthew and Mark do not blame Judas alone; they imply that several or all disciples were taken

---

[1] Matthew XXVI, 6–10; Mark XIV, 3–9; John XII, 1–7. Cf. also Luke VII, 36–48.
[2] Cf. John XII, 6.
[3] Cf. Luddy, loc. cit., pp. 198 et seq.

aback by the Magdalen's 'waste'. But if this is so, then they were taught a sublime lesson on this occasion, which the man from Karioth refused to learn.

The truth is that we have so far given only a partial picture of the circle around the Founder. We have only considered the Master's relationship to His disciples, and that alone can be called ideal. We have now to investigate the relationships of the disciples to each other, and they – as the Gospels witness – fell far short of perfection. In the earliest germ-cell of the Church, as in the later full-fledged organism, the archetypal – noumenal and the merely phenomenal, the exalted and the ordinary, gold and dross were equally intermixed. Today as in the year A.D. 31 or 32, the axial reality within the body of believers is their love of their Lord; where that is absent, Christianity is absent, too. And today as in the year 31 or 32, secondary relationships cluster around that axis which are lesser in love, lower in temperature, though, we may hope, still somewhat warmed by the heart-life of the group which, as a religious group, must be considered by its adherents – in so far as it preserves something of the Founder[1] – to be somewhat more than human. True, ideally, according to the Founder's command, even the circle that had lost Him, even the far-spreading and therefore unavoidably impersonal Church of the future, was to be informed by *agape*. 'A new commandment I give unto you: that you love one another; as I have loved you, that you also love one another. By this shall all men know that you are my disciples, if you have love one for another' (John XIII, 34 and 35). The plea, indeed, is here, and it is clear. The response has ever been but partial. The fact is disappointing, yet it is unavoidable because human beings are involved. If the Church was in its Founder more than human (as faith assumes), it has at all times been nothing but human in the human beings – the human beings *as such* – who compose it.

Even the circle around the Founder was therefore in a manner split: it carried within its circumference the unheard-of and the commonplace (*das Alltägliche*, as Weber called it) at the same time. And this has *ever* been the condition of the Church: a stream of pure love has gone up to heaven, while only an impure, in the sense of imperfect, sentiment has linked the members horizontally on this earth. The relationship between the two qualities, the ideal and

[1] On this point, cf. below, pp. 114 et seq.

the sub-ideal, can best be described in Platonic–Neoplatonic terms. The ideal is the pure divine 'Idea' (in this case, the idea of what a society should be like), in which the sub-ideal merely 'participates', but with which it never fully coincides. At the same time it is and remains the command and the challenge which it has ever been – the aim towards which the society of believers must try to move. Like all other human realities, the Church must endeavour to *become* what it *is* – it must endeavour to become *in fact* what ideally it is *in design*. This conception is diametrically opposed to that of Weber: Weber sees an unavoidable, irreversible sinking down; the Catholic Christian sees an ever-difficult, yet never impossible, rising up. Friedrich Heiler was, like Max Weber, a Lutheran, yet he understood the relation between ideal and real which is embedded in the bases of the Catholic Church's self-understanding: 'All religious Catholics are in the last resort Platonists (even if they are in their philosophy and theology Aristotelians). They see in the phenomenal world imperfect mirrorings – mirrorings deformed by *hyle* [materiality] – of perfect divine originals; and they have the admirable gift of recognizing the pure designs of the Deity even in their most impure appearances and in their coarsest distortions.'[1]

As the charismatic-caritative circle around the Founder conceives of itself as the highest form of society, it is but logical that it should claim absolute priority over all other human attachments. Economic and professional ties, for instance, are broken by it: Simon-Peter is called away from his fishing, Levi-Matthew from his money-counting; in a negative instance, the rich young man is denied entry because he cannot cut loose from the cash-nexus which binds him to another kind of life (Mark X, 17–28). More dramatic still is the setting aside of familial ties; yet on this point Jesus, as the Gospels depict Him, is firm: 'If any man come to me and hate not his father and mother and wife and children and brethren and sisters, yea and his own life also, he cannot be my disciple.' Or again: 'And another [who was called] said: I will follow thee, Lord; but let me first take my leave of them that are at my house. Jesus said to him: No man putting his hand to the plough and looking back is fit for the kingdom of God . . . And another of his disciples said to him: Lord, suffer me first to go and bury my father. But Jesus said to him: Follow me, and let the dead

[1] Heiler, loc. cit., pp. 332 and 333.

bury their dead' (Luke XIV, 26, and IX, 61 and 62; Matthew VIII, 21, 22.)[1]

These strongly, even at first sight shockingly strongly, negative words can, however, be rightly understood only if two germane doctrines are fully taken into account. While the charismatic-caritative circle ranks above all other social formations and therefore breaks their claims, it also offers itself as their model and thereby strengthens their claims. The prime example here is the marriage bond. The Mosaic Law allowed divorce (though not without provisos and safeguards); Jesus forbade it: 'What God hath joined together, let not men put asunder' (Mark X, 9).[2] Rightly does Maurenbrecher, in his comment on this passage, interpret it as a universal precept: 'A community, once it has been taken up, binds the human beings comprised in it together for all time to come.'[3] 'The family reflects, as no other social institution does, the mystery of the Church, her real union with Christ,' writes Karl Adam, and refers to Ephesians V, 32, for his authority.[4] Because of this similarity to the charismatic circle, Christianity has ever protected the marriage bond; witness, for instance, St. Gregory the Great's condemnation of the imperial law which permitted a husband or wife to engineer a divorce by entering a monastery or convent.[5] But if the family is singled out for special mention, *all* human relationships are ultimately meant to be transformed into *communitates totius vitae*, as the Roman lawyers liked to call the supreme forms of social life, societies of total fusion, as Leopold von Wiese described them in his system of sociology.[6] The circle around the Founder does not, therefore, claim a permanent privilege; it is merely set up as the light for men to steer by until they reach the harbour of ultimate all-embracing harmony.

That this is indeed the meaning of the Gospel passages which we have quoted can be seen from the missionary command which Jesus gave to His disciples, originally on the occasion of their first apostolic journey,[7] and then again as His parting instruction: 'Go ye into the whole world and preach the Gospel to every creature' (Mark XVI, 15). This is the second of the doctrines which

---

[1] Cf. also Luke IX, 59 and 60; VIII, 19–21; Mark III, 31–5; Matthew, 47–50.
[2] Cf. the whole passage, ibid., 2–16.
[3] *Von Nazareth nach Golgatha*, as quoted, p. 92.
[4] Adam, loc. cit., p. 151.   [5] Workman, loc. cit., p. 170, note 2.
[6] Cf. loc. cit., pp. 254 et seq.   [7] Matthew X, and parallels.

countermands the apparent negativity of the above passages, especially the one about 'hating' one's father and mother. If all men are to be loved maximally, there remain no blood-relations that could be 'hated' – or, for that matter, preferentially loved. Jesus was, if we may use the word, imperialistic in His intentions. He looked beyond the narrow circle around Him towards a charismatic-caritative world society. It is in this sense that we can call Him the Founder of the Catholic Church, a Church which must be apostolic, so that it can become truly catholic. The point is sociologically crucial: Christianity had indeed at first the outer position of a sect, but in its inner kernel it was from the inception laid on as a world-wide community[1] – a church both apostolic and catholic, with the ambitious aim of filling all humanity with the spirit which pervaded the circle around the Founder in its supreme moments. As we have seen at the end of the last chapter, it was the universalist Princes of the Apostles, Paul and Peter, who continued the work of Jesus, not those sectarian Judaeo–Christians whom they had to conquer at the Council of Jerusalem.

This vision of an all-embracing communion of all is, of course, the uttermost limit which social idealism can reach in its boldest flight. We can hardly imagine that it will ever be realized by creatures of flesh and blood. What we have before us is, in Platonic language, an image laid up in heaven, not a scheme which human endeavour can easily construct on earth. But even if we descend to a lower level, there remains something unrealistic about the Christian ethos. The charismatic-caritative circle around the Founder filled by love is claimed to be the germ-cell of the Church; but the Church – the full-fledged organism – as we know it empirically, as we can see and observe it, is not filled by love as that circle was; it has its human – its all too human – weaknesses; it appears as a society like most others, no worse perhaps in its inner tone, but not much better either. Does this contrast not suggest that Max Weber's concept of the routinization of charisma is correct after all? In nature, there is upward development: from the ugly caterpillar springs the beautiful butterfly. Has not the opposite happened here, in the history of Christianity? Has not the beautiful butterfly turned into an ugly caterpillar? Are we not moving on an inclined plane which leads from a family of faith to an impersonal, face- and soul-less organization?

[1] Cf. St. Thomas Aquinas, *Summa Theologiae, pars III, quaest. 8, art. 3.*

Certainly, as we are turning our eyes from Jesus and His relations to the Twelve to the interrelations among the Twelve themselves, we are confronted with the picture of a simple human society. Simple human societies are characterized by the presence, not of love, but of competition, by the constant manœuvring of individuals for place and position. And of this there is ample evidence in the Gospel accounts of the conduct of the Apostles. For instance: 'James and John, the sons of Zebedee, came to Him saying . . . Grant to us that we may sit, one on thy right hand, and the other on thy left hand, in thy glory . . . And the ten, hearing it, began to be much displeased at James and John' (Mark X, 35, 37, 41). It was on this occasion that Jesus explained to the circle how love – how *agape*, the perfect love – has ambitions diametrically opposed to those which actuate the unregenerate man: it tries to be great by being humble. 'Whosoever will be first among you, shall be the servant of all. For the Son of Man also is not come to be ministered unto: but to minister and to give his life a redemption of many' (44, 45). As we have shown in vol. III, this sublime lesson entered, however imperfectly, into the ethos of Spanish kingship, as it entered into the ethos of chivalry of which Spanish kingship was one of the forms and flowers. In so far as it did enter, not only the programmatic ethos, but even the practical conduct, of human beings in later ages – and the historical records have their patches of light here and there – the passage of time brought evolution, not involution, of *charisma* and *caritas*, a rising up towards the divine archetype, and not a falling away from it.

The evidence for the similarity of the earliest and the latest Christian communities, so far as human behaviour is concerned, is so substantial that pages upon pages could be filled by it. But there is no need to waste our space.[1] Men have always been men, as they always will be. Instead, we should direct attention to a technical point which also militates against the Weberian law of religious entropy. Routinization, as Weber sees it, implies bureaucratization; bureaucratization, however, implies a division of functions, indeed, is the implementation of a division of functions. Yet the division of functions is not the result of a gradual falling from grace, of a

[1] Cf. especially Mark VI, 52; VIII, 14–33; I Corinthians I, 11, and III, 3; Galatians V, 15; Philippians I, 14–18; Acts VI, 1; further all the passages enumerated by Meyer, op. cit., vol. I, pp. 268 and 269; cf. also vol. III, p. 496, for this historian's general judgment.

charisma-involution and caritas-degeneration. It is present from the very beginning and involves the Founder Himself. We have the authority of Joachim Wach on our side and can pit it against that of Max Weber. 'The tendency towards organization,' Wach writes in his *Sociology of Religion*, 'is never absent, being apparent to a certain degree even in the "circles".'[1]

We are not thinking so much of some detail, as the carrying of the purse by Judas Iscariot, though even that is significant; we have in mind a sociologically far more important duality which divides and structures the original circle, and not only that around Jesus, but also that around Gautama, for in this particular the parallels are amazing. All the four Gospels are plainly agreed that two of the Twelve Apostles occupy a special position: Peter and John. But the pre-eminence which they share is less important than the differentiation in function which divides them: Peter is from the beginning the representative of humanity rather than a personal companion of Jesus, while John is the personal companion of the Lord rather than a representative of humanity. The Buddhist Peter is Sariputta, the Buddhist John is Ananda. At the Master's death, John and Ananda are present, Peter and Sariputta are not. Peter's face is turned outward, so to speak, John's inward. The differentiation of which we are speaking is present from the very first minute of discipleship, from the very first second even. Mark describes the formation of the apostolic circle as follows: 'And going up into a mountain, He called unto Him whom He would Himself. And they came to Him. And He made that twelve should be with Him and that He might send them to preach' (III, 13 and 14). They 'should be with Him', His fellow-wayfarers: here we have one function; 'that He might send them to preach': here we have another. As yet, the roles are not visibly divided, but soon they will be: and already the figure of Peter points forward to preacher, priest and pope, active servants in and of Christendom, the figure of John to soul-companion, mystic and saint, especially the cloistered kind of saint, for whom the loving contemplation of the Godhead is a point of arrival and not a point of departure, a state of rest and not a pre-paration for further duty. Cullmann, whose discussion of the sources is particularly enlightening in this field, points out that according to Mark, Jesus always calls the fisherman Peter after He has renamed him (III, 16) – with one exception. The exception is

[1] Loc. cit., p. 141.

109

the reproach on Gethsemane: 'Simon, sleepest thou? Couldst thou not watch one hour?' (XIV, 37). Peter's weakness on this occasion is purely personal. It has nothing to do with the function which he is called to fulfil.[1]

If the analysis of Wach and Cullman is correct – and there is no reason whatsoever to impugn it – then any sharp confrontation between the apostolic circle and the later Church is exaggerated. The ideal-typical distinction which we have used as the heading of the present chapter, and which, as the reader will soon see, dominates the argument of the present chapter, the distinction between those who are more priests than saints and those who are more saints than priests, can be traced to the reality of the narrowest and innermost circle during the Founder's own life-time. Indeed, it is He, the charismatic leader *par excellence*, who gives one role to Peter and another to John – He who initiates the prime division of labour which characterizes the Church at all stages of her development. If it be said that Peter's role is open to routinization and John's is not, then everybody will have to agree. If the Church consisted only of administrators, then, indeed, the fate of bureaucratization would have been unavoidable and Weber would have been right. But the Church has never consisted of administrators only; she has always had her saints; and these saints have prevented the ossification of her organism because they have ever poured new life into her veins.

The specific differentiation of roles and functions which we have now discussed is not, however, the only feature – the only differentiation – which proves that the apostolic circle was on its human side similar in social character to ordinary (*alltägliche*) societies. There is the further significant fact that, like ordinary societies, it had an inner core, a prestigious praesidium, one might almost say, if a sober and secular term is permitted in the orbit of sacred history, a committee – Peter, James and John. At the transfiguration, in the garden of Gethsemane and at the awakening of the daughter of Jairus – that is to say, at the three most momentous happenings – they are present, the other disciples are not (Mark IX, 1; XIV, 33; V, 37). And while Peter, James and John are thus a wheel within a wheel, the Twelve, too, are collectively such a narrower circle within a still larger circle, the Seventy soon to be called, and indeed

[1] Meyer had made the point before Cullmann, cf. vol. I, p. 150. Generally, cf. Cullmann, loc. cit., pp. 31 et seq., and Meyer, vol. I, pp. 135 et seq. Cf. further Wach, *Meister und Jünger*, as quoted, p. 31.

the less definite, but no less real multitude of anonymous followers. 'In the Kingdom,' writes St. Chrysostom, 'the honours were not equal . . . but three were above the rest . . . for one star differeth from another star in glory. And yet all were apostles,' all were stars. 'Nor were all the disciples equal,' yet all were disciples.[1] If we may change our metaphor and bring our exposition closer to sociological terminology, we may say that the Christian community, even while Christ was yet present, was *structured*. That structuring did not prevent the Divine Love (as we may say in a theological aside) from being indiscriminately lavished on all, but it did make the society of believers, considered apart from that Love, comparable to, indeed identical with, other, ordinary societies.

The fact on which we are insisting, namely that organization, with all that it implies, is not a later evolution, or rather a later degeneration, but an unavoidably present trait of the society of believers in all its developmental stages, even the very first, appears to be widely admitted. Max Weber's concept of the routinization of charisma was modelled, as he himself indicates,[2] on Rudolph Sohm's assertion of the progressive legalization of the Church. Yet Lowrie had this to say in his Preface: 'The most distinctive feature of my representation of the subject (which is Sohm's) is the proof that the whole development of Catholic [i.e. legal] institutions was conditioned by ideas which, perverted as they were, may be traced back to the very beginnings of Christianity.'[3] In this sentence, two parts have to be distinguished – the phrase 'perverted as they were', and the rest. The phrase 'perverted as they were' is a pure value-judgment based on an ultra-individualistic conviction that there is *no* appropriate organization for a religious grouping, that *all* organization is mortal to the religious life properly so called. This is, to say the least, a begging of the decisive question. The statement we have quoted becomes, when it is freed from this valuational content, entirely factual: 'The whole development of Catholic institutions was conditioned by ideas which may be traced back to the very beginnings of Christianity.' This is precisely what we are saying; this is precisely what we have been proving. Our essential disagreement with Sohm and Weber should therefore be clear: they are thinking in terms of a radical change, over time, in the

[1] Cit. Chapman, op. cit., p. 76.
[2] *The Theory of Social and Economic Organization*, as quoted, p. 328.
[3] Loc. cit., p. XIV. Heiler has a parallel passage (op. cit., p. 43).

society of believers, we are thinking in terms of a gradual unfolding of its indwelling characteristics. Their stance is critical, ours descriptive. It should be obvious who is conforming to the ideal of a value-free social science.

What we have discussed so far are the circumstances which obtained while the Founder was still with His disciples. He (we repeat it) called the Twelve from the milling multitude, He called the Three from within the Twelve. And He, too, gave one task to Peter and another to John, turning the one more man-ward, the other more God-ward, making one an administrator, the other a mystic. The Founder's death obviously marks an epoch. We must now see what happened after it. There is only one supplementary remark which we have to make on the subject of the 'circle'. The first group of Franciscans or Passionists or any other founded religious movement, Protestant or Catholic, must be imagined as filled by charismatic and caritative sentiments comparable to those identifiable in the apostolic community. We have hardly any sources which would compare with the Gospels and would allow us to do for other circles what we can do for the apostolic group; but in so far as we have them, for instance in the primitive writings of Franciscanism, they convincingly bespeak the presence of a similar spirit. This is anything but surprising, for what was the essence of the great secondary founders if not their Christlikeness? Books like Bartholomew of Pisa's *De Conformitate Vitae Beati Francisci ad Vitam Domini Jesu*[1] are merely the development, the stylization as it were, of a basic fact. Here again, Platonist conceptions can help us to clarify reality. There is only one divine idea of what a rose really is, but there are always new roses which more or less replicate or reduplicate that archetypal image. There is only one Rome seated upon seven hills, but cities like Prague, and even the English Cambridge,[2] did their best to mirror its qualities as a Saint mirrors the Saviour's spirit. So also with the charismatic circle. Indeed, it seems impossible even for the poetic imagination to conceive of a religious founder-and-disciple relationship in

[1] Cf. our vol. III, p. 302.

[2] For the architectural device, with the help of which Christoph Dientzenhofer contrived to move one of Prague's outlying mountains closer to the others, the nearer six, cf. Schürer, O., *Prag: Kultur, Kunst, Geschichte*, ed. München und Brünn 1939, p. 364. In Cambridge, Peas Hill and Market Hill are about as flat as they can be, but to townsmen who loved to regard their township as a little Rome, nominal hills were better than none at all.

radically different terms. Gerhart Hauptmann's great novel, *Der Narr in Christo Emanuel Quint*, which describes the formation of a Pietist sect in his native Silesia,[1] shows, in a glass darkly, the same features as the human circle around Jesus Christ.

THE DEATH OF THE FOUNDER AND THE ISSUE OF CONTINUITY

Every circle is broken if one of its links is lost; every system is shattered when the kingpin which holds it together is withdrawn. We have described the love of the Master for His disciples as the axial reality of the apostolic group, compared with which the clustering human relations among the co-disciples, i.e. the social relations in the narrower sense of the word, constitute merely a secondary phenomenon. If the axis is removed, the result would have to be – so it would seem – an almost total collapse of the community.

Almost total, so most would say, but yet not quite total. For the dying Founder leaves behind him a memory, and this can enter into the changed situation and provide a fresh social cement. After all, the followers of Jesus, who on Good Friday scattered to the four winds, reassembled again before many days were over. Yet the new bond is not like the old: the memory of a man is not like his personal presence. The new society will therefore be but a shadow of the old. Form will remain rather than substance. In a consistently individualistic world-view, things must necessarily appear in this light. It can be seen, how deep the roots of the concept of an unavoidable routinization of charisma are, not only in Weber's mind where they have found formulation, but in all modern mentality which is pre-eminently person-centred and cannot envisage an abiding relationship beyond the grave.

But not only individualism leads to the conviction that the Founder's death and disappearance must substitute an inferior for a superior form of society: axiomatic unbelief must do so likewise. In positivism, even the religiously tinged positivism of Auguste Comte, death is the end of everything; it is *a fortiori* the end of everything in a pure positivism without a tinge or trace of religiosity as was that of Weber. Yet for the religious man, if he is to deserve this description at all, death is not, and cannot be, the end in any

[1] Cf. our vol. II, p. 9.

sense of the word: belief in the immortality of the soul is absolutely basic to, and integral in, *any* form of religious belief. 'For those who are of the faith', says the Preface of the Mass for the Dead, 'life is changed: it is not taken away.' Jesus, too, underwent a change of life when He was crucified and buried; yet His life was not thereby taken away, nor was He taken away from His followers, quite apart from any possible miraculous reappearances such as those asserted in the Gospels. 'I know that my Redeemer liveth', proclaimed Handel in his *Messiah*. But that means that, to the religious believer, the tie between the Master and the disciple is not terminated by the former's (or the latter's) death. Therefore, the axial reality around which the human relationships in the apostolic circle revolved, was fully preserved even after the catastrophe of Calvary, and the Church of the future could carry within her the same heart which had held together and animated the Twelve.

So far as the scientific sociologist of religion is concerned, it cannot make the slightest difference whether he personally believes in the survival of the soul or not, or indeed whether he believes in anything at all. This belief is simply part and parcel of his data, of the religious reality which he has to study, and he must allow for its objective efficacy, even if he subjectively entertains the conviction that he is confronted with nothing but superstition. Indeed, this is a good instance for the application of Max Weber's own principle of objectivity.[1] *Anybody* who, without prejudice, sees the facts as they are, must acknowledge that believers *do* believe in the continued existence of the Founder. This is really a matter of logic and definition, for if they did not carry that belief within themselves, they clearly would not be believers. But given the belief, there is little reason to assert that the Founder's physical removal must totally transform the community around Him.

There is, however, more. Christians down to, and including, Martin Luther, i.e. both Catholics and the early Reformers, assumed *two* incarnations of the Divine Principle of Love: one in the historical body of the man Jesus of Nazareth, and the other in the body of bread which constitutes the Sacrament of the Lord's Supper. But this Eucharistic sign (which is more than a sign because it mediates, for faith, a 'real presence') is ever renewable, and therefore there is, for this part of Christendom, even a *physical* form in which they have their Lord and hold Him at all times in their midst. Luther's

[1] Cf. Stark, W., *The Sociology of Knowledge*, London 1958, p. 127.

transition from the Catholic dogma of transsubstantiation to his own doctrine of consubstantiation makes no difference, so far as trust in the Lord's real and continued presence amid His followers is concerned. Only in Calvinism's re-interpretation of the Sacrament of the Altar as a meal of remembrance do we find a serious weakening of the credal element which we are discussing: only Calvin substitutes memory for the real presence. Indeed, as a closer consideration of his theology would show, even he retains something of the old mysticism; even for him the Lord is *in fact* among those who assemble in His name. It is therefore doubly wrong to overestimate the change which came with the death of Jesus Christ: His spiritual survival in the beyond and His sacramental re-incarnation down here below both show that, for the Church of the latter times, the bond of union is near-identical with that of the earliest days.

We are here up against a difficulty which is inherent in modern man, or, as we might or should perhaps formulate it, in the modern languages. Precisionists as we are (witness the chronometers which we carry around with ourselves on our wrists), precisionists as we must be in our type of economy and society, we are better equipped for the description of an individual moment than for that of a lasting state. Yesterday and today, 'that was' and 'this is', are for us sharply distinguished, if not, indeed, mutually exclusive, concepts. It was different in the epoch when Christianity first formed, and when Hebrew and Greek were the idioms which not only expressed, but even formed and informed, human thought. 'In a Latin language of today', writes an outstanding philologist-historian, 'we find present, future and past tenses, each of them referring to a well-defined segment of time. But the . . . viewpoint of Hebrew grammar is . . . quite different . . . The flow of time is what counts, not its successive states . . . Jesus, along with the other Jews of His time, had an idea of time which may still be found today in isolated Jewish communities . . . To . . . the Ashkenazi Jews of Central Europe . . . the present moment knew no limits, but was part of a continuum stretching from the beginning to the end of time . . . Their life was not led on a chronological basis, for the patriarchs, kings and prophets of the Old Testament were always at their side . . . So it is that for a Jew every fleeting moment has something of the savour of eternity. Present, past and future run together.' Therefore it is, within these linguistic cadres, easy to conceive of 'an action that may be repeated any number of times but never finished'[1] like the Jewish Seder or the Christian Eucharist, especially the Catholic Mass, in which the Founder of Christianity finds ever new entry into the life of His people.

Another great philologist-historian, Eduard Meyer, to whom this volume owes so very much, makes the same point with regard to Paul's Hellenistic Greek, and he joins to his authority that of a most prestigious theologian. The reference in the following quotation is to I Corinthians XV, 4: 'He rose again the third day.' 'Rightly does Harnack emphasize,' writes Meyer, 'that, in contrast to the other fact-recording aorists, ἐγήγερται is in the past tense (Perfectum). The resurrection is a happening which is continually effective (*dauernd wirksam*); even now Christ is the Risen One.'[2] The very last words prove *how* much of a strait-jacket our languages are, for they do not sufficiently convey that in one sense, an important sense, the rising from the dead is as yet 'effective', i.e. not quite over.

As the thought of Jesus was embedded in this linguistic matrix, in this implied metaphysics, it is not surprising to find that He took a definitely positive view of tradition: tradition is valuable, if not invaluable; it does enshrine and preserve the genuinely sacred. This was a point on which He sided with the Pharisees as against the Sadducees.[3] 'The scribes and the Pharisees have sitten on the chair of Moses,' runs a logion recorded by St. Matthew. 'All things therefore whatsoever they shall say to you, observe and do: but according to their works do ye not. For they say, and do not' (XXIII, 2 and 3). What these sentences condemn is the partial, the purely formal, carrying on of the religious traditions: the traditions themselves are upheld.[4] It was easy for St. Paul to develop his own concept of tradition as he had so firm a basis to build on. 'I delivered unto you,' he writes to the children of his heart, that 'which I also received' (I Corinthians XV, 3). Campenhausen, who acknowledges

---

[1] Aron, R., *Jesus of Nazareth: The Hidden Years*, New York 1962, pp. 54–6.

[2] Meyer, loc. cit., vol. III, p. 209, note. The Harnack reference is to a paper in the *Berichte der Berliner Akademie*, 1922, pp. 62 et seq. ('Die Verklärungsgeschichte Jesu, der Bericht des Paulus, und die beiden Christusvisionen des Petrus').

[3] Cf. Kümmel, W. G., 'Jesus und der jüdische Traditionsgedanke', *Zeitschrift für die neutestamentliche Wissenschaft*, 1934, pp. 105 et seq., especially pp. 116–21.

[4] Cf. especially ibid., verse 23, which makes the meaning perfectly clear. Cf. also Adam, loc. cit., pp. 76 and 77.

that Paul 'knows and accepts the concept of tradition to which, as a Jew, he was antecedently close', emphasizes at the same time that the Apostle mentions as yet no office-bearers whose special task it would be to preserve the traditions.[1] That is true. But such office-bearers are at least foreshadowed in Paul and in the Gospels themselves. Granted that no specific functionaries are traceable in the earliest days, the specific functions are, and so their appearance can not be seen as anything but an unfolding of a primitive pattern. It would be absurd to cry 'perversion!' here.

But Jesus was not merely positive in His general attitude to tradition; He was even preoccupied with the stability of that tradition. The metaphor which He used when He appointed Peter to the primacy among the Apostles – 'Thou art Peter [Kepha][2] and upon this rock I will build my church' (Matthew XVI, 18) – was used by Him before as the same Gospel records: 'Every one therefore that heareth these my words and doth them, shall be likened to a wise man that built his house upon a rock. And the rain fell and the floods came and the winds blew: and they beat upon that house. And it fell not, for it was founded on a rock' (VII, 24 and 25). Catholics can hardly be blamed if they link the two passages, i.e. if they see the institution of a priesthood and of the papacy as the creation of instances entrusted with the preservation (and even with the stabilization) of tradition.[3] Protestants will, not surprisingly, be inclined another way. Some of them have denied the authenticity of Matthew XVI, 17–19; others, however, have upheld it, especially Oscar Cullmann.[4] But whatever the ins and outs of this question, Matthew VII, 24–5 cannot very well be impugned; for this is the end of the Sermon on the Mount, by common consent the most authentic of all tradited material, and the two verses cannot be jettisoned without endangering the best attested passages of the Gospels and the ones which ring more true, and to *any* believer, Protestant *or* Catholic, convey the Christ-spirit in greater purity and intensity, than any other. But these verses

---

[1] Campenhausen, loc. cit., p. 164; cf. also 165 and 166. Campenhausen agrees with our own point of view. He underlines that the usual confrontation of 'a living spirit' and 'a dead tradition' is not primitive or patristic but modern, and that for Paul tradition *is* living because it is inspirited.

[2] This is the Aramaic word for rock.

[3] Cf. Butler, loc. cit., pp. 194 and 105.   [4] Cf. loc. cit., pp. 215 et seq.

extol stability, at least stability in itself, apart from any stabilizing agency.

Eduard Meyer has considered the scene before the gates of Cæsarea Philippi, when Peter confessed to the Galilean: 'Thou art Christ, the son of the living God' and was, for his part, re-named The Rock (Matthew XVI, 16 and 18), the *peripatia* in the drama which was to end on Mount Calvary. He writes in one context: 'With the acknowledgment that He is the Messiah, the Christian community is founded. Thus Jesus can face the fulfilment of His earthly fate and set out on the road to Jerusalem.' And in another he adds, calling the Petrine confession 'the decisive turning point': 'Now Jesus has a band of enthusiastic followers at His side; now He can endeavour, with their aid, to tackle His work, to convert the whole nation to which He is sent to a belief in the Kingdom of God, in a grand manner. This demands His appearance at the spiritual centre of the nation, not, as formerly, far away in the provinces. And so He begins at Caesarea His Journey to Jerusalem.' The revolutionary act which soon follows, the chasing of the traders from the Temple, is an outward manifestation of the inner strength which the collection of supporters and the credal declaration of the head of them had given Him. The disciples in the widest sense of the word are thus brought prominently into the picture: Jesus reckoned on their backing. But Meyer, after a strict examination of the sources, also asserts that Jesus foresaw the sorry end of His irruption into the citadel of orthodoxy, and we must therefore assume that in His consideration of the more distant developments, too, the disciples must have figured prominently. 'He could not be in any doubt,' Meyer opines, 'that He also had to expect the destiny which had overtaken all who had preached the word of God before, that He, the Son, would not fare better than the servants, i.e. the prophets. As recently John, the returned Elias, had been unable to carry out the task to which He was called, but "they had done to him whatsoever they would", so also would He be handled.'[1] If this is true, and there is no reason to dissent from the judgment of the great historian, then Jesus must have reckoned on His disciples, not only in His planning of the nearer, but also in His planning of the further, future: He must have had His eyes on those who would survive Him; He must have had a

[1] Meyer, loc. cit., vol. I, p. 116, and vol. II, pp. 449–51. The scriptural allusions are to Mark XII, 1–8, and IX, 10–12.

mission for those who would survive Him. And that mission could be no other than the prolongation of His own work – indeed, the prolongation of His own self. Thus there is laid on, from the very beginning, the thought-form in terms of which the Church has ever interpreted herself and her very being. As a collectivity, as the living body of those who are not separated off by their sins, as the living body of those who are truly saved, she is the Immortal Jesus, so far as He remains on this earth. The words which Paul heard when he was thrown off his horse on the road to Damascus – 'Saul, Saul, why persecutest thou me?' (Acts IX, 4): not: my followers, but *me* – demonstrate that this was the solution to the problem of the continuity of charisma which Christendom embraced, and which is one of its profoundest characteristics.

If it be said that this is a specious belief, not a sober fact, we should remember once again that we are in the area of faith and must, as describers and analysts, take what we find as a datum, however we may privately feel about it. Yet sober facts are not entirely missing, and we should adduce them in support here. Among the shorter stories of Anatole France there is one which depicts Pontius Pilate in his old age. He is asked whether he remembers Jesus the Nazarene, but he cannot. There was a lot of trouble in those days, he says, but the detail he has forgotten . . .[1] *Se non è vero, è ben trovato.* Memories *are* short. Why then was it that men of another age or generation had heard of Jesus and desired to know about Him? Because they had met with, or even been absorbed in, the Church. 'A visible society of human beings,' writes Butler, 'does in fact appear to be the one direct outcome in history of Christ's life on earth'[2] – direct and tangible. If it is urged that the Gospels rather than the Church have carried the knowledge of the Founder down the stream of time, then we have to consider that these accounts, invaluable as they are, were written for the Church and are thus secondary to her, as Butler also emphasizes.[3] Furthermore, the Gospels, though agreeing in substance, are diverse in detail. For the survival of the *one* historical person, there had to be *one* unitary – in this case, also unifying – spirit, and that spirit could only be that of a historical community, in so far as it was filled by the Founder's abiding selfhood.

[1] 'Le Procurateur de Judée', in *L'Etui de Nacre.* Cf. *Oeuvres Complètes Illustrées d'Anatole France*, vol. V, Paris 1944, pp. 217 et seq.
[2] Butler, loc. cit., p. 101.   [3] Ibid., and pp. 114 and 115.

Because this is the initial and continuous self-understanding of the Church, a tendency on her part – difficult to accept for modern man, but easy for ancient and all medieval mentality – to see herself as a collective person, a 'real' body in the sense of the philosophy of realism,[1] was almost unavoidable. The metaphor of Galatians IV, 19 – where Paul says: 'I am in labour again, until Christ be formed in you' – sets the tone: the taking shape of the Church is like birth pangs, and the birth is the birth of the undying Christ. If this poetical rendering of the basic conception suggests a chain of births of the same person, so much the more effective is it in the formulation of the carrying conviction: the charisma of Christ was not tied to His death-committed personal body, but prolonged itself, and remained present, in a collective body not destroyable by death, in many lives which – in so far as they are His life – are 'in reality' but one life, the life of one being.

Marie-Joseph Congar has emphasized that this identification of a holy One with the many is thoroughly in line with Jewish conceptions, and that the theme can be found, in anticipation of the Christian version to be formulated later, in the Book of Daniel. 'What is foretold,' he writes, 'is an eternal Kingdom of God. But then, who will receive the benefits which this will bring with it? It will be at one and the same time an individual being who "comes upon the clouds as a Son of Man" (VII, 13), and to whom are given "power, glory and a kingdom" for all eternity, and also "the people of the holy ones of the Most High" who receive too the rule and the power and the greatness of kingdoms which are under all the heavens (ib. 27). Here we find already,' Congar adds, 'in an extremely remarkable way, one of the characteristics which were to become dominant and even decisive in the Christian idea of the Kingdom and the Church – the real identity of one and all: . . . all belongs to one, and yet all is realized in a collectivity . . .'[2]

Oscar Cullmann has added to this evidence from the Old Testament even more valuable observations from the New. A comparison, he tells us, between Matthew XI, 4 and 5, and Matthew X, 7 and 8, is deeply revealing; he is right. For in the one passage Jesus speaks of the deeds which He Himself has performed, and in the other of the deeds which the apostles are to perform – and the two

[1] Cf. above, pp. 14 et seq.
[2] *Esquisses du Mystère de l'Eglise*, Paris 1941, p. 14. We have quoted G. Webb and A. Walker's English translation as given in Cerfaux, loc. cit., p. 284.

are identical. Perhaps we may use sociological jargon here and say that the same *function* that He has fulfilled is to be fulfilled by His disciples also, and that therefore there is but *one* work which the one and the many share. 'Even during Jesus' own life,' Cullmann insists, 'fulfilment takes place not only in His own person, but God's people has begun to realize itself in these men' – the disciples whom He calls to be fishers of souls and reapers of the Lord's harvest (Mark I, 17, and Matthew IX, 37). According to Matthew XVI, 18 – giving the assurance that the gates of hell shall not prevail against the Church – the whole *ecclesia* (so Cullmann interprets) enters into the saving work of Jesus. 'What is, during Jesus' lifetime, committed to the disciples as a messianic function . . . that is here laid on the whole *ecclesia* . . . It is said of the *ecclesia* founded on Peter as the rock that, though it will remain in the present dispensation which is still dominated by death, it will yet participate already in the power of the resurrection which is the property of the Kingdom of God.' Summing up, the great Protestant bible scholar declares these interpretations to be part and parcel of his intimate convictions. Speaking in the first person he writes: 'I accept the idea of a prolongation of the work of Christ in a visible earthly Church because I find it as the central assertion above all in the whole Gospel according to St. John.'[1] Eduard Meyer, who was what is often called a free spirit, indeed, something of a sceptic, also agrees that the historical sources must be so understood. He goes so far as to assert that the Gospel according to St. John[2] ascribes to Jesus and the Church the same teaching authority, indeed the same infallibility.

We are adducing these facts for one purpose, and one purpose only: to show that the issue of continuity which was a great problem for Max Weber, was nothing of the kind for the early Christian community. The difference does not lie in the 'scientific' attitude of the one and the 'fideist' commitments of the others; if that were all, matters would be simple; it lies basically in the individualistic preoccupations of the modern observer and in the collectivistic, philosophically 'realistic' *imago mundi* of the first followers of Christ

---

[1] Cullmann, loc. cit., pp. 226, 227, 232–7, 268. Cf. also Cerfaux (whose fine distinctions we cannot, and need not, discuss), pp. 268, 269 (note), 323, 325, 342–5, and Campenhausen, loc. cit., p. 137.
[2] His references are XIV, 18 et seq., and XVI, 6 et seq. Cf. Meyer's vol. III, pp. 646 and 647.

and co-founders of Christianity. If he is to do justice to the alien culture-complex which he is studying, today's sociologist of religion will have to empty his mind of the subconscious metaphysics of his own age; otherwise he will assuredly not achieve that inner 'understanding' which, to Weber himself, was the perfection of scholarly endeavour, and for which he was always pleading. For a generation which has lived less with the canons of individualistic philosophy and more with the insights of social anthropology, the task should not be too difficult. After all, the death of a chieftain does not bring an automatic and unavoidable deterioration of clan life, for that life remains: it is the life of a whole clan, not that of one man. True, Christ was not merely a chief, He was the Founder, the fount of the collective life. But this makes little difference. To St. Paul, He is the head from which the life streams into all members and the soul which inspirits them. Absence in the flesh did not mean absence in the spirit, as presence in the flesh had not necessarily meant community in the spirit either.

But enough of that; the point has been made. If the death of Jesus wrought a major difference on the sociological (as opposed to the personal) level, it was by giving the disciples, frightened as they were, a feeling of opposition to the world such as sects normally entertain and this feeling, composed of both an inferiority and a superiority sentiment, is a potent social cement. What is often called the apostles' communism of consumption had its roots in this opposition-feeling.[1] But this was merely a passing phase. It could not be more than merely a passing phase, a brief interlude, because Christianity has in it, or Christianity *is*, a total *élan vital* and *élan religieux* which (as the first volumes of this work have shown) cannot be contained even in large empires, let alone in a small sectlet. Once the converted Pharisees of Jerusalem were vanquished, who had been prepared to accept sect-like encapsulation and would have led Christianity to denominationalization or death, once Peter and Paul had succeeded in steering the Christian community into the open waters of history and on to a journey towards world-conquest, not opposition and self-restriction, but missionary work and expansion became the key-note of the Church. Finally, she could freely unfold. A study of that unfolding is our next task.

[1] Cf. Acts IV, 32–7.

THE UNFOLDING OF THE CHURCH

The first fact which characterizes the unfolding of the Church, as that of any other society, sacred or secular, is the sheer growth in numbers. A small roving band of evangelists living by alms is one thing, a far-flung movement of whose members the vast majority remain within their regular occupations is another. According to the Hegelian dictum that a change in quantity, when it goes beyond a certain point, becomes a change in quality, we should indeed have to expect a total transformation of Christianity, and this is precisely what Sohm and Weber are saying. Sociologically speaking, this transformation, whose reality is not to be denied, consists in the replacement of an élite group by an anonymous mass, the waning of a personal, and the waxing of an impersonal, mode of co-existence. Logically, therefore, those who are tied to élitist conceptions – and most intellectuals are so tied, even if they are democrats in politics – are prone to consider the whole evolution as an involution, to see the gain in quantity as a loss in quality. Discussing the decay and fall of ancient civilization, Michael Rostovtzeff ends his *Social and Economic History of the Roman Empire* with the following sentences which express a mood parallel to, or identical with, the one which possessed Sohm and Weber when they contemplated the drift of Christianity from the post-apostolic age onward: 'The evolution of the ancient world has a lesson and a warning for us. Our civilization will not last unless it be a civilization, not of one class, but of the masses . . . But the ultimate problem remains like a ghost, ever present and unlaid. Is it possible to extend a higher civilization to the lower classes without debasing its standard and diluting its quality to the vanishing point? Is not every civilization bound to decay as soon as it begins to penetrate the masses?'[1]

The dilemma posed in these rhetorical questions is indeed real. A world church cannot be like a circle of friends who are always in each other's company and share the last morsel of bread they eat. Love, when spread too widely, is apt to get thin. In St. Paul's Epistle to the Galatians, there is an exhortation which shows the quandary and proves that it occupied the Apostle's mind: 'Whilst we have time, let us work good to all men, but especially to those who are of the household of the faith' (VI, 10). Where does the emphasis in such a statement lie? On the second half-sentence which

[1] Ed. Oxford 1926, pp. 486 and 487.

more or less legitimizes the restriction of love to a narrower circle, or on the first which enjoins its extension to all members of the vast human race?

The answer is that for the Christian the emphasis lies, and must lie, on the first half-sentence: let us work good to *all* men, 'The word of the Lord came to me, saying . . . Behold, *all* souls are mine,' writes the Prophet Ezekiel (XVIII, 1 and 4), and St. Paul would not have rejected this religious intuition: it was too deeply part and parcel of the teachings of his master, Jesus. In all probability, it was not the principle of love but merely the practice of alms-distribution which the Apostle had in mind when he spoke as he did. However that may be, the idealism of Jesus was such that it knew no half-way house on the road: nothing less than the transformation of all humanity into one family was His aim. Any élitism is therefore out of the question for the Christian. This is where the impossibility of a sectarianism which is genuinely Christian lies: this is the fulcrum which enabled Paul and Peter to propel Christendom out of the cramping shell of a small conventicle into a world-wide frame.

Of course, it will be said here that principle means little and practice much; that the decay of religiousness consists in this that a small group can practise the principle and a large one cannot. Yet why could the apostolic circle achieve a high degree of charismatic-caritative integration? Because it was small? Surely not. Ordinary societies, when they are small, are as likely to be filled by personal antipathy and hate as by sympathy and love. Restrictedness, face-to-face-ness, leads to an intensification of whatever sentiments there happen to be, not to the conquest of negative and the victory of positive attitudes. Is there anything more distressing than a bad marriage or two hostile brothers? The real reason that we can figure the apostolic circle as filled by love, in so far as that is humanly possible, was the presence in it of the axial reality of the charismatic-caritative I-and-Thou relationship between Jesus and each individual disciple. It was this which irradiated all the other human relations: multiple love sprang from a mutual, two-poled devotedness. Differently expressed, the co-disciples loved each other 'for Christ's sake'. But this axial reality, on the existence of which all Christian *agape* hinges, is as possible now as it was then, and is as possible in a vast society as it is in a small group. Arnold Rademacher's fine formulation: 'The closer the relations of man to God, the warmer also the relations of men to each other,'[1] expresses a universal truth in the area of the sociology of religion, one might almost say, a law. We have admitted that the growth in numbers made a difference to Christendom, that the widening of the circle rendered the practice of the basic virtue more difficult. But what kind of difference? The very words '*more* difficult' show that it was one of quantity only, and not one of quality. The key-reality, after all, has remained the same: now as before, there must be the inspiring love of two persons for each other; the number at the core has not changed; it is only that the warmth engendered in the heart must travel to a more distant circumference. Yet however far away that circumference may be, it still encloses *one* body. Christianity cannot contract out of its collectivism and universalism: it is committed to all-inclusiveness, as it is to absolute idealism.

Of course – who would deny it? – only the committal to the principle is total, the practice is woefully inadequate. To remain within our metaphor, which is that of all Catholic Christianity, the warmth of the heart-region is not high enough, not sufficient to supply the outlying tissues: it is cold out there; we all know it. But is this because of the growth in numbers, the widening of the circumference? Hardly. It is because of men's *individual* incapacity to experience love beyond a certain measure of intensity, because of an abiding weakness at the personal centre. And this weakness is genetic and generic; it is simply human. Assuredly, there has been no upward development in this area; but it is very unlikely that there has been serious loss. If it be said that in Christianity's passing semi-sectarian period, the brother-Christians were closer to each other than their successors were after the end of the age of persecution, this is true enough and has to be admitted. But the argument is self-defeating, for the heightened love for the insider was based on, and bought at the price of, a heightened hate for the outsider, and the sum-total of love (which is all that matters) was no greater than before or afterwards. The over-all loss of lovingness which has been asserted as a concomitant of the outer unfolding of Christendom[2] can only be realistically assessed if two associated

[1] Loc. cit., p. 48.
[2] We refrain here from giving exact references as we are dealing with a widespread opinion which is 'in the air' rather than with one or more individual authors. Intellectually, of course, Sohm and Weber, with whom we deal a little later (cf. pp. 136 et seq.), are fathers and foci of the anti-Catholic, not to say, anti-Christian views we are reviewing.

errors are avoided: a tendency to romanticize the apostolic circle, whose members were, after all, ordinary men; and a tendency to underestimate the effort of later generations to wring from themselves a more intense response to the call of the Founder. If justice is done on either score, perhaps it will be seen that the balance sheet did not change too much. Love is a stranger to the world now, but it always has been.

If the growth in numbers is, to some extent, a process whereby the bond between the co-religionists is relaxed, the exaltation of the Founder after his death – and this applies to minor founders more than to Jesus Christ – is a concomitant but countermanding development which makes that bond more tight and taut. The apostles preached Christ; they spread the knowledge of Him; and they lifted Him up so high that all men could see Him. This, surely, was a society-building activity, and one should, prima facie, expect that sociologists of religion would see it in a positive light. This is not so, however. Even here the tendency is to discover, or at least to assert, involution.[1]

The reason that a deterioration is assumed to take place is very simple. While the Founder, or a founder, was in the flesh, he could be seen in his *de facto* features; a truthful image of him could be entertained; ideas about him could be checked against reality. As soon as he is dead and buried, however, fancy may begin to enter in and start a process of falsification. Legends will spring up and spoil everything. In the end a tissue of absurdities may result, and this cannot but be booked on the debit side of the historical account. So runs the argument, and it is a powerful one. It has, however, its own problematic. It obviously rests on a firm, if hidden, conviction that the *literal* truth is always and in all areas and in all circumstances preferable to any deviation from it. It is better to believe that the square root of 9 is 3, than to accept the proposition that it is 4 or even that it is 2·999 or 3·111. It is, of course, entirely correct that the square root of 9 is 3 and neither more nor less, and no man in his senses will gainsay it. Nevertheless, the argument is naïve. It assumes that there is only one form of truth, the form which we find in mathematics and rational mechanics. But this is not so. Insistence that it is so and must be so would destroy large areas of science as well as religion. The propositions of botanists and zoologists are different in character from those of geometricians,

[1] Cf. Wach, *Meister und Jünger*, as quoted, especially p. 42.

and yet they are true. It is merely that they are true in a different sense.

Not literal truth, but symbolic truth is what matters in religion.[1] Differently expressed, a legend, though incredible on the level of literalness, may well convey in an allegorical fashion a very hard and fast fact. Let us take a concrete example – the famous tradition that St. Francis preached to the birds and that the birds listened to him.[2] The pure rationalist will raise his eyebrows. Childishness, he will say, if he is rude, childlikeness, if he is polite. But if this is all his reaction, he will have missed the point of the story. What it conveys is not only, and, indeed, not so much, that a certain historical event took place, the address of St. Francis to the assembled animals at the Carceri above Assisi, but rather that the Poverello brought with him an entirely new attitude to reality which ended a millennium of estrangement between nature and man. Mountains were largely meaningless to medieval man; perhaps they were only nuisances to him; certainly he did not love them; but Francis did. Witness his fondness for Monte Alverno, for instance. He saw their beauty as he saw the beauty of the Umbrian plane and indeed of all creatures, wolves and sparrows and lilies and fire and water. Francis was, so to speak, on good terms, on speaking terms, with the things around him: it is only a slight exaggeration, if we put matters in this way. True, he expressed himself in poetical terms, but what of it? The essential point is that he loved, where his predecessors had been indifferent, that he *saw* where they had been blind. Behind him, there appear figures like Leonardo da Vinci and Albrecht Dürer, draftsmen who would depict natural objects as they really were, and thereby lay the foundations for even more sober scientists who could perfect the transition from poetic to literal truthfulness.[3] Wrapped up in the *legend* of the sermon to the birds is therefore the *fact* that Francis initiated a new approach to man's subhuman environment, a truth not much inferior, given the differences between the science of mathematics and the science of history, to the proposition that twice two is four. Our age is

[1] Cf. Stark, *The Sociology of Knowledge*, as quoted, pp. 158 and 159.
[2] Cf. especially chapter 16 of the *Fioretti*. Workman gives the text, loc. cit., p. 306. We are not discussing the possibility or impossibility of a miracle as such a matter falls outside our present frame.
[3] Cf. Stark, *The Sociology of Knowledge*, as quoted, pp. 114 and 115 (especially *re* Max Scheler's analysis) and 'The Socio-Religious Origins of Modern Science', *Revista Internacional de Sociologia*, 1962, pp. 322 et seq.

impatient with such wrappings, but it is foolish to throw away a good kernel because it is enveloped in a coloured shell. The growth of a legend may therefore mask an advancement in insight rather than a recoil in rationality, provided, of course, that the core of truth remains identifiable, as it is in the instance which we have given. As modern observers vowed to objectivity we must reconcile ourselves to the fact that earlier societies, including those in whose matrix the basic unfolding of Christianity took place, preferred an imaginative to a non-imaginative presentation of their ideas and insights. It would hardly be a convincing sign of devotedness to truth if the pursuit of it were declined because there are analytical difficulties. To see, at once and automatically, involution rather than evolution in the proliferation of legends is therefore simple prejudice.

Furthermore, it must not be thought that the filling-out of the image of a founder is either an undirected or an unrestricted process, as if the imagination could go in any direction or to any lengths. First of all, it is not undirected for it stems from a very definite effort, namely the desire to understand the charismatic personality which has moved across the mental screen of his followers, to plumb his mysterious depths, to interpret his higher meaning. It is well known that there is a difference between the three synoptic Gospels and the Gospel according to St. John, and again a difference between the latter and the Epistles of St. Paul. John is later than Matthew, Mark and Luke, and therefore there has been time for some meditation on the mystery and the mission of Jesus, a fact which does not fail to show up in the text. The Epistles of St. Paul are in all probability not later than John, but another factor pushes in the same direction: Paul was a disciple of the 'second hand'; he may have seen Jesus, but he did not know Him. His image of Christ is therefore not one of a man but rather that of the God-Man, the Messiah, the Great Priest. This, say the rationalistic critics, is the locus of falsification: what is needed is demythologization. Yet not two terms need to be compared here, fact and fancy, but three – fact, faith, and fancy. The simple identification of faith and fancy is permitted to the scholar in his private capacity as an unbeliever, if he is an unbeliever, but it is not permissible to him in his public capacity as a scientist. A sociologist of religion must know that religion *is* faith. To dissolve the credal element clustering around a founder in, or the Founder of, Christianity, is simply to dissolve the subject-matter with which the sociologist is supposed to deal. The first fruitful question which has to be raised if accretions to a tradition are sociologically considered is, not how much falsification of fact there is (textual criticism will deal with this aspect), but how well these accretions manage to enhance the coherence of the movement involved by unfolding, or making conscious, the religious, including the mystical, meaning of the events to which it owes its existence.

In view of the fact that this volume contains a sustained critique of the Sohm–Lowrie thesis, it is important to note our agreement with these two scholars on the point we are considering just now. 'The full notion of the Church – in particular its religious significance – could not possibly be realized so long as Jesus remained with His disciples upon terms of human, social intercourse,' writes Lowrie. 'It was only when He passed again into the heavenly, invisible sphere, and *religious* intercourse was begun with Him there, that the highest conception of the Church could be realized, in particular, that the disciples would comprehend what was meant by assembling *in His name*. This affected not only the idea of the spiritual or invisible unity of the Church, but its concrete organization; for to this spiritual community of the Church with Christ – no longer merely with Him, but *in* Him – there could not but correspond a closer religious and social unity among the members.' 'St. John's Gospel throws light upon this subject,' Lowrie says a little later. 'This is pre-eminently the Gospel of discipleship.'[1] And discipleship, or rather a deepened apprehension of discipleship, is also the theme of Paul's essential letters. 'He speaks of fellowship in the *sufferings* of Christ (Philippians III, 10) and of the fellowship of the Holy Ghost (Philippians II, 1),' whereas 'St. John [in his Epistles] uses the word only in the general sense of fellowship with God or Christ and with one another (I, 1, 3, 6, 7).'[2] It would be difficult to put this point more forcefully than Lowrie does, and the point is that the exploration of a founder-figure's meaning is socially constructive, evolution and not involution.

What is added to the facts, then, is the upshot of speculation, but of a fact-bound rather than of a fancy-free speculation. And the anchoring of the speculation in the facts is soon made more

---

[1] Lowrie, loc. cit., pp. 115 and 116. Italics in the original.
[2] Ibid., p. 129. Our italics.

secure. Christianity is, as Mohammed often emphasized, a 'religion of the book'. The Gospels give us the testimonies of witnesses in a written form, and that means that deviations from what they are saying become increasingly unacceptable, not to say impossible. The fate of the apocryphal literature is characteristic. Wach draws attention to this truth-preserving agency: 'In the moment of the first literal fixation, something entirely new is created, a minimum, so to speak, to which . . . even the boldest allegorical interpretation, the most miracle-minded and phantasmagoric account must forthwith keep.'[1] The observation is correct, and it is intriguing. It shows that, when a founder has died, *two* processes ensue, not one: one is a process of development, of unfolding, the other a process of preservation, of potential ossification. History pits the two against each other and works by checking the tendency by the countertendency and vice versa. As we shall soon see,[2] this duality reveals a basic – nay, *the* basic – fact of the sociology of religion. It must remain masked for the unself-critical rationalist describer for in his view both tendencies are reprehensible: the one as ratiocination which may go beyond the facts, the other as routinization which may cramp the freedom of the spirit. But in so far as the one holds sway, the other cannot advance. We shall return to this subject when we finally confront genuine and official charisma, saint and priest.

One final point remains to be made about legends. Let us assume that there are some – and many would assert that all belong into this category – which convey neither a hidden truth in a poetical form nor a truth-tied exploration of a mystical meaning, but are simply fancy, fairy-tale inventions of child-like minds.[3] It does not matter in the least for our argument how many fall into this group; the percentage is irrelevant. What matters is a proper understanding of the causes and of the effects of such truth-defying traditions. Why do they arise, if and where they do arise? Surely because of the love of the people at large for their subject. We tell anecdotes about those who interest us, not about those to whom we are indifferent; and we tell nice, heart-warming anecdotes about those of whom we are fond. Our exaggerations are proofs of our devotion. Love is thus the cause of some legends, and love is their effect. When one of our heroes has died, how else can we keep his

[1] *Meister und Jünger*, as quoted, p. 44.   [2] Cf. below, p. 165.
[3] Cf. especially Workman, loc. cit., p. 36, footnote.

memory fresh and induce others, especially upcoming generations, to give him a place in their hearts also? Only by recounting his life, his deeds, his excellences. *Fama crescit eundo*: so be it. But the kernel of fame is still fact, albeit laced (as we here assume) with fancy, fact which has become embroidered and embellished. Or perhaps we should say that it is fact laced with love, for love is the leaven which makes the facts germinate. In science, legends would be out of place, but is it the same in religion? Indeed, can religion live without them? When two young persons fall in love, they are loving (as everybody knows) not each other's factual, but each other's idealized image. 'Demythologization' would mean destruction of the sentiment. Religious devotion is no different in this respect than romantical infatuation. At a later stage neither romantic nor religious love may need the rosy light of fond deception – though this is doubtful. At the beginning at any rate it is indispensable. We are touching here upon one of the deepest and potentially most distressing aspects of human evolution: can scientific soberness spread without compressing the capacity for emotion? Can the reasonableness of technology gain the ascendant without destroying the ecstasies of love? Is a St. Francis or a St. Teresa thinkable in a computerized age? Such questions cannot be answered by an *obiter dictum*. But one thing is clear: the phenomena of religion can only unfold in a world in which rationality is not alone in possession of the field.

Our very last words already imply a judgment of the next issue which must necessarily come up in any study of the unfolding of Christianity: the development of a technical – and this means unavoidably: of a rational – theology. As such a science is in essence a commentary on the Founder's dicta and other sacred texts, and later a commentary on the earlier commentaries and so on, it easily slips into a certain verbalism and thereby into a distressing aridity which may be grotesquely at variance with the majesty of the message with which it is formally concerned. Not that this has to happen: but it is apt to happen and has happened often. Much of the Judaic–Rabbinical lore was of this character, and the new religion soon learned from the old. Already 'the teachers of the second century are no enthusiasts: they are Scripture-experts', says Campenhausen and he adds, as a revealing detail, that some of them, like Justin and Tertullian, liked to don the black gown, the philosopher's professional garb. 'In these circles, the confessional acceptance of the revelation in Christ is being combined with an appeal to philosophical . . . reason.'[1] The text which almost automatically springs to mind when such a rationalistic desiccation of religion is considered is from St. Paul: 'The letter killeth, but the spirit quickeneth, (II Corinthians III, 6). This terse statement has not only all the prestige of the great Apostle who made it, it has also the backing and the convincingness of common sense.

If the ensuing rationalization of religious thought were an undirected and an unrestricted process, there would indeed be dire consequences. But, as in the case of legends, so in the case of dogmas, this process is neither undirected nor yet unrestricted. It is not undirected because, once again, it is the exploration of given material, of those ipsedixitisms (as Bentham called them) which the Founder left behind in the memory of His hearers and which then form the canon of His doctrine. Already in His life-time, His teachings afford a focus of attention which is distinct from, and above all more objective than, His personal magnetism. His personality is beyond discussion, but His doctrine is not and cannot be. Certainly, in so far as the words of Christ partook of His being which was charismatic, it is hurtful to see them treated like mathematical or similar lifeless and loveless propositions, and this is where the danger of desiccation lies. But one ought to remember here Cardinal Newman's distinction between paper logic and the logic of life.[2] Both drive forward from premise to conclusion, but only the former is in basic contradiction to the spirit of religiosity; the latter is not. And the latter is not, because it is more beholden to the content of the religious dogma than to the demands of formal logic. An example will make perfectly clear what we mean. Theology started out with the conviction that Jesus Christ was both God and man. Paper logic, rationalistic as it is, will prove unable to live with this contradiction. It will drive towards an interpretation which will make the God–man God rather than man or man rather than God. These rationalizing theologies mushroomed in the first centuries and had to be fought off. They were fought off by mainstream theology, and could be fought off by it, because it

---

[1] Campenhausen, loc. cit., pp. 211 and 212.
[2] Cf. *Apologia pro Vita Sua*, ed. London 1895, pp. 168 and 169. Cf. also Stark, W., 'Towards a Theory of Social Knowledge', *Revue Internationale de Philosophie*, 1950, p. 302.

used the logic of life which knows, and reconciles itself to, the fact that irreducible contradictions are of the essence of reality. Yet even these irreducible contradictions have their implications which must be thinkingly unfolded and displayed, and this is precisely what happened. The effect was an exploration of mystery, not its disappearance, a digging deeper, not a sanding-up of the source. To write the whole of theology off as dry-as-dust rationalization is unrealistic. In any case, only excessive rationalization is destructive to religion, a modicum and measure of it is not. On the contrary. The wild prophesying which seems to have gone on in some of the earliest Christian communities is not likely to have afforded a better atmosphere for the systematic plumbing of the depth-dimensions of the Gospel doctrines than the somewhat more settled moods of the next generation. Reasonableness has its uses, even in religion.

Yet it is and remains true that reason and love are antithetic, and that the systematic assertion of the former may bring a dimming, and lead to dying, of the latter. If the theologizing of the Gospel message had meant a technicizing, and if that technicizing had progressed unchecked, a literalism would have resulted which would have destroyed the spirit, the very soul, of Christianity, which is not dogma, but *agape*. No doubt, Christianity has had its scribes and its Pharisees, even its Sadducees, just like Judaism, but these small men, whose names are not remembered, were unable to achieve an out-and-out rationalization. Their influence has been persistent, perhaps even pervasive, but certainly not decisive. If the greater names are considered, the names of commanding intellects who have given direction to Christian thinking, it is seen that they did not press rationalization beyond a certain point. In Antiquity, Clement of Alexandria was such a figure. Eduard Meyer has depicted him as a rationalist: 'He not only tried to prove that Christianity in its basic features was identical with the highest doctrines of Greek philosophy, above all Plato, he even attempted to transform it altogether into a philosophy.'[1] This was an attempt at rationalization, no doubt. But the tendency was arrested in mid-passage, even in Clement's own mind. Campenhausen, who knew him well, showed the other side of his thinking, his mysticism. 'He was aware of the inexhaustibleness in content of the sayings of Jesus which, as he expressed it in one passage, give birth to truth

[1] Meyer, loc. cit., vol. III, p. 539.

for the whole world and yet remain for ever virginal.'[1] A man who could write these words was not likely to reduce the Sermon on the Mount to a string of arid quasi-mathematical propositions. In the Middle Ages, St. Thomas Aquinas drove the rational formulation of Christian truths to considerable lengths, and it should be conceded that his treatment, in the *Summae*, even of the mysteries themselves was not without its formalism and coldness. But not only was his relative rationalism counterbalanced and corrected by such contemporary mystics as St. Bonaventure, he himself counterbalanced and corrected it by his own mysticism.

> 'Loving I adore you, hidden deity,
> Who beneath these symbols art so near to me . . .'

In his hymns, such as the one from which we have just translated,[2] the great Master of the Schools appears, not as a manufacturer of definitions and deductions, but as a man afire, and it is difficult to decide what one should admire more: his powerful intellect or his delicate tenderness.

St. Thomas's hymns are best known through their use in an act of worship known to Catholics as 'Benediction of the Blessed Sacrament', of which he was the virtual author, and this brings us to our text topic, the evolution of ritual. Needless to say, this too has been interpreted as a loss in essential religiosity: the argument runs that in the beginning, there is true prayer, prayer from the heart, which needs no form, indeed, repels all form, and in the end there are merely substitute actions (such as the taking of holy water on entering a church), which are at best symbols and at worst superstitions. Religion seems therefore to throttle religion: religion's worse self seems to throttle religion's better self. This appears to belong to the very core of the phenomenon called the routinization of charisma.

Let us note, first of all, that the evolution of ritual stands in an inverted relation to the evolution of rationalization: we have again two tendencies which hold each other in check. All through history, rationalism and empiricism have been in a tension, and engaged in a tussle, with each other. A technical theology, needless to say, falls under the heading of rationalism, an elaborate ritual,

---

[1] Campenhausen, loc. cit., p. 228. The reference is to *Stromata*, VII, 16 (also quoted VII, 94, 1); cf. *Patrologia Graeca*, as quoted, vol. IX, Paris 1890, cols. 529–32.

[2] *Adoro Te devote.*

on the other hand, belongs to the area of experience, of experiential life. If both the development of theology and the development of ritual are condemned, then there is less than logic in the attitude of the condemner. Or rather, there is only the logic of a total rejection of religiosity, rejection of all its aspects. But this is hardly scientific; it removes the very object of a sociology of religion from the scene.

Next, it is important to realize that ritualism belongs to the essence of religiosity as moisture belongs to rainfall or dryness to sunshine. He who asserts that Jesus stood for a prayer-life free from all ritualism is not acquainted with the facts. He nowhere condemns the Temple worship, and He repeatedly presupposes the conscientious fulfilment[1] of its formal duties. The Last Supper was in all probability a formal Seder. Thus old rites were duly celebrated in the apostolic circle. What happened in the early history of Christianity was merely that new rites developed to enshrine, express and preserve the new religious spirit – a most natural process, the absence of which would have betokened lack of life, not its presence. Out of the Jewish Seder came the Christian Eucharist. There was a transformation, but neither loss nor gain, so far as ritual is concerned. Indeed, in so far as each distinct religion needs its own forms, in order to act out its own inspiration, there was gain rather than loss.

The whole assertion that ritual is routinization rests on the assumption that rites are external acts without either internal cause or internal effect. To a rationalistic mentality, they necessarily appear in this negative light: to a man who is little more than intellect, or who values nothing but intellect, they must seem meaningless, and he will conclude that they are meaningless in themselves, meaningless in the objective sense of the word. But for a religious person – and a sociologist of *religion* is concerned only with them – they carry a deep meaning. If there is love in his heart, he will have the spontaneous desire, nay need, to express it by overt acts (Pareto's residue number III), and he will as naturally genuflect to the altar as he will kiss his bride. But such genuflection, as such a kiss, will not only enact the sentiment, so to speak, it will also make it endure and increase. It is simply of the life of the emotion; perhaps we can even say it *is* the life of the emotion; certainly, without it, the emotion will decay as eyes which are not used will grow blind or

[1] Cf. especially Matthew V, 23 and 24, and XXIII, 16–21. Cf. Oesterley, W. O. E., *The Jewish Background of the Christian Liturgy*, Oxford 1925.

muscles which are never exercised atrophy. To say that the evolution of rites is the involution of religion is therefore profoundly wrong. True, who can overlook it, there are ritual acts which are, by some persons, done mechanically, as kisses are also sometimes given, and in these specific cases, there *is* a downhill trend. But to say that *all* ritual acts are empty is merely a bad case of the *pars-pro-toto* fallacy. Surely, if ritual acts were meaningless to those who perform them, they would not continue to perform them. Inertia alone could not keep them in being. But however that may be, the creation and loving perfection of a rite, like the unfolding of the Mass in the early centuries, is a sign of religious inspiration and upswing, not of a deadening formalization and decay. Forms, once established, it is true, may last for a long time. Such was the Kiddush which Jesus said, such is the Lord's Prayer which He taught His disciples. In such instances it is the rationalist's suspicion – a suspicion which easily hardens into a conviction – that there simply must be routinization, a mechanical recitation of dead words learnt by rote. What is forgotten is that development is refinement, nay search for perfection, as Sumner showed in his folkway analysis and as Newman showed for the religious sphere. The Kiddush and the Lord's Prayer, and the Mass also, are forms optimally adjusted to their religious content. They endure because they afford lasting satisfaction to the need and desire to give outer expression to inner religious states.

To sum up: the growth in numbers, as the growth of legend, dogma and ritual, are processes which bring their problems, but they do not change the evolution of Christianity into an involution of genuine religiosity. They check each other and thereby safeguard the essence of the whole; and none of them necessarily goes so far as to become a danger by itself.

But we have not yet wholly explored this subject. Indeed, we have yet to confront the essential aspect of it – essential, if the prevailing and most prestigious part of the literature is to be believed. The tragedy of the unfolding of Christianity consisted, according to Rudolph Sohm, in the replacement of love by law, and according to Max Weber, in the ousting of genuine by official charisma. The two assertions are really one: charisma is love, and bureaucratization is a form of legalization, namely legalization by means of an administrative code. Weber merely concentrated on those who were to execute its norms, while Sohm concentrated on the norms which were to be executed: the phenomenon meant is in either case the same. But we can consider one author and his thesis after the other. We shall deal first with the older man, and then with the younger.

Sohm, says his American interpreter, Walter Lowrie, 'sees in the legalizing of Christian institutions a radical departure from primitive ideals'. 'A legal constitution (whether *jure humano* or *jure divino*) is opposed to the nature of the Church. It is here the visible Church that is meant, the Kingdom of God, which "is not of this world",' we are told. This kingdom 'never can be ruled by worldly means (by a polity conformable to the kingdoms of this world), but only by God's Spirit'. 'The veritable apostolic doctrine, drawn from God's Word, is this: *that the organization of the Ecclesia is not a legal but a charismatic organization.*'[1]

The keynote of Sohm's attitude is thus an assumed contrast in nature between charisma and law, and it forms in his mind the basis for a further contrast in nature – that between Christianity and Catholicism. 'In the subjection of the Christian society to the terms of a legal institution, Sohm sees the essence of Catholicism,' Lowrie writes. In another context Sohm's approach is put by Lowrie into parallel with 'a kindred spirit of revolt against the Catholic externalizing of the idea of the Church' which showed itself already in the early days and in the fullness of time led to the Protestant Reformation.[2] Both the original and the 'cleansed' forms of Christendom are thus for Sohm non-legal and anti-legal.

A sociologist might be inclined to see in the development of the first centuries merely the tightening of a basic pattern, a tightening of the *same* pattern, to be exact. He might regard such legalization as takes place as a formulation of the folkways inherent from the beginning in the Christian community – hence only as a clarification of the patterning norms, without a change in the norms themselves. It is not so that Sohm visualizes the process. To him it is perversion, and he tells us with all desirable openness wherein this perversion consists, in his opinion: 'A spiritual conception dominates in Church history, the conception of the visible Church, a conception which is determined by the content of the Christian faith. Where is Christ, the Lord of Glory? Where the people of Christ (the

[1] Lowrie, loc. cit., pp. 12, 9, 147. Italics in the original. Cf. also pp. 4, 156, 163.
[2] Ibid., pp. 11 and 15.

Ecclesia), in whose midst Christ is with all His spiritual gifts? Where is the visible Church? where the true Christianity? All turns upon the answer to this question. The answer which maintained its credit unquestioned throughout the first century,' and which is therefore the true answer, Sohm asserts through Lowrie's pen, 'is recorded in the Gospel (Matthew XVIII, 20), "Where two or three are gathered together in my name, there am I in the midst of them." Catholicism defined: Where the bishop is, there is the Catholic Church... The whole development of Catholicism lies implicit in that answer...'[1] What Sohm suggests is clearly this, that an episcocentric is substituted for a Christocentric society: a man usurps the place of the God–man and the circle is no longer filled by divine love but merely by human law. As the bishop is essentially a law-officer, i.e. a bureaucrat, Sohm comes to exactly the same result as Weber: the unfolded Church is an entirely impersonal structure, not a set of spiritual and therefore intensely personal relationships, an administrative mechanism, not a self- and soul-engrossing dyad of master and disciples.

The reference to Matthew XVIII, 20 is crucial, not only because Sohm makes it so in his own argument, but above all because it links him, more clearly than anything else, to the tradition from which he has sprung: that of Lutheranism. Luther, too, based much, if not indeed all, on this logion. It is therefore of overwhelming importance in our context and in itself, to understand it aright. Luckily for us, an outstanding scholar, Ernst Kohlmeyer, has recently subjected it to a new searching interpretation: his article 'Charisma oder Recht?', published in the *Zeitschrift der Savigny-Stiftung für Rechtsgeschichte*,[2] brings all the resources of historical science to bear on the passage, and the result of the investigation is absolutely fatal to the assumptions and assertions of Rudolph Sohm. Far from proving that the first Christian community gathered around Jesus was innocent of law, it demonstrates in a peremptory fashion that it conceived itself, and was conceived by its Founder, in legal terms.

Kohlmeyer's procedure is as simple as it is unassailable. He refuses to tear Matthew XVIII, 20 from its context, but on the contrary reinstates it therein. He asserts – and who would criticize

---

[1] Ibid., pp. 12 and 13. Cf. below, p. 157, where the correct interpretation of the sentence *ubi episcopus, ibi ecclesia*, is discussed.
[2] Kanonistische Abteilung, 1952, pp. 1 et seq.

him for it? – that the preceding paragraphs must be used for the elucidation of the verse concerned. Now the preceding verses (15–17)[1] run as follows: 'If thy brother shall offend against thee, go and rebuke him between thee and him alone. If he shall hear thee, thou shalt gain thy brother. And if he will not hear thee, take with thee one or two more, that in the mouth of two or three witnesses every word may stand. And if he will not hear them, tell the church. And if he will not hear the church, let him be to thee as the heathen and publican.' It would be difficult to find a passage anywhere in the four Gospels whose import is more fully and more clearly legal than this. First of all, its content is a conflict between two neighbours, such as it is at the bottom of every law-suit; and, furthermore, its prescription is procedural, i.e. an indication of the steps which should be taken in order to bring the conflict, the law-suit, to a proper conclusion. There is therefore in this passage both an element of material and an element of formal law. Perhaps the latter is even more important than the former. What Jesus recommends is that the damnified party should first plead with the wrong-doer, and the plea, we can be sure of that, was envisaged as a loving appeal to his higher nature. But if this method fails, pressure is to be brought to bear on the guilty head, *increasing* pressure; and if that is of no avail, a sentence of banishment is to be pronounced before the community, and by the community,[2] as this judgment, if just, will be subscribed to and validated by all. If this is not law, nothing is. Of course, it can always be argued that these legalistic, i.e. offending, sentences are later interpolations which should be dropped from the canon. But how would it be possible to cut out verses 14–18 and yet retain verse 20 with which they form a meaningful whole? This surgery would be much more hurtful, from Sohm's (and Luther's) point of view, than the trouble which it is meant to cure.

However, reinserting the text into the texture of its chapter is only half the work. The chapter and its constituent ideas must be reinstated into the context of contemporary life, and Kohlmeyer does this for us, too. He shows us that Jesus, on this occasion, as so often, upholds and reinforces a tradition current in his Jewish environment, the power of the community to discipline a delinquent member in their midst, and, if necessary, to banish him. 'In the

[1] We shall presently speak about verse 18. Verse 19 is an aside.
[2] Kohlmeyer, loc. cit., p. 6.

Jewish ban,' Kohlmeyer writes, 'we have before us, not the inspiration of a charismatic personality, a prophetic pronouncement concerning an isolated case . . . but a precisely regulated law . . . Its equivalent in the primitive Christian community shows no trace of difference . . . The character of this disciplinary power is, if we accept Sohm's antithesis, legal and not charismatic.'[1] And in making this statement, Kohlmeyer reminds us, as he has every right to do, of a logion from the Sermon on the Mount which may well find a justified application here – Matthew V, 18: 'Amen, I say to you, till heaven and earth pass, one jot or one tittle shall not pass of the law, till all be fulfilled.' It is not the ceremonial law that is meant, therefore, in this passage; that Jesus abolished; and He could abolish it, because it had become merely mechanical, almost dead; rather the logion refers to the living law which every society needs if, and as long as, there may be conflict between man and man, the law which sees to it that strife is minimized and ultimately resolved by the action of all against the rebellious one.

Yet it was not merely a mundane law that Jesus was highlighting and covering by His authority as a teacher. In a community totally devoted to the service of God, every crime, nay every injustice to a brother, is a sin as well. Sins, however, have to be purged if the sacredness of the group is to be maintained. Therefore the community acting against an evil-doer was not only looking after its own peace and quiet, but also ensuring its peace and amity with the Deity who is Righteousness Itself; it was not only executing its own sentence, it was also executing the judgment of God. This religious aspect of the power of discipline, of the power of jurisdiction, fully explains Matthew XVIII, 18: 'Amen I say to you, whatsoever you shall bind upon earth shall be bound also in heaven: and whatsoever you shall loose upon earth shall be loosed also in heaven.' What Jesus pronounced in these words was the identification of the community's disciplinary and jurisdictional authority with the ultimate authority, Authority Itself, the authority of the Lord of Heaven and Earth.

These considerations, whose historical basis is of the firmest, also shed light on Sohm's (and Luther's) most beloved quotation and bring out its real and intended meaning. 'Where there are two or three gathered together in my name, there am I in the midst of them,' does not only mean that Jesus will be there if two or three

[1] Ibid.

pray; it means that, as the intervening verse 19 indicates; but it means also that Jesus, the Judge, will be there if two or three concern themselves with the unity and the sinlessness of the community, or if they, despairing of a peaceable outcome, have to take sterner measures and enact the separation of the offending limb from the body of the community. That this is not a fanciful interpretation can be seen from the fact that this decisive logion is an echo of a passage from the *Pirke Aboth*, or Sayings of the Fathers, which form the oldest part of the Mishna and therefore of the Talmud: 'If two sit together and interchange words of Torah [i.e. The Law], the Divine Presence abides between them.' Jesus knew this piece of Hebrew lore. He approved of it; and He wished His followers to accept it as the truth, as the pious Jews did, of whom He was one.[1]

The thinking of a large section of Christendom is at the present moment characterized by a certain tendency to Pelagianism and indeed to sentimentalizing the image of Jesus: He is seen as the ever-forgiving, the never-angry, indeed, as One incapable of sternness and condemnation. It was not so that the early Christians saw Him; to them He was a hater of sin as well as a lover of souls, a hater of sin as well as a lover of sinners. He was the world's appointed judge, awful in majesty and terrifying by dint of His very justice. Rightly did François Mauriac, in his admirable *Vie de Jésus* (1936), remind a weakling generation of these harder features of One whom they should fear as well as love. Nor would it be true to say that a punishing God could not be all-loving. The condemnation of the unrepenting sinner is not God's – or the community's – work, it is the sinner's own. *He* cuts himself off from the community whose spirit and mode of action is not his own. Technically expressed, the sentence of banishment pronounced by the community on a hardened wrongdoer (as God's judgment on him after death and on the Last Day) is in its whole nature declaratory, not constitutive. It does not drive him from the ranks of the blessed into those of the condemned or the damned: he himself has taken his place on the wrong side of the fence. That is how the first century really thought: Sohm's idea that the primitive Christians felt no need to reprove sin and, if necessary, to ostracize the sinner, is

[1] Cf. ibid., p. 7. For *Pirke Aboth* III, 3, cf. *The Authorized Daily Prayer Book*, revised ed., transl. Hertz, J. H., New York 5717 [i.e. 1957], pp. 647 and 649. The saying is attributed to Rabbi Chananya ben Teradyon.

profoundly unrealistic. But to deal with sin, you need law, a special kind of law, to be sure (we shall presently discuss *what* kind of law), but still *law*, and that is why Sohm's whole thesis falls to the ground.

We can see this law in action in a concrete case when we turn to I Corinthians V, 1–5. But before we consider this incident which fully confirms Kohlmeyer's whole analysis, we have yet to draw attention to a more general matter. Matthew XVIII, 20 is Sohm's mainstay, and it is that of all Protestantism, whereas Catholics have based their ecclesiology on Matthew XVI, 19, where Jesus is reported as saying to Peter: 'Whatsoever thou shalt bind upon earth, it shall be bound also in heaven: and whatsoever thou shalt loose on earth, it shall be loosed also in heaven.' The coincidence of this passage with Matthew XVIII, 18 is striking. In either case, the jurisdictional power of human agents is said to be supported by the power of God, only that the human agent in the one context (XVIII, 18) is a collectivity, the community, whereas in the other (XVI, 19) it is a single person, Simon Bar-Jona, to be called the Rock. (In so far as Peter is to be the representative of the collectivity, an idea to be presupposed as a matter of course in the context of contemporary, largely collectivistic modes of thinking, the difference is very small.) In either case, Jesus institutes a law-enforcement agency. And this is not to be wondered at, for how can any human society survive without such an authority? 'How could one even think of giving to Christendom, to the body of Christ, the organization of a secular society?' asks Sohm in a rhetorical flourish.[1] More soberly, we can formulate the opposite question: How could one even think of not giving to Christendom, the body of Christ, the organization of a secular society since it was not a *corpus purum*, like the communion of saints in heaven, from which sin is for ever removed, but a *corpus permixtum* in which sin is yet firmly established and has to be repressed and excised? If it is 'the point which Sohm presses with the utmost vigour', that law 'is not merely . . . not included in the idea of the Ecclesia', but 'positively excluded by it',[2] then the opposite proposition must be pressed with equal vigour. And it can be pressed with superior realism and reason. For the Church, for all its metaphysical qualities, is a human society, and a human society, as every sociologist knows, can neither arise nor exist nor yet perdure without norms and the enforcement of norms.

[1] Lowrie, loc. cit., p. 149.   [2] Ibid. p. 156.

St. Paul found this out – to his sorrow, we may assume, rather than to his surprise – when he watched over the development of his beloved congregation at Corinth. A member had become guilty of what at the time passed for incest (cohabitation with his step-mother) and his case had to be dealt with. Paul tells his friends that it would be best 'that he ... that hath done this thing ... might be taken away from among you', otherwise sinfulness might spread: 'A little leaven corrupteth the whole lump.' He advises the congregation to exercise its inherent judicial power and pronounce a sentence of excommunication on the guilty man: 'You being gathered together ... in the name of our Lord Jesus Christ ... with the power of our Lord Jesus,' he writes, should act 'to deliver such a one to Satan' (I Corinthians V, 1–6). The form of words chosen is extremely revealing. Paul's epistle fully squares with the teaching of Jesus as reported in Matthew XVIII, 20, the salient point being that the community constituted as a law-court is assembled in the name of Jesus and Jesus is in their midst. Moreover, the nature of the judgment given by the community-court is also made perfectly clear: it is a judgment 'with the power of our Lord Jesus', i.e. a judgment upheld by the higher authority of the Ultimate Judge who acts here through human instruments – indirectly, so to speak, but yet personally all the same. The mouth which pronounces the judgment, so we may also render the decisive assertion, is the mouth of men, but the authority is the authority of God. The consequence of the condemnation is not physical, as it is in the instance of a secular court, where it may be confinement to jail or some such visible and tangible punishment; the consequence is metaphysical: the culprit is thrust out of the circle of the redeemed and thereby 'delivered to Satan'. The effect of the procedure lies in eternity, not in time (though Paul allows that the sinner may yet be saved ultimately 'in the day of our Lord Jesus Christ', i.e. at the Second Coming).

What do we have before us in this concrete application of the principle of Matthew XVIII, 20? Kohlmeyer gives us a convincing answer: criminal justice on the part of the congregation, but a criminal justice which 'partakes of the supernatural'. We have *law* before us, but it is 'sacred law'. Kohlmeyer speaks of the 'existence of a sacred law ... which inserts God into the legal relationships, refers the breach of the norm directly to divine law and invokes a supernal power of punishment'. And he shows us that nothing could be less surprising than the presence of such ideas in Paul's mind. Both Jews and Greeks thought in these terms: in fact, we have here one of the important points of confluence which made the Judaeo–Hellenic culture-synthesis which we call Christianity possible. So far as the Jews were concerned, we have no need to say any more, although for instance Günther Holstein's work, *Die Grundlagen des evangelischen Kirchenrechts* (1928), would yield historical material a-plenty. As for the Greeks, it was a well-established, and is a well-attested, tradition to 'dedicate' one who has outraged the gods and men, to the 'infernal powers', i.e. to condemn him, in human terms, and to leave the execution of the sentence to more-than-human agents whose existence and co-operation was assumed as an article of faith.[1]

In sum, then, the Christian community lived, from the beginning, by a sacred law which lay parallel to the sacred law of the synagogal and the hellenistic traditions; by norms, as Kohlmeyer splendidly expresses it, which 'referred everything to God'. As a rule, the Spirit brings grace and sanctification; but in cases where it is needful, It can also bring curse and perdition; and in either instance, the instance of blessing or the instance of damnation, Its gift flows to the individual through the community. Sohm's construction, Kohlmeyer tells us, is too narrow, and Kohlmeyer is right. His article is called: Charisma or Law? But he finds that the alternative – Sohm's alternative – is wrongly posed and presented. For what we find in the primitive Christian congregation, in the primal cell of the Church, is 'a sacred law which rests on the Church's charisma'[2] – a *charismatic law*, as we may perhaps more simply, but no less truthfully, express it.

We are making Kohlmeyer's analysis entirely our own, and we are doing so because he seems to us to have understood the nature of the original sacred society gathered around the Founder far better than Sohm did. That society referred *everything* to its Risen Lord. It prayed in His name; it blessed in His name; would it not also judge, where it had to judge, in His name? To raise this question is to answer it in the affirmative. What, after all, is a group of believers if not a circle which identifies itself *in everything* with Him in whom it believes?

But we would go a good deal beyond Kohlmeyer. His is essentially a factual and historical critique of the Sohm position; but a

[1] Kohlmeyer, loc. cit., pp. 6 et seq.   [2] Ibid., pp. 10, 16, 24.

more theoretical and logical evaluation of it is possible and necessary as well. The concept of law with which Sohm worked seems to us as faulty as his interpretation of the Gospel texts and other given sources.

Sohm's attitude would be justified only if by law one meant a set of norms necessarily alien to the believing community and unassimilable by it. This is logical, for only under this assumption is submission to it perversion and involution. What is behind Sohm's argument is therefore the same basic idea which is also behind Max Weber's theorizing: law is in its inmost nature rational; religion is in its inmost nature irrational; hence the two are mutually exclusive. But only some law – only *made*, or, to use a somewhat value-laden term, manufactured, law, first thought-out and then *imposed* law – comes close to being rational; *grown* law is rather different. Grown law is no more rational than, for instance, grown language; and everybody knows how non-rational grown language is, and how well it serves life just because it is so. But the canon law of the Catholic Church is almost exclusively grown law; even the Codex Iuris Canonici of 1917 is only an attempt to marshal the masses of custom which history has thrown up and deposited in the unwieldy Corpus Iuris Canonici which held undisputed, and very difficult, sway before; it is, so to speak, a key to the Corpus and to the customs.[1] Sohm and Lowrie concede 'the importance of custom as the expression of Christian consciousness and the regulation of Church life'. 'The early canons,' they write, 'for the most part were designed merely to formulate and affirm customs already prevalent in the Church . . . The function [of authority, in this case] of the synod, was merely to *ascertain* what doctrines were conformable to the truth and what customs were agreeable to God's will. But,' they add, 'from the first the tendency was to supersede customary law by canon law.' What happened was that authority *confirmed* custom, for its validity 'could not but seem incomplete until it was confirmed by enactment'. By this confirmation, we are told, custom became customary law, something entirely different, something entirely new. This is a crudely formalistic argument which misses the whole point; in fact, it is hairsplitting. If customary law is confirmed custom, then it is still custom; then it is still not made or manufactured law, still no rational pattern that is

[1] Cf. Stark, W., 'The Routinization of Charisma: A Consideration of Catholicism', *Social Analysis*, 1965, pp. 203 et seq., especially pp. 207 et seq.

alien to life and imposed upon it from the outside; then it is still the precipitate of that life and grown inside it and out of it; then the action of authority is merely declaratory and not constitutive. It may be doubtful whether the term 'legalization' is applicable to the development of the Catholic norm system; but it is *not* doubtful that the term 'rationalization' is *in*applicable to it. Sohm and Lowrie have to admit that Kahl's *Lehrsystem des Kirchenrechts* (1894) is consistent 'in treating custom as though it were equivalent to customary law'.[1] Why should the great canonist not so treat it, as customary law *is* equivalent, in any but the most formal sense, to custom? Since when has 'yes' made a difference to the proposition to which it is applied? But custom is the scion of life and in no sense its adversary.

Yet another theoretical point has to be raised here. For those who, like Sohm and Weber, have been brought up in the Rousseauan and Kantian tradition, law is essentially impersonal – the impersonal and supra-personal norm which confronts, controls and coerces the personalities who live under it. The development of law must therefore necessarily mean depersonalization, the substitution of objective principles for subjective relationships, the replacement of a live give-and-take by a set of dead paragraphs. But this idea of law, important as it has been in history and grandiose as it still is in conception, can claim no universal validity. It has its time-bound character written all over it; it could only arise and have full meaning at the moment when it was actually formulated: on the eve of the French Revolution when the personal will of the monarch was being replaced by a supposed impersonal will, the will of the mystical power called The Law. Yet even Rousseau realized that The Law is really the *volonté générale*, the will of all, in the sense of all upholders of the social bond and the social constitution. There is thus no depersonalization at all. In a case like that of the incestuous man at Corinth, what was pitted against each other was the will of the congregation bent on sanctity and the will of an individual bent on sin. And so it will always be. There may be impersonal laws in nature, but there are none, and can be none, in society for social laws need backing. What determined Sohm and Weber to think as they did, and particularly to think of the unfolding of the Church as depersonalization and deperition, was less their high regard for religious values (as they imagined) than their low estimation of the

[1] Lowrie, loc. cit., pp. 179 et seq.

social whole, their philosophical nominalism.[1] 'The unit of the Church is not the congregation, but the individual believer,' they maintained; indeed, they maintained that in religion 'each [is] a denomination by himself'.[2] In a word, they did not see the forest for the trees.

These are, to some extent, sophisticated arguments, but a much simpler consideration might be even more telling. We can bring it in with the help of a home-spun comparison. A young man and a young woman fall in love; in due course they get married. That they get married signifies that their relationship is being legalized. Does this mean that their love has now to dry up? If we are to believe Sohm, this is so, this must be so, for law and love are in his opinion mutually exclusive realities. Yet such an assertion flies in the face of all experience. Far from destroying the attachment of the partners, the legalization of their union makes it secure for the future and ensures its fulfilment, the fulfilment of its purpose in the great scheme of things. In a marriage, law is merely a distant, entirely unobtrusive helper: it guarantees a stable framework within which the appropriate sentiments can freely develop. We say freely, for law only coerces and cramps the deviant, not the loving and law-abiding person. What a strange idea of law Sohm has! It is to him a killer, not a protector and preserver. This is more than individualism – this is in tendency anarchism. In any case, this has little to do with reality. In the reality of the Church, as in the reality of the home, the existence and even the enforcement of order is the necessary condition, rather than the fatal inhibition, of spontaneity.

Eduard Meyer saw things in this light, and this is remarkable for – unlike Sohm – he was, as we have noted a short while ago, a

---

[1] As we have spoken about this at length in our introduction, we say no more here, apart from emphasizing that Sohm was as extreme an individualist as Weber. Even social functions are to him exclusively individual tasks and no more. Cf. Lowrie, loc. cit., pp. 147 et seq. and 237 et seq. Cf. also pp. 152, 106–108, and 110. In the latter passage Sohm–Lowrie miss the point of Jesus' parable of the mustard seed (Mark IV, 30–2) which contains His acceptance of an organismic sociology, as the description of Israel as a vine in Psalm LXXIX incorporates and expresses the Jewish tradition's holism. Plants are integrated bodies just like animal organisms. Cf. also John XV, 1–6, where the solidarity of Jesus with this Jewish philosophy of society is made absolutely plain. Cf. further Kohlmeyer, loc. cit., p. 15.

[2] Lowrie, loc. cit., pp. 100 and 155.

sceptic. 'For the truly pious man,' he writes where he speaks of
Jewish religiousness in the age of the scribes and Pharisees, 'com-
pliance with the divine law is the presupposition, accepted as a
matter of course, of a truly God-devoted life . . . In their circles,
the law is being conquered precisely by being conscientiously
obeyed. It has become flesh and blood, but it forms the beginning
rather than the end of religiosity.' And he points out that some of
the finest flowers of the Jewish faith, for instance the prophecies of
Isaias, have sprung from this soil.[1] Heiler, for all his Lutheranism,
argues in a similar vein. His main example is the coming of a settled,
i.e. law-established and law-supported, liturgy. Does it choke
piety? By no means: 'It is true that the Catholic liturgy, at least
according to its conception, is throughout a communal service;
not the individual, but the holy assembly, indeed, the whole
ecclesia, enters into direct contact with God and the glorified
Christ. Nevertheless, the Catholic Church has succeeded in giving
to the individual soul hungry for God that calm and solitude, that
separation and freedom, which it needs for communing with God
. . . The Catholic cult leaves far more latitude for the individual than
the Protestant . . . It permits a distance between him and the priest;
it leaves a distance even between his prayer and liturgical prayer;
it does not tie him to the words of the priest, but allows him freely
to pour out his inner thoughts and feelings; and even if the pious
man joins in the hallowed prayers of the priest, he can let his innermost self flow into the wide and rich formulae of the liturgy.' The
same, so Heiler emphasizes, is true even of the celebrant himself.
He has to go through certain prescribed forms, but the content he
lays into them is his own. Indeed, even the rubric, i.e. even the law
itself, helps him in this respect, for instance when it advises him
to pray for those whom he intends to pray for, or to stop a moment
in meditatione sanctissimi sacramenti. Heiler rejects the whole Weberian
idea of routinization: 'The frequent recitation of [prescribed]
prayers creates firm external pathways along which internal contemplation, petitioning and adoration can move with safety. In
consequence of a certain mechanization, energy is no longer needed
in order to apprehend and comprehend the prayers of the liturgy;
and so all energy becomes available for the prayerful pursuit of
certain spiritual implications of the texts during their outward
recitation . . . The fixed schema is only the shell of free prayer.' And

[1] Meyer, loc. cit., vol. III, p. 17.

as Heiler rejects the reproach of routinization, so he does that of legalization. 'The recitation of the liturgical texts imposed [by law] as a duty [on the cleric],' Heiler says, 'does not rob him of his freedom, of a personal intercourse with God. These sacred texts are so rich in high and deep thoughts that they continuously trigger ever-new religious impulses.'[1] What is said here of one piece of legalism, the hard and fast obligation to read the office or the breviary, is true of all legality. It is meant to 'trigger ever new religious impulses', as the lawful and dutiful implementation of the legal schema of marriage triggers ever new impulses of conjugal or familial love. Law is not, as Sohm seems to have felt, outside life: it is in it, of it, and around it. And for that reason its coming in the Church is evolution and not involution.

It is obvious that a faulty idea of what law is and what law does must be fatal to a book whose title and subject is *Kirchenrecht* – Ecclesiastical Law. And yet we would not regard this misconception as the main strand in the etiology of Sohm's errors. Even more important is his habit of looking only at one aspect of the Church's unfolding and completely overlooking all others, for among these others there is one which counterbalances, indeed, cancels, the associated drifts towards routinization and legalization – the development of mysticism in the wider sense of the word. One of the most outstanding modern historians of Church life, Christopher Dawson, has drawn attention to this fact. Catholicism, he has insisted, is characterized both by intense universalism and by intense individualism, and, he says, 'if we attempt to look deeper into the causes of this combination of universality and individuality which lies at the heart of Catholicism . . . we shall find it in the economy of the sacraments. It is evident from the history of Catholicism that the development of the ecclesiastical polity, the growth of canon law, and all the other forms of external organization, have been accompanied *pari passu* by a development of the sacramental system which brought the whole ecclesiastical order into immediate contact with the psychological experience of the individual . . . Here the Church is seen not as a ruler, lawgiver, or guardian of orthodox tradition, but as the mother of a reborn humanity, each member of which is the heir of the divine promises, recipient of the gift of the spirit.'[2] Granted therefore that the Church is, in the

[1] Heiler, loc. cit., pp. 409 and 410. Our translation.
[2] Dawson, loc. cit., pp. 292 and 293.

course of time, becoming more like secular societies (and this is Sohm's essential complaint), she is also, and in a step-by-step parallelism, becoming more and more unlike them. The blunder which Kohlmeyer identified – taking one text, Matthew XVIII, 20, out of its context – is identifiable, in a more general manner and on a much more universal scale, in Sohm's taking the whole of ecclesiastical law out of its context, the total unfolding of the Catholic Church.

We are touching here once again upon an essential point of our investigation. We have asserted throughout that Catholicism is a third type of religious society, alongside sects and ecclesial establishments. At first, the circle of believers in Jesus Christ, and more especially the congregation around James in Jerusalem, was sectarian in character. Paul and Peter changed this. Why then did the Church not become establishmentarian? Tendencies in this direction were undoubtedly present, for were Paul's Epistle to the Romans and Peter's First Epistle not brimful of loyalism?[1] And yet there was no settling down into the established scheme of things. That came only later, and only in the East, in Byzantinism. The West escaped. Why? It escaped because the Church saw itself more and more in mystical terms – as in this world, but not of this world, as even here and now a monarchy under Christ the King; this devalued the secular state and made its sacralization impossible, nay more, this implied a critical attitude to the surrounding world and thus carried the sect's negativism, the sectarian revolutionism, on into the future. One comparison which was dear to St. Paul was that between the Church and the Jews in the desert.[2] But in the desert the Jews were wanderers, *peregrinantes*, present in, but alien to, the forbidding environment in which they happened to find themselves. And this became the decisive self-conception of the Catholic Church[3] from which she did, indeed, sometimes stray, under the influence of her conservatives or quasi-establishmentarians, but to which she was ever called back by the voices of her revolutionaries or quasi-sectarians.

If the Gospels are carefully studied, it appears that there are *two* tendencies which put a distance between society at large and the sacred society of believers, the incipient Church. One of these two

[1] Cf. our vol. III, pp. 1 and 2.
[2] Cf. especially Cerfaux, loc. cit., pp. 97 et seq.
[3] Cf. Stark, as just quoted, p. 12.

tendencies is indeed clearly sectarian. It centres on the expectation of an imminent end of the world, and, after the execution of Christ, on the anticipation of His early return in power and glory 'to judge the living and the dead'. Thinking is here in terms of time – a shortened time, a speeded-up time, so to speak, but yet in terms of *time*. The twenty-fourth chapter of St. Matthew's Gospel is characteristic of this mood. But alongside such passages there are others, and many of them, for instance, Luke IV, 21, and XVII, 20–21, and Matthew XII, 28,[1] which see in the Incarnation of the Divine Principle of Love a *breakthrough of timelessness* into time. The revolutionary act *kat exochen* is not the awaited Second Coming; it is the realized First Coming. Salvation is not something which we have yet to receive; it is something which is already within our grasp.[2] The concept of a Second Coming may be retained as a vision of the end of time – time which is still flowing in the wider world, even though timelessness has already been reached within the narrower enclosure of the Church, as the ultimately supervening *dénouement* of the world's history, but it loses its commanding place in the interpretation of the present. In this theology, the return of Christ is not so important, for in a sense He has never departed. He has ascended *physice*, but He is ever among us *mystice*. Did He not say to His disciples, on the day when He was taken up, according to the self-same Gospel of St. Matthew (XXVIII, 20): 'Behold, I am with you all days, even to the consummation of the world'?[3]

When the Church is conceived along these latter lines, it ceases to be a sect, but it does not, and cannot, become an establishment either. Joining the Church, or rejoining her after penance when membership has momentarily been lost through sin, through a personal lapse from timelessness into time, is of necessity a revolutionary act, a contracting-out of the world. This includes a partial

[1] Cf. also Corinthians VI, 2; Galatians IV, 4.
[2] It is not for us to say which element in the Gospels is more important, but we would quote Harnack's opinion that the belief in the imminence of the Last Judgment and the world's end belongs to the enkindling [*zündenden*] rather than to the abiding [*ruhenden*] ideas of Jesus. Cf. Heiler, p. 22 (no further reference given).
[3] Cf. Cullmann, loc. cit., pp. 224–6; Adam, loc. cit., pp. 79 et seq.; Cerfaux, loc. cit., pp. 92 et seq., 352, 377; Campenhausen, loc. cit., pp. 60 and 61; Bultmann, loc. cit., pp. 220 et seq.; Meyer, loc. cit., vol. III, p. 645; Kümmel, W. G., *Verheissung und Erfüllung, Abhandlungen zur Theologie des alten und neuen Testaments*, No. 6, Zürich and Basel 1945.

contracting-out of the state which, even if it is not satanic, is yet merely a piece of passing time, a helper of the mortal body perhaps, but no help to the immortal soul. Within this ambit of ideas, a total legalization, i.e. secularization, of the Church is unthinkable. The worldly apparatus, the outer shell, of the body of believers may indeed drift in this direction and must do so, if it is to hold its own in the environment in which it is placed. But it is only partially so placed. The otherworldly life, the inner core, must remain impermeable to, nay untouched by, that development.

It will perhaps be said that this mysticism which, as we claim, places narrow limits on routinization, rationalization, legalization and mechanization, is impossible to maintain, that mysticism is merely another word for enthusiasm and enthusiasm evaporates. But this is a misapprehension. Heiler has called 'the idea that Christ lives on in His community' the core-conception of St. Paul's 'Panchristism'.[1] But St. Paul was no enthusiast. It was not volatile emotions that he engendered, but a deep philosophy, a philosophy which could last and did last. Protestants like Sohm are somewhat handicapped here in their capacity to understand the unfolding of Christianity with which our present chapter is concerned, for their Christology is centred either on the historical Jesus or on the eschatological Christ. (We could show this, if we had enough time and space, by a study of that greatest of twentieth-century Protestants, Albert Schweitzer.) But, as one author has expressed it, 'between the historical and the eschatological Christ, there stands the Christ alive in the Church'.[2] Here, for the Catholic, is the true *crux fidei*, the core of his faith. And here lies the real change that comes over the brotherhood of believers as it emerges into the apostolic and post-apostolic age and on into an indefinite future: 'The place [within belief] of the immediately imminent return of Christ is taken over by His eternal presence in the community.'[3] There is thus a mystical Church as well as a legal Church, and Sohm saw within Catholicism only the latter. And he would have seen even the latter very differently, if he had been at all prepared to do justice to the former.

But he was not prepared to do justice to the former, and Max

---

[1] Heiler, loc. cit., p. 575.
[2] Blazovich, A., *Soziologie des Mönchtums*, Wien 1954, p. 117.
[3] Maurenbrecher, *Von Jerusalem nach Rom*, as quoted, p. 171.

Weber, if possible, was even less prepared. This is easily explained. The seat of mysticism is not, of course, in the administrative machinery of the Church, but in her prayer life, and that was of little interest to these two men. Consequently, they could not possibly discover it. The case of Heiler is very different. He knew all Catholicism, not only the shell but also the kernel, and he could therefore write the following remarkable words: 'Where it is the liturgy that occupies the centre of thought and life, there casuistry and ecclesiastical politicking, canonistic and scholasticism must of themselves sink down into insignificance.'[1] This is something of an overstatement; the outer, secular form of the Church (her man-ward aspect, so to speak) is one half of her being, alongside the inner, metaphysical content (her God-ward aspect); but in its essence, Heiler's statement is true. And so we have left it to one Lutheran to controvert the other.

It is, of course, mainly in the Mass that the continued presence of Christ is made real for the Catholic believer. This is not the place to enter into a deeper consideration of this *mysterium fidei*, but we must insist, once again, that the credal content of the rite (the doctrine of the 'real presence') be taken as a datum by the sociologist of religion. It must be so taken by him, if he is to do justice to his material. The Catholic believes that, at the Last Supper, Christ instituted, under the appearance of bread, a symbol of Himself which would be more than a symbol, which *would be* Himself, though not, of course, naturally, but supernaturally, not physically, but metaphysically – and yet – in the eyes of faith – really and truly. The Catholic therefore who goes to Church on Sunday and partakes of Holy Communion also believes that he has been in contact with – that he has received – The Lord. He believes even more. The Catholic believes that if he visits the church building, he enters the presence of the Lord who abides in the tabernacle there. The very layout of the structure is focused on the mystery. 'The centre of the whole system,' writes Lowrie, thus proving that he knows the bare facts, 'is the Holy Table. Without it, the arrangement would be accidental and inorganic. In this the ritual found its centre, and even the architectural lines of the building were ordered with predominant reference to it.'[2] What Lowrie, with Sohm as his instructor, does *not* comprehend is that a community thus tied to a mystical life could not become a dead legal or bureaucratic mechanism; it

[1] Heiler, loc. cit., p. 430. [2] Lowrie, loc. cit., p. 286.

had a heart in it, and to the extent that that heart continued to beat, it was and remained an organism, that is to say, something alive and therefore resistant to mechanization in any form and shape, even the mechanization which is called routinization, rationalization and legalization. Mechanization – the transmutation of an organism instinct with life into a corpse bereft of it – could only supervene, if the mystical core of the Church were totally eaten out. But that Lowrie, Sohm and Weber have not asserted; nor would it matter much if they did make the assertion, for they, as outsiders, would hardly be qualified to judge. And as they maintain that the assumed decay of the Church took place, not at the end of the second millennium, but already at the beginning of the second century (if not indeed before – sometimes even St. Paul's 'pastoral epistles', Timothy and Titus, are taken as evidences of it),[1] they would have to show, in order to make their case convincing, that live mysticism was already lost in the age of the martyrs, a truly impossible proposition.

There is a context in Lowrie's book where he touches upon the unity of the legal and the mystical Church, and what he says there is very characteristic. 'It was in connection with the Eucharist and the Eucharistic assembly,' he writes, 'that a legal conception of the congregation and the ministry was first formulated . . . The reason . . . is this that the Eucharistic assembly was the assembly which exhibited the congregation in its most definite and exclusive character and the ministry in its most definite and exclusive functions.'[2] Very true. On the facts, then, there is no quarrel, only their interpretation is at issue. Lowrie and Sohm assume that the developing law overwhelmed the charismatic and devotional content of the communal assemblies, but this is an entirely unwarranted assumption. Do the Christians, even now, after nearly two millennia, not still assemble to offer up the sacrifice, to pray, to worship, to meet and to receive their Lord? We can take Lowrie at his word here. As he describes the development in the passage which we have quoted, the Eucharistic assembly is there first and forms the basis of what happens later. What happens later, a kind of legal firming-up of things, is therefore merely secondary and adventitious; the Eucharist – the Mass – remains the warm heart around which an admittedly cooler and harder shell begins to form – without, however, destroying that heart: indeed, far from destroy-

[1] Heiler, loc. cit., pp. 61 and 62.   [2] Lowrie, loc. cit., p. 267.

154

ing the heart, the shell protects it, for this is the function of any shell around a living organism.

The indissoluble unity of the legal and the mystical Church, by dint of which the mystical element keeps the legal in check, as the legal prevents the mystical from dissolving – from, so to speak, evaporating – the community, is traceable in all the predominant doctors of Catholicism. Heiler draws attention particularly to St. Augustine and St. Thomas Aquinas. 'The legal and juridical element in Augustine's religion,' he says in his summing up of the great Bishop of Hippo, 'is kept in a healthy equilibrium by the spiritual, evangelical and mystical' counterweight. And in his discussion of St. Thomas he writes that the scholastic 'art of logical harmonization makes it possible for the Aquinate to hold fast to both the contrasting concepts of the Church which through the centuries have struggled against each other for pre-eminence, the spiritualistic and the institutional'.[1] Thus the two sides of the coin are always seen together, as indeed they ought to be.

However, this reference to theory is not entirely convincing, if it is left standing alone; what matters is practice, for men's professions are not always consonant with their conduct. What we must find out is whether the yoking together of a mystical element with the legal one has softened legalism in the Church, has made it less legal than the legalism of the world. And this is indeed so. Every Catholic knows this, as the well-informed Protestant Heiler knew it, though the ill-informed Protestants Sohm and Weber did not. Heiler discusses the most important aspect – the sacrament of penance. The activity of the confessor, he points out, is juridical and jurisdictional; he is in every form of law the *iudex ecclesiasticus*. Yet, he adds on the next page, there is a *complexio oppositorum* even here. 'The mystical element of piety cannot be absent.' The aim of the 'legal process' which runs off inside a confessional box is *contritio* – loving reconciliation of the sinner with the loving and therefore forgiving God.[2] The existence of a *forum internum* or court of conscience is indeed of supreme importance in a discussion of the so-called legalization of the Church, and the fact that they turn a blind eye towards it, shows all the weakness of the Weber–Sohm position.[3]

---

[1] Heiler, loc. cit., pp. 101 and 116.   [2] Ibid., pp. 122 and 123.
[3] Cf. Stark, 'The Routinization of Charisma', as quoted.

We do not, however, have to remain in the darkness of the confessional box to see that the mystical element redresses and thereby redeems the legal: there is open and public evidence enough. In the first days, the possession of *pneuma* (of inspiration) is demonstrated in wild manifestations, ecstasis and glossolaly, for instance, and Weber lays great emphasis on this fact. The primitive Christian is for him somebody like the fierce berserker Cuchulain of Irish fame, always ready to run riot and foam at the mouth.[1] Later, quieter forms are found for the expression of the pneumatic or inspired state, and this precisely is seen by Weber as the 'routinization of charisma'. But it is in fact the very opposite: the release of charisma. 'According to Paul,' says Rudolf Bultmann, who has given this matter particular attention, 'the *pneuma* does not show itself as a magical power in the believer but – and in this he decisively influenced the further development – as a *norm for his practical conduct.*' And what is practical conduct for the Christian? The fulfilment of the law of love – love pure and simple. 'He that loveth his neighbour hath fulfilled the law,' Paul tells the Romans (XIII, 8), and also the Galatians (V, 14): 'All the law is fulfilled in one word: Thou shalt love they neighbour as thyself.' What is more truly charismatic then, the foaming at the mouth of the over-excited period or the caritative attitudes of the quieter days thereafter? Not only St. Paul, but already St. John give an unambiguous answer, and there is no need to spell out what it is.[2]

But it is not only the coming of a more settled mood that makes for a release of charisma, of that spirit of brotherliness which *is* charisma, it is also the coming of a more settled magistracy. Who, according to all experience, is more likely to show mercy to an errant brother – a multitude of men or one alone? Unless the one is a sadist, the answer is hardly in doubt. Whatever one may think of the Reformers' general claim to have gone back to primitive Christianity, they certainly did go back to the most primitive condition of the Church when they substituted 'the stool' for the confessional – that stool on which the culprit had to stand and hear his case dealt with by minister, elders and congregation. It is today acknowledged on all sides, including the successors of the one-time collective judges themselves, that love was rarely in

---

[1] Cf. *From Max Weber: Essays in Sociology*, as quoted, p. 245, and *The Theory of Social and Economic Organization*, as quoted, p. 359.
[2] Cf. Bultmann, loc. cit., pp. 227–233.

evidence on these occasions. So far as transition from the first open congregational tribunals to the later closed and confidential priestly ones is concerned, we can once again call in an outstanding expert to help us elucidate the matter – Hans von Campenhausen. As this excellent scholar shows, the early Christian communities worked with a list of crimes which either could not be forgiven at all, or could be forgiven only once so that the recidivist, even if his repentance was genuine, was left without hope. This hard state of affairs began to change as soon as the power of discipline drifted from the hands of the assembled multitude into those of the presiding officer, the bishop. While laymen like Tertullian fought for the retention of the old, unyielding policy, leading clerics like Dionysius of Corinth or Agrippinus of Carthage quietly introduced a softer, more charitable line.[1] Of course, this development would be put down by many as a sign of decay; old-style Calvinists, for instance, would be sure to feel that way. But in the case of Christians, decay would logically have to mean a falling away from Jesus Christ. Christ, however, when asked how often one should forgive a wayward brother, had answered: not seven times, but seventy times seven times (Matthew XVIII, 22). In this instance, therefore, the 'legalization' and 'bureaucratization' of the Church brought an approach to the authentic Gospel spirit, and not a retreat from it. It is of Tertullian, not of Dionysius or Agrippinus, that Campenhausen can say that 'the legalistic conception has swallowed up the evangelical spirit'. Indeed, he gives it as his opinion that an insight into the 'evangelical meaning' of the power to discipline 'has remained operative in the frame of an official system and more especially of episcopal privilege'. 'Only so,' he adds, 'can one understand the strong upward development which the episcopal office was everywhere to receive in the course of the third century.'[2]

We are now in a good position to return to one of Sohm's most basic and most bitter formulations, his condemnation of the adage, '*ubi episcopus, ibi ecclesia*'.[3] If this saying really meant what he assumes it to mean, namely: 'where the administrative official is, there is the Church', its currency would indeed betoken a sad fall from grace.

[1] Campenhausen, loc. cit., pp. 240 et seq. Cf. also Steidle, B., *Die Regel St. Benedikts*, Beuron 1952, p. 213.
[2] Campenhausen, loc. cit., pp. 256, 257, 260. Cf. also pp. 269 and 270.
[3] Cf. above, p. 138.

But this is a misconception; indeed, it is not much more than a mistranslation. The significance the four words really carried, the assertion they contained, was 'where the Eucharist is, there is the Church'. For the men of the first century, as for the true Christian even now, the bishop or the priest is not primarily concerned with administration; that may be one of his activities, but is not the centre of his function: the centre of his function is to lead the community in worship, to lead them in their ritual re-establishment of contact with the divine, in their religious renewal. Perhaps it is natural for men like Sohm and Weber to think of the clergy in essentially bureaucratic terms; it is certainly unnatural for believing Christians to see them in this light. 'The first thing that becomes obvious,' when the facts of history are investigated, writes Kohlmeyer, 'is that the offering of the Eucharist is the kernel of the official duties, and soon also rights, of the bishop ... This right is his most important and decisive right ... The office is cultic.' Why did St. Ignatius of Antioch fight so determinedly for a monarchical episcopate? Why did he say that only he who acknowledges the one bishop can be regarded as a true Christian? Because he wanted to secure the unity of the cult.[1] '*Ubi episcopus, ibi ecclesia*' means therefore: where the common worship is, there is the Church. And this in turn, remembering the early Christian and continuing Catholic belief in a real presence of the Godhead in the cultic congregation, i.e. the congregation 'gathered in His name', ultimately means: where Christ is, there is the Church. It is truly difficult to see what exception Sohm, or anyone else, could possibly take to this wrongly incriminated adage. Nothing could be less of an indication of a process of degeneration than these words. And nobody could have been less of a bureaucrat than the very same Ignatius to whom these words can be traced. 'The ideal conception of the [episcopal] office which is to be found [in this man] could be called both spiritual and cultic ... The bishop is the centre of the spiritual mystery of the Church ... We have before us a characteristic interpenetration of pneumatic and official or ecclesiastical thought.' So writes Campenhausen.[2] We can close our consideration of Sohm with his statement. It brings out what we have urged all along, namely, that the development of a legal

[1] Kohlmeyer, loc. cit., pp. 27–32. Cf. also Meyer, loc. cit., vol. III, p. 579 (note), and Campenhausen, pp. 105 et seq.
[2] Pp. 115 and 113.

order in the Church runs parallel to, indeed, is one process with, the development of a mystical conception of the Church, and that only both together make up the reality with which the historian and sociologist of religion is concerned.

In discussing the bishop and his office, we have already battled with Max Weber as well as with Rudolph Sohm, for this precisely is the point at which their respective analyses overlap. Yet the concept of 'official charisma', in contradistinction to genuine charisma, is more specifically Weber's contribution. His classical formulation is to be found in a passage from *The Theory of Social and Economic Organization*.[1] He discusses there 'the concept that charisma may be transmitted by ritual means from one bearer to another' – transmitted, we must understand, in a sort of a way, for true transmission is excluded by the personal nature of the endowment. 'The conception was originally magical,' Weber adds. 'Charisma [properly so called] is a phenomenon typical of prophetic religious movements . . . in their early stages. But as soon as the position of authority is well established, and above all as soon as control over large masses of people exists, it gives way to the forces of everyday routine.'

In these lines, official charisma is condemned twice over – firstly because of its assumed pre-Christian antecedents, its supposedly magical character. With this aspect we shall deal a little later.[2] And secondly, because of its post-Christian emergence, its supposed connection with a Christianity which has already lost its soul. Significantly, Weber, in another, equally crucial context, equates official charisma with a substitute or sham, with an *ersatz* charisma, if this unhappy wartime hate-word be permitted here. This is what he writes: 'Charisma may be either of two types. Where this appellation is fully merited, charisma is a gift that inheres in an object or person simply by virtue of natural endowment. Such primary charisma cannot be acquired by any means. But charisma of the other type may be produced artificially in an object or person through some extraordinary means.' 'The most important example,' so we may complete the exposition by a quotation from an earlier context, 'is the transmission of priestly charisma by anointing, consecration, or the laying on of hands.'[3]

[1] As quoted, pp. 366 and 370. [2] Cf. below, p. 238.
[3] *The Sociology of Religion*, transl. Fischoff, as quoted, p. 2; *Theory of Social and Economic Organization*, as quoted, p. 366.

The operative words in these statements – the terms which bring out the contrast to be established – are 'fully merited' and 'produced artificially': the difference is one in quality, in genuineness, in value. Official charisma is but a counterfeit.

This heart-piece of Weber's sociology of religion is highly characteristic of his whole system of sociology.[1] If there is one trait which distinguishes his thinking from other contemporary and competing theories, for instance that of Emile Durkheim, it is its consistent nominalism or individualism, a philosophy which Weber not only rationally embraced but also passionately believed in and propagated. If a quality, for instance a virtue, is ascribed to a person, then it is real for the person is real; if the same quality, the same virtue, is predicated of a collectivity, then it is unreal for collectivities are fictions whose 'reality' we merely accept or rather assume because of the tangibility and of the emotional connotations of certain symbols, the crown in the case of England, the flag in the case of America, and so on. Scientifically, there is no England, there are only Englishmen, no America, only Americans. It is not necessary to fall into the opposite Comtean or Durkheimian error of reifying collectivities and denying the reality of concrete persons in order to see that this social philosophy is exaggerated. In the order of nature the self is certainly superior, ontologically, to society which is physically only a collection of bodies; but in the order of culture society is as certainly superior, ontologically, to any self or all selves for mentally these selves are essentially the products of their society and its pre-existent culture-complex. It is therefore as possible for a society to be a *fascinosum*, in Weber's language, to have the specific compelling appeal which he calls charisma, as it is for a personality. When we speak of a university, Weber urges us, we must not allow ourselves to be caught by the fact that there are university buildings. These buildings, which give our unweary minds the delusion that a university is a real entity, merely cover up the decisive truth, namely that a university is *not* a real entity but merely a place where some men lecture and others listen and learn. So also of the Church, Weber says – but he is wrong. When somebody steps over the threshold of the Cathedral of Chartres, he feels (if he is not 'religiously unmusical' as Weber confessed to be) in the presence of a culture and indeed of

[1] Cf. Stark, W., *The Fundamental Forms of Social Thought*, London 1962, especially pp. 245 et seq.

a community which is different from others, which has its own self and its own soul. And this culture, this community, is as capable as any other of entering into individual personalities and making them its own. There can therefore be as real and as genuine a collective charisma as an individual one. To deny this is sheer narrowness and prejudice.

Once this is admitted, it becomes obvious that what we should distinguish is not genuine and fake charisma, but collective and personal charisma.[1] A man may be obeyed because of what he *is*, or because of what he *stands for*. In the former case, the prestige he enjoys is due to personal charisma, in the latter to his representation of, or participation in, collective charisma. In religion we call the one type a saint, the other a priest. When a young recruit is inducted into the army and instructed in its customs, he is invariably told that when he salutes an officer, he evinces respect 'not for the man, but for the charge'. Behind the officer there is the army, behind the army the king or the nation, and it is *their* aura that lies on the young lieutenant – *he* probably has none of his own. It is the same with a priest. Behind the priest there is the Church and behind the Church (for the believer) Jesus Christ. And Jesus Christ is, according to the thinking of all religious traditions which go back beyond the year 1500, according to Catholic as well as Orthodox conceptions, both individual and collectivity, both a holy person and a hallowed community – for even the Church is the mystical body of Christ. There can be no objection to Weber's distinction between two variants of charisma; that is justified and realistically seen; but there must be a determined rejection of his value-laden terms 'merited' and 'artificial'. It is a difference *in kind*

[1] In introducing the concept of personal charisma, we are not, of course, retreating from the position which we have taken up earlier in the book. We have maintained, and continue to maintain, firstly, that the mysterious quality known as charisma can attach to collectivities as well as to individuals, and that, in the Christian–Catholic orbit, it attaches to a collectivity rather than to individuals; secondly, that, in so far as it attaches to individuals, these need not be conceived as radically incomparable, but can be thought of as forming a family, and that the saints in the Christian–Catholic orbit reflect, and to some extent replicate, the charisma of Jesus Christ, thus evincing a family likeness to each other. Yet, in spite of this, the charismatic personalities of the Christian–Catholic tradition can still be legitimately described as unique, and we shall so describe them (cf. below, p. 192). Where, in music, you have a theme and variations, every variation is unrepeated and unrepeatable, even though it is linked to others by the common theme.

with which we are confronted here, not a difference in value. We must try to see both phenomena in their own terms and judge them, not by each other, but by their own inherent nature and possible perfectibility.

Scholars who are not given to Max Weber's personal prejudices have for a while been moving towards the point of view which we have just set forth. Carl J. Friedrich, for instance, in the article from which we have already quoted,[1] writes this: 'Instead of the personal inspiration of the faithful by the founder of a religion, there develops the impersonal inspiration of the religious teachings of the founder . . . The impersonal inspiration is still inspiration in the true sense.' And a few pages before this passage he makes an incidental remark which is even more helpful for the sociologist of religion: he speaks of the necessity of drawing a 'distinction between the initiating and the maintaining form of charismatic leadership and power'.[2] Nothing could be more to the point. The man of personal charisma, the saint, is the initiator, the revolutionary – Jesus Christ, St. Francis and all like them, great and small. The priest, on the other hand, is the maintainer; he is not personally holy, and if he is, he belongs in the other category or in both; but he is holy by dint of his work – and only for this reason is the pope, for instance, described as the Holy Father. But if he does what he is supposed to do; if he makes himself into an organ of the charismatic community which he serves, then the charisma of that community will, so to speak, shine through him and radiate from him, and he will receive the obedience which, for another reason, is given to the spontaneously arisen saint. Edward Shils has brought this out well in another important article.[3] 'Charisma not only disrupts social order, it also maintains and conserves it,' he says.[4] 'An attenuated, mediated, institutionalized charismatic propensity is present in the routine functioning of society. There is . . . a widespread disposition to attribute charismatic properties to ordinary . . . roles, institutions, symbols and strata or aggregates of persons.' Shils speaks in fact, in this last sentence, of 'ordinary secular roles', but what he says is, of course, applicable *a fortiori* to the priest whose role is by definition more than merely secular.

---

[1] Cf. above. p. 31.   [2] Loc. cit., pp. 20 and 17.

[3] 'Charisma, Order, Status', *American Sociological Review*, April 1965, pp. 199 et seq.

[4] Ibid., p. 200.

By calling the priest (or bishop or pope) an *organ* of the Church, we have introduced an appropriate simile which will repay elaboration. The pejorative implications of the term 'official charisma' are ultimately due to the conception that the administrator is a bureaucrat and the bureaucracy is 'a machine', hence something mechanical and dead, which can have no place in a living organism like the Church. We do not stay to inquire whether this opinion is fair to officialdom in general; should one ever allow the abuses of an institution to colour one's estimate of its uses? But in view of the profoundly and consistently organological tradition of ecclesiological thinking, we would point out that even a body like our own has in it servo-mechanisms which support the vital functioning of it and are indeed indispensable. Who could live without bones? Who could work without muscle or tendon? And yet bone, muscle and tendon are not fully vital parts. Granting the possibility that there may be and have been ecclesiastical administrators who not only had no personal charisma, but had not even a tangible share in the Church's collective charisma, they would yet be able to go through the appropriate motions and thereby help the stream of life to continue. Death would only supervene, if there was nothing left but such types: only then would the warm organism turn into a cold skeleton. But that has not happened and will not happen until the last person has said his last prayer.

We have now shifted the discussion on to new ground. We have begun to consider our subject-matter from the point of view of *functionalism*. Our next section will envisage saint and priest from precisely this angle of approach. We shall show that both are equally essential to the Church. This will be more of a constructive and less of a critical task. In taking leave of Sohm and Weber, we have finally to point out that Weber's fault was identical with Sohm's: he also saw only half of reality, and this was his general weakness, for in general sociology, too, he put all the emphasis on the reality of the individual and none on that of institutions. But without institutions there can be no individuals, and without priests there can hardly be saints. Saints – and this, humanly speaking, is true, as we have already shown,[1] even of Jesus – emerge out of an ongoing stream of tradition. They may turn against that tradition, they may change it inside out, they may

[1] Cf. above, p. 9.

revolutionize it, but they yet presuppose it, as the child presupposes his parents and the institution of the family. A family is more than husband and wife: it is a union with the purpose of producing offspring. The Church is more than a number of priests: it is a number of priests with the purpose of producing saints. This Weber never knew, for his idea of the saint was that he came into the world without progenitors, a unique self-generated phenomenon, almost an inexplicable freak. He saw the saint only in the singular: he never discovered that there is in reality a chain of saints (plural) which stretches from age to age and is not likely to break off. But this, it must be said, is poor sociology, even if it is good, very good, individualism.

Looking back over one thousand nine hundred and fifty-eight years, Christopher Dawson has emphasized the ever-presence, in history, of both individual and collective charisma. 'The Catholic Church,' he writes, 'is a charismatic as well as a hierarchical society, and its universal mission is carried on not only by the organizing work of the great religious orders and congregations but by the unpredictable intervention of saints like Bernadette of Lourdes or Jean-Baptiste Vianney of Ars who are the representatives of the common Christian people – the *Plebs Christi*.'[1] This is a true, but not a new insight. Christians, it appears, realized at all ages that what their religion needs is not only inspiration but also organization, and not only organization but also inspiration. Campenhausen's great work illustrates this from the sources of the earliest period of Christendom: it is called 'Ecclesiastical Office and Spiritual Power in the First Three Centuries'.[2] Already on the opening page, Campenhausen rejects Max Weber's specific view of genuine and official charisma. The idea of a fated degeneration and descent from the former to the latter is 'too schematic'. But what is it, so we must ask, that Campenhausen puts into the place of Weber's scheme? It is, in a word, the conviction, inspired by a study of the facts, that in history there is a *tension*, an *abiding* tension, between ecclesiastical office on the one hand and spiritual power on the other. The term 'tension' is used already in the first line of the investigation, and it enunciates both the basic theme and the

[1] Dawson, loc. cit., p. 289. Cf. also Lowrie, loc. cit., p. 366, where this kind of opinion is acknowledged to be widespread.
[2] Cf. above, p. 81.

164

essential content of all discussion in the book and all development in reality.

We cannot enter into the detail here; we cannot, for instance, show how at the beginning of the third century in Hippolytus of Rome (or, for that matter, in Clement of Alexandria) 'the pneumatic-charismatic and the official-sacramental conceptions still run side by side without any great difficulties'.[1] Only the principle must be established and secured. Campenhausen calls it 'a double law of validity in the realm of religion' that 'official authority and personal power . . . support each other' – and the term *law* is chosen deliberately. Not that Campenhausen is oblivious of the difference between the two: official authority is conferred, personal power, however, is indwelling; not that he is oblivious of the conflicts which may pit the two against each other: priests and prophets have often clashed and fought.[2] But, in the last analysis, if we envisage the outline of history as a whole, they are (as we have already formulated it) like the two sides of a coin. The saint alone would dissolve the sacred society, the administrator alone would deaden it. 'In the reality of historical life, both are dependent on, and must accept, each other.' It will not do, Campenhausen insists, to divorce inspiration and tradition. They are one reality. There is a 'firm correlation', a complementarity, an 'equilibrium of forces' between them.[3]

The unfolding of Christianity is therefore a double process, a development in two directions. Officers, i.e. priests, appear and form a system; but saints also arise and form a chain which, for all its discontinuity, is yet a unity as well. Jesus Himself, and Jesus alone, is both saint and priest.[4] It is true that we are all inclined to see Him as a figure of genuine charisma rather than as a bearer of official charisma. But He Himself has corrected this onesided interpretation, for He insisted that He was sent, and that in the same meaning of the word in which He was sending others.[5] One who is sent, however, carries the authority of another and not, or not only, his own. After Jesus, the Apostles are still between the two

---

[1] Campenhausen, loc. cit., pp. 192 and 193.
[2] The relation may be, and often is, of course, entirely irenic. Cf. the picture given by Hermas of the conditions in his community, Campenhausen, pp. 103 and 104.
[3] Ibid., pp. 1, 2, 324, 325.   [4] Ibid., p. 325.
[5] Cf. above, p. 100, *re* John XVII, 18.

archetypes, saint and priest, as Campenhausen shows in some detail,[1] his main point being that they are, because of their historical position, more representatives of the person of Jesus than of the 'body of Christ', i.e. that their mission is derived from an individual, rather than from a society. That they must not be regarded as purely charismatic figures in the Weberian sense of 'heroic in themselves' and 'impressive for others', that they are, in spite of their indubitable inspiration, ordinary men and therefore precursors of the appointed priesthood rather than archetypes of self-standing sanctity is clear from the whole picture of the Twelve – small and timid men – which we are offered in the Gospels. Here indwelling and imputed charisma are still together under the same roof, so to speak. With the third generation, however, the division of functions finally takes place, and henceforth we see a duality which, though it is often a duality-in-conflict, is essentially and enduringly a duality-in-unity. There is, of course, no contradiction in this assertion. The contrast between priesthood and sainthood is simply a dialectical antithesis similar to, and perhaps identical with, the confrontation between established and sectarian religion. The conservative and the revolutionary principle, form and content, will always have to face, and to contend with, each other. But life – and especially the life of Catholicism – is an ever renewed synthesis.

It is true that Campenhausen discovers at the close of the third century an ascendancy of the priestly over the saintly element,[2] and this proves that all was not well then. But the end of a particular period is not the end of all time, and it is not justifiable to stop the story there. If we widen the purview, as we must, we discover precisely then the powerful forces which were presently, and ever again, to correct the temporary unbalance. St. Anthony of the Desert was born in 251 or thereabouts. He and his monks revivified the Church which had become too bureaucratic and opened a period of renewal, or rather a series of renewals, which not only arrested but even reversed the process of routinization and struck again and again new fire from the ever-cooling but also ever-glowing ashes. We have told this story in the third

---

[1] Ibid., pp. 325, 326, also pp. 23, 24, 28–30, 35 (note 1), 171. Paul considered himself as called rather than as endowed with charisma. Cf. Wobbe, J., *Der Charis-Gedanke bei Paulus*, Münster 1932.

[2] Ibid., pp. 328 and 331.

volume and need not repeat it here. What the saints of the ages brought was not only the external liberation with which we were concerned there, but also an internal reformation as we are studying it here, indeed, a total rebirth which shook the Church free from the chilling hand of that spiritual entropy which, to Sohm and Weber, paradoxically was the supreme law of life.

PRIESTLY AND SAINTLY CHARISMA: THEIR COEXISTENCE, CONFLICT AND CO-OPERATION

The comparison between body physical and body social must not be driven beyond a certain point, if realism and reason are to be preserved. But it is true and undeniable that the two do have some basic features in common, and among them the most important is the fact that both carry, deep within them, an elementary desire to survive. Surprising though it may sound, collectivities are about as alarmed by the prospect of death as individuals are, and will do as much to stave it off as individuals will. The discussion about the undesirability of routinization started by Max Weber is therefore to a large extent academic. Even if it had to be admitted (and this book does not admit it) that routinization and its attendant phenomena are sheer and unrelieved loss, it would yet have to be accepted, for that loss would merely be the price of continued existence and hence of the supreme good, the securing of which justifies almost any sacrifice. 'The *routinization* of charisma,' writes Thomas O'Dea, 'is . . . a process which also involves the *containment* of charisma.'[1] This is true, but everything depends on the correct interpretation of the word 'containment'. Clearly, it is an ambiguous word. It suggests, first of all, a stemming back and wearing down, as we might say, for instance, that an army has contained its enemy. But it also suggests, at the same time, a preservation and prevention of loss, as in the phrase that water is contained in a pitcher or wine in a cask. Both meanings apply to O'Dea's phrase, not only the negative which the Weberian tradition would foist on us. To carry the teachings of Jesus or even the knowledge of Him into the future, it was not sufficient to collect followers; that alone would assuredly not have been enough; it was necessary also to form an integrated and abiding following out of these followers. For

[1] Cf. *The Sociology of Religion*, Englewood Cliffs, N. J., 1966, p. 50.

individual followers without organization would sooner or later have scattered to the winds.

What we are asserting here is not the result of specious speculation, but demonstrable truth. The Quakers set out to be merely 'a society of friends', i.e. a group bound together by the feeling of brotherliness, and not bound together by anything else. The Spirit was to have it all its own way, so far as their circle was concerned; law was not to enter in. There was, for instance, to be no preaching unless the Spirit moved a believer to speak; if this did not come about, there was to be unbroken silence. What happened after a very short time is an open secret. There were not only embarrassed and often prolonged silences which made nonsense of the whole habit of gathering for worship; there were also equally embarrassing (and often very prolonged!) preachments by brothers who were less than inspired, who either mistakenly thought themselves 'moved by the Spirit' or quite simply liked to hear themselves talk. Soon there was a clear-cut alternative: either to see the meetings cease or to organize some content for them. But that is routinization, whether the term be used, and admitted to be justifiable, or not. 'They learn the great truth repeated in every revival, that no church can be built up on mere experience.' The words are Herbert Workman's and they refer to the early Franciscans.[1] But they are equally applicable to the early Quakers; indeed, they are of universal validity.

Workman also provides us with some clear-cut descriptive material culled from the history of monasticism, and as there are close correspondences between the inclusive roof-society, the Church, and the included sub-societies, the Orders, much can be learned from it. Benedict, as everybody knows, was the great organizer of conventual life; what had happened before he appeared on the scene to undertake his epoch-making, world-historical task? Two tendencies had shown themselves, and although they were diametrically opposed to each other, they were both fatal to the cause of monasticism: a tendency towards dissolution and a tendency towards ossification. South Gaul, the area around Marseilles, was one of the chief venues where monasticism developed, and there the tell-tale term of *Gyrovagi* was soon used to describe the brothers. Workman openly characterizes them as 'vagabonds' and says that they 'confused vagrant laziness with religious contemplation'. But

[1] Workman, loc. cit., p. 310.

even where there was some willingness to settle down, 'monasticism . . . remained . . . amorphous, prone to many of the diseases of
hysterical subjectivism'. The words are deserved. A movement of
this description could not possibly flourish and last. Without
Benedict, the West would not have had an abiding monasticism
at all. As for the East, at which a side-glance is entirely in order at
this point, an abiding monasticism did indeed appear, but of what
kind! Twice Workman calls it 'stereotyped'. 'Perched on the sum-
mits of precipitous rocks, to which the only access was by means of
a windlass, as in the monastery of Barlaam in Meteora, a handful
of monks live out monotonous lives . . . a barren asceticism without
history or contribution to history.' Deir Mar Makar, where the
great Macarius of Alexandria is buried, still has its convent, and
'the life, in its outer guise at least, is scarcely altered since the dawn
of monasticism'. But 'the high ideals of the early recluses are long
since levelled with the dust', and 'their heroic enthusiasms have
sunk down to a dull stagnation'.[1] This is at best a shadow of monasticism, not its own living self.

What was to be done to preserve that precious living self?
Experience provided a clear and unimpugnable practical answer:
regulation was required – not the kind of regulation which is
tantamount to strangulation, of course, but yet real regulation,
enough of it to forestall indiscipline and to preserve form, that form
without which content must necessarily evaporate. Benedict was
only the last and greatest of the monastic legislators, but the need
for legislation was felt much earlier and its efficacy in healing the
weaknesses inherent in coenobitic life had been proved long before
he was born. If monasticism was a success anywhere, it was at
Marmoutier near Tours because the Bishop of that see, Saint Martin,
knew not only how to inspire but also how to control the assembled
hermits; and a century later, Cassian first provided a definite rule
which could become the model of Benedict's *Regula*. This latter
solved the problem of monasticism. 'In the sixth century, Monasticism in Gaul, in spite of the renown given to it by St. Martin, as
elsewhere, presented symptoms which must inevitably have issued
in decay, had it not been for the new life given to it by Benedict of
Nursia.' A comparison with Irish monasticism is very instructive.

[1] Workman, loc. cit., pp. 120, 134, 155, 152, 153, 154. The description of
Deir Mar Makar is taken from A. J. Butler's *Ancient Coptic Churches of Egypt*,
Oxford 1884, vol. I, p. 287.

'Unfortunately, the enthusiasm of these Celtic missionaries was not combined with equal resources of administration.' How did they save themselves? Very simply: by adopting the Rule of St. Benedict.[1]

Benedict, therefore, was the saviour of monasticism, and he saved it by giving it a legal constitution. For that is precisely what the *Regula* provided: any other description of it would be technically at fault. Indeed, the Holy Rule (as it is usually called) comes much closer to a fairly narrow definition of law than canon law at large, for that, as we have emphasized,[2] is very largely grown law, custom, rather than made law, statute. The *Regula* is statute from beginning to end. It was all systematically thought out beforehand and rationally formulated and therefore similar, in essentials, to the contemporary Codex Justinianus or to the Code Napoléon promulgated nearly thirteen centuries later. Yet Workman regards it as a life-preserving, not as a death-inducing document: 'Monasticism in the East retained its individualistic basis,' he writes, 'and remained little more than an aggregation of units; in the West, through the influence of Benedict, it became an organic whole wherein were maintained those fundamental virtues without which society itself must dissolve.'[3]

Workman is half inclined to deny, or at least to play down, the legal character of the Benedictine constitution. 'It is in [its] emphasis of inner principle, rather than in any enforcement of a definite organization, that we find its secret of power,' he says.[4] 'An organization would have waxed old and perish; an inner principle can adapt itself to changing needs.' We have no quarrel with the factual content of this statement and with the sentiment it expresses; rightly did this most competent observer feel that there is no deadening legalism in St. Benedict's masterpiece. But the absence of a deadening legalism does not imply the absence of a sane legality. When the maker of Monte Cassino is called lawgiver of his Order, and he is often so described, it is correct and not poetical language that is applied to him. The Holy Rule is and remains in its inmost essence *law*.

Trying to find a brief formula to express what precisely the Holy Rule did for the Benedictine family and for occidental monasticism in general, Workman asserts that it was designed to correct both

[1] Workman, loc. cit., pp. 120, 121, 132, 135, 211.
[2] Cf. above, p. 145.　　　[3] Ibid., p. 153.　　　[4] Ibid., p. 148.

'rigid asceticism' and 'reactionary laxness'.[1] This is true. As we saw a minute ago, rigid asceticism spoiled the monks of the East, reactionary laxness threatened, and continued to threaten, those of the West. We may say therefore that the basic monastic code promulgated by Benedict stabilized conventual life between the extremes and thereby preserved its self and its sanity for centuries to come. Antinomianism was avoided, and so was what might be called nomianism, enslavement to statute, legalization in the bad sense of the word, routinization of charisma.

We should not, however, forget the small causes of legal regulation over the large ones. To give but one example: the Benedictines, in accordance with an old religious principle, would turn nobody hungry from their doors. But if they fed (and cleaned and housed) every hobo, what was there to prevent colonies of loafers from forming around their gates and ruining the whole establishment? To obviate the very real danger involved, some such rule as the restriction of hospitality for any one person to a week was needed. We may regret this and even speak with some sort of justification of legalization and routinization here. But in a world as we know it, in the conditions within which even the saints have to operate, the norm was both unavoidable and healthy.

Monasticism is apt to bring out yet another problem which creates the need for legal and authoritative control in and of the religious community. In *The Brothers Karamazov* Dostoevsky shows us two kinds of charismatic man: the sane as well as saintly Father Zossima and the also in a sense saintly, yet at the same time decidedly insane Father Ferapont.[2] Ferapont, a marvel of asceticism, has visions and revelations and his repute is high; yet he is a nuisance in the monastery, mainly because humility does not rank too highly in the catalogue of his virtues. So much are we all imbued with the conviction that the 'genuine' charismatic is superior in every respect to a person possessed merely of 'official charisma' that we easily forget that the genuine charismatic may, in spite of his sanctity, be vain or domineering, or evince other quite natural human weaknesses. In the early days of Christendom, the problem was very great, as Campenhausen has emphasized.[3] Even saints need to be controlled. Even Jesus submitted Himself to the Law and the laws.

[1] Ibid., p. 149.   [2] Cf. pt. II, bk. IV, ch. 1.
[3] Campenhausen, loc. cit., p. 77.

A well established technique for identifying the function of an institution is to think it away and see what loss its omission is likely to cause. If Benedictinism had not been legalized to the extent to which it was legalized, what would have happened? The answer to this question need not be completely speculative: the case of the Grandmontines can be brought in to serve as a term of realistic comparison. These monks adopted the Rule of Camalduli and to that extent they, too, were 'regulated'. But they anxiously avoided all concern with secular matters which were left entirely in the hands of the lay brethren.[1] The result was less than satisfactory. Where are the *Bons Hommes de Grandmont* now? They are but a memory. But St. Benedict's sons still go strong all over the world. His spirit (and we can take this word in a very full sense) has endured.

In all this, there is surely no surprise for the sociologist: he knows full well that societies are systems of social control and that they *are* only because, and so long as, they remain systems of social control. The practical problem lies, as always, in the length to which control is driven. Where Benedict of Nursia succeeded, Benedict of Aniane failed. 'In his efforts to secure reformation,' Workman reports, 'Benedict of Aniane made one fatal mistake: he sought a renunciation which should express itself in rigid uniformity. Meat, drink, the cut of the dress, the order of services were to be exactly alike, the products of an almost mechanical mill. Even prayer and praise did not escape his machinery . . . The activity which for the moment blazed up in the monastic systems of Europe was bound from the first to flicker down into ever more sombre ashes. The mechanical can never be anything else than short-lived; the swaddling-clothes of a rigid uniformity never fail in time to crush out the new-born enthusiasm and power.'[2]

Over-regulation is therefore very bad, and our libertarian age will not find it difficult to assent to this proposition. But so, too, is under-regulation, and this is where one must today expect determined dissent. Yet the facts speak an unambiguous language even here. Accusing the Christians of Rome of a 'spirit of legalism oblivious of love,' Heiler bitterly complains of Pope Victor I (189–198): he 'dared to renounce communion with the churches of Asia Minor, as if they were heretics, because of their deviation from an external ecclesiastical custom, the solemnization of Easter'.[3]

---

[1] Workman, loc. cit., pp. 250 and 251.
[2] Ibid., pp. 226 and 227.   [3] Heiler, loc. cit., p. 292.

What was involved, was not so much the solemnization of the feast, but the method for computing its proper date – an apparently even more petty, purely formal matter. The deviants concerned wished to celebrate Easter on Nisan 15, i.e. according to the Jewish calendar. They were 'Quartodecimans'. Is this not, as Heiler suggests, an indifferent point, where everybody could be safely allowed to have his own head? A closer consideration shows that this is by no means so. In fact, the Quartodeciman movement carried in it two mortal menaces, not only one. It was, first of all, Judaizing in tendency, and in combating it, yet another blow was struck against the Hierosolimitan sectarianism with which St. Paul had contended, and in favour of the Pauline vision of a world church – surely no petty enterprise. But, secondly, the Quartodecimans were inclined towards rationalism and thus a storm-signal, the harbingers of that Arianism which, as we have seen in volume III, would have ruined Christianity beyond repair. Victor's action was not the sign of an unbecomingly domineering attitude; if it was a sign of anything, it was a sign of solicitude for the future. *Principiis obsta* . . . Surely, Heiler should have understood this. In our context, it is necessary to insist that under-regulation is at least as dangerous for the preservation of Christian institutions as over-regulation.[1]

But a final question arises here. Granted that Christian institutions, whether it be a monastery or an Order or the whole Church, cannot endure without adequate legal stiffening, would their failure to survive be really catastrophic for religion in the narrower and proper sense of the word, for *spiritual* religion? Is it not true, after all, that law is necessary only for the preservation of the outer form and relatively indifferent so far as the vital content is concerned? The answer must be unhesitatingly in the negative. We have discussed and decided upon this matter already when we analysed and defended the role of 'the Second':[2] without him, the work of the first, of the Founder, would have decayed and disappeared. The saint is the successor of the Founder rather than of the Second and the priest is the successor of the Second rather than of the Founder, but that does not mean that he is dispensable. Far from it. Conservation may be a 'lower' function than creation, but it is a vital function all the same. We might as well say that a man needs his heart more than his liver or his spleen! He cannot do

[1] Cf. pp. 256 et seq.   [2] Cf. above, p. 79.

without either. Countless souls have longed for salvation even in the days when charismatic leaders were thinly sown; the appearance of personal charisma is in its nature discontinuous, but the need for religious leadership is continuous. In the interstices official charisma must provide a medium for the propagation of the Gospel message, as there is no other. Yet we are not thinking in terms of a circulation of *élites* here, as if the carriers of personal and official charisma were like the lions and foxes in Pareto's scheme: when the ones are in, the others are out, and vice versa. We are thinking in terms of coexistence and co-operation. If a simile is needed to clarify the impression which we have received from the study of the facts, it would be that of foreground and background on a stage. The carriers of personal charisma, the saints, while there are such, occupy the foreground; they receive the limelight, and rightly so. The carriers of official charisma, the priests, who are always there, occupy the background; they are most clearly seen if and when there is nobody else who would be more resplendent. But they are essential, too, because the scene must never be empty. Salvation is a drama which brooks no interruptions – life brooks no interruptions either, and salvation *is* religious life in the fullest, the most spiritual, sense of the word.

The simile of foreground and background is sociologically sound because it tallies well with the general situation in the social system where great individuals are forever standing out from the less eye-catching, if more massive figures which form the collectivity. Historically, saint and priest have shaded into each other; conceptually, they are ever in sharp contrast. A short philological aside can prove both. Basilius Steidle has subjected the word 'abba' or 'father' to a closer inspection and found that at first it describes the 'genuine' charismatic, i.e. the religious leader who imposes himself on his followers by dint of his own indwelling authority. After a while, however, the referent of the noun changes. The community begins to feel the need for more permanent leadership and while it will raise the relatively most charismatic man (still in the sense of the 'genuine' gift) to a position of authority, this authority is now to some extent at any rate conferred. It is not, or not essentially, indwelling. The personal qualification is more of a precondition of leadership in the new circumstances, not its essence: express bestowal is required. 'Thus the name "abba"', which at first indicated the possession of a spiritual gift or personal holiness, becomes spontaneously the name of the paternal office, [the office] to lead and to guide a *coenobium* or a *laura*, a colony of monks.'[1] The *abba* turns into the *abbas* or *abbot*.

This change does not, however, mean the disappearance of charisma. Charisma remains as real as before. Its locus is altered, even its source, but not its existence and efficacy. The magnetism which we call charisma was originally due to the mystery of a personality or assignable personalities; later it is due to the mystery of a whole community, an ongoing stream of life.[2] That is where the contrast between *abba* and *abbas* lies; not in the holiness of the former and the bureaucratic character of the latter. No mystery hangs about a bureaucrat (unless the state he serves is itself seen, by its subjects, as a *mysterium*, as an *arcanum* as it was sometimes expressed – but then the state is a church as well and circumstances are similar to those in the Church): an abbot has his aura, as nobody can deny. No rationalization has therefore taken place. A bureaucrat properly so called is a functionary of an administration bereft of any but mundane functions. Comparison with a priest whose functions are anything but mundane is therefore out of the question. We must, as sociologists of religion, make our way towards a *positive* definition of the priesthood. The negative definition which is restricted to saying that a priest is not, as such and necessarily, a saint, is not sufficient.

A quotation from J. M. Cameron's searching book, *Images of Authority*,[3] will quickly lead us to the heart of the matter. 'In the earliest civilizations,' he writes, 'the ruler was simultaneously king, priest and god. What distinguishes Christianity, even the Christianity of the later Middle Ages, from these apparent historical parallels is that one who holds authority is himself under the judgment of Divine authority. *The authority he has is not intrinsic, but sacramental; rather than possessing authority, he is possessed by it.*' The words we have italicized are indeed the core around which a realistic concept of the priesthood has to be constructed. In case 'sacramental' is equated with 'magical' – we shall have to return to this subject later[4] – Cameron adds that this characterization of sacred authority makes no difference to its derived, and in the final analysis

---

[1] Steidle, loc. cit., pp. 87–9. Quotation from p. 88.
[2] Cf. on this point the article by Edward Shils, quoted above on p. 162, especially pp. 206 and 207.
[3] New Haven 1966, p. 3.   [4] Cf. below, p. 238.

collective, nature: 'Magical power is something at the disposal of the one who holds it. The authority that goes with an office in [the] Church . . . is not at the disposal of the holder of the office; rather, the holder of the office is at the disposal of the authority of which the office is a sign.' Cameron echoes in these statements thoughts of Martin Heidegger – thoughts which belong to the deepest this eminent philosopher has conceived: 'Man never possesses existential authority. It is existential authority that possesses man.'[1]

If it be said that this introduces a mystique or mystification into a scientific subject, then the two words used must be rejected as too value-laden. But the presence of mystery has to be conceded. One simply cannot speak about a religious phenomenon at all without this dimension which is co-constitutive, and unavoidably so, of religious phenomena in every shape and form. Yet for the sociologist mystery is only a remote reality. He is more concerned with the tangible foreground of things, with the hard and fast facts, and such are by no means missing. Prime among them is the easily observable circumstance that Catholics down the ages have paid a respect to their clergy which was in all normal cases (in all cases in which the clergyman concerned did not possess a personal as well as an official charisma, i.e. did not happen to be a saint) well in excess of what was due to their personal qualities. They have saluted in them, as we have already expressed it, not the man, but the charge.

'Not the man, but the charge' means, of course, 'not the isolated individual, but the integrated functionary', the organ of the community. An element of sociological (in the sense of philosophical) 'realism' must be admitted here. It is only a very slight exaggeration to say that respect shown to the Catholic priest is in effect respect shown to the Catholic Church. That Church, as a collectivity, is in a manner concretized in the office-holder; perhaps we could even say, she is reified in him. The use of the female pronoun 'she' instead of the impersonal 'it' in speaking of the ecclesia is in itself characteristic: 'her' comparison with, nay identification as, a quasi-person is obvious. Extreme individualists and nominalists are sure to protest and to complain of fiction-mongering; but extreme individualists and nominalists are bad sociologists. Even

[1] Cf. Boelen, B. J., 'The Maturity Concept as a Basic Factor in the Problem of Authority', *Humanitas*, Pittsburgh 1965, p. 128.

in speaking of modern society, i.e. associational society, middle-of-the-road sociologists distinguish between social roles and social role-players, social functions and functionaries fulfilling them. The mayor's office is one thing, the mayor is another: the office remains, but the mayor changes. Durkheim was more realistic about this than Weber. And if Weber was still relatively realistic with regard to modern associations in which the 'we' is but shadowy and certainly weaker than the 'I' and 'you', he was absolutely unrealistic with regard to ancient communities in which the 'I' and 'you' are weaker than the 'we' and the 'we' is very largely what matters. The Catholic Church, however, is the ancient community, or simply community, *kat exochen*. If the assertion of the phenomenological philosophers that in, with and under the concrete we perceive the abstract and universal, the idea and the ideal, is exemplified anywhere, it is within her house. The authority of the Roman clergy is theirs not as persons nor even as role-players but decidedly as roles. A man is The Pope rather than Eugenio Pacelli or Angelo Roncalli or Giovanni Montini.

The truth of what we have just said can best be seen in the painful cases in which discrepancies between the role and the role-player, the office and the man, become apparent, and in the manner in which such conflicts are handled. Dante had no qualms about placing individual popes in hell. Nicholas III, for instance, is head down, feet up, in the third pit of the eighth circle, to burn for the sin of simony. Dante inveighs against him, but he does not forget the office over the person. The person is condemned and damned, but this does not – as he makes perfectly clear – diminish Dante's *riverenza delle somme chiavi*, his reverence for the Supreme Office of the Keys.[1] Even clearer than this unhappy picture from the *Inferno* is a much happier one from the *Paradiso*, set in the context of the poet's paean to St. Dominic. Dominic has to appeal to the contemporary pope, Boniface VIII, placed by Dante, as yet another simonist, with Nicholas III: but Boniface's sinful ways do not interfere with Dominic's saintly work. It is the Holy See with which the Saint co-operates, not its accidental occupant; he co-operates with the ideal papacy, not the actual pope. Dante expresses all this with his unique brilliance:

[1] *Inferno*, canto XIX, lines 46 et seq., Temple classics ed., London 1932, pp. 204 and 208.

The vineyard
Soon loses colour, if the workman is at fault.

But though the leaves turn yellow, the soil remains as good and
fertile as ever, waiting for a new hand to do it justice and bring
forth noble fruit. The land itself, the basis of all, is not in jeopardy.
So also of the papal office:

The Holy See, which once was kinder
Unto the poor, degenerates not in itself,
But only in him who is seated on it.[1]

What matters is the abiding institution, not the deviant individual.

There is, however, a second and different, if kindred, reason
that the failings of a role-player must not be thought to attain the
role itself, in addition to the sociological realism so deeply built
into Catholicism, and this is of especial importance here where we
are trying to show the distinction between, and the co-operation
of, priests and saints. It arises from the first half of the great double
function which the priesthood has to fulfil: to impart stability to
religious life. If this part of the function is to be fulfilled, if stability
is in fact to be imparted to religious life, if the priest is to be what
Joachim Wach rightly calls him,[2] 'the guardian of traditions', the
keeper of sacred knowledge and cultic techniques, then his work
must be so organized as to withstand the changes which the process
and progress of life carries with it, and more especially the coming
and going of the generations. A deeply conservative character
is therefore to be presumed in, and regularly found to be connected with, a clergy, evoking an unfortunate, but at the same
time unavoidable, anticlericalism on the part of the reforming
forces.

We shall see in the next chapter just how the conservative function of the priesthood is fulfilled. Here where only the definition,
the *differentia specifica*, is up for discussion, we have to emphasize
that the priesthood is a calling, a profession, one might almost say,
a craft. What it takes to make a good, even a perfect priest, can be
learned, and more specifically learned with the aid of routinized
teaching methods. Priests, like physicians or lawyers, can be pro-

[1] Ibid., p. 206 (*re* Boniface); *Paradiso*, canto XII, lines 86–90, same ed.,
p. 146. Our translation.
[2] *Sociology of Religion*, as quoted, p. 373.

duced, and this is necessary because the supply must never fail. Saints, unlike physicians or lawyers, cannot be made to order, and if it is true that every generation has had its own saints, its own charismatic personalities, there was yet no uninterrupted flow of them in the past, as there was out of the seminaries, and there certainly is no guarantee of continued sainthood for the future. Furthermore, priests can be, and are, shaped according to a pattern, one might almost say, made according to specifications, and therefore they become easily interchangeable. True, parishioners rarely like to see their pastors leave, but in principle the next incumbent can do the work as well as the one whose position he takes. This is again a guarantee of steadiness, of stability. But saints are not interchangeable. Who can take the place of a Francis or a Theresa, or even of a Vianney? Such extraordinary persons cross the human scene once, and once only. Still, the contrast between 'replaceable' and 'not replaceable', 'producible' and 'not producible', 'reproducible' and 'not reproducible', though both real and essential, must not be exaggerated. It would be quite wrong to say that saints do not learn from each other. 'Aspiring persons live largely in the imagined presence of masters and heroes to whom they refer their own life for comment and improvement,' writes Charles Horton Cooley in *Human Nature and Social Order*,[1] and he is right. St. Bonaventure was a great saint by any and every standard of judgment we may care to apply, yet it is clear that he had modelled himself on St. Francis. The difference between saints and priests must be somewhat more subtly conceived. We have discussed it already, and if the reader will turn back to p. 101, he will find all that he needs. Between priests and their educators, the relationship is that of between teacher and student; between saints and their models, that of between master and disciple. The priest's response to the training which is his, is an ordinary man's ordinary response.

The distinction we are labouring becomes particularly obvious if attention is concentrated on one crucial moment, the moment of entry into priesthood and sainthood. Nobody can say when a saint's sainthood commences or comes to be acknowledged, and even the simple word 'or' which we have just used carries with it, in this context, something of the mysterious. Saints, in fact, appear from nowhere; it is only a slight poetical exaggeration to say that

[1] Revised ed., New York, Chicago and Boston 1922, p. 242.

they fall from heaven. But the case of the priest is prosaic and clear –
as prosaic and clear as that of a civil servant. He passes his examinations; he takes his vows; he is formally admitted, the rite of admission being characteristically called 'ordination', being placed within
an *ordo* or rank or office. Nobody can appoint a saint; the very idea
is the height of absurdity; but every priest is appointed to his charge
and unavoidably so.

Saying that the priesthood is a calling, a profession, an office,
almost a craft, is saying that the priest is *set aside* for his task. In
the Middle Ages when a man's 'art' was expressed in his clothing,
when one could tell at the first glance whether a man was poet or
peasant, a cleric was immediately identifiable by his get-up, and
part of this distinctive garb has remained, notably the clerical
collar. The priest needs some such means of identification for,
again, he is an ordinary man. The saint has no such accoutrements
and he does not need them, for he is distinguished by other marks
of recognition. There is 'something about him', a *je ne sais quoi*; it
may be his passionate nature; it may be his quiet authority; it may
be his irresistible kindness; it may be his unfeigned humility.
Whatever it is, it is strictly individual and inherent, not like a collar
or cincture which anybody can put on; either a man has it or he
does not have it; certainly it cannot be acquired in a shop. But here
again we must beware of overstating the contrast. Just as saints are
a little like priests in that they, too, are in a tradition and learn from
others, albeit in a peculiar way, so priests are a little like saints. They,
too, have something of the unique about them, in that their calling
is no ordinary mundane one (here the parallel to physicians and lawyers breaks down), but is set in the framework of a sacred, indeed,
supernatural, society, in that they serve a Divine Master and a
divine mystery, albeit in a more prosaic and technical way than do
saints. The most important mark of distinction in the religious
communities which understand the priest radically as 'a man set
apart', a *sacerdos in aeternum*, is, of course, celibacy.[1] From the
religious point of view, this trait betokens that the Lord who has
taken a man as His servant, can have nobody with whom He would
have to share his allegiance. Johann Adam Möhler, who could
speak with great authority on this subject, called the priestly

---

[1] I had hoped to devote a special section to this subject, but scarcity of space
makes this impossible. I intend to publish a paper on celibacy in some journal
later on.

avocation an 'undivided service'.[1] Nothing like that is expected of any other functionary, public or private. Sociologically, celibacy means *total* integration into an *undying* corporation; and we are italicizing the two words because they are both equally essential. By being totally integrated, the cleric is with finality set apart; and by being so integrated in an undying corporation, he fulfils, in solidarity with his brethren, the priesthood's first function, or part-function, of imparting stability and permanence to religious life, in contradistinction to the saint who is a person rather than part of a collective structure and so must die, thereby posing the problem of instability and impermanence which the institutionalization of religious life in a Church is meant to solve.

Before moving on to a consideration of the second half of the priestly function, we have yet to draw attention to one further implication of the first. If it is indeed the main purpose of an institutional clergy to give uninterruptedness to the process of religiosity, and if we must for this reason see that clergy as a collective unit rather than as a collection of individuals, then the personal failings of an individual clergyman cannot be allowed to threaten the essential stability and permanence of religious life. If only 'pure' priests were to be allowed, for instance, to dispense the sacraments, it would never be possible to know with any degree of assurance whether the sacraments have in fact been dispensed. Poetically expressed: there might be holes, and invisible ones at that, in what ought to be a seamless robe. The deeper a layman's belief, the higher would be his anxiety. In discussing the Cathari, we have seen how painful a problem this potentially is.[2] In the Catholic Church it is therefore clearly understood that the subjective weaknesses of the *operator* do not destroy the objective validity of the *opus operatum*.[3] This is, however, nothing that is exclusive to Catholicism; rather is it a logical implication, and that one of great practical bearing, of the whole concept of a permanent and professional clergy, as our analysis cannot have failed to demonstrate. Yet stronger than any demonstration by analysis is undoubtedly a demonstration from the facts of history. In the complex tissue of grievances which induced the Reformers to revolt, the charge that the Catholic clergy was 'corrupt', e.g. guilty of 'riotous living',

---

[1] Title of a book (1825).　　　[2] Cf. vol. III, pp, 345 and 346.
[3] For the problematical speculations, but practically sound conclusions of Origines, cf. Campenhausen, loc. cit., pp. 289–291.

formed a purple strand that stood well out and struck the eye. Yet when Luther came to organize his community, he was naturally led to enunciate the same – the Catholic – principle; and if he had not spontaneously followed the needs of life in this respect, he would sooner or later have been forced to do so. If one thing is surprising about his pronouncements on this head, it is the extremity of the language which he uses. Assuming the Devil could manage to secure a regular appointment, and assuming that he were to dispense a sacrament, for instance, baptism, in outward accordance with Christ's institution, Luther asserts, even he, Old Nick himself, could validly dispense it. Both *Der 82. Psalm Ausgelegt* (1530) and *Von den Konziliis und Kirchen* (1539) powerfully make the same point. 'Those estates which are instituted by God's Word,' Luther writes in the former treatise anent verse 6, 'are all holy and godly (*göttliche*) estates, even if the persons are not holy. For example, father, mother, son, daughter, master, mistress of the house, serving man, serving woman, preacher, parish priest etc. are holy estates, even if the persons within them were knaves and scoundrels.' Already before, under verse 1, he had laid it down as a principle that 'abuse does not disturb or destroy the office, the office remains lawful,' as in the State, so also in the Church.[1] At this juncture, the Protestant Luther vividly reminds one of the Catholic Shakespeare. 'Thou hast seen a farmer's dog bark at a beggar? And the creature run away from the cur?' *King Lear* asks.[1] 'There thou might'st behold the great image of authority: a dog's obeyed in office.'

What we have said so far is not likely to come up against great dissent. Few would deny that the clergy *are* the conserving, and therefore, in tendency, the conservative, element in religious life. The fact has been stressed, and indeed overstressed, on all hands. What has been far less understood and acknowledged is the associated and equally undeniable fact that the priesthood has always been instrumental in releasing the reforming and indeed revolutionary forces which are contained within the flocks over whom they presided. This is the second half of the double function which the clergy as a class has to fulfil, and we must remember here the distinction so vital to any and every functionalist analysis –

---

[1] *Werke*, vol. XXXVIII as quoted, pp. 240 and 241, and vol. XXXII as quoted, pp. 217 and 196.
[2] IV, 6.

the distinction rightly drawn and elaborated by Robert Merton, between subjective intention and objective consequence.[1] It may but rarely be the subjective intention of a preacher to evoke a response which might turn against him and the thing he stands for, in this case preservation of the *status quo*. It is none the less often the objective consequence.

How does the call come to a saint – that call which is very different from, above all much more soul-shaking than, the first envisagement of a calling, even the calling of the priesthood? In lieu of a general consideration, we shall give here a specific example, and this will take care of the general case at the same time. We have chosen it at random; almost any other would have done as well. Maria Droste zu Vischering attended, when she was seventeen years old, the solemn vesting of some new sister in a convent. When she entered the chapel, she had no idea yet, not even a suspicion, that her future would turn out to be different from that of any other teenage girl of her family, class or country. Yet when the preacher announced his text, her old world collapsed and a new world was rising before her eyes: 'Hearken, O daughter, and see, and incline thy ear: and forget thy people and thy father's house. And the King shall greatly desire thy beauty; for He is the Lord thy God' (Psalm XLIV, verses 11 and 12). 'It is impossible for me to explain,' she related later, 'what happened within me. The plan of my life lay fully elaborated before me. I heard the voice of the Saviour who called me, to forget the creatures in order to belong only to Him, to forget my parents, brothers and sisters whom I loved dearly. He humiliated Himself so much that He asked me to be His bride. "The King shall greatly desire . . ." These words deeply affected my heart . . . Already I was no longer my own; totally, totally, I was His . . . I can find no words to express what occurred between Him and me.'[2]

What had occurred was the coming of the call and its willing acceptance. And the call was exactly the same as the one which Peter had received by the lakeside or Matthew in his counting house – with one difference: it was conveyed, not by the Founder's voice, but by the voice of one of His (or His community's) functionaries, an ordained priest. The preacher, so we can express it,

[1] Cf. *Social Theory and Social Structure*, ed. 1962, pp. 50 and 51.
[2] Chasle, L., *Schwester Maria vom Göttlichen Herzen Droste zu Vischering*, cf. this German ed. of the French original, Freiburg i. Br. 1907, p. 17.

was a messenger, a messenger (as faith would formulate it) between God and a soul destined to sanctity. This brings to mind a story from Livy[1] which Søren Kierkegaard liked to tell[2] because it illustrates precisely what we are discussing here. Tarquinius Superbus wished to subjugate the city of Gabii, but neither a direct assault nor a subsequent siege succeeded in the execution of this design. 'So he finally had recourse to the un-Roman and disgraceful method of deceit and treachery. Pretending to have abandoned hostilities ... he arranged for Sextus, the youngest of his three sons, to go to Gabii in the assumed character of a fugitive from the intolerable cruelty of his father ... Sextus was soon admitted to the councils of state ... Everything he said or did was so nicely calculated to deceive that confidence in him grew and grew until he was finally appointed commander of the armed forces ... At last he was able to feel that he had the town, as it were, in his pocket ... Accordingly he sent a confidential messenger to Rome to ask his father what step he should next take ... Tarquin was not sure of the messenger's good faith: in any case, he said not a word in reply to his question, but with a thoughtful air went out into the garden. The man followed him, and Tarquin, strolling up and down in silence, began knocking off poppyheads with his stick. The messenger at last wearied of putting his question and ... returned to Gabii supposing his mission to have failed. He told Sextus ... what he had seen his father do: the king, he declared, had not uttered a single word.' But Sextus needed no express communication: he realized at once that Tarquin was advising him to exterminate the city-fathers of Gabii, to 'make them a head shorter'. This tale appeared to Kierkegaard to hold a deep meaning for the Christian. God's message is like Tarquin's: His sons (the saints) will comprehend it, but to the strangers (i.e. ordinary men, even if they are parsons) it will be for ever incomprehensible. Yet such strangers may and must be the deliverers, like mailmen who carry letters to us from our friends whose contents are hidden from them.

The simile implied in this story – the assertion that the saint is like a son in God's family and the priest like a servant – is not

[1] *Historiae Romanae*, I, 52–5, *The Early History of Rome*, transl. de Sélincourt, A., Penguin ed., Baltimore, any printing, pp. 76–8.
[2] Cf. Kierkegaard, S., *Fear and Trembling*, transl. Lowrie, W., ed. Princeton 1945, p. 2. (Kierkegaard's reference is to Hamann, but the ultimate source is Livy, as above.)

entirely wrong. In the saints there resides, and from the saints there radiates, something of the charismatic power which also dwelt in, and went out from, Christ Himself, and therefore they are assumed to be closer to Him than ordinary men, be they in orders or not. It is the general judgment that they understand His spirit better and speak more authentically in His accents than others. Yet the comparison is not entirely right, if and in so far as the roles of son and servant are conceived as incompatible, as mutually exclusive. God's call (Kierkegaard came to see this very clearly)[1] is for *all*, saint, priest and laity alike. However much we may stress that their level of religious attainment is different, they remain one household, speak one language, and serve one Master. Contrast there is, but it is once again a dialectical contrast. The saint calls forth the priest as his antithesis, and the priest, for his part, calls forth the saint. They are a little like the sleeping and the waking hours. When the priest predominates, there is rest, but forces are gathered which will provide the energy for new spurts of activity and advance. When these are achieved, and they are achieved under the leadership of saints, new periods of rest are imperative for every organism must settle down after a great effort, restore and reorganize itself and assimilate the newness that has come from it and to it. And thus it is that life can both perdure and progress.

The real test of the Church, world history's judgment of her performance, is not therefore how well she has preserved the Founder's Gospel, for preservation alone is something of a contradiction in terms: that which is merely being preserved is, in the absence of further growth, no longer quite alive. Nor yet is it, how far she has progressed from her Founder's Gospel, for progress alone is also something of a contradiction in terms: that which progresses without concomitant preservation incurs loss as well as gain and may be impoverished in the end. The real test is how well preservation and progress have been combined. The salient question is: how have the saints fared through the centuries – those saints who are the agents of renewal as the priests are the defenders of the citadel against disruption?

An answer is given by Friedrich Heiler, the Protestant who knew Catholicism more intimately than anybody else of his persuasion. In the passage which we are about to quote, he speaks expressly only of the mystics, men like Jacopone da Todi and St. John of the

[1] Cf. Stark, W., *Social Theory and Christian Thought*, as quoted, pp. 102 et seq.

Cross whom he mentions more particularly, but what he says of them applies *a fortiori* to all other saints, for the mystics are the most retiring and therefore the least influential of all men of God. 'The influence of mysticism on Catholic religiosity is immeasurably wide and deep,' Heiler states. 'All believing Catholics have drunk from the waters of mysticism, some more, others less; but to all mysticism came to mean much. Yet it gave sustenance not only to the individual believers – the whole organism of the Church received without interruption vital juices from it . . . Mysticism is one of the great spiritual forces which bestow on Catholicism immortal life. It is the strongest possible counterweight to all the hard and rigid institutions of ecclesiastical law and ecclesiastical legalism, an invincible barrier against the rationalism of theology. Like a vestal priestess, mysticism guarded the holy fire of divine mystery – guarded and preserved it from all contamination by rationalistic speculation and hierarchical world domination. It triumphantly overcame the immense danger which threatens every ecclesiastical institution, and the most extended and powerful more than any other, of confounding churchly, cultic and dogmatic forms with the inexpressible mystery of the divine. It knew and preached unceasingly that all ritual, legal and rational forms are but the outer wrappings of a naked purity, shadows of the eternal light . . . A Church which did not forget this sublime truth could never perish in externals, for in it breathed the spirit of all real religiosity, awe and amazement in face of the totally incomprehensible.'[1]

Such was the influence of the men of prayer and poetry. That of the men of action we have discussed in the second half of our third volume where we have shown how the founders of the successive religious Orders have collected their armies of renewal and reform, to do battle with, and invariably rise superior to, the entrenched forces of inertia and decay. Our argument there is part of our argument here.

The word 'battle' which we have just used must not be interpreted too restrictively and metaphorically. It is easy for the sociologist to speak of a division of labour between saint and priest (though, objectively, this is entirely correct); it is just as easy for the historian to assert that there has been an ever-impeded, yet also never-arrested forward development (though, again, this is

[1] Heiler, loc. cit., pp. 551 and 552.

objectively entirely correct); the fact remains that conflict between
the conservative and reforming forces was always an actual threat
and sometimes even a dire reality. Alexander Pope's word that
'discord' is 'harmony not understood' and 'partial evil, universal
good'[1] is too glib to be acceptable in an honest view of what in fact
happened during the Church's pain-punctured millennial march
through time.

A fuller study of the relationships between saints and office-
holders would have to range from such early cases as the hostility
of the priest Brictio to St. Martin of Tours or of the priest Floren-
tinus to St. Benedict,[2] to the life of St. Theresa of Lisieux, still
within living memory, who 'was persecuted in the true sense of the
word by a Mother Superior'.[3] Materials would not be missing, and
yet they would not be over-rich, for all men are a little like the
citizens of Perugia who once captured St. Francis in a local squabble
and kept him in captivity for a while, but were sorry for it ever
after and tried almost desperately to hush the matter up, even
though it had all happened long before Francesco Bernardone was
more than one of the youngsters from Assisi. Difficulties of documentation and interpretation would arise at every step: it is under
any and every circumstances a hazardous task to try and reduce
hagiography to sober fact. Needless to say, we cannot turn aside
here to give this unhappy aspect of Church history closer consideration. But we have to include at least one illustration, if for no other
reason than because we do not want it said that we have hurried all
too quickly over an objectively important but subjectively distressing chapter. We have chosen the case of St. John Bosco, founder
of the Salesian Order, whose trials and tribulations have not remained a secret and can be easily and faithfully recounted.

Like others of his fettle, Don Bosco was not precisely a sober
man; indeed, he was an enthusiast, an extremist, a heart afire. Some
were uncomfortable with him; others were afraid of him. How
could one live with such a fellow? The first attempt to get him out
of the way was a scheme to confine him to a lunatic asylum. 'The
rumour went round that he was indeed in need of treatment, a few

---

[1] *An Essay on Man*, Epistle I, lines 291 and 292. Cf. *The Works of Alexander
Pope*, ed. Elwin, W., vol. II, ed. New York 1967, p. 370.
[2] Cf. Workman, loc. cit., pp. 103 and 104; Blazovich, loc. cit., p. 119.
[3] Moulin, L., 'Policy-Making in the Religious Orders', in *Government and
Opposition*, October 1965, p. 29.

weeks' rest as it was euphemistically called, and two canons were constituted the mouthpiece of their brethren in the clergy,' one of the biographers reports. 'Don Bosco was perhaps not surprised to receive a visit from them and underwent a little examination at their hands: they cross-questioned him about his projects' in which they decried evidences of megalomania, though the future was to show that his early dreams were to be far surpassed in reality. 'A few days later two other canons called on him and . . . invited him to accompany them in their carriage – a drive in the country would do him good.' The saint realized that he was to be taken to a mental hospital, but he was not dismayed. 'In a few moments the three went down to the carriage. Naturally Don Bosco allowed the two venerable canons to get in before him, but no sooner were they seated than he slammed the door and called to the coachman. "Quick," he shouted, "the asylum. These two gentlemen are expected there." The coachman who had been ordered to take a passenger to the asylum whipped up his horse and lost no time *en route*. On arrival the two canons had some difficulty in talking themselves out of their predicament and had to await identification by the chaplain before being allowed to depart. No more was heard of Don Bosco's madness; a man who could entertain the whole town with a joke like that was in no danger of being thought mad.'[1]

Later troubles were not as easily sidestepped. Successive archbishops were annoyed with Bosco, and it is understandable that they were, because the best young men who wanted to serve God joined the new institute and not the regular clergy. 'The chief difficulty concerned the ordination of the Salesians . . . Mgr. Riccardi di Netro . . . opposed the Congregation on the ground that he could not tolerate in his diocese clergy who were not subject to him and trained in his seminary.' Riccardi di Netro had at first been friendly and changed only when he began to look at Bosco with an archbishop's eye. Unfortunately, the same was true of his successor, Gastaldi, who had even been an active supporter of Don Bosco's at one time. 'It was not long before Don Bosco suffered from the prelate's autocratic dealings. Gastaldi has been excused on the score . . . that he suffered from a liver complaint, but it was a hard trial indeed that Don Bosco should be the chief victim of the archbishop's liver. The truth of the matter is probably . . . that he was too ready to listen to the tittle-tattle in the archi-

[1] Sheppard, L. C., *Don Bosco*, Westminster (Maryland) 1957, pp. 63 and 64.

episcopal curia where jealousy of Don Bosco's success had from the beginning produced covert opposition to him. Pinpricks, and something more, became his daily lot.' It would be tedious to rehearse the detail: it was all a sign of that pettiness which, in a superior, can thoroughly poison a subordinate's life. Most hurtful was refusal of the *imprimatur* to a pamphlet which set out the saint's aims: it had to be secured and the pamphlet published at Fassano, and rejection of a scheme to open a house for late vocations, which in the end had to be located at Genoa, not Turin. 'Don Bosco bore it all unmurmuringly for many years; in the end he was compelled to defend himself at the Roman court and sent in a detailed account of all that he had been obliged to bear. The Pope, the Congregation of Bishops and Regulars, all did their best to make the archbishop see sense and peace of a sort was patched up, but it was not until the death of the archbishop in 1883 that this trial was removed.'[1]

In a history of conflict like the one which we have just surveyed, it is very difficult not to take sides, and especially not to take the side of the saint against the priests. Yet fairness and sober truth demand that we keep the balance straight even here: *audiatur et altera pars*. It is not the sanctity of the saint which, in most cases, arouses resistances against him: that sanctity is in any case not yet proved. Nor yet is it his morality which may be unimpugned. It is basically his desire to innovate, and to press innovation with a passion which takes no account of dangers and difficulties. The voices raised against the firebrands were as a rule not only the voices of conservatism in the bad sense of the word, the voices of unreasoning neophobia, but also the voices of conservatism in the good sense, the voices of caution and consideration. 'There is always a certain anarchy in the founders of new Orders,' writes Leo Moulin, an outstanding expert in the field. When we quoted him before, we did not give the whole quotation and must complete it now: St. Theresa of Lisieux was not simply 'persecuted . . . by a Mother Superior', but 'by a Mother Superior who was otherwise of the highest character'.[2] This makes a difference. It is the weakness – the 'ideology' – of authors of leftist leanings to argue that history pits against each other champions of new values and defenders of old unvalues, promoters of the light of tomorrow and protagonists of the darkness of yesterday, and the day before. The case is in fact

---

[1] Ibid., pp. 101 and 113–15. [2] Moulin, loc. cit., pp. 44 and 29–30.

almost always very different. The parties which meet and fight are both champions of values, both defenders of good as they see it. Therein precisely lies the tragedy of their combat. Two of Franz Werfel's finest plays – 'Paulus unter den Juden' and 'Juarez und Maximilian' – show this in a most moving manner. The heart-rending scenes which he displays have plenty of parallels in the drama of Christianity's development, only that the outcome is not as catastrophic for the conservatives: unlike Gamaliel and Maximilian, they do not have to die. As for the progressives, theirs is undoubtedly all too frequently (as our account of Don Bosco has already shown) a life of trials and tribulations. Cases like St. Francis, who had his bishop on his side and generally encountered little hostility, are rare.[1] Even death may be the innovator's lot: the heartbreaking case of St. Joan of Arc – condemned and then rehabilitated – springs to mind at once. Yet her story does not belong in this chapter and volume which is concerned with the *micro-sociology* of religion, i.e. the *inner* life of religious societies. Her martyrdom was caused by the contemporary – the Hundred Years' – war. It was an incident in European rather than in ecclesiastical history. From the stake of St. Joan to that of John Hus is but a small step: the period is the same, and so is the reason for his execution. Protestants are likely to present their *acta martyrum* at this point. Those who fell a victim to the Inquisition (which was an institution of the state, though clerically staffed) and similar courts, met their fate, not so much because of a specifically religious, as because of an all-round revolutionary attitude – which does not mean that their elimination was justified or even justifiable. We are simply not concerned with them here. What we are concerned with are clashes *inside* the Church, like that between Netro and Gastaldi on the one hand, Bosco on the other, conflicts between the values and ideals of organization and conservation, and those of progression and reform, within the bosom of *one* unbroken and abiding Church.

Of course, the conflicts in question are not only due to the clash of values and ideals, they are also due to the clash of generations and personalities. Moulin has drawn our attention to the former aspect: 'In most cases, the founders and innovators were young and necessarily had to deal with old administrators who possessed a sharp sense of the requirements of both the hierarchy and . . .

[1] Cf. Workman, loc. cit., pp 308 and 309.

government.'[1] There is nothing accidental about this occurrence and recurrence of something like the father–son confrontation. A young man, a son, is not likely to be a bishop; an old man, a father, has usually made good and is beyond criticism and attack. The conflict of generations is therefore a regularly appearing, one might almost say, an essential feature of the dealings between saints and priests. But far more important still, and just as unavoidable, is the conflict of personalities in the narrower and narrowest sense of the word. Saints are by definition 'peculiar' people; they are not even 'normal' people in most instances; often they are downright 'odd'. If we go back to the very first glimmerings of the tension between sainthood and priesthood, to the apostolic and immediate post-apostolic age, we find the later troubles foreshadowed in the differentiation between the sedentary teacher and the itinerant prophet. We have drawn attention, in volume II,[2] to the mutual dislike between the Quakers Howgill, Burrough and Audland on the one hand and their 'friend' Collinson on the other; we have seen that Collinson, a stay-at-home, resented the intrusion of the wanderers Howgill, Burrough and Audland. This simply repeated an early phenomenon and is revealing to the typologist. Those who drift from place to place are not, psychologically, the same kind of people as those who settle down and stay put, and there is little to surprise one in the fact that they usually do not like each other. Harnack has explored and emphasized this fissiparous tendency and has shown that its implications are deeper than might be expected: an itinerant is inclined to see himself as belonging to everybody and nobody; he will think in universal terms; a sedentary man will conceive himself as belonging predominantly, if not exclusively, to his parish or diocese; he will think in local terms.[3] Most saints' troubles, up and down the centuries, were with the 'ordinary', i.e. the bishop of the locality. We have seen this, for instance, in our study of the Cluniacs and the Redemptorists.[4] This throws into high relief the great importance of the papal office – an office, to be sure, but not one that would induce its holder to sink down into a local-temporal pattern and to become over-conservative thereby. The world-wide character of the papacy has

---

[1] Moulin, loc. cit., p. 44. [2] Pp. 261 and 262.
[3] For a summary of Harnack's researches, cf. Lowrie, loc. cit., pp. 94, 99, also 246.
[4] Cf. vol. III, pp. 269 and 313.

also, in its best representatives, engendered wider, more generous attitudes towards innovators, i.e. saints. Their appeal has often been to the Holy See.

While these are some of the more specific strands in the etiology of the conflict between saints and priests, the most general cause is simply the fact that saints are more than life-size: whatever they are, they are to a superlative degree. It may be intellectuality, as in the case of St. Thomas Aquinas; it may be lack of intellectuality, as in the case of St. John Baptist Vianney; it may be almost any trait, as long as that trait is truly outstanding or rather standing out. The saint is by definition the man to whom everyday standards cannot be applied; the priest is the man to whom everyday standards can be applied, and, even more importantly, who tends to apply everyday standards. Here lies the last root of the case of Bosco *versus* Gastaldi or Gastaldi *versus* Bosco, and of the innumerable parallels which, if we knew all the details, would fill tomes as voluminous as the *Acta Sanctorum*.

No study has more convincingly argued the individuality and individualism of the saints in contradistinction to the collectivity and collectivism of the priesthood than Albrecht Dürer's last and, by common consent, greatest canvas (incorrectly known as) *The Four Apostles*. Not only do the portraits sharply underline the distinctions between age-categories, but each presents its subject as extremely characteristic of his generation: John of youth, Mark of early manhood, Paul of later manhood, and Peter of old age. But this is the least of the contrasts between the Apostles, and hence the smallest indication of their incomparability, brought out in this sublime work of art which tries to interpret apostleship as such and hence sainthood. There is a sharp confrontation between the left-hand panel of John and Peter and the right-hand panel of Paul and Mark: the former pair is a pair of contemplatives, the latter a pair of activists. Peter and John's prayerful nature is as magnificently communicated as Mark and Paul's impatience to do and fight. Yet if the distinctions between age-categories and directions of religious activity still have something of the general or typological about them, the final, most impressive and most expressive discrimination which the picture establishes shows us the four 'apostles', and, by implication, any and every saint, as unique personalities.[1] Many historians call the masterpiece not *The Four Apostles*, but *The Four*

[1] Cf. above, p. 161, note 1.

Temperaments: John is the sanguinic, Peter the phlegmatic, Mark the choleric and Paul the melancholic. The lesson which the painter wants to convey – and which a factual-historical, descriptive and documented comparative study would convey with equal convincingness, though hardly with equal brilliance – is negative rather than positive: these men cannot be brought on to a common denominator. They are extraordinary; they are – we must repeat it, there is no other word for it – unique.[1] And what is extraordinary and unique fits ill into the mechanisms, and even the organisms, of practical life.

There is, so we must conclude, something inescapable, something fated and fatal, about the conflict of saints and priests. One might be inclined therefore to shrug one's shoulders and say: this is human nature all over, or *c'est la vie*. And he would be right. Nevertheless, the strain and the struggle is not entirely commonplace, simply because the saints are not commonplace. We have seen above[2] that it is the distinguishing mark of religious, in opposition to political, charisma that it avoids the use of worldly means, that it fights by not fighting, that, in St. Paul's words, it confidently asserts: 'Power is made perfect in infirmity' (II Corinthians XII, 9). The conduct of the saints when beset by persecution was similar to the conduct of Christ Himself. The priest Brictio, who never tired of slandering St. Martin of Tours, might have been removed from office by the latter's intervention, but he would do nothing towards this end: better to suffer than to inflict suffering, he thought. 'If Christ bore with Judas' – these were his words according to Sulpicius Severus – 'why should I not bear with Brictio?'[3] Roughly fifteen hundred and fifty years lie between the birth of Martin and the death of Bosco, and innumerable instances of saintly forbearance in the face of priestly pressures might be culled from them. We cannot display them all, but the reader may take our assertion for provable and indeed proven, though the detailed proofs are scattered through hundreds of biographies. We have given one example from the fourth century; let us take the other from the nineteenth. When Cardinal Cagliero testified to the holiness of the Founder of the Salesian Order, this is what he said about the saint's differences with his archbishop: 'This cross

[1] Cf. Grote, L., *Dürer*, Geneva 1965, pp. 113 et seq., and Brion, M., *Dürer*: *His Work and Life*, New York 1960, pp. 286 et seq.
[2] Cf. p. 32. [3] Workman, loc. cit., pp. 103 and 104.

which the Lord laid upon his shoulders, never drew a groan from
his lips, nor an exclamation of impatience, nor any attempt at
retaliation. And God knows the time he spent merely in self-defence.
He bore the burden with courage, calmness, and humility, without
losing his interior peace for a moment, without interrupting his
apostolate for a minute. Such cheerfulness of mind and such enduring union with God amidst the hardest trials is indeed the mark
of the saints.'[1]

Outwardly, at a first glance, it might appear that the non-
combativeness of the saints is due to their weakness, their despond-
ency, but this impression turns on closer inspection into the very
opposite: they are too strong, and above all too confident, to take
attacks on them all too seriously. They know they will win in the
end. When Don Bosco undertook to build the church of Our
Lady, Help of Christians, in Turin (a tremendous enterprise which
may well have inspired the rumours that he was megalomaniac and
mad), and soon there was no cash with which to carry on, he was
not in the least ruffled. 'He never worried . . . He was sure that it
was part of his work in this world to build that church; if, then, he
did all in his power to bring it to pass, God would do the rest.'[2]

The greatest evidence of saintly strength lies not, however, in
their ability to manage technical tasks like the building of a magnificent church without adequate money to pay for it, it lies in their
ascendancy over men. Don Bosco was mainly an apostle of the
young, and boys took to him, discipline and all, as if it were the
most natural thing in the world. 'Everything in him seemed
ordinary, quite ordinary,' one of his pupils later reported, 'yet he
could have led us wherever he wanted. It must have been God who
spoke to us through him and bound us to the man.'[3] In case this
sounds too theological, let us slightly change the wording and say
that Love spoke through him – for the Christian the two terms are
identical in meaning anyway. But a man who is love personified is,
by definition, in possession of genuine charisma, a charismatic
leader.

It is, however, one thing to captivate trusting boys and quite
another to impress mistrustful men, confirmed anti-clericals for
instance, but Bosco managed that equally well. In 1865, the rela-

[1] Cit. Sheppard, loc. cit., p. 115.
[2] Ibid., pp. 162 and 163. Cf. also p. 85.
[3] Cit. ibid., p. 163. Cf. also p. 85.

tions between the Curia and the Italian government (then in Florence) were at a low ebb indeed. Some old bishops were in exile; some new bishops were prevented from entering their office; and there were no fewer than one hundred and eight vacant sees. Whom did Pius IX choose, to prevail on the political power-holders to change their obstructive attitude, to begin to co-operate? One of his many refined diplomats supposedly expert at this sort of thing? By no means. He called on Don Giovanni Bosco, to all appearances a slightly ridiculous village *parroco* with bulging pockets, one of them usually full of candy for children, the other full of half-read proof sheets for some printer. Would men like Cavour or Crispi or Lanza even deign to talk to a type like that? Not only did they talk to him, but they showed him a deference that was simply amazing. The exiled bishops were at once allowed to return; by 1871, the number of vacant sees was under seventy, and Bosco – Bosco, in law a little nobody! – was asked to draw up a list of nominees for all of them. Characteristically – paradoxically – Bosco used to say: 'My political views are those of the Lord's prayer.' This, surely is the height of naiveté. Yet this did not prevent him from wielding more power than professed politicians. The solution of the conundrum is simple: it was the authority indwelling in his person – in other words, his personal charisma – which allowed him to impose his will on others, friends and foes alike.[1]

Jumping back across the centuries and coming once again to St. Martin of Tours, our other chosen example, we have not, of course, the same abundant documentation, but Sulpicius Severus is a sufficient witness all the same for it is, in this context, about his own experiences that he speaks. When he, in his *Vita* of the Saint, describes his visit to him, he recalls how Martin insisted on serving him, even to the extent of washing his feet. Naturally Sulpicius was embarrassed and mortified – how could he allow this? Yet he was too paralysed to do anything about it. 'I did not have the courage to refuse and to resist – so much was I in awe of his mighty personality,'[2] he recalls, and we may believe him. One does not say 'no' to a man like Martin of Tours.

In *The Two Sources of Morality and Religion*, Henri Bergson has

[1] Ibid., pp. 107, 117, 118.
[2] *De Vita Beati Martini Liber Unus*, 25, *Patrologia Latina*, as quoted, vol. XX, Paris 1845, col. 174.

started a most intriguing question to which, in the nature of things, there can be no detailed and documented answer.[1] What has been the relationship of saints and priests in the confessional? The outer facts are clear; at the inner explanation we can but guess. 'As to theological teaching in general,' Bergson says about the mystics, men and women with a direct vision of God, like St. Teresa of Avila and St. John of the Cross, 'they seem to accept it with utter docility, and in particular to obey their confessors'. Friedrich Heiler and Evelyn Underhill, whose knowledge of the history of mysticism was still wider, fully confirm this observation.[2] 'It would indeed be interesting,' Bergson writes, and one cannot but agree with him, 'to study closely the relations between the spiritual adviser and the soul seeking counsel.' In all probability, 'it would be found that, of the two, he that has meekly acquiesced in yielding to guidance has more than once, no less meekly, become the guide'.[3]

But we do not have to grope in the darkness of confessional boxes for proof of the ascendancy of the saints: we can clearly see it in broad daylight. Where are their opponents now? Who indeed would know today that there ever was a priest called Brictio, if it were not for the undying glory of Martin of Tours? Who would know that there ever were archbishops called Riccardi di Netro or Gastaldi, complete as they were with mitre, infula and crozier, if it were not for the fame of simple and humble Don Bosco? If we may venture a bold simile, we should say that attempts to check the saints in their courses are like attempts to contain a mighty river: it may be held back for a while, it may be forced to rise higher, but in the end it will overflow all obstacles and be on its predetermined way, an elemental force which nobody and nothing can restrain.

But at this point our argument is in jeopardy. Have we not vastly overstepped the mark? Have we not seriously overstated the power of the charismatic man? Is it not true that priests decide who is, and who is not, to be called a saint? And is this decision not reached in and by a legal process, the process of canonization, which runs through precisely predetermined phases (*venerabilis, beatus, sanctus*) and leads up to a formal judgment, and, in favourable cases, to a no less formal promulgation? Do not the four ugly words and things – routinization, bureaucratization, legalization and formalization –

---

[1] Paperback ed., Garden City, N.Y., n.d., p. 247.
[2] Heiler, loc. cit., pp. 537–9; Underhill, loc. cit., p. 126.
[3] Bergson, loc. cit.

reappear here and demand, with an especially strident voice, and with an especially well-founded claim, their due – acknowledgment as descriptive and truthful labels of what has happened in reality? Let us see.

First of all, a word on terminology. In this treatise we have, as is right and proper, used the expression 'saint' in its established sociological sense, the sense which we share with Max Weber, to describe a man in possession of a decidedly personal charisma. In ecclesiastical usage, two different definitions are current, one considerably wider, the other somewhat narrower. According to the former, every friend of God is one of His saints – every man who is on the way to heaven, who finds himself in a 'state of grace'; and, of course, every man who has made it to heaven, who has departed in a state of grace. Here no extraordinary qualities are presupposed; on the contrary. According to the latter definition, not every friend of God, and not even every charismatic man, is a saint, but only such as the Church has singled out as possible inter-cessors for their fellow-men, i.e. individuals of such outstanding merit, e.g. of such heroic virtue, that their charismatic power not only *was* great among men, but still *is* (in faith) great – even with God. 'The Catholic saint,' so Delooz has summed up the essential criterion, is 'a personality to whom the Church accords an official cult.'[1] The men of personal charisma, the born religious leaders, are seen as a pool, so to speak, from which some are selected in order to be 'raised to the altar'. That not every potential saint (in this official sense of the word) has advanced from *de facto* to *de jure* sanctity is obvious from the fact that new names are from time to time placed on and in the calendar, occasionally names of persons whose death occurred several centuries ago. There are even cases where such final promotion has now become rather unlikely, for instance that of Fra Matteo da Bascio who initiated and for a moment headed the Capuchin Order.[2] Clearly, the step from saint in the sociological sense, saint with s, lower case, to Saint in the ecclesiastical sense, Saint with capital s, is not automatic. What is needed, in addition to the qualities displayed in life, is their valida-tion by a Church court, differently expressed, the seal of authority, and this is the point where the power of the priesthood over the

---

[1] Delooz, P., 'Pour une Etude Sociologique de la Sainteté Canonisée dans l'Eglise Catholique', *Archives de la Sociologie des Religions*, 1962, p. 18.
[2] Cf. our vol. III, p. 388.

saints appears to lie. The question is only whether it is more real than apparent or the other way round.

In order to be quite sure that we shall do justice to this aspect of Church life, we must descend to the very root of things, to the formative period of Christendom, for it is a genetic analysis which, here as so often, holds and yields the key to the truth. And if we proceed in this manner, if we penetrate to the period when the division between personal and collective charisma first took form, we encounter not only saints and priests but also an undesirable third party – the charlatan. Swindlers, alas, have played a considerable part in the history of religion: Sabbatai Zevi, for instance, among the Jews. Their presence even in the apostolic age is an unhappy certainty – witness the First Epistle of St. John (IV, 1): 'Dearly beloved, believe not every spirit, but try the spirits if they be of God: because many false prophets are gone out into the world.' Similar in implication is a passage from St. Paul's First Epistle to the Thessalonians (V, 21): 'Prove all things; hold fast that which is good.' In a document called *Didache* or *Teachings of the Apostles*, which may not be much younger than the Pauline letters, a thoroughly nasty type makes his appearance: the *Christemporos* or 'man who makes a good thing – a business – out of Christ'. These were wandering prophets who had the tendency to stay in a place so long as the brethren would house and feed them, and who would unconcernedly move on when no more was to be got from the local congregation. The *Didache* suggests, no doubt realistically, that board and lodging should be restricted to two or three days. Thereafter the 'saint' should work. When he resumed his journey, he should be provided with provender but not with cash, for cash is precisely what the *Christemporoi* seek. All this is said to divide the chaff from the wheat. The respect expressed for the true saint in the *Didache* is undivided and undiminished. Yet he must submit to judgment at the hand of the community. The community, so the document says, 'will understand on the right hand as well as on the left', i.e. it will know how to divide what is genuine from what is false.[1] In these words we have before us, in a most tangible form, the inception of important later developments up to and including the process of canonization. The holiness of the holy man is not to be doubted, but it is to be tested and tried. And why should it not be? The truth will out: *magna est veritas et prevalebit.*

[1] Meyer, loc. cit., vol. III, pp. 253, 261, 577; Campenhausen, loc. cit., p. 78.

The technical term used to describe the investigating function of the community is 'the discernment of spirits', a word inspired by I John IV, 1, quoted above. The need to test and prove the prophets loomed very large in the life of the early Christian communities, and Campenhausen has given it his closest attention.[1] What strikes the reader who goes through his fact-filled, well-documented pages is a certain contradictoriness. On the one hand, the congregations are fully and painfully aware of the difficulties of the task; on the other hand, they show a supreme confidence in their ability to meet its challenge.

As for the difficulties, they were due to the fact, or rather the belief, that evil spirits could perform whatever good spirits could. Demons, for instance, might work miracles or at least deceive men sufficiently to give them the impression that there had been an inexplicable happening. The same applied to the traditional hallmark of prophecy-prediction of future events. Demons could either see into the future or shape the future so as to fit in with the prophecy, or, again, at least create the delusion that the forecasts have been confirmed by subsequent constellations. In face of the failure of these tests, the congregations fall back on more sober observations. Was the 'saint' in question interested or disinterested in material gain? And what was his general style of living? Did his conduct, especially in the ordinary affairs of everyday life, give evidence of that deep morality by which we can know the true friend of God and man? The general guide-post was, of course, the Gospel: 'Beware of false prophets who come to you in the clothing of sheep, but inwardly they are ravening wolves. By their fruits you shall know them. Do men gather grapes of thorns or figs of thistles?' (Matthew, VII, 15 and 16).

It is difficult to believe that it was in every case easy to be certain. Both the evidence used and the conclusions drawn from it must at times have been rather problematical. Yet it was, and it remained, the deep conviction of the congregations that they were not deceived, at least not for long, that they knew a hypocrite and a charlatan when they saw one. This confidence is reflected in the *Apocalypse*: 'Unto the angel [i.e. the bishop] of the church of Ephesus write: These things saith he who holdeth the seven stars in his right hand, who walketh in the midst of the seven golden candlesticks: I know thy works and thy labour and thy patience

[1] Loc. cit., especially pp. 202 and 203.

and how thou canst not bear them that are evil. And thou hast tried them who say they are apostles and are not: and hast found them liars' (II, 1 and 2). The basic conviction was that the true saint would willingly submit to scrutiny by the community, whereas the faker would tend to shun the light of day: he would operate in corners and conventicles, whereas the true saint would expose himself freely and fully to the judgment of all. Beneath this policy and political philosophy, there were two beliefs very different in character: one commonsensical, one might almost say, Benthamite, the other metaphysical and profoundly religious. The commonsensical and Benthamite belief was trust in the power of public opinion: publicize the facts and you have done all you need to do to insure that the truth will prevail. The metaphysical and profoundly religious platform was the conviction – part and parcel of the often unexpressed, yet ever present Catholic creed – that the community as a collectivity is the seat of divine wisdom and truth. We have seen what the Gospel words 'Where there are two or three gathered together in my name, there am I in the midst of them' mean.[1] But they yet understate the basic Christian–Catholic belief. Christ is not only *with* His Church, He *is*, in a sense, His Church, for the Church is the Body of Christ. The words which Paul heard on the road to Damascus – 'Saul, Saul, why persecutest thou me?' (Acts IX, 4) – imply a *total* identification of the Founder with His Foundation. Therefore, the community will not err; therefore, also, the community has the right to examine, and to pass judgment on, all aspirants to religious leadership. The 'discernment of spirits' is a charismatic gift in the possession of *all* believers *collectively*, as the power to impress the masses is a charismatic gift in the possession of some personalities individually. Only together do the two constitute the whole Church.

This, then, is the deepest root of all later dealings with emergent saints, up to and including the process of canonization. But the control of the holy community over the holy individual was not restricted to the testing and to the confirmation of a man's personal charisma. Characteristic is also, for instance, the manner in which glossolaly – the 'speaking in tongues' – was handled. The assumption was certainly that in and through an inspired man, the Holy Spirit Himself was speaking. Yet it was a concomitant and complementary conviction that in the believing group the Holy Spirit was

[1] Cf. above, pp. 138 et seq.

also present and enabled them to interpret and indeed to judge –
to accept or (if the inspiration was not genuine) to reject – what they
had heard. Once again, Campenhausen can be our expert witness:
'The prophet, as Paul sees him, never stands alone; he stands in a
closed rank with other prophets who possess the same power and
is, by his spirit, connected with them and the whole community . . .
The prophets should not contradict, but complement each other
. . . The last decision, however, rests always with the community as
such and is not left to the individual . . . It is significant that Paul,
where he calls for watchfulness and the testing of spirits . . . never
addresses a special class or group of persons . . . In principle, there
is no *élite* in the congregation and the men of the spirit do not form,
for Paul, a "pneumatic aristocracy" . . . The authority which they
exert, is not absolute . . . This applies even to their witnessing [their
predication] which . . . is to be judged from case to case and to be
tried for its truth . . . The "men of the spirit" are, precisely as
carriers of charisma, referred to the community in which and
through which the spirit of Christ asserts itself, and this Spirit
alone is sovereign.'[1]

Even the small and to us uninteresting word *amen* has in this
context its definite significance. It betokened originally the assent
of the congregation to any act or prayer or preaching: 'So be it.'
If it has shed its liveliness, this is due, not so much to our loss of
rights or religiosity, as to our possession of forms of worship (in
the widest sense of the word) which have been proved and tested
already, and which must be – like gold that has been refined to the
last degree of perfection – acceptable to everybody. Originally it
was the great collective safeguard against the vagaries of ejacula-
tory prayer which (as later sectarian experiments have amply
shown) is apt to lead to results which are embarrassing rather than
elevating. But who was it who said *amen* and thereby confirmed an
act, a prayer, or a preaching? The people accidentally present? By
no means. To think so is to think in individualistic-nominalistic
terms and these are at variance with the Church's ingrained collectivism and philosophical realism. No, *amen* is said by the
community as such, the community which is more than the sum of
its members, which is the Body of Christ, which *is* Christ. 'To the
angel of the church of Laodicea write,' says *The Apocalypse*, 'These

[1] Campenhausen, loc. cit., pp. 67 and 68. Cf. also Meyer, loc. cit., vol. III,
p. 221, and Kohlmeyer, loc. cit., pp. 33 and 34.

things saith the Amen, the faithful and true witness, who is the beginning of the creation of God' (III, 14). It is, of course, Christ who is called *The Amen* here:[1] they, therefore, who say *amen* in the true spirit truly confirm the truth, for their voice is divine.

We see here once again what we have seen several times before, namely that the Church is indeed what she calls herself, a *societas perfecta*, a perfect society, in the sense that she has the basic unity-within-multiplicity or individuality-*versus*-collectivity which is characteristic of all human societies. But with Catholicism at any rate, the emphasis lies on unity and collectivity rather than on multiplicity and individuality. It was therefore soon the common conception and conviction that a judgment, in order to be true, would have to be a universal judgment: *securus iudicat orbis terrarum*, St. Augustine proclaimed,[2] and not long afterwards St. Vincent of Lerins asserted, in a happy formulation, that we should believe *quod ubique, quod semper, quod ab omnibus creditum est.*[3] This principle, which has all the diversity and all the unity, in a word, all the catholicity of Catholicism behind it, deeply influenced the confirmation of the sainthood of the saints. From the local congregation, the right to judge drifted to the dioceses, and from the dioceses to the world community. On February 2, 993, Pope John XV canonized St. Ulrich of Augsburg. This was the earliest known papal canonization. It marks a milestone in the history of the veneration of the saints. Another is the year 1234, in which the Supreme Pontiff reserved to himself the exclusive right to proceed to canonizations.[4]

Soon stricter safeguards were introduced. There was not only what might be called the test-by-space, the insistence that all parts of the Church, wherever situated, would have to approve of the promotion of a person to saintly status, there was also a parallel test-by-time, a delay sufficient to ensure that a man's *fama sanctitatis* or odour of sanctity was not a mere one-day-wonder, as quickly dissipated as it was asserted. And there was above all the use of judicial methods in the preparation of the final judgment. It is a

[1] Cf. also II Corinthians I, 19 et seq.
[2] 'The entire world should speak in judgment', *Contra Epistolam Parmeniani*, III, 24, *Patrologia Latina*, as quoted, vol. XLIII, Paris 1865, col. 101.
[3] 'What has been believed at all places, at all times, and by all', *Primum Commonitorium*, 2, *Patrologia Latina*, as quoted, vol. L, Paris 1865, col. 640.
[4] Delooz, *loc. cit.*, p. 19; Workman, loc. cit., p. 193.

common human experience that nothing serves better to elicit the facts, and thereby the truth, than a contest – the pitting of defence against attack. That alone creates the tension which induces the parties to put forward their best efforts, to mobilize all their forces. In the process of canonization, *causae promotor* and *fidei defensor* (the figure jocularly known as *advocatus diaboli*) are matched in this way. Humanly speaking, there is no better safeguard of success in the endeavour to ascertain whether or not a man or woman deserves to be raised to the altar.

The detail does not concern us. What does concern us is the question as to whether this evolution has delivered the saints up to the priests, and the answer is very clearly in the negative. Perhaps we can use here, for purposes of exposition and explanation, a comparison with the academic establishment. It has happened from time to time, and we must be glad that it did, that rank outsiders, men with no formal schooling or at least no final degree, made signal contributions to scientific and technological endeavour. A. J. Cronin discusses an instance in his great novel, *The Citadel*, which, far from being a mere piece of fiction, is in fact a medical man's impassioned indictment of the medical profession.[1] In such cases, the professional brotherhood was as a rule at first thoroughly hostile to the intruder; sometimes he was met with sarcasm and ridicule, sometimes with legal or even physical interference, sometimes indeed with both. But if he stood his ground, carried on with his work, and finally succeeded in demonstrating the value of his innovation, he could no longer be treated in this way. At this juncture, the fact that he has no schooling and degree begins regularly to be regarded as doubly embarrassing: embarrassing to him because he is exposed as a self-made man and because something is seen to be missing in him; but embarrassing also to the profession as a whole because something is seen to be missing in them, because one of their limitations has been exposed, not to speak of their lack of generosity and slowness in recognizing a great contribution when it comes along. In this situation a special fig-leaf is conveniently used to cover both nakednesses: an honorary doctorate is conferred and, presto!, everything is changed. The outsider has become an insider; he can feel that his success is now not only complete, but also confirmed; and the profession has re-established its precious prestige: now it is one of their number who

[1] Cf. ed. Boston 1938, pp. 311 et seq. and 397.

has done the great deed, and all advances which have been achieved in the field are due to them, and none to a stranger. Of course, this will only happen if and when the amateur's triumph is absolutely overwhelming, when it is impossible and unthinkable for the professionals to ignore him any longer. Nothing else and nothing less will force them to pay tribute to one who first had painfully disturbed their circles.

We have said: nothing else and nothing less will force them to pay tribute to him. We might as well have said, with a little poetizing and exaggeration: nothing else and nothing less will force them to raise him to the altar. For the case of the canonized saint lies precisely parallel to that of the *doctor honoris causa*, as against the seminary priest or the ordinary graduate who has gone through the academic mill. In either case, the near-impossible has come true, the weed of the common has flowered more beautifully than the blooms in the garden. Only one parish priest, it is said, has ever been canonized: Jean-Baptiste Vianney, the man who failed in all his seminary examinations, was ordained by a kindly (or inspired) bishop against the advice of his teachers, and given the worst parish in the whole of France, the (then) dreadful hamlet of Ars – a fine exception with which to confirm the rule. Only one parish priest has been canonized: but the number of hedge preachers who have come to be included in the calendar is legion.

Sometimes there has even been an attempt to pretend that this charismatic man or that, though to all appearances a hedge preacher, has in reality been a priest. St. Benedict of Nursia and St. Francis of Assisi, for instance, were, according to some legends, in holy orders. Historical research has made this very unlikely.[1] It matters little whether formally they were or not. Neither, surely, was in fact a typical priest. Francis in particular cannot, by any stretch of the imagination, be forced into this category. A vagrant cannot be compared to a parish administrator, nor can an angel in human form. The Reverend Francesco Bernardone – the very idea is absurd. And because it *is* absurd, because there must be a place of honour for the revolutionary leaders as well as for the conservative hierarchy, a *different* place, a place of their own, the class of canonized saints was developed by the Church at large and is attended to and tended by the priesthood.

[1] Cf. Workman, loc. cit., p. 19; Blazovich, loc. cit., p. 123; Cowley, P., *Franciscan Rise and Fall*, London 1933, p. 59.

In the study of canonization which we have already quoted,[1] Pierre Delooz has spoken of a 'triumph of the groups which the episcopate would have liked to eliminate'.[2] There is some exaggeration to this statement, but it is substantially correct all the same. We do not have precise statistics – much is still to be studied in this field – but even a cursory reading of the calendar will reveal that most saints have come from the world of religious protest, the world which has produced the revolutionary orders, and only few from the world of religious respectability, the strata which have maintained the ecclesiastical machine. But what is still more significant is the fact that (as Delooz points out) the organization (i.e. routinization, bureaucratization, legalization and formalization) of the canonization procedure has led to an *in*creased, and not a *de*creased, number of founders and foundresses of orders or institutes being raised to the status of official saints.[3] And, on closer consideration, this will prove to be easily understandable.

For what is it that forces a name through the dark and tortuous alleyways of the canonization procedure and ensures that it will in the end emerge into the sublime light of official sanctity? Where do the energies come from which make a person into a *venerabilis*, and a *venerabilis* into a *beatus*, and a *beatus* into a *sanctus*? They rise up from the very depths of the Universal Church, from the anonymous masses of the faithful. It is not really the power of the priests which decides who does, and who does not, become a saint; they are merely the executors of a stronger one's will; and that will is the will of the community, the general will as Rousseau called it. It is precisely in the context of canonization that we can clearly see that the hierarchy, who superficially look like the controllers, are in reality controlled.

We have quoted Delooz to the effect that the Catholic saint is a personality to whom the Church accords an official cult.[4] This is true, but a somewhat more complex formulation of the same definition will be much more revealing. The Catholic saint is a personality in whose case an unofficial, but broadly based and toughly persistent popular cult is followed and confirmed by an official, i.e. ecclesiastically recommended, veneration and invocation. The cult *de facto*, so we may also express it, leads to a cult *de jure*. Those who sit in judgment on a *causa* of canonization do not

---

[1] Cf. above, p. 197.   [2] Ibid., p. 29. Cf. also Moulin, loc. cit., pp. 52–4.
[3] Delooz, loc. cit., p. 29.   [4] Cf. above, p. 197.

make a decision, they only put it into words; they may appear to be leading, in fact, however, they are following a leader. More technically formulated, their verdict is declaratory, not constitutive. What constitutes a saint's sainthood, even a saint's formal sainthood, is the general will. In this area, nobody can speak with greater authority than Christopher Dawson, a truly top-ranking Church historian. He asserts the presence of a 'democratic element' in the making of sainthood and writes: 'It is always the voice of the people that counts. In distinction from the hierarchical character of the Church, recognition of saints comes from the laity: the popular cult precedes the Church's recognition.'[1] Delooz, in his more narrow and technical investigation, has fully confirmed this thesis. He speaks of *un problème d'énergétique sociale*, i.e. of a case in which the elementary power of the community asserts itself, and says: 'An unorganized popular pressure remains very generally the motive force in the official consecrations of saints.'[2]

In fact, if we have so far confronted the fruitful tensions between saints and priests, we begin to see here another, if kindred, antithesis as fruitful as the first: the tension between priesthood and laity. The archetypal situation is an initial clash between a popular demand for canonization on the one hand and ecclesiastical, or rather hierarchical, resistance on the other. Subjectively, this opposition or obduracy may be no more than simple neophobia, a negative trait, but objectively it has an entirely positive function to fulfil. If we step for a moment outside the Christian culture area, we see what is apt to happen: a cult – possibly problematical in character – may quickly spring up and quickly die down again. In *A Passage to India*, that profound study of both the English and the Muslim and Hindu minds, a certain Mrs Moor has won the hearts of the natives: she has taken the side of an unjustly accused Indian against his accusers, her own people. While the drama approaches its climax, while the court is sitting which will decide the fate of the victim (happily only half-victim) of injustice, strange sounds are heard floating in through the open windows:

> 'Esmiss Esmoor
> Esmiss Esmoor
> Esmiss Esmoor
> Esmiss Esmoor . . .'

[1] Dawson, loc, cit., p. 291.   [2] Delooz, loc. cit., p. 28.

An invocation: a saint had been born in the popular mind. Later, 'a legend sprang up that an Englishman had killed his mother for trying to save an Indian's life – and there was just enough truth in this to cause annoyance to the authorities . . . At one period two distinct tombs containing Esmiss Esmoor's remains were reported: one by the tannery, the other up near the goods station. Mr. McBryde visited them both and saw signs of the beginning of a cult – earthenware saucers and so on. Being an experienced official, he did nothing to irritate it, and after a week or so, the rash died down'.[1] This account may be taken from a book of fiction, but it is none the less entirely factual. The people of India, as the natives of South Africa, and many, many others, have often reacted in precisely this way to potential prophets in their midst.

The 'discernment of spirits' has been very much more effective in the West, and there are several reasons for this superiority, above all, of course, the West's greater all-round rationality. But one of them, and not the least, has been the salutary intervention of established authority. We have mentioned the year 1234 as one of the turning points in the history of canonizations. The detail is instructive. Some time after 1170, Pope Alexander III intervened in far-away Sweden to inhibit the formation of a cult: the supposed saint around whom it was gathering was known to have been an alcoholic. By his action, the Pope did not wish to intimate that the candidate was not a saint in the wider sense of the word, a soul that would see blessedness in heaven, for it is permissible to hope that ordinary human weaknesses will be forgiven; nor did he necessarily deny that the candidate had admirable qualities as well as less admirable ones, like a craving for strong drink; even the power of religiously inspiring the masses was not expressly doubted; but Alexander felt that an acknowledged saint is being offered to the human race as a model, and to serve as a model – to deserve to serve as a model – a man had to be beyond reproach in *every* respect. More simply expressed, the Holy See, in the situation which we have described, insisted on standards, and insistence on standards is indeed the *raison d'être* as well as the hallmark and the secret of the canonization procedure. There was no autocratic intervention; there was much rather, to use a traditional phrase, an appeal from the people ill informed to the people well informed; the principle of decision – the legal norm, if one will – on which administrative

[1] Forster, E. M., *A Passage to India*, ed. New York 1924, pp. 225, 256, 257.

action was based was the common ethos of the Christian–Catholic Church. And the masses validated the negative verdict of the Curia by simply dropping the half-formed cult. Indeed, so obvious was the reasonableness of Alexander's step that his decree was, about sixty years later, under Gregory IX, inserted into the collection of decretals which formed the abiding substance of canon law, and thereby became one of the permanent bases on which the 'discernment of spirits' has rested ever since.[1]

To sum up: in no sense can it be said that the priestly bureaucracy *makes* a saint; it merely *identifies* him; and even in the act of identification it follows the lead of the faithful. To use religious language: it is the clergy which responds *amen* to the people's voice. That voice is raised first and it also has the last say.

The study of priesthood and sainthood, and of their relationship, brings the sociologist in the end up against the simplest and yet greatest of all social phenomena – the division and integration of labour. It is one task to preserve what has come down from the past: it is another to introduce what will lead forward into the future. Therefore there must be priests as well as saints, and saints as well as priests, and a laity which will listen to both. Catholicism has always accepted the principle of the splitting and sharing of functions: we see it here, and we shall see it again. Protestantism has demurred and resisted. And yet it was a leading Protestant, the Methodist Herbert Workman, who has most clearly felt the truth of the matter. Distinguishing the normalist (or conservative) and the enthusiast (or reformer), this is what he says in his classical book: 'The presence of a norm is one of the most constant phenomena of Church life. This it is that so often crushes the reformer with that sense of opposition within the camp, worse than any opposition from without. This it is that so often leads to a species of civil war within the Church itself, when the swords of the normalist and the enthusiast are turned against each other rather than against the common foe. In this also, more than anything else, we may see the source of the schisms and splits which have furrowed deep in both the Anglican and Nonconformist Churches. But in the case of Rome

[1] Delooz, loc. cit., p. 28. The date of the decree *Audivimus* is incorrectly given as 1190. It should have been 1171–1180. Cf. *Regesta Pontificum Romanorum*, edd. Jaffé, P., *et al.*, vol. II, Leipzig 1888, p. 355, No. 13546. For the decretal of Gregory IX, cf. *Corpus Iuris Canonici*, ed. Friedberg, E., Leipzig 1881, vol. III, col. 650.

It is interesting how much quotation there is from Dr Herbert Workman an almost forgotten Methodist historian!

it has been otherwise . . . The Church of Rome would have used Wesley and Booth to found new orders within herself, whose zeal and enthusiasm would have strengthened rather than weakened the Church.'[1] This statement is, surely, more than hypothetical. The likes of Wesley and Booth in the Catholic fold – their opposite numbers, as we might colloquially say – have, in point of fact, founded new orders and have become canonized saints.

The institution of a canonized sainthood, however, as indeed the institution of an ordained priesthood with a *character indelebilis*, comes up against a basic Protestant principle: that of religious equality. All, so Protestant doctrine, at least in its purest form, runs, are called to the same consummation: Christian perfection. Differences are therefore invidious. And yet at this decisive point the Methodist Workman sides with Rome against Wittenberg and Geneva (and even his own denomination). 'Are all called to be ministers?' he asks. 'Are all called to be missionaries? Is the same measure of self-sacrifice demanded from every child of God? . . . Is the sacrifice of Abraham – "thy son, thine only son Isaac" – an incident in every life? Is the command: Go sell all that thou hast and give to the poor, of universal application? Are there no martyrs whose glorious end we could no longer imitate, however much our desire? When put in this form, the question answers itself.'[2] There is an organic place for an *élite*, or even for two *élites*, in Christian life.

The questions which Workman so emphatically raises have indeed been answered unambiguously by the Catholic communion. Speaking of the conflict between subjective sanctity and objective authority, one of her most widely acclaimed protagonists in the twentieth century, Karl Adam, has asserted that 'both these factors are necessary for the life of the Church. The Spirit of Pentecost must always and will always awaken new life. Ever and anon it will touch the depths of the Church's soul and set free mighty impulses and stirring movements. But so that these movements may not come to nothing, but may be permanently fruitful, they must be guided by Church authority by means of rules and laws, fixed ordinances and regulations. So personal piety requires that the Church regulate it, and define it and give it strict form, if it is not to ebb uselessly away. But on the other hand the form needs the flow of experience if it is not little by little to be-

[1] Workman, loc. cit., pp. 333 and 334.   [2] Ibid., pp. 335 and 336.

come rigid and crusted over . . . In the right co-ordination of these two factors lies the secret of the Church's vigorous life'.[1]

Of course, the difference, in this detail, between Catholicism and Protestantism is far from absolute. Catholicism, too, demands that all – all without exception – should try to put on Christ, to become saintly and saintlike, if not technically sainted. This is the reason why the Holy Man from Assisi is so often held up as the model of models, for – as the medieval *Meditationes Vitae Christi* have it – 'St. Francis became, as it were, the picture of Christ and was transformed at all points into Jesus, completing and finishing this work by the impression of the stigmata.'[2] But Catholics take their clue from the mercy of their Lord: they know that more than a very remote and partial identification is beyond the power of most men, and they are prepared to forgive, if not to forget, men's creaturely weakness. They are also by tradition inclined to make a distinction between the personal and the functional. Personally, there is no contrast, no wall, between God's children. A layman or a priest can rise up into the ranks of acknowledged sainthood, and many have done so, from humble country girls like Bernadette Soubirous to exalted aristocrats and hierarchs like Carlo Borromeo. Already under the Old Dispensation, priests like Ezechiel and Zacharias could turn into prophets;[3] why should it be otherwise under the New? But, in the Church as in the State, the uniformity of basic civic duties is in no way incompatible with a multiplicity of specific higher functions. All cells are in a manner equal in nature and importance, and yet they form, and belong to, very different individual organs. Societies, be they secular or sacred, are, like bodies, systems within which associated and antagonistic sub-systems cohere, conflict, coexist and co-operate.

We have said above that the study of priesthood and sainthood, and of their relationships, brings us up against the simplest and yet greatest of all social phenomena, the division and integration of labour. That is true; yet it leads us even deeper and further. For behind the division of labour, there hides the fact that a society is in its essence a multiplicity, a collection of individuals ever ready to go their own way, and behind the integration of labour is the

---

[1] Adam, loc. cit., p. 256. [2] Cit. Dawson, loc. cit., p. 212.
[3] Wach, J., *Sociology of Religion*, as quoted, p. 369. On this topic, cf. also Berger, P. L., 'Charisma, Religious Innovation, and the Israelite Prophecy', *American Sociological Review*, 1963, pp. 940 et seq.

concomitant fact that it is in its essence at the same time a *holon*, a vital system, a collectivity determined to preserve its unity and its essence. The priesthood is one feature in this double face, as it were, the saints are the other. The priesthood is linked with order and persistence and hence with integration, the saints with freedom and progress and hence with diversity. And so it is that the Church shows us, as in a mirror, the great image of all sociality: like her companions, she is an antithesis-in-synthesis, a paradoxical and yet viable solution of the problem of the many and the one.

3 · MONK AND PREDICANT

Of the two figures whom we have considered in the last chapter, saint and priest, the priest is of closer and more immediate concern to the sociologist as sociologist, even though the saint may be – indeed, we are tempted to write: must be – much more meaningful and attractive to him as a man and especially as a believer. However interested the sociologist is in individual actions, his main assignment is the study of collective institutions, of those abiding structures only in relation to which individual actions assume a lasting and social significance; and the Church as such a structure is grouped around the priestly hierarchy. We therefore turn now to a study of that hierarchy, but in doing so and in entering into that study we must not for a minute, or even for a single second, forget that the priesthood is not identical with the Church. The fundamental error of Sohm and Weber was precisely that they saw, at least in medieval and modern Catholicism, nothing but bishops and other administrative officials, and disregarded the saints and even the saintly laity who lead the prayer life, and consequently the true life, of the ecclesiastical community.

A preliminary point to be settled in this context is, naturally and necessarily, why the society of Christians separated out a special group of clergy in the first place, and why it did not abide by the informal arrangements of its earliest days when, like any other sect, it did not have an established priesthood. To us this is a problem, for the Reformation has made it one; but to the primitive Christian community it hardly was so. The development of a set of office-bearers is simply a reflection of the principle of the division of labour which operates within any and every social circle, and the Christians of the first centuries would as little have hesitated to set apart certain persons to subserve their communal purposes as they would have to acquire a specific place of worship different from their private dwellings. Harnack tells us that it was Antioch which led the way. The cult was regarded as all-important in that infant church, and the centrality of the cult brought with it the centrality, and even the ascendancy, of the priest or bishop who performed it with and for the laity. The latter was seen in terms of relative passivity. Harnack adds, however, in the same breath, that the Antiochene model was matched, and to some extent counterbalanced, by the Alexandrian. In Alexandria the emphasis was on the religious layman, the monk, the virtuoso, i.e. the amateur rather than the professional, the 'true gnostic' as Harnack has it, using the term in the wider sense of a man who has penetrated to the divine mysteries rather than in the narrower sense in which we sometimes speak of the heterodox gnostic sects. If Antioch was priest-centred, Alexandria was saint-centred, and the universal Church, as it ultimately evolved, became a synthesis of these two germinal forms. In the literature we can follow the synthesizing process through Methodius, Gregory of Nyssa and Macarius to Dionysius Areopagita, 'the great unknown', who on the one hand 'conceived cult and priesthood as an earthly parallel to the heavenly hierarchy,' but on the other hand took over and carried all 'the individualism of neo-platonic mysticism'.[1]

The democratic, not to say unstructured, character of the Christian assemblies of the apostolic age has, not surprisingly, been especially emphasized by those researchers who belong to denominations which either reject, or at least minimize, the principle of hierarchy. In his book, *The Minister in the Reformed Tradition*, Goodykoontz analyses, on the basis of the fifteenth chapter of the *Acts of the Apostles*, 'the first great church conference', namely the meetings at Jerusalem which were called to consider if circumcision was a necessary preliminary to Church membership and hence to salvation. 'Paul and Barnabas as well as Peter and James were influential in the discussion,' he writes, 'but in the end it was the decision of the whole group . . . James the Lord's brother gave his judgment, which was, however, merely a summary of the convictions that the assembly had reached, not a dogmatic utterance which the gathering had to swallow . . . From the beginning therefore, when major decisions had to be made, the church in congregational meeting . . . made the decisions. Not one apostle, not even all the apostles together, but the apostles along with the elders made the decision at the Jerusalem assembly.'[2]

Yet these very words show how the Church, which can hardly

[1] Harnack, *Grundriss der Dogmengeschichte*, as quoted, pp. 173 and 174.
[2] Goodykoontz, Harry G., *The Minister in the Reformed Tradition*, Richmond (Virginia) 1963, p. 28.

be said to have been born as yet – the time is still before the year 50 – is already structured, and thus not radically democratic. The apostles with the elders make the decisions, not the whole *plebs Christi*. And Goodykoontz himself concedes the point, for what he really writes is: 'when major decisions had to be made, the church in congregational meeting, or more likely the church through its chosen representatives, made the decisions'. The most that can be claimed therefore is that the Apostolic Church was a representative democracy. But a representative democracy is not a pure democracy: it is already split into rulers and ruled.

In the sequel, Goodykoontz discusses the whole broad development up to the martyrdom of Peter and Paul, and it is surprising to see from what he says just how rapidly an official structure forms within the body of Christendom, even though it is still young. He approaches the *Epistles* of Paul and Peter, as well as the *Acts of the Apostles*, with two concepts in mind, 'functions' and 'offices', or (what amounts to the same) tasks and titles. And he finds, by a very painstaking investigation which puts every word under the microscope, that there is a definite, and definitely undelayed, transition from function or task to office and title. 'The conclusion of this study is,' so he sums up the result of his close considerations, that while the connotation of terms like apostle, prophet, evangelist, pastor and teacher is 'primarily and immediately functional, the hints of office grow stronger until with Ephesians we are on the threshold of office, if not across it.' The decisive lines are versicles 7, 11 and 12 of this Epistle's chapter IV: 'To every one of us is given grace, according to the measure of the giving of Christ . . . And he gave some apostles, and some prophets, and other some evangelists, and other some pastors and doctors, for the perfecting of the saints, for the work of the ministry and for the edifying of the body of Christ.' 'This is the classic passage on the ministry in the New Testament,' Goodykoontz writes, and it 'almost certainly names *offices*.' And he adds: 'The main point is that one of the great gifts of the ascended Christ to his church is the gift of ministry, and of *specific persons* carrying out definite functions of ministry with manifest connotations of ministerial office.' In any case, and remaining as sober and non-theological as possible, there is evidence of 'a transformation in the concept of the ministry from function to office'.[1]

[1] Loc. cit., pp. 33 and 32. Our emphasis.

It is therefore only a slight exaggeration to say, against Weber and those who think like him, that the singling out of a definite class of officers and officials is less the consequence of a process of evolution or involution than an aspect and implication of the act of constitution, the birth-act, so to speak, of the Christian Church.[1] It took time, of course, for everything does take time; but it took very little time; and though it took more time for the structure to gain consolidation and to settle down into the forms which we still know, the principle at least of a permanent priesthood was there from the very beginning. However that may be, the fact is that the power of the community and the power in the community shifted and drifted into the hands of the office-bearers and became anchored there. The right to discipline erring members, for instance, and the further right to excommunicate them when the need arose, wandered from the local assembly to its presiding officer and finally to the monarchical bishop who could act alone and regularly did so.[2] Catholicism became an autocratic church in which the laity is ruled, not ruling, so far as administration is concerned, and it was this which aroused, not only the protest of the Protestants and of their disciples, among whom we must number Max Weber, but even the ill-will of many Catholics and generated the important and undying phenomenon of anti-clericalism.[3] What is surprising in all this is how little opposition the concentration of power in the bishops aroused in the post-apostolic age. Campenhausen, whose *Kirchliches Amt und geistliche Vollmacht in den ersten drei Jahrhunderten* (1953) represents, as we have seen before, the most authoritative study of these matters in recent times, asserts that there was not a trace of resistance against a hierarchy conceived as a legally established set of rulers.[4] And he gives us the underpinning conceptions which carried the whole development: the *plebs Christi* is a community within the world, almost a state within the state, and the *episkopoi* and *presbyteroi* are the princes who

[1] Goodykoontz goes so far as to write (on p. 24): 'The story of the election of an apostle to replace Judas shows that the Twelve was an office and not simply a function.'

[2] Cf. Kohlmeyer, loc. cit., especially pp. 13, 18, 35.

[3] Anti-clericalism turns out, on closer analysis, to be a rather complex phenomenon, and a satisfactory account of it would unavoidably demand a long excursus. We must therefore reluctantly pass it by here, just like the case of celibacy, hoping to deal with it in some periodical later on.

[4] Cf. especially p. 272, note 8.

rule over it. They are the leaders of God's holy people, the judges who keep it clean, the torch-bearers who light its way. As one source particularly movingly expresses it: the Church is the way-side inn to which Christ, the Good Samaritan, brings mankind, wounded as it is and bleeding from all limbs. But the bishops are the keepers of that inn: they, more than all others, look after the mangled body which God has placed under their care.[1]

Such sentiments are evidence of a deep and widespread loyalism. They sound strange in an age like ours which has engendered a permanent revolution against authority, both secular and religious and even familial, and especially against clerico-hierarchical authority. The doctrine known as 'the routinization of charisma' would seem to suggest that the change in attitude towards the power-holders is due to a change of quality in the power-holders: they were saints at first and therefore willingly obeyed, they are sinners now and therefore rightly resisted. Such an opinion is unrealistic, for the problem of authority, namely the danger that those who have the charge may prove unequal to and unworthy of it, exists the very minute authority itself exists. Campenhausen depicts Cyprian of Carthage as the ideal 'overseer' of the early, heroic days – rightly so, for, like the Good Shepherd, he laid down his life for his flock. The communal and charismatic character of the primitive Christian brotherhood is fully alive in him.[2] But at the very same time, Origines already protests against the shortcomings of some of Cyprian's colleagues. Black and white therefore coexist; they do not follow each other in a time sequence like night and day. And who would, who could, forget that even St. Peter, the chosen one, betrayed his Lord thrice before the cock crowed! Bishops are very human now and therefore apt to blunder; that is true; but they were human beings already in the first centuries and liable to fail even then. The striking contrast between acceptance of authority and suspicion or rejection of it (which is, in tendency at least, the contrast between antiquity and the middle ages on the one hand and modern times on the other, and also, of course, with some restrictions and modifications, the contrast between the classical Catholic and the Protestant worlds) has deeper reasons than purely personal ones which could in any case never be more than accidental. It has reasons which root, and

[1] Ibid., p. 262.　　　　[2] Ibid., pp. 307 and 308. Cf. also p. 318, note 6, and Ibid., pp. 278 and 279.

root deeply, in the soil and subsoil on which the Roman Church
and the non-Roman churches appeared and evolved. It reflects
constitutional differences between the two basic types of society,
community and association, and between the basic conceptions,
the implied metaphysics, with which they are respectively connected.

Perhaps the quickest as well as the clearest way of explaining the
contrast is to say that the very same public figure, and indeed the
very same private person, appears in an entirely different light in
the two societies: he is the Right Rev. Dr. Proudie rather than the
Bishop of Barchester in the one; he is the Bishop of Barchester
rather than the Right Rev. Dr. Proudie in the other. The latter is
the case of the older forms of Christianity and especially Catholicism (and Anglicanism as well, as our example from Anthony
Trollope, or better the facts which his fiction reflects, can show);
the former is the case of the newer, the post-Renaissance forms of
Christianity and especially of the radical sects. The latter is the
case of community, the former that of association. Even the terms
functions and offices, or tasks and titles, must be interpreted in this
way. There can perhaps be functions without offices or officers in
the precise meaning of the word, but – sinecures apart – there
cannot be offices or officers without functions. The contrast
between the older and the newer forms of church organization
consists in this that in Catholicism the function shows much more
clearly through the office than in Protestantism, particularly
extreme Protestantism, where a man is a man and no more, even in
the highest positions. Only where the social, the ecclesiastical,
whole is conceived as an organism can a clergyman appear as a
functionary with indwelling rights rather than as a hired man with
imposed duties. Only an organism can have organs and the
organs, functions: everything is dependent on the basic idea or
ideas. But we do not need the terminology of organicism nor even
that of Tönnies to make the matter clear: we can follow Sir Henry
Maine and speak of 'status' and 'contract' and their essential
contrast. Catholicism thinks of its priesthood pre-eminently in
terms of status, Protestantism in terms of contract. Or rather we
should say (for we must not forget here that Protestantism, apart
from the radical sects, has not fully embraced the principle of
association and hence also that of contract) that in the mixture
of community and association, function and office, status and

contract, with which the mentality of the two great Reformers worked, the official-contractual element received a relatively stronger emphasis. To the Catholic, the priest is one who controls the community rather than one who is controlled by it; to the Protestant it is, in principle, the other way around, even though in practice the power of especially the Presbyterian ministers over their flocks (beginning with the stern Jehan Calvin himself) has sometimes been considerable.

The mention of status and contract, and even simply of the name of Sir Henry Maine, reminds us that we are confronted here with a generalized phenomenon and not merely with a phenomenon of organized religion. Up to the French Revolution, status dominated the state as well as the Church; since then contract has largely, not to say fully, taken its place, as it did to some extent already before 1789 in the Protestant world, which was in this as in so many other respects the harbinger of modernity. In the ancient and medieval periods, democracy seemed possible, even for purely technical reasons, only in restricted circles such as the polis. Aristotle simply could not imagine a democratic world state and not even a democratic constitution for a larger area. Where small communities formed within her womb, the older Church also applied democratic methods: witness the election of a Benedictine abbot; witness above all the Dominican constitutions which effectively pioneered in this field and thereby prepared both the Protestant half-democracy and the fuller general democracy of post-revolutionary days.[1] A church forming, as Catholicism did, in the early centuries of the Christian era and spreading, by a deep-laid inner impetus, to the very ends of the earth, could not but become authoritarian, with permanent and irremovable office-bearers.

Catholics are for those reasons possibly somewhat more willing to bear with the human weaknesses of their clergy than Protestants are: they see the canonicals, cope and crozier, mitre, ring and infula, in one word, the essential *dignitas*, rather than the accidental person invested with it. But, of course, the difference must not be exaggerated. The problem of social control, the vexed question as to how you can make and keep the private person fit faithfully to fulfil public duties, has ever existed and still remains:

[1] Cf. Barker, E., *The Dominican Order and Convocation. A study of the growth of representation in the Church during the thirteenth century*, Oxford 1913.

it is a crux and a cross of *all* societies. Catholics rely on control from above: the bishop disciplining bad priests, Protestants rather on control exerted sidewise or from below: the fellow ministers reprimanding, or the congregations dismissing, unsatisfactory predicants. Yet both confessional groups know, as we all do, that the only desirable safeguard is (in Durkheimian-Parsonian language) the internalization of the proper norms in the office-bearer. This is the line of endeavour which the Catholic Church has ever pursued in her effort to make her authoritarianism something higher and finer than what even a full democracy can provide – to turn the power-holder into a loving servant of those over whom he holds power, to change the master into a slave, remembering the injunction of Jesus: 'He that is the greater among you, let him become as the younger, and he that is the leader as he that serveth' (Luke XXII, 26) – remembering even more the shining image of the Founder: 'I, being your Lord and Master, have washed your feet; you also ought to wash one another's feet. For I have given you an example that as I have done to you, so you do also' (John XIII, 14 and 15; cf. further Matthew XX, 28, Mark X, 42–45 and Isaias LIII).

Speaking more practically, the Catholic Church has endeavoured to create a priesthood which would have only one interest in life – the Church, not to say a priesthood which would invariably prefer the interest of the Church, and that means, in an ideal vision, of redeemed humanity, to any interests of their own, especially personal ones. The experiment has been largely based on an optimistic estimate of the possibilities of education. This is a point where we see very clearly the deeply Platonist character of Catholicism. It has not been emphasized in the literature, and yet it is immediately obvious to the informed observer, that the Church has tried to implement the scheme set forth in the *Republic*: to have a class of rulers bereft of private property and a family life of their own, so as to make them nothing but servants of the community. As, by definition, ordinary human beings are involved, it is obvious that such an experiment can never be more than a partial success, and the same must necessarily be said of other, newer, more democratic methods of ministerial education and placing. It is not for the scientific sociologist to say which denominations have better and which worse servants: an objective yardstick for measuring their quality has never been invented. Yet any realistic student of the scene must know and may assert that such variations as exist (if any do exist) can hardly be more than differences in the degree of worthiness, or better unworthiness, for the charge. Who, indeed, is worthy?[1] Those who cannot bear a cleft between the ideal and the real in this matter must embrace the only radical solution that lies open. the solution selected by the Quakers and other marginal groups like them: to get rid of functionaries and office-bearers and of a church-like organization altogether and settle for unstructured, purely localized face-to-face conventicles.

THE MONK AS AN ARCHETYPE

The brush against a one-time confessional polemic, the raising and dashing of the question as to which half of Christendom has succeeded in providing a more satisfactory clergy, was necessary in order to make it quite clear that Catholicism and Protestantism are in this field definite alternatives, however great their common Christian possessions may be in other respects. There is really no 'better' and 'worse' here: there are, sociologically speaking, incomparable and mutually exclusive 'ideal types'. A priest acting for an integrated community is one thing, a preacher acting on an assembled multitude is another. However much the two may in practice shade into each other, in principle they are clearly contrasting. Our task is therefore to take them in turn, to look first at the Catholic priest as the older phenomenon and only then at the Protestant predicant as the newer development, and to identify the salient characteristics of each as best we can.

So far as the hallmark which distinguishes the Catholic priesthood is concerned, this is a point at which a détour will amply repay the effort which it involves. The fund of Catholic ideas, overt or covert, from which all ecclesiological conceptions flow, can be much more convincingly demonstrated with the help of the figure of the monk than with the help of the figure of the priest, even though it is true, as we have emphasized on an earlier occasion, that monks as a group are laymen, notwithstanding the fact that individually they are, most of them, priests.[2]

---

[1] Cf. Bouëssé, loc. cit., pp. 144 et seq., and especially the quotations from and references to, St. Thomas Aquinas there.

[2] Cf. our vol. III, pp. 408 and 409.

What, then, is a monk? In trying to answer this question we are, once again, confronted with the difficulty with which we are forced to battle throughout the pages of this volume, the spurious attempt to interpret products of an age of community in terms of the dominant reality and the predominant ideas of our own age, which is an age of association. Seen within the context of a decidedly individualistic culture, he is a man who pursues a specifically personal religiosity, who wishes, in and for his own person, to reach an exceptional degree of religious perfection. And so he has been seen by many. But such an impression is deeply misleading, is, to say the least, but partial and therefore distorting. Even the monk, even the Carthusian in his lonely cell, is a social functionary; even he fulfils a task which is essentially communal.

We have, in many contexts, quoted the admirable study of Herbert Workman, *The Evolution of the Monastic Ideal*; we have seen over and over again how deeply this Methodist could enter into the spirit and the achievements of a group of men whose very existence his denomination thinks unjustified. But when it comes to the final question, to the deepest meaning of monkhood, his individualism betrays him. This is how, in one passage, he formulates the supposed categorical imperative of the coenobite as well as of the anchorite: 'Live as if you were alone in this world with God.'[1] And in another he writes: 'Throughout its history, monasticism has been too intent upon the part to be conscious of the whole.'[2] Or again: 'Against the essential solidarity of the Catholic Church, as against the all-pervading tyranny of the organization of the Empire, the monk placed that individualism which must lie at the root of all conscious renunciation. His was the protest of the individual against the collectivism which tended, both in Church and State, by its institutions and functions, to lose sight of his value. The monk, whether in the East or West, was the voice in the wilderness crying the lost truth of the worth of one soul.'[3] Commenting on some paleo-Christian literature from the mental orbit of the monks, Workman finally remarks: 'Life is viewed from an individualistic standpoint complete enough to satisfy the crudest disciple of Hume or Rousseau ... The question is argued from the standpoint of spiritual Robinson Crusoes; no conception even of a possible Man Friday, to whom the Christian

[1] Op. cit., p. 272.   [2] Ibid., p. 13.   [3] P. 23.

may owe a love that is something more than charity, ever seems to cross the mind . . . The social instinct, social claims, that larger altruism which forms today the hope of the age, seems altogether wanting.'[1] The diametrical opposite of 'large altruism' is 'narrow egoism', and Workman all but implies that it was rampant in the conventual communities as well as among the isolated hermits whom he describes.

So intent is Workman on this point (which, it must be allowed, is all-important) that he even tries to assemble Catholic witnesses in support of it. Thus he quotes Montalembert: 'Historians have vied in praising Benedict's genius and clearsightedness; they have supposed that he intended to regenerate Europe, to stop the dissolution of society, to reconstruct public order, and so on . . . I firmly believe that he never dreamed of regenerating anything but his own soul.' There is further a passage from Cardinal Newman to the effect that 'the monk proposed to himself no great or systematic work beyond that of saving his soul. What he did more than this was the accident of the hour.'[2]

These are formidable authorities, and yet it is necessary to withstand them to their faces. We are sometimes fortunate in gaining, as in a momentary flash, a really deep insight into the monkish mentality, and when we do so, what we find is anything but the spirit of a man who wants to go to heaven alone or merely side by side with his brethren. One such occasion is offered by the foreword of St. Bernard's essay known either as 'The Glories of the Virgin Mother' or 'Homilies on the *Missus Est*'. The saint explains that he is ill in bed, and that it is therefore impossible for him to take part in the community's normal activities. Thus he is 'able to enjoy a little leisure', and he wishes to use it well 'to write something that would satisfy my devotion to the Mother of God'. Surely, such a desire must be unexceptional in a religious man. But Bernard is uneasy. And why? Because, he says, 'this is not rendered imperative by any necessity of my brethren whose advancement in virtue I am bound to promote, nor even recommended by any hope of benefiting them particularly'. Will they not

---

[1] Workman, loc. cit., p. 58.
[2] Ibid., p. 12. Workman's references are as follows: Montalembert, C. F. R., *Monks of the West*, ed. Gasquet, F. A., London 1896, vol. I, p. 436; Newman, J. H., *Historical Sketches* [presumably ed. London 1906], vol. II, p. 452 and 453.

have the right 'to complain of me for indulging my own devotion'? To us, this scruple looks like the height of over-conscientiousness and we feel almost relieved when we hear and see St. Bernard laying it to rest.[1] But that he should have entertained it at all shows, and most convincingly, that his was not an individualistic mentality.

Still, this is merely a splinter of evidence, not enough of it. But there *is* enough of it, and all that is needed is to give it its due weight. What monasticism was, and what it was not, must surely be decided by an investigation of the *end* which it set out to pursue, of the purpose for the sake of which it came into being. And that end, that purpose, consisted, according to Cardinal Newman himself, 'if not in reverting to the original condition of man', then at least in doing so 'as far as the changed circumstances of our race admitted'.[2] In saying this, the great theologian merely echoes the words of the great monk whom we have just encountered, the holy man who can, without exaggeration, be described as the flower of monkhood, St. Bernard of Clairvaux. When some religious from St. Peter's Abbey at Chartres asked him various questions about the calling of the monk, especially what its last implication and meaning might be, he answered that 'it restores in man the original image and likeness of God'.[3] And he goes on to compare the rite of profession to the rite of baptism. Both cleanse him who receives the sacrament, but whereas, in children of the world, the stain of sin almost unavoidably soon returns and has to be washed off again and again by confession and penance, the son of St. Benedict undertakes to try to remain free from blemish and indeed to make that endeavour the main content of his life. Monasticism was therefore something like an experiment in sinless living – an experiment to be undertaken, even though it seemed well beyond our human capacity. This was to be the monk's peculiar *imitatio Christi*, the cross which he laid upon his shoulders and promised willingly to carry throughout his life.

And why this painful experiment which goes so much against the grain of men? Is it in order to achieve a personal sanctification

---

[1] Luddy, loc. cit., pp. 86 and 87. Cf. *Patrologia Latina*, as quoted, vol. CLXXXIII, Paris 1854, col. 55.
[2] 'The Mission of St. Benedict', *Historical Sketches*, as quoted, vol. II, p. 377.
[3] Luddy, loc. cit., p. 469; cf. pp. 458 and 459.

and only that? Surely not. What the monk really undertook to do was to prove to Almighty God that the human race, though fallen, has not fallen so deeply as to be unable to rise up again towards the Summit of Perfection, even if that Summit remains forever far away – to prove to Almighty God that the human race, at least in some of its representatives, is capable of reversing the tendency unhappily evinced by our first parents, and as unhappily continued by their offspring, the ordinary run of men, the tendency to drift away from God, to embrace, in St. Augustine's words, the love of self to the contempt of God instead of the love of God to the contempt of self with its indwelling sin. What the monk did, there-fore, was done on behalf of *all* men. He may not have had an office, but he certainly had a function. His model was Abel whose offering was well received by God, and not Cain who denied that he was his brother's keeper. Indeed, his model was Adam – Adam, the obedient son, before his temptation and disgrace. This is what Cardinal Newman really teaches about the monk.

The point which we are trying to make was developed with particular felicity and convincingness by P. Notker Würmseer in a paper published in the *Benediktinische Monatschrift* and called 'Vom Sinn des Mönchtums' (the meaning of monkhood).[1] Any concep-tion of the monk, the author begins his analysis, which sees in him merely a man devoted to personal sanctification, is too narrow; indeed, it fails to appreciate the deepest significance of monasticism and could hardly yield as much as a bare justification of its existence. That justification can spring only from a con-sideration of the religious achievement of the cloistered life. Now, religious man has always tried to please and pacify Almighty God by sacrifice: such were the firstlings of Abel's flock which were found acceptable on high. But even lambs are only possessions, only things, something which man can surrender without too much pain to himself. Yet he has something better to offer up than that: his own *self*, and that too he owes and should give entirely to God. For ordinary man this is difficult, if not impos-sible, for he is absorbed in the struggle of survival and cannot totally devote himself to penance and prayer. But it is different with the human race as a whole. 'The human race as a whole has the possibility of laying before God a much more appropriate

[1] Vol. VI, 1924, pp. 107 et seq.

symbol of its devotion by surrendering the secular services of some of its members, especially their participation in the procreation of offspring and in the production of commodities, and by therefore separating them off from the rest and dedicating them exclusively to the immediate service of God.' Obviously, this monk's idea of monkhood is collectivistic, not individualistic, and it is so to a supreme degree. He himself spells this out with all desirable clarity: 'We find in the end that the God-given mission of monasticism is the fulfilment of the sacrificial duty of humanity as a whole. *The meaning of monkhood is to be humanity's sacrificial offering*, a sacrifice in the name of humanity and for the sake of humanity, with all the purposes which sacrifice in its widest connotation subserves . . . above all expiation. This last-named element provides monkhood with its special characteristic: it becomes a communion of penitents who do penance for their own sins, but equally for the guilt of the race.'[1] On this last point, Würmseer might well have quoted St. Bernard: 'To punish in himself both his own sins and the sins of the world – such, he told his religious, is the vocation of the monk.'[2] And he might further have quoted St. Benedict himself. Penance, Benedict knew and preached, is suffering, and suffering is Christ-like. Hence 'by persevering in the monastery until death, we shall become partakers in the sufferings of Christ'.[3] But Christ suffered for all, for all Adam's children sunk in sin.

We need not follow Würmseer much further for perhaps we have now made our point. Only one detail may still be helpful and should be mentioned. To sacrifice oneself means above all to sacrifice one's will, for the will of fallen man is the seat, as it were, of his rebelliousness. Obedience therefore is of the essence of the monk's life. By developing this virtue, he becomes less imperfect and thereby sanctifies his soul. This, if any, would be the context in which the supposed individualistic nature of monachism should be stressed, if it really existed. But Würmseer stresses the very opposite. Of course, the monk, like any man, should strive to save and sanctify himself; that much is obvious; but his is a special case. 'From his sacrificial character flows an

---

[1] Loc. cit., pp. 107, 108, 109. Author's emphasis.
[2] Luddy, loc. cit., p. 45.
[3] Cit. Luddy, loc. cit., p. 467. The words are the closing passage of the Proemium of the 'Holy Rule'.

additional reason for the obligation and hence an additional motive for the pursuit of sanctity. He must sanctify himself not only for his own sake, but also for the sake of his fellow men.'[1]

The voice we have heard is the voice of a Benedictine, and it might be thought that later communities felt differently. Yet such an impression would be false. St. John of Matha's Trinitarians and St. Peter Nolasco's Order of Our Lady of Ransom had to all appearances a rather sober aim: to buy the freedom of Christians who had fallen into Muslim hands. Yet the basic fund of ideas in these men was similar to that of St. Basil and St. Benedict and St. Bernard of Clairvaux. The Trinitarians lived a life of very great austerity. They did so because, Chateaubriand tells us,[2] 'if there had to be victims of God's wrath, it was hoped that the Almighty would accept the hardships of these religious in exchange for the sufferings of which they were to free the captives'. The basic concept, then, was the concept of vicarious satisfaction, and nothing more un-individualistic can be imagined than that.

This should be amply sufficient to rebut Herbert Workman's individualistic interpretation. It is true, and we have emphasized it ourselves:[3] monastic movements were regularly anti-clerical. They could not be otherwise for theirs was a protest against an all too close identification of the (official) Church with the world, and the recurrent reform of the clergy was their historical effect as well as their strategic aim (whatever Workman may assert to the contrary).[4] 'He recoiled from the growing conception of the kingdom of God as an organized society,' Workman writes of the monk,[5] but even if there is a small element of truth in this statement, there is yet much more that is erroneous about it. The monk may have recoiled from the growing conception of the kingdom of God as an *organized* society, but he certainly did not budge an inch from the established conviction that the Church, and that

[1] Würmseer, loc. cit., p. 110.
[2] Chateaubriand, F. R., *Génie du Christianisme*, ed. Reboul, P., paperback ed. Paris 1966, vol. II, p. 199.
[3] Cf. our vol. III, especially p. 409.
[4] Cf. especially his p. 12, where he controverts himself by mentioning the name of Gregory VII, the great monk who did reform the Universal Church.
[5] Cf. p. 23.

mankind, is an *organic* whole. Perhaps it would be best to say that successive generations of regulars turned away from the mechanism of the Church, but they never ceased to consider the Church as an organism. Organicism was the essence of the age in which monasticism appeared, as it is of the essence of Catholicism down to this day. To speak, in a book entitled *The Evolution of the Monastic Ideal*, of 'an ideal altogether outside the ideal of the Catholic Church'[1] is simply unhistorical; indeed, it is well-nigh illogical, for in this sentence something is declared to be un-Catholic which has ever been pronounced *most* Catholic, and by nobody more than by Workman's fellow-Protestants.

The words which we have just quoted and criticized refer more specifically to the hermits, but they are not applicable even to them, for even the deserted fathers, for all their physical isolation in the sandy wastelands of the Thebaid, did penance for all mankind and not only for themselves. They are, however, still less applicable to the cloistered and communal monks, the coenobites, and we must briefly point this out though it means, regrettably, opening an aside within an aside. The great proof, undertaken by the monks of the Benedictine tradition, that it *was* possible for men, ordinary men, to lead a largely God-pleasing life, whatever the difficulties involved, included, according to intention, an *ad oculos demonstratio* that it was possible for them to live in concord, the word taken in its deepest implication, namely, being 'of one heart' (*con-cors*). Already St. Augustine, himself the author of a famous Rule, had, in the first chapter of that Rule, described this aim as absolutely essential: 'This is what we command you who are in the cloister: the first task of your common life is to dwell together in amity, to be in God of one heart and one soul,' as the apostolic community was according to Acts IV, 32. In another context, Augustine dramatizes the same demand by a little imaginative philology: monk, he says, the Latin *monachus*, comes from the Greek *monos*, one. 'Those who live in oneness (*monos*) should form one man, so to speak, and they should, as the Scripture has it, in truth possess but one soul and one heart.' Elsewhere again he compares, in his incomparable way, the cloister to a harbour or haven: it is open on one side and so sin can still enter in. But those who have taken refuge there are, so long as they can prevent the waves from breaking over the walls, at peace. Ships do

[1] Workman, loc. cit., p. 24.

not need to jostle each other inside their anchorage.[1] St. Benedict fully shared these sentiments. In the sixty-first chapter of the Holy Rule he calls the monastic community the *corpus monasterii*, as St. Basil had defined entry into a *coenobium* as a *sociari corpori congregationis*.[2] But the simile which Benedict uses most frequently to explain the ideal character, and especially the coherence, of a monastery is a comparison with the domestic circle. 'The distinguishing mark of the Benedictine abbey,' so writes one who has made the study of these matters his special concern, 'is its likeness to a family.'[3] Already the second chapter of the Holy Rule begins with the words: 'The abbot who is worthy to be the head of a monastery must always remember what his name is.' His name, however, is abbot which comes from abba, father.[4] This sets the tone, as it were, of the whole *Regula*. It is the fundamental theme which is presented in many variations.

This peace of the cloister, this *pax Benedictina*, is again not meant merely to subserve the happiness, or the religiosity, of the monk or monks. The implication is once more decidedly and strongly collectivistic.[5] The purpose of Christ's coming was to bring peace to all mankind. It has not yet been achieved. But within the Church there is more peace than in the world at large, for she is the body of Christ, and hence filled by His charismatic spirit, the spirit of love. Yet even the Church is still in the world. Making use of St. Augustine's inspired metaphor, we can say, she is a vessel at sea, not a vessel home in port, and therefore she is buffeted from all sides. The monastery is different. It *is* a harbour within which a deeper calm prevails, in which brotherliness can spread and intensify, thus lifting those within it up towards that perfect and divine *Agape* which was made manifest in Jesus

---

[1] Cf. *Patrologia Latina*, as quoted, vol. XXXII, Paris 1877, cols. 1377 and 1378; vol. XXXVII, Paris 1865, cols. 1732 and 1733; ibid., cols. 1276 and 1277. Cf. also letter CCXLIII, vol. XXXIII, Paris 1902, cols. 1055 et seq., especially col. 1056. Cf. also Steidle, loc. cit., p. 61, note 1, *re* Pseudo-Dionysius who expresses himself much as Augustine does (*monasterium = monas*).

[2] Cf. Blazovich, A., *Soziologie des Mönchtums und der Benediktinerregel*, Wien 1954, p. 64.

[3] Ibid., p. 159 (and often).

[4] On the depth of meaning connected with this word, which cannot but be surprising to modern man, cf. Steidle, as quoted, Excursus I (pp. 84 et seq.).

[5] Cf. Steidle, loc. cit., *passim*, but especially. pp. 265, 329, 330.

Christ. The three narrowing circles – the world, the Church and the cloister – could, of course, be thought of as simply examples to each other, the cloister teaching, and, as it were, beckoning on the Church, the Church teaching and beckoning on the world. But such a conception would be too weak, and above all too modern, too much in the spirit of a merely associational society, to do justice to the essence and aspiration of monasticism. No, the brotherly love of the monks for each other, if and to the extent that it is realized, is a realization of the lovingness possible for all men, an achievement of mankind in and through some of its members. It raises the *whole* race, by a necessary reflex as it were, up to a more exalted level.

In all this there is something very deeply, and very specifically, Catholic, not to say un-Protestant. All Christians believe that Christ, through His sacrifice on Calvary, reconciled God to man; all also believe that that sacrifice was final and perfect in the sense of all-sufficing. Yet Catholics, in opposition to Protestants who are inclined to regard the efforts of Adam's kind in the religious sphere as unavailing, feel that men need to, and can, associate themselves with Christ's redemptive deed, even though they are but men – even though they are but born as sinners. Under the cross stood Mary and her pain mingled with that of her Divine Son. Under the cross stood John; under the cross stood the Magdalen; under the cross stood Benedict and Francis and an uncountable multitude. They all help in a manner to redeem mankind – they are all partakers in the *one* work of salvation. In the words of St. Paul (Colossians I, 24), they fill up, by their sufferings, 'those things that are wanting in the sufferings of Christ'. Being the continuing Body of Christ, they are not only redeemed, but also redeeming, and, what is most important in a sociological view, they redeem each other, or rather help to do so. This is the collectivistic background against which even so sober a figure as the priest must be seen. As the monk by his action, be it penance or prayer or labour (which is also penance and prayer),[1] acts in behalf and for the benefit of the whole people of God, so does the parish pastor or the diocesan bishop or the pope, only their actions are more of an administrative kind, more sober, more technical, more of every day routine.

[1] Cf. Steidle, loc. cit., pp. 53 and 54, footnote 3.

THE OFFICE OF PRIEST

The development of a special class of monks is as characteristic of Catholic conceptions and, indeed, of the whole Catholic culture, as its condemnation and virtual disappearance is of the modern Protestant dispensation. We have hinted at the final reason for this already in the opening lines of this chapter: Catholicism, together with the other older forms of Christianity, such as Orthodoxy and even Anglicanism, did not oppose the operation of the principle of the division of labour in the religious sphere: to them it was as natural that some men should make the service of God their special concern as it was that some should be cattle-breeders rather than all-round agriculturists or conveyancers rather than all-round lawyers. The Protestant churches, on the other hand, though they formed and matured in a world which pushed the division of labour in general, and especially the economic and technological division of labour, to formerly unheard-of and even undreamed-of lengths, resolutely rejected it, so far as the religious quest was concerned. And that was but logical. For if it is not mankind as a whole which collectively strives back towards the God whom they have, in Adam, collectively forsaken, but men, individual men (plural), then there is nothing to divide here. Everybody is to be on his own way, as Bunyan's Christian was, when, in *The Pilgrim's Progress*, he set out from home in response to a call which had sounded in his inmost heart.

More theologically expressed, Catholicism embraced, and Protestantism condemned, the distinction between general precept and counsel of perfection,[1] between those who would, and those who would not, make total sanctification their direct and indeed exclusive aim in life. But it is on this very distinction that monachism rests. Jesus both by example and by word had recommended to the inner circle of his followers the virtue of poverty: 'If thou wilt be perfect, go sell what thou hast and give to the poor and thou shalt have treasure in heaven.' He had recommended to them the virtue of chastity: 'There are eunuchs who were born so from their mother's womb: and there are eunuchs who were made so by men: and there are eunuchs who have made themselves eunuchs for the kingdom of heaven. He that can take, let him take

[1] Cf. Butler, Cuthbert, *Benedictine Monachism*, ed. 1924, reprint Cambridge and New York 1961, pp. 38 and 39; Blazovich, loc. cit., pp. 17, 18, 34, 38, 39.

it.' And he had recommended to them even more strongly the virtue of obedience when he prayed in the garden: 'My father, if it be possible, let this chalice pass from me. Nevertheless, not as I will, but as thou wilt' (Matthew XIX, 21, 12, and XXVI, 39). These three, poverty, chastity, and obedience, became the evangelical counsels, and they constituted the vows which the postulant had to take, solemnly, before entering a religious order. They were not thought to be binding in the same way on laymen who remained in the world; above all, they were not thought to be included, in all their stringency, in the baptismal vow.

There existed in this manner a division between the common run of men and religious specialists (this ugly term will, it is hoped, be forgiven) who made the realization of the counsels of perfection their business, so to speak, their profession, their function. It is with this separation of a minority in active pursuit of sanctification and a majority more passive in relation to religious values, that Protestantism had a serious quarrel, especially in its earliest, perfectionist days. Was there any evidence, the Reformers asked, that Jesus had addressed his threefold advice only to some and not to all? Had he not expressly exhorted the assembled multitudes, in his most self-revealing sermon, the Sermon on the Mount, to be perfect, even as our heavenly Father is perfect? (Matthew V, 48). How then could some be allowed to content themselves with the implementation of those reduced duties which are called general precepts and be excused from the full obligation involved in the counsels of perfection? No, what was binding on one, was binding on all. A division of labour in this field appeared to Lutherans and Calvinists equally invidious, the proof of low standards in faith and ethics.

The contrast in this respect between Catholicism and Protestantism must not, however, be exaggerated. Even according to Catholic principles, the counsels of perfection are and remain binding on all men. The differentiation does not lie there at all. It does not lie in the end pursued, but merely in the paths chosen, the means applied. The layman works towards perfection in the world, the monk in the cloister, and therefore, it was assumed, the monk had a better chance to get ahead in this quest than the layman had, or, indeed, could have, circumstanced as he was. True, fulfilling the counsels of perfection, or rather trying to, was an obstacle race for both, but the obstacles were smaller for the

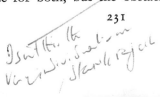

monk who had, at the outset, withdrawn from economic and family ties and entered a community in which obedience, being practised daily, would become relatively easy, if not indeed second nature. Even so, the greatest lights of monasticism never doubted that there would be plenty of laymen who would reach the goal of sanctification, in so far as it can be reached, before many of the monks with whom they vied in this religious competition. When Paphnutius, after practising self-denial for a long time, asked God to show him a person who had achieved a richer measure of sanctification, there appeared before his mind's eye the vision of a certain merchant in Alexandria, who was as concerned about the poor as he was about his business. This was a lesson to Paphnutius, and it was not lost on other monks either, as the *Vitae Patrum* testify.[1]

We have introduced these considerations into a section which is to deal with the priest, and especially the secular priest, the parish pastor, the bishop and the pope, because they lead us to yet another basic conceptual distinction which must be established before the detail can be attacked: the distinction between universal and special priesthood, i.e. priesthood in the narrower and now current sense of the word, which can also be described as ministerial, operational or official. In its widest connotation, a priest is a man who serves God. But the pious person – every pious person – serves God without ceasing. 'You give praise,' writes St. Augustine, 'when you do your daily work; you give praise, when you eat and drink; you give praise, when you take your rest on your couch; you give praise, when you sleep. When then do you not give praise?'[2] In this sense a monk who honours his vows is a priest, even though he is not in holy orders. In this sense a layman is a priest (provided, of course, he is not in mortal sin and does, whatsoever he does, in the right religious spirit) even though, by definition, he cannot be in holy orders. Priest is thus, on any but the colloquial level, where it describes the man with a round collar, an ambiguous term. Equally ambiguous are other, kindred terms. *Liturgia* means, according to Webster's New World Dictionary, 'prescribed ritual for public worship', i.e. what the clergyman does in church on Sunday. But the philological expla-

[1] Cf. Blazovich, loc. cit., especially pp. 132 and 133.
[2] Commentary on Psalm CXLVI, cf. *Patrologia Latina*, as quoted, vol. XXXVII, Paris 1865, col. 1900.

nation given refers to *leos*, people, and *ergon*, work, hence the people's work, what all do throughout the week. Even that can be sacrifice and worship and hence priestly, and so we can only achieve a proper definition of the specialized priesthood if we clearly and cleanly identify its distinctive character.

The formulation which will help us to bring clarity into this matter, provided it is properly understood, is to say that the man who is God's servant in all things and hence a member of the universal priesthood, sets out to *be* something rather than to *do* something, whereas the man who has entered into the ecclesiastical hierarchy and become part and parcel of what Lucien Cerfaux has called the *sacerdoce ministériel* or *sacerdoce de fonction*,[1] must *do* something as well as try to *be* something. Of course – it is hardly necessary to spell this out – he, too, must try to be what the servant of God in the world and in the cloister is, namely one who leads a totally theocentric life. Indeed, the Church has always demanded and, since the great Gregorian reform, adamantly insisted that he take the three vows of poverty, chastity and obedience, for in his own way he is also a 'religious specialist', just as the monk is. But his obligation – his specific and distinctive obligation – does not end there. He has incidental duties which make him what he is, and we can well characterize them by quoting from E. O. James's wide-ranging study of *The Nature and Function of Priesthood*: 'The primary function of the priest is to offer sacrifice'; he must also 'reveal, conserve and guard sacred learning and knowledge'; and finally he must 'absolve the penitent and exorcize and expiate the forces of evil'.[2] More simply expressed, the priest is concerned with the cult, with preaching, and with the discipline of his flock.

By attending to these three typical tasks, the operational or official priest becomes one set aside, whereas the 'priest' of the universal priesthood is not set aside, is, on the contrary, merged into the undifferentiated multitude of believers. What must strike anyone who works through the literature on monachism, including even the classical writings from the pen of the pioneers themselves, is the recurrent insistence that the monk as such has no ecclesiastical purpose to fulfil, no office which he can call his

[1] 'Regale Sacerdotium', reprinted in *Recueil Lucien Cerfaux*, vol. II, Gemblous 1954, pp. 283 et seq.
[2] Op. cit., pp. 208 and 293.

own.[1] 'An abbey is not one of the many utilitarian organizations of the Church which are set up to pursue a definite goal,' writes Steidle in his commentary on St. Benedict's Holy Rule. 'The last and the deepest meaning of the abbey is not the dignified and solemn presentation of the liturgical services nor the cultivation of choral singing or of scholarship, research, instruction and education, the cure of souls, missionary work, art and craftsmanship, or the erection of model enterprises . . . It cannot be sufficiently stressed that the final significance and purpose of the abbey lies in the formation of a community which is inspired and vitally filled by Christ's Holy Spirit . . . The only duty of the abbey is to make the monastic vows [of its professed monks] a reality.'[2] We know from Gregory the Great's *Vita* of St. Benedict that he took an active part in the cure of souls among the laity around him; indeed, we do not go too far when we say that he did a good deal of straightforward parish work. Yet parish work is not even mentioned in the Holy Rule. It was but secondary to the sacred mission of the monastic communities. When modern students of Benedictinism, under the influence of conceptions bred by and characteristic of our activistic society, tried by hook or by crook to foist a defined and definite 'purpose' on the Order, when they insisted, for instance, that it came into being to tend and foster the liturgy – the so-called *propter chorum fundati* theory – they were decidedly opposed by the spokesmen of Benedictinism itself. Indeed, that opposition at times assumed considerable intensity, a strong proof that something truly profound was involved.[3]

Comparing the ideal priest and the ideal monk, St. Thomas Aquinas points out, in his little work *De Perfectione Vitae Spiritualis*, that both are at one in so far as both seek growth in godliness through the practice of charity. But charity is twofold: it is divided into love of God and love of neighbour, even if the two ultimately coincide. The ideal monk pursues, to the utmost of his forces, the love of God, and he serves his neighbours precisely by loving God; the ideal priest, on the other hand, has to concentrate on his service to his flock, and he loves God precisely by serving

[1] The point is very strongly made by Dom Cuthbert Butler. Cf. loc. cit., especially pp. 28, 29, 368.

[2] Steidle, loc. cit., pp. 48, 49, 47.

[3] Ibid., loc. cit., p. 241 (note 2); Blazovich, loc. cit., p. 106; Butler, loc. cit., pp. 29 et seq.

them. In another context, namely in the *Summa Theologiae*, St. Thomas uses a quotation from St. Gregory's *Regula Pastoralis* to illustrate the essential difference: 'Isaias wishing to be of profit to his neighbour by means of the active life, desired the office of preaching, whereas Jeremias who was fain to hold fast to the love of his Creator exclaimed against being sent to preach.' Jeremias was thus the type and predecessor of the clergy regular, Isaias of the clergy secular. In the passage which we have just quoted, the contrast is almost expressed by the confrontation of 'active' and 'passive', and though these words must obviously be used with caution in this context (for the monk cannot, of course, be entirely passive, if he is to do his work, the *opus Dei*), they do explain what is involved, and they have therefore been, in tradition, repeatedly employed to point the distinction.[1]

Perhaps the reader will see now more clearly what we meant when we said that the monk endeavoured to *be* something rather than to *do* something. The case of the secular clergy is very different, indeed, diametrically opposed. The parish priest has work to do and his whole *raison d'être* lies in doing that work. He is by definition the executive, one might almost say, the manipulatory, instrument of the Church in its day-to-day operations.

At this point it is almost unavoidable to draw a parallel between the Church and the State. The clergy has often, nay invariably, been characterized as a kind of bureaucracy and it is obvious that there is some truth in this comparison. The laity of the Church, including, so far as Catholicism is concerned, also the clergy regular, the monks, corresponds to the citizenry. The priesthood on the other hand corresponds to officialdom, to what, in the English language, is so strikingly described as the civil service. In one sense, the laity *is* the Church, as the citizens *are* the State. They provide the body as it were, and the health of the whole depends on their quality. Yet in another sense, the bureaucracy is the State as the hierarchy is the Church, for it is they who act on behalf of the collectivities concerned. It would not be difficult,

---

[1] Cf. Bouessé, loc. cit., pp. 147 and 148. *De Perfectione*, 2, 11, 16, 17; *Summa*, IIa IIae, qu. 185, art. 2; *Regula Pastoralis*, I, 17. Cf. St. Thomas Aquinas, *The Religious State*, ed. Father Procter (no first name given), St. Louis 1902, pp. 8, 9, 48–52, 87–95; The *'Summa Theologica' of St. Thomas Aquinas*, transl. by Fathers of the English Dominican Province, vol. XIV, London 1922, p. 184; *Patrologia Latina*, vol. LXXVII, Paris 1896, col. 20.

starting from this definition of the priesthood as a bureaucracy, to spin out the metaphor involved, and to follow it, point for point, in a lengthy disquisition. Some light might thereby be shed on the phenomenon; and yet it is impossible to see how a really realistic sociology of religion could be achieved in this way.

For the Church is not, in her inmost nature, like the State. The 'administrative work' which she does is not secular, not rational, not utilitarian. If she 'administers' anything it is the sacraments, and the sacraments are loaded with mystery, a fact which gives the term 'administration' in this context a curious – indeed, we should not hesitate to say, an improper – meaning. If a parallel must be drawn between the priest in the Church on the one hand and some outside figure on the other, it would lie much more in line with religious and especially Catholic (and that is to say, organological) thinking to liken him to a physician who administers some medication than to a bureaucrat who administers a department of state, the roads or the railways or whatever. Yet even this comparison would fail in the last resort. The priest should, like anybody else, be seen in his own terms, otherwise only a distorted picture can result.

Starting therefore from the *differentia specifica* of the Catholic priest himself rather than from any *genus proximum* in his environment under which he might conceivably be subsumed, we would, at least in a preliminary way, define him as one who serves the sacraments, for serving the sacraments is the office as well as the function with which the community has entrusted him. To the believer, he is in the first place the man who says mass, i.e. administers the sacrament of the altar, who imposes a penance and pronounces absolution, i.e. administers the sacrament of forgiveness, who gives the last rites, i.e. administers the sacrament of extreme unction, and so on. Yet the tie between the priesthood and the sacramental system is even closer. Priests in a sense 'make' the sacraments, but they are themselves made by a sacrament. You become a *sacerdos* by receiving the sacrament of ordination. Everything must for these reasons depend on a proper understanding of the idea of a sacrament.

It is our hard fate to be, once again, forced into a polemic with Max Weber, but it is all too clear that this cannot be avoided, if an unprejudiced and adequate account of the priesthood is to be achieved. To Weber, the Catholic priest could be understood best, if his cultic or mystical rather than his sober bureaucratic side is to be considered, not by looking at him, but by looking at somebody else, not by looking at a medieval and modern figure, but by looking at a primitive one – the wizard, the medicine man, the magician. This personage had loomed very large in our race's superstitious past: he was thought to be loaded with occult energies, potent for evil, yet potentially also a promoter of good. The Catholic priest presented, in Weber's opinion, something like a faded picture of this dire devil-man: working for the assumed supernal rather than for the dreaded infernal powers, he was yet like his predecessor in that he, too, was 'loaded', i.e. in possession of a supernatural potency – in that he was, to say the least, capable of doing what other, ordinary men could not do. The sacrament of ordination was, to Weber's way of thinking, the occult act of 'loading' the priest, that is to say, taking him out of the human race and making him into something more – precisely a kind of wizard, medicine man, modern magician, or rather magician whom the intellectual inertia of the masses had allowed to stray into the modern age.

The parts of *Wirtschaft und Gesellschaft* which deal with this subject, and which Ephraim Fischoff has translated and published under the title *The Sociology of Religion*, provide ample proof that our summation of Weber's curious conception of the Catholic priest is correct. They evince little of that 'value-free' attitude, of that absence of all prejudice, which Weber never ceased to preach, but which he – at any rate on this occasion – honoured in the breach rather than in the observance. This is what he writes in a rather decisive passage: 'The crystallization of developed conceptions of supernatural forces as gods, even as a single transcendent god, by no means automatically eliminated the ancient magical notions, not even in Christianity . . . A [divine] power conceived by analogy to [the power of] living persons may be coerced into the service of man, just as the naturalistic power of a spirit could be coerced. Whoever possesses the requisite charisma [i.e. the requisite indwelling dynamis] for employing the proper means is stronger even than the god whom he can compel to do his will. In these cases, religious behaviour is not worship of the god but rather coercion of the god, and invocation is not prayer but rather the exercise of magical formulae. Such is one ineradicable basis of popular religion, particularly in India. Indeed, such coercive religion is universally diffused, and even the Catholic priest continues to practise something of this magical power.' While these sentences refer mainly to the 'miracle of the mass', i.e. the sacrament of the altar, a later context brings parallel assertions concerning another sacrament, that of penance: In primitive societies 'the diviner is consulted when sickness or other blows of fate have led to the suspicion that some magical transgression is responsible, making it necessary to ascertain the means by which the aggrieved spirit, demon or god may be pacified. This is also the source of the confessional which originally had no connection with ethical influences on life . . . Pastoral care may later assume diverse forms. To the extent that it is a charismatic distribution of grace, it stands in a close inner relationship to magical manipulations'.[1] These are hard words. The friendliest statement to be found in the text is to the effect that 'in practice, the viewpoint of the Catholic church has oscillated between a relatively magical and a relatively ethical orientation'.[2] This does not, however, countermand the earlier and more basic assertion that 'the concept of the priest includes a magical qualification'.[3]

It must, surely, be obvious that magic, as Weber (in our opinion correctly) conceives it, namely as an attempt to *coerce* the higher powers, is diametrically opposed to religion – to *every* religion, whatever its shape might otherwise be. For religion properly so called is man's humble submission to the gods or to God; its attitude is one of prayer and petition, not one of demand and command. Rightly, therefore, the leading experts in the science of religion have protested against the careless confounding of the two phenomena of which Weber's argument is an example. 'It is only permissible to speak of magic,' writes Friedrich Heiler, one of the finest minds in the field, 'where the relation of man to the mysterious forces lacks devotional awe and where ritual practice has turned into a rational quasi-scientific technique . . . The wide connotation of the terms "magic" and "magical" has caused great confusion in so far as the use in high mystical piety of the sacraments has been described by and condemned in it. It would be desirable to restrict the employment of these terms so far as

[1] Fischoff, loc. cit., pp. 25 and 75; cf. also pp. 14 and 186. On this latter page, there is another reference to the sacrament of the altar. Through it, Weber tells us, 'some host' is 'magically transformed into the body of a god'.
[2] Loc. cit., p. 188.   [3] Ibid., p. 28.

possible and to apply them only to those degenerate forms of belief . . . which have broken loose from the core of religiosity and, in their divorce from it, have undergone complete corruption.'[1] E. O. James, too, feels that perhaps 'the time has come to drop the use of the term "magic" altogether,' especially if it is given a wide compass, for there are in reality 'two fundamentally distinct kinds of thought, action and intention'. The magician properly so called 'acts exclusively on his own authority and initiative', while the priest 'supplicates and conciliates forces superior to himself': 'the one officiates in his own name and by his [own] occult methods; the other serves at the altar . . . as the representative of the community in its relations with . . . the unseen world.'[2]

These are apposite and appropriate remarks. The assertion that there are, or have been, or can be Catholic priests who think, or feel, or imagine, that they can actually *coerce* God, e.g. *force* Him to come down on the altar, when they speak certain words, is so utterly fantastic that it is impossible to spare Weber the unqualified reproach that he knew next to nothing about the religious tradition which he was discussing and condemning with so much blandly self-arrogated authority. Even the barest basic facts are disregarded. To them belongs the presence of the Catholic's, as any Christian's, bedrock conviction that man is absolutely dependent on God, even for the simple continuance of his life, that he is a creature who was not only made by God but could not even draw another breath unless God continually sustained him, along with the whole universe in which he is included. From a theology of this complexion, no magical conclusions can ever be drawn. How could a thinking reed impose his will on the Lord of Heaven and Earth? The very idea must, to *any* Christian, whatever his denominational ties, necessarily appear outrageous, not to say the height of outrageousness. The assumption, attributed by Weber to the Brahmins, of the possibility of an 'effective magical coercion of the gods',[3] of a *manipulation* of God, is totally abhorrent, and necessarily so, to every theist who deserves that name. The explanation of the Christian and Catholic sacramental system must clearly be sought and found along different lines.

Before trying to elucidate the true concept of a sacrament, and

[1] Heiler, loc. cit., p. 167.
[2] James, loc. cit., pp. 14 and 33; cf. also p. 26.   [3] Ibid., p. 14.

thereby laying sounder foundations for the definition of the priestly office, the office, that is, which consists pre-eminently in the administration of the sacraments, we should note the abuse of the term 'magic' of which Weber renders himself guilty. Social anthropologists, when they wish to explain to their students what the term connotes, are apt to tell them some story which can serve as an illustration. An old woman, they will say, gets hold of a lump of wax and moulds it into the likeness of a man, a definite man in the tribe. Either the puppet will look like that man, or it will at least 'mean' that man; it will be identified with him in some way. Then the old woman, the witch as we may begin to call her, takes a needle and thrusts it through the chest of the doll in the belief, or in the expectation, or at least in the hope, that now the man meant, the chosen victim of the black art, will collapse and die, as if he had in fact been stabbed through the heart. That is magic. The underlying idea is indeed the conviction that a human being loaded with occult power can coerce nature, can, by his will, or perhaps simply by the recitation of an occult-power-laden formula, impose himself on the forces of reality and make them do his imperious bidding. What the necromancer tries to do, then, is to insert himself into the natural nexus of cause and effect, to introduce his wish, his subjective whim, into the objective texture of events. He regards himself as a new cause that will bring a specific new effect, but it is all to take place in the framework of the given, workaday world.

It is because of this enclosedness of the magical operation in the physical universe, both so far as the supposedly causative act and the anticipated emergent effect are concerned, that it cannot, by any stretch of the imagination, be compared to the sacraments. For the sacraments are physical acts which have *meta*physical, not *physical*, consequences. We may also say that they are deeds done on earth which are valid in heaven, or deeds done in time which are valid in eternity. The baby whom the priest has baptized in water and the ordinand on whom the bishop has laid his hands remain in every respect, physically, chemically, organically and ethically, the human beings they have been before. The *character indelebilis* of which theology speaks and which faith accepts as real, is impressed on the soul, not on the body, and the same applies, *mutatis mutandis*, to the particles of bread and wine which, on the altar, undergo transubstantiation, i.e. a change in their invisible essence, not one in their visible accidents, colour, weight, taste or whatever else it may be. To overlook this truly decisive difference, this difference between phenomena which are lightheartedly compared and lightheartedly confused by Weber, but which are in fact literally worlds apart, shows, to say the least, that he operated with very blurred concepts.

It is not this conclusion, however, this attempted commingling of fire and water, to which the sociologist, as a sociologist, must most vigorously take exception. Rather, it is once again the individualistic substructure of Weber's thinking and the consequent one-sidedness and limitation, not to say falsification, of that thinking itself with which the sociologist must needs disagree. It is for Weber a matter of course that the priest does whatever he does, whether its results be physical or metaphysical, of this world or of another, by his own inherent charisma (a word used, in this context, in a slightly deviant sense, denoting less a personal capacity to impress, as it usually does with Weber, than a kind of *mana*, an occult potency and power on the part of the consecrated individual). It does not even occur to him that the underlying conception may be *toto coelo* different; he has no knowledge and no inkling of the fact that it is for Catholics in truth not the priest himself who administers the sacraments but the Church, the Church as a collectivity, as *one* body, and indeed as the Body of *Christ*, so that it is in the last resort God who administers the sacraments and not man at all – neither man as an individual nor yet men as a collectivity. 'Jesus is the principal cause (*causa principalis*) of all functions exercised by the Church, their ultimate source and the basis of their efficacy,' writes Karl Adam, using the language of the Scholastics. 'Man is only an instrument,' he continues, 'the *causa instrumentalis*, through whom Christ Himself acting in the Church teaches and sanctifies and governs. And so in the functioning of the Church, the human self [of the priest], the human personality, the individual as such, falls wholly into the background. Not any human personality, but the redemptive might of Jesus controls the Church.' What is true of the living instrumentality, the priest, is true, *a fortiori*, of the dead instruments, the sacramentals. 'According to the Scotist view which is now advocated by many theologians, the sacrament itself possesses no strictly "physical" causality in any way immanent in its sign. On the contrary, the sacramental grace flows directly from Jesus into the soul of the believer. The sacrament is no more than an appointed sign of Christ, an objectivization of the gracious will of Jesus, a visible and perceptible "I will, be thou made clean".[1] There is thus a lot of faith in sacramental thinking, faith in the total identity of the Church and Christ, the Redeemer and the redeemed, but there is little magic; in fact, there is none at all. If Weber had wished to understand all this, he would have had to read some such book as Abbot Columba Marmion's classical study, *Christ in His Mysteries*. But that is precisely what he disdained to do. To judge from his references, or rather from the absence of them, he stood by the maxim still widely current in the Protestant Germany of his day, *Catholica non leguntur*. But this is hardly the way to inside knowledge or to a sociology which is 'value-free' and 'understanding'.

One thing, of course, is true and should be emphasized because it explains why it is easy for an inherently unsympathetic and potentially hostile observer from the outside to jump to the conclusion that something like magic survives in the sacraments. These rites have their manipulatory side, and the manipulation involves material objects, for instance water in the case of baptism, oil in the case of ordination and extreme unction, bread and wine in the case of communion, sound patterns (the words of absolution) in the case of confession. The metaphysical effects are therefore in a manner dependent on physical things and their ritual handling. But it would be wrong to conclude from these externals that we are after all confronted with a form of sorcery: it is right, on the other hand, to identify, even in these bodily acts, a spiritual, and nothing-but-spiritual, meaning. It is true that faith must be stretched even further here than we have just seen it stretched; but faith in God's help is not belief in occult, impersonal machinations and formulae. Chateaubriand strikes the correct note and strikingly summarizes the Catholic position when he says, the use of materia things is a divine concession to the *grossièreté de nos sens*, the crudity of our mentality.[2] He also quotes in this context the atheist Denis Diderot. 'Suppress all the visible symbols,' the *Encyclopédiste* writes in his *Essais sur la Peinture*, 'and the rest will soon be reduced to a metaphysical rigmarole which will assume as many bizarre shapes as there are heads.' Pictorial presentations are

[1] Adam, loc. cit., pp. 24 and 29.
[2] *Génie du Christianisme*, as quoted, vol. II, p. 68.

necessary, he insists, if religion is to have any effect on the people.[1]
Man – so we may continue in this vein – is not a spiritual being;
he is sunk in a body and in a bodily universe and only that which
is tangible will be truly real to him. In order to operate in a world
such as we know it and such as we are made for, metaphysical
values must find physical embodiment, otherwise they simply will
not count. 'It is natural to man,' writes St. Thomas Aquinas, 'to
attain to intellectual truths through sensible objects, because all
our knowledge originates from sense.'[2] 'By visible things to the
invisible: that is the fundamental principle of the whole system of
the Church,' writes Karl Adam nearly seven hundred years after
St. Thomas, but in exactly the same spirit. 'It is the function of
Christ and Christianity to bring the love and grace of God to
sense-bound man under the veil of visible and evident signs . . .
The seven sacraments are God's appointed means whereby man
shall ordinarily experience . . . the elevation of his being into the
stream of God's life and love.'[3] That, then, is why, according to
Chateaubriand, Christ instituted sacraments tied to physical
symbols before He left the earth: He knew us and yet He wished
to help us. The connection of an inward grace with an outward
form, and even with an outward thing, the objectivation of it, so
to speak, is therefore in the eyes of faith the moving evidence of an
overflowing divine love which meets man in a manner acceptable
to, profitable for, and manageable by, him. It is, to express it in a
terminology which we have used before and which is surely most
appropriate here, part and parcel of the *agape* of the Godhead, His
coming down to *our* level so that in the end we may rise up to *His*.

These conceptions are not discussable by the sociologist as a
sociologist, i.e. as a man of science. They must be taken by him as
givens which he may like or dislike, but with which he has to
reckon because they are present in, and of the essence of, his field
of observation. If he does not reckon with them but chooses to
disregard them, he will assuredly never understand what a priest
is, and we have introduced an account of them here for one reason,
and one reason only, namely precisely this – the proper understanding of the essence of (Catholic) priesthood. In a study dealing

---

[1] Chateaubriand, loc. cit., p. 303 and 304 (note XLI).
[2] *Summa Theologiae*, Ia, qu. 1, a. 9. Cf. The '*Summa Theologica*', as quoted, vol.
I, London 1911, p. 15.
[3] Adam, loc. cit., pp. 79 and 206.

exclusively with the Radical Reformation, the Quakers, for instance, they would hardly have had to be mentioned at all. Yet it should be remarked in passing that what we have said is necessary also, though to a lesser extent, for the proper understanding of the essence of the Protestant ministry. We see here again what we have seen before, that the true alternatives, in the sociology of religion, are not Catholicism and Protestantism *tout court*, but rather Roman Catholicism and the Radical Reformation. As for Lutheranism and Calvinism, they certainly reduced the sacramental system, and the kind of thinking that goes with it, to a bare minimum, but the salient point is that they never cast it off altogether. Luther, after some uncertainty about confession, ended up with two sacraments, Baptism and the Lord's Supper. So far as the latter is concerned, he weakened the traditional dogma of transsubstantiation into his own doctrine of consubstantiation, but that is still a kindred form of mysticism. Only the Swiss Reformers replaced the 'real presence' by the concept of a memorial meal. Yet even they held fast to baptism as a 'supernatural blessing' and therefore there is, as we shall see in due course, still a sacramental element (albeit sensibly diminished) in their predicants, as there is in the Lutheran pastors.

The reduction of the sacramental system which we have just noted, and which had as its reflex a change in the character of church services and church servants, must not be thought of as merely a shift in fideist positions. On the contrary, it had very 'real' antecedents, and these were sociological in the narrowest sense of the word. So long as the matrix of the Church was a community according to the Tönnies definition, a man would be an organ of the whole rather than an independent personality. When the background was transformed and society in general became more associational, with a constantly growing emphasis on the uniqueness of the individual, he would be conceived as one acting *on* others rather than as one acting for others, and the image dominant before of *all* acting in and by *one* person would be considerably weakened, not to say driven near the vanishing point. It was the very same process which, by a kind of feedback, further undermined the sacramental style of thinking. Where man is essentially a symbol of the clan (a 'representer' of it, as the older Scots tongue so finely has it), where he is a MacDonald rather than Ian or Seumas, it is easier to comprehend that a piece of bread 'is' the body of Christ than where men and things are seen in their ultimate selfhood, and a piece of bread is simply a piece of bread with no possible reference beyond itself. Indeed, it could be argued that the whole sacramental system – the very inception and conception of it – is to be seen, in the light of the sociology of knowledge, as an outgrowth of the form of life known to sociologists as community. Community bears in itself the seed of a symbol-setting mentality, and sacramentalism is one of its fruits bred true to type. The coming of an associational society puts the process into reverse gear, replaces a 'realistic' philosophy by a nominalistic one, that is to say, replaces thinking in terms of archetypes by thinking in terms of the ultimately and irreducibly particular and thereby deprives sacramentalism of its plausibility. Theologians, of course, see the origins of the sacraments in their direct divine institution. The sacrament of the altar, for instance, the Eucharist, is traced back to the Gospel according to St. Matthew, chapter XXVI, verses 26–28, and parallels, and to I Corinthians XI, 23–26. Yet in addition to these starting points in sacred history there are also the starting points in collective psychology, in the collective subconscious as we may say in reference to Carl Gustav Jung, whose theory of archetypes is directly relevant here. Water and wine, bread and oil are not only physical objects as science knows them, they were for centuries, down to the dawn of the scientific age, carriers of religious meanings as well, and to many men they are so still. When Jesus instituted the sacraments, he did not choose their outward signs at random; rather did He draw on a deep well that had gushed up as soon as the human race had developed any mentality at all and continued to flow strongly until very recent times. To say the least, therefore, there was no resistance, in the older forms of society, to the development of a generally symbolic and specifically sacramental world-view. It was truly 'natural' in and for them to symbolize, and even to effect, the admission of a man into a special functional-occupational grouping by imposition, on his head, of the hands of those who were already established in it, just as it was natural for them to develop special functional-occupational groups in religion in the first place. With the arrival of the budding age of modernity, of the day of Luther and Calvin and George Fox, there is, not only, as we have seen, resistance to the development of special functional-occupational groups in religion, or rather insistence on their restriction and reduction, there is also, in connection with and in prolongation of this retro-action, a stage-wise withering away of symbolistic philosophizing and of its credal component, sacramentalism. These are deeper connections which we intend to explore in the fifth and final volume of this work. Here they are merely meant to help in explaining the ideal foundations of the specifically Catholic conception of the priest as one who (while himself the creature of a sacrament) is administering the sacraments on behalf of all, of the whole Body of Christ, and hence of Christ Himself.

Having hammered and, it is hoped, driven home the point that the *sacerdotium* of the older forms of Christianity is, in every one of the connected meanings of the word, an institution of *community*, we can proceed to present some of the illustrative and corroborative evidence. The chain of witnesses stretches from the first to the last ages, a sure proof that we are confronted with an abiding and essential trait.

Among the writers in whom the speculations of the patristic age came, so to speak, to a head, Cyprian of Carthage occupies an especially splendid place, for his mind is like a bright mirror in which we can see much, and see it sharply. This great summarizer achieved in one of his epistles a very neat formulation of the ecclesiological and soteriological conception which interests us here: 'You must know,' he writes to his addressee, Florentius Pupianus, 'that the bishop is in the Church and the Church in the bishop.'[1] Nobody will have any quarrel with the first half of this statement ('the bishop is in the Church') which indeed sounds quite trite. But it is different with the second half which alone gives point to the whole sentence ('the Church is in the bishop') – an assertion which is totally unacceptable to Protestants and must sound strange to any modern ear. Yet Cyprian meant precisely what he said. And other great spokesmen of the early Church were with him, for instance Ignatius of Antioch. As Ignatius sees things, the ecclesiastical community is the place in and through which all men receive the Spirit; but that Spirit is concentrated, as it were, in the bishop. He is therefore the 'focus' of the community, and the proper function of a focus is to draw all the rays into one. Rightly does Campenhausen, in his dis-

[1] Cf. *Patrologia Latina*, as quoted, vol. IV, Paris 1891, col. 419. My translation.

cussion of Ignatius, speak of an interpenetration of pneumatic and official or ecclesiastical thinking. The Church has a soul, and that soul is (pre-eminently, substantially) in the official or ecclesiastical head, the bishop.[1] When he acts, therefore, *all* act.

A thousand years or so later we are with St. Thomas Aquinas. His background is city life, and in a city collective ties invariably weaken and individualistic ideas wax strong. Yet the basic conception is no different from Cyprian's, as we can see from the following quotation out of the *Summa Theologiae*: 'When the priest consecrates the Eucharist, he does so in the person of the entire Church, as is evident from the fact of his putting up all prayers in the person of the Church.'[2] On an earlier page, the Saint expresses the same conviction in a slightly different form: 'The priest both offers and consumes the blood on behalf of all.'[3]

Since the High Middle Ages, collective ties have weakened further and individualistic ideas have waxed stronger still. Yet, once again, the basic conception is the same as in Cyprian and Thomas, and it must be so, for the Catholic Church is and remains a community in the sense of Tönnies. She may reform herself in a thousand and one different ways and still remain herself; but if she were ever to drop the idea that one can act for all, she would no longer be what she had been before. Indeed, she would not only cease to be Catholic then, she would (according to her own tradition) cease to be Christian, for was not Christ, too, one who acted for all? 'Nowhere else, in no other society, is the idea of community, of fellowship in doing and suffering, in prayer and love, and of growth and formation in and through such fellowship, so strongly embedded in doctrine, morals and worship, as in the Catholic Church,' writes Karl Adam, and what he says determines the contents of the concept of a priest as well. For 'the priest does not offer [sacrifice] for himself alone. Nor does he merely offer [it] as the people's representative, so that as in the ancient sacrifices there is only a moral unity between priest and people. On the contrary, the unity between priest and people is a

---

[1] Cf. Campenhausen, loc. cit., pp. 109-10, 113-14, 124.
[2] IIIa, qu. 82, a. 7. The '*Summa Theologica*', as quoted, vol. XVII, London 1914, p. 424.
[3] IIIa, qu. 80, a. 12. Cf. loc. cit., p. 402.

mystically *real* unity.'[1] Such quotations could be indefinitely prolonged. But it is hardly necessary. Perhaps it would be best to sum it all up with the help of the great simile to which discussions of the Catholic Church have ever a tendency to return – the simile of the body. The priests are *the hands* of the Church. She acts where they do.

They are the hands, and they are the tongue, too. With this statement we leave the first of the three functions which, with E. O. James, we have enumerated, the cult, and turn to the second, preaching. But is preaching – to which we may add teaching – really only the *second* of the priest's functions, is it not, and necessarily, the first? Are the sacraments, on the other hand, not unavoidably, logically, secondary in relation to it? Must there not be an effort in education, in moralization, in sanctification, before there can be a community in which, and on behalf of which, mass, for instance, may be said and the other sacraments sought and given? Common-sense would seem to say so, and common sense is usually right. But in this case it is not, perhaps, as right as it would seem. Or perhaps we had better say that much depends on the circumstances – that the common-sense of one age is not necessarily that of another. The common-sense of an age of association is not necessarily the common-sense of an age of community. Let me explain.

The Catholic Church does not see herself only as a church; she sees herself also as a total culture, an *inclusive* culture, to be correct, and her historical experience of the Middle Ages has confirmed her in this belief. If we may borrow, for a moment, St. Cyprian's authoritative words, we should say that the Church is in a Catholic culture, and the Catholic culture is in the Church. But a culture, a total culture, is not handed on by preaching or, more generally, by word of mouth. It is a stream of life and we learn to live in it simply by living in it. Basically a child is not told that he must get up at 7 o'clock in the morning; he does so because those around him do so, and he picks up the conviction that it is right to do so in the same manner, unwittingly, unsuspectingly, quasi-automatically. There are several traditional phrases which correctly, if metaphorically, describe the process. We say that a child 'sucks something in with his mother's milk', or that he 'breathes it in with the atmosphere', the vital air around him. Prodding is

[1] Adam, loc. cit., pp. 9, 147, 148. Our emphasis.

necessary, even a talking-to now and then, as we all know. But such prodding, such sermonizing is, surely, only secondary. Nor would it be at all effective if it could not appeal to a feeling in the youngster who finds it difficult to get out of bed that he should do so, that it is his duty to comply with the order of life, including the clock-order, which is established around him and, by habituation, even in him. Sociologists are wont to call this the 'internalization of values', and since Durkheim and Parsons they know that there can be no abiding social system without such internalization. Catholicism has ever lived by this principle. The Church has ever asked the parents to bring their children to mass on Sunday morning, even if they do not understand yet what is going on. For well before they will or can understand what is going on, they must have a sense, so to speak, of the sacred cult and its meaning – a meaning which is not fully explicable in words anyway. Differently expressed, the Church has never placed total reliance on rational teaching. Rational teaching narrows man into an intellect with a vital adjunct, but real man is more: he is a vital whole with an intellect given him merely as a piece of equipment, a convenient tool. It is at that vital whole, at that total man, at that personal centre that Catholic culture transmission has ever aimed. Even her greatest rationalists have done so. St. Thomas Aquinas' hymns have converted more hearts than his arguments, including the best. Indeed, the whole life-effort of that great rationalist must be seen in this light. He did not think that the proofs for the existence of God would ever sway, or simply reach, a man who was, in Max Weber's phrase, religiously 'unmusical' or deaf. What Aquinas undertook was merely to elaborate more formal proof for a proposition – 'there is a God' – which was, in his world, beyond material doubt anyway.[1]

A small illustration will show more clearly what is involved. Until very recently it was a Catholic custom to genuflect in church when, in the recitation of the creed, the words *Et homo factus est* – 'And He was made man' – were reached. Such genuflection inculcated, indeed, incorporated, in the faithful a deep, deeper-than-rational respect for the mystery of the Incarnation, and it is highly doubtful that any preaching, however effective otherwise, could

[1] Cf. Stark, W., *Social Theory and Christian Thought*, London 1959, pp. 150, 151, 161. (The paper on Max Scheler, on whose philosophy the arguments in the text are based.)

get so much 'under the skin', or, we should rather say, into the heart, as this simple custom. The Catholic community down through the centuries has always responded to this mode of expressing inward states by outward acts, precisely because these acts would not only express the sanctifying sentiments which they showed forth but also create them, i.e. strengthen them in those who already had them, and evoke them in those who did not yet have them, the young, the next generation. When Mozart elaborated, in his mass music, the four credal words, when he embroidered them, so to speak, when, for instance, he made a coloratura aria out of them, he responded to a religious need (more felt by him, we can be sure, than known), the need to find techniques of character-formation which can dispense with words and penetrate more deeply than they can. Non-Catholics have often found Catholics very opinionated, stubborn, 'fanatical' etc. The reason for this is that religious education among them does not rely on the school and the pulpit only, as it does in some of the Reformation and post-Reformation churches (not in all, as we would emphasize – not in Methodism, for example), that it mobilizes all methods of access to the innermost recesses of the mind and heart. But if such is the Catholic tradition in culture-transmission, preaching can only be a relatively secondary strand, not comparable to the practice of the sacraments whose reception is experiential, not merely rational. The sacraments are the carriers of life and not merely arguments.

Intellectuals, with their naïve, if understandable, over-estimation of the intellect and of ideas have often, nay invariably, shown a tendency to underestimate the power of acts, or actions, to convert, convince, compel and dominate; they place their reliance on verbal pleas, even from the pulpit, even in religious matters which are yet sub- or super-rational (whatever one wants to call them). But the greatest of them have understood. Pascal, for instance, discusses the question as to how a non-believer can bring himself to believe, and he advises him not to expect true conversion from a study of the proofs for the existence of God. This is what he writes: 'You would like to attain faith and do not know the way; you would like to cure yourself of unbelief and ask the remedy for it. Learn of those who have been bound like you . . . and who are cured of an ill of which you would be cured. Follow the way by which they began; by acting as if they believed, taking the holy water, having masses said etc. . . . . This will naturally make you believe . . .'[1]

Henri Bergson felt exactly like Blaise Pascal. In a decisive context of *The Two Sources of Morality and Religion*, he asks whether the common-sense opinion is correct according to which something (an idea, a conviction, a creed) is introduced into us when we are religiously converted, and he answers that it is much rather the other way round – *we* are introduced into something outside of us, namely a stream of life, as passers-by may be drawn into a street dance.[2] The simile is apt and characterizes the underlying philosophies – that of Bergson and that of Catholicism – to perfection. The individual is not primary: primary is the existing socio-cultural system, or, better still, the ongoing socio-cultural process, and growing up is simply the fitting of the self to, and into, that system and process. In the case of a church, and especially of the Church, growing up, growth into full-fledged membership, religious maturation, is essentially a gradual conversion. If it can take place without prodding and preaching, *via facti* as it were, all the better.

We are not, in saying all this, forgetting that Catholicism has produced mighty preachers whose work has been essential to her work. Broadly speaking, she has developed, and, in some favoured individuals, perfected two great homiletic styles – the rationalistic style aiming at the head and the emotional style aiming at the heart. The Dominicans, officially described as the *Ordo Praedicatorum*, represent the former, the Passionists, founded to preach Christ 'and Him crucified', represent the latter. Yet the appearance and mighty unfolding of these movements merely confirms what we are saying, for their efforts were directed outward, towards the unconverted and the lapsed, those not yet won and those lost – the Cathari in the case of the Dominicans, the *fuorusciti* of all kinds in the case of the Passionists.[3] Preaching, then, has its prime place in the missionary effort of the Church, while it can only be subordinate in the proper, the very own, inner life of the community.

[1] *Pascal's Pensées*, Dutton paperback ed., New York 1958, p. 68. For the puzzling end of the passage quoted, and the explanation of the puzzle, *see* Stark, *Social Theory and Christian Thought*, p. 73.

[2] English transl. by Audra, R. A., and Brereton, C., paperback ed., Garden City, N.Y., n.d., p. 40.

[3] Cf. our vol. III, p. 308. *Fuoruscito* means outlaw, but in a wider sense it means all outsiders.

That life is a life of love, love of the God who graciously comes to meet those who seek Him in the guise of the sacraments, and love has never needed many words: where it exists, silence is as pregnant, or more so, than talk. This, certainly, was the opinion of St. Ignatius of Antioch. It is, indeed, generally surprising how little store this model bishop set by sermonizing.[1]

More recently, too, the absolute primacy of the sacraments has been strongly underlined by competent writers. Thus Bouessé states: 'Whatever the place of the priest, whether or not he is concerned with the cure of souls, he is above all sent to offer the Eucharistic sacrifice: that is his (as it is the Church's) first activity, and it is his last . . . All other activities . . . insert themselves between one such sacrifice and another.'[2]

However, it is precisely the realization that the voice which speaks for her is more important for the Church's relations with her neighbours than for the relations with those who inhabit her own house, which leads us after all to a high estimation of the preaching function, the second function of the priest. Christianity has the whole world to convert: if the love of God is its first concern, love of neighbour is a near-second, and the task of drawing the stranger into its ambit is, in a deeply social religion of this kind, an inescapable duty, nay, an inner psychological necessity to the believer himself. It must be so, for Christ the Archetype felt that necessity also, and, indeed, it shows forth His very essence – to be a lover of *all* souls, even of those yet far from Him. This is what we read in the first chapter of the Gospel according to St. Mark (verses 35–38): 'Rising very early, going out, He went into a desert place, and there He prayed. And Simon and they that were there with him followed after Him, and when they had found Him, they said to Him: All seek for thee. And He saith to them: let us go into the neighbouring towns and cities, that I may preach there also; for to this purpose am I come.' To this purpose He also called His apostles and sent them out evangelizing. He made them 'fishers of men',[3] and the net which they threw out was often woven from words. Thus preaching was initiated by the Founder Himself and will remain essential until all men are collected into one fold. When the faith started and missionary work was the very making of the Church, it could even be placed above the sacra-

[1] Campenhausen, loc. cit., p. 110.
[2] Bouessé, loc. cit., p. 139. Cf. also p. 161.   [3] Matthew IV, 19.

ments as it was in one context by St. Paul: 'Christ sent me not
to baptize, but to preach the Gospel,' he told his (and his
Master's) disciples (I Corinthians I, 17). But, surely, he wanted ?
to preach only so that in the end he could baptize: we sow
only so that we may reap. Preaching is a means to an end, albeit
an indispensable means, while the sacraments are the end, in
so far as through them the love of God, ascending as well as
descending, is mediated and both objectively and subjectively
realized.

By emphasizing that preaching is in principle an outward-
directed rather than an inside-anchored function of the priesthood,
that it belongs more to the missionary than to the parish pastor, we
do not, however, even for a single second, deny that it is in practice of the essence of the parish pastor's work also. For nobody is
enough converted, whether or not he is baptized, whether or not
he is assiduous at receiving the sacraments, and even whether or
not he loves, for the love of man is but weak even at its best, as the
great saints have ever emphasized; everybody therefore needs
prodding and preaching. In times of great moral malaise powerful
preachers have arisen whose chosen mission field was their home
pitch, their country, their city or their parish. Such was Berthold
of Regensburg, such also was Geiler of Kaysersberg. Men of their
mettle are needed now, as they were always needed. So long as our
race is inclined to waywardness and folly – and that is to say, so
long as they remain the creatures we know, so long as the waters of
history continue to flow – they will need exhortation, and if its
voice should ever fall silent, religion would be doomed to total
involution, to decay and death.

We have, in what has gone before, drawn a fairly definite contrast between the sacraments and the sermon, the priest's work at
the altar and his work in the pulpit, and we do not propose to do
anything to blur the dividing line. Yet, lest a false impression be
created and the unity of the priestly function be misunderstood,
we must point out the similarities also. To these similarities
belongs above all the fact that both are collectivistic in character.
We have, two pages or so back, heard St. Thomas Aquinas say
that the priest is 'putting up all prayers in the person of the
Church'. It is the same with the putting out of his exhortations.
The voice that comes to the church-goers on a Sunday morning
between the Gospel reading and the Creed, is not one man's voice,

but that of the community. Or rather, what is good and strong and convincing is from the community, and ultimately, for the believer, from Christ, while what is false and feeble stems from the individual as such. Rightly does Schelkle[1] draw our attention to the fact that when the Twelve were sent out, as later when the Seventy-two were sent, it was arranged that they should go two by two (Mark VI, 7, and Luke, X, 1). This was not an accidental or an incidental arrangement: rather was it an assertion and application of the principle of sociality, the safeguard of an essential element. Not that the message should be spread, but that it should be *rightly* spread, was Christ's concern, and as every individual is liable to error and aberration, it is agreement with the collective mind (if the term be allowed), that guarantees proper preaching. But he who speaks in agreement with the collective mind, speaks the collective mind, and this is what the priest, barring accidents, actually does.

Furthermore, a man does not speak only by his tongue, he also speaks by his gestures, and the most meaningful gestures of a priest are to be seen, not in the pulpit, but away from it: they are liturgical rather than homiletic. When the celebrant, at the beginning of the Mass of Good Friday, throws himself down and lies prostrate on the ground in wordless prayer, he is, at least potentially, much more eloquent than if he uttered a thousand words. We say potentially rather than *de facto* because modern man has little ready understanding for the cultic *gestus*, unlike medieval man who was well attuned to it. Yet if religion is to survive at all, symbolism has to survive as well, for material symbols convey and carry religious meanings much more effectively than mere language does, and it is, of course, the sacerdotal class whose mission it is to preserve the traditional symbolism, be it in objects or actions, vestments or vessels or signs of hand or whatever else. Seeing a cultic pattern performed – *any* cultic pattern – is therefore a little like hearing a sermon preached. Those who speak of a 'ministry of the word' might just as well speak of a 'ministry of vision'.

In this way, a sacrament is a little like a sermon, but a sermon is inversely also a little like a sacrament. This is a truth of which Martin Luther was more fully aware than any other religious man, and we shall have to return to this matter when we come to discuss

[1] Schelkle, loc. cit., pp. 74 and 75.

him and the Protestant conception of the ministry generally.[1] Yet
Catholics were and are by no means unaware of the semi-sacra-
mental character of the Word of God which loomed so large
in the Reformer's thinking. For a man's utterances contain and
convey his will, and if this will is mighty, the words that express it
will not and cannot be ineffectual in the external world either. But
God's will is almighty and therefore all-effectual. When hearing of
'the Word of God', the religious consciousness cannot but be
referred back to the origin of all things, to the creative act *kat
exochen*, and this creative act was commanded by the divine word:
'And God said: Be light made. And light was made' (Genesis I, 3).
Truly, therefore, can it be asserted, by and to the believing mind,
that 'in the beginning was the Word' (John I, 1). However these
words are interpreted – and Christians of all denominations have
never doubted that they refer both to God the Father and His
creative deed and to God the Son and His redemptive deed, that
the two Persons of the Godhead are one, that Christ is the Word
Incarnate – their aura of sacredness and power will, for the
believer, surround every sentence of Holy Writ. And it will also
surround, albeit with diminished strength, every sermon that
expounds Holy Writ. 'When the Catholic priest proclaims the
word of God,' writes Karl Adam, 'Christ Himself preaches
through him. Certainly, this authority of Christ is most plainly and
most strikingly expressed in the doctrinal pronouncements of His
Vicar; but it is present also in the preaching of the simple parish
priest in his remote village church.' After making these statements, Adam, in order to confirm them, jumps back across a
millennium and a half to St. Augustine, himself one of the mightiest
voices ever to be heard from the pulpit. 'Christ Himself speaks
through His disciples,' the great Doctor asserted. 'His voice is
heard through those whom He sends.'[2] And again, more directly
still: 'It is Christ who teaches . . . The head teaches the members
and the tongue speaks to the feet. It is Christ who teaches: let us
hear, let us fear, let us do what we are bidden.'[3] Consistently, the
Saint calls the sacrament literally *verbum visibile* and the words in

---

[1] Cf. below, pp. 307 et seq.
[2] *In Evangelium Ioannis*, XLVII, 5. Cf. *Patrologia Latina*, vol. XXXV, Paris
1902, col. 1735.
[3] *De Disciplina Christiana*, XIV, 15. Cf. *Patrologia Latina*, vol. XL, Paris 1887,
col. 678.

effect *sacramentum audibile*.[1] Adam might well have added to Augustine's sayings those of Paulus where he praises the Thessalonians (I, II, 13): 'When you received of us the word of God, you received it not as the word of men, but (as it is indeed) the word of God', as the word of fullness and of power (*ib*. I, I, 5). In the last resort Jesus Himself had laid the foundations of Pauline and Augustinian and generally Catholic convictions on this head when He told His apostles: 'It is not you that speak, but the Spirit of your Father that speaketh in you' (Matthew X, 20). If it is a definition of a sacrament to say that it is a channel through which the power of the Creator and the love of the Redeemer flow into human life, the sermon, too, must, in spite of the larger share of creaturely weakness that enters into it, be acknowledged to be akin to the sacraments properly so called.

Normally, the voice of the priest (behind which there stands the community, behind which in turn there stands, for the believer, Christ) is a voice of blessing. 'For Christ therefore we are ambassadors, God as it were exhorting by us,' says St. Paul. 'And he hath placed in us the word of reconciliation' (II Corinthians V, 20 and 19). But the very term exhortation is ambiguous, especially if it is used in connection with the term reconciliation. We are indeed reminded by the Apostle, as by many preachers since, that we are, as a race, reconciled, that is, redeemed, but we are also reminded that our personal case is not yet closed, that we may yet fall. The power-laden Word of God may dash down as well as raise up. It is necessary to remember the sterner Old Testament here as well as the milder New. 'I desired mercy and not sacrifice,' so Osee interpreted the mind of God. 'But they, like Adam, have transgressed the covenant . . . I have slain them by the words of my mouth' (VI, 6, 7, 5). The word of God, and the word spoken in the name of God, may therefore be one of judgment as well as one of blessing, a sentence of condemnation as well as merely a call to conversion or re-conversion. This is an important fact, and it brings us to the third strand in the priestly function, office and avocation: the administration of discipline.[2]

[1] Cf. *Patrologia Latina*, vol. XXXV, Paris 1902, col. 1840, and vol. XXXVIII, Paris 1865, col. 969. These passages are not quoted by Adam.

[2] We have discussed this already in connection with our elucidation of the concept of sacred law and with our rebuttal of the theory of progressive desacralization through legalization, and must send the reader back to pp. 141 et seq. above.

In passing from the administration of the sacraments *via* preaching to the administration of discipline, we are stepping over a broad dividing line, nay more: we are going from one pole of a dialectical relationship to the other, from thesis to antithesis. The priest who offers sacrifice on behalf of the community is in a humilific position: he abases himself and us because he prays, he implores, he spends incense, he immolates a victim. The priest, on the other hand, who takes a sinner back or holds him off, again on behalf of the community, is in a honorific position: he acts as one in authority, as for instance the judge on the bench who has an ultimate power to back him up. Theologically speaking, the priest represents the two aspects of Christ: the Christ of Gethsemane and the Cross, borne down by the load of mankind's sins, weak, suffering, even defeated, and the Christ of Easter Day, the Risen Christ, the Christ triumphant, He to Whom 'all power is given in heaven and in earth' (Matthew XXVIII, 18).[1] To this duality-in-unity (ultimately the duality-in-unity of the two natures in Christ, the human and the divine) there corresponds, of course, as ever, a cleavage in the Church and of the Church, which is in this respect, too, the Body of Christ, identical with Him. The Church is on the one hand a communion of sinners who have been laid low, and on the other hand a communion of saints who have been raised high. This essential and inescapable ambiguity or brokenness has always characterized the place and the position of the priest as well. It could not be otherwise, for he *is* the Church; the Church is 'in him'. Respected at some times and by some, he has been reviled at other times by others, or indeed by the same.

The social theorist who knows the wider history of his subject will at this point be vividly reminded of the way in which St. Augustine handles the basic institutions of secular society, notably government and property.[2] Both are the results of sin: government of men's desire to lord it over each other, property of their determination to possess more than the next fellow. Yet both are also the remedies of sin as we see very clearly when, in a thought-experiment, we think them away: without a settled government, without kingship, without police, and without legalized ownership, without a firm, respected and enforceable distribution of material goods, there would be more mutual hate

[1] Cf. Bouessé, loc. cit., pp. 74, 75, 98, 99.
[2] Cf. Stark, *Social Theory and Christian Thought*, as quoted, pp. 19 et seq.

and more fratricidal fighting than there is now. The institution known as priesthood lies somewhat parallel to the two basic institutions, the two pillar institutions, of society at large. We have priests, and we have to have priests, because we sin: and we have priests, and have to have them, so that we may sin less. It is in the context of the sacerdotal power to punish and to absolve that this becomes particularly obvious.

In the early days of the Church, the absolute unity of the pastor and his congregation lay open before all eyes, because penances were public. We still have a phrase which helps us to understand the situation then prevailing. 'In these circumstances . . .', we say. The circumstances were originally the *circumstantes,* literally those standing around the presiding officer, in this case the presbyter or bishop, and they made the decision; one might almost say, they laid down the law. The presiding officer himself merely voiced the decision made – excommunication in some instances, re-aggregation in others. The subsequent change which concentrated the judicial power in the clergy and the still later change which made most penances confidential and private seem in retrospect to have lessened or even broken the co-operation of the many and the one in this matter; indeed, they seem to have deprived the many of their rights and role. But appearances are deceptive. The ethical standards which the bishop as the *judex ordinarius diecoeseos* and the parish priests as father confessors apply are, of course, the precipitate of communal thinking, its codification in an agreed tradition. And if there is loss, there is gain as well. For crowds, according to experience, tend to be merciless, while the truly religious man, the Christian, is merciful like his Lord and Master. As discipline is handled now, it applies, not this or that congregation's momentary whim, but all Christendom's sifted and settled ethos. Here, too, we can say, with St. Augustine: *Securus judicat orbis terrarum.*[1]

It is for the historian, not for the sociologist, to give a detailed description of the process which reduced the part played by the congregation and magnified the part played by the priest in the area of discipline. Only one aspect has to be insisted on by the social analyst, namely the fact that the transformation was an uncontested, to all intents and purposes even unconscious, development. The Gospel according to St. Matthew speaks twice in

[1] Cf. above, p. 202.

short succession of the power to bind and loose, i.e. to expel a sinner from the ranks, with dire consequences for his fate in eternity, and to re-admit him and thus re-instate him in his assurance of salvation. In chapter XVI (verse 19) the power of the keys (as it is usually called) is given to one man, Peter; in chapter XVIII (verse 18) it is given to all, to the whole community. Logically, there is contradiction, but it was not experienced as such: one and all were simply one hand. Speaking of a 'monarchical' and a 'democratic' version, Campenhausen yet insists on their coincidence: 'The two forms may quietly be placed side by side, for it is one and the same power which is used, now by Peter and the Apostles, now by the Church in its entirety.'[1]

It is an often observed phenomenon that groups try to get rid of their duties, or to ensure the more efficient realization of them, by entrusting them to smaller committees, and that then, on a higher level, the same process is repeated again: after committal to the committee comes committal, *de facto* or *de jure*, to the committee's chairman. With the lapse of time, a monocratic constitution then results. If this happens without protest, it is a sign that an implicitly agreed development is taking place – something like the formation of a folkway. We get a custom-based concentration of obligation and entitlement. To modern man, ever aware and ever jealous of his individual rights, it is well-nigh incomprehensible that his forefathers should have allowed the clergy to 'usurp' the power of magistracy. Yet the early Christians, with their community spirit, neither objected nor even noticed, for was the congregation not still acting – namely acting in, by and through one? And a further development strongly supported the first, the devolution, by default, of the power of the keys to the clergy: the formation of domestic courts inside the Church. In their feeling of opposition to the surrounding world, the early Christians tended to avoid the secular-heathen courts, local, provincial and imperial. If they had a conflict among themselves, they tried to resolve it by arbitration.[2] We cannot be surprised that the arbitrator, the peacemaker, habitually chosen was the man about the altar, the priest. Thus he became in time something like a civil judge; and this position reacted on the penal practice and, by a kind of contagion, helped him to become the criminal judge as well.[3] We are saying, in time:

[1] Campenhausen, loc. cit., p. 143.   [2] Cf. Corinthians VI, 1 et seq.
[3] Cf. Campenhausen, loc. cit., pp. 160, 237, 238, 238, 259, 260.

though time is always relative, we might as well say: in a short time. For already the so-called Pastoral Epistles show the clergy as the normal judges of the community. There is only one explanation for the considerable speed of the shift: the absence of retarding opposition, the supporting consensus of the congregations.

The important source from the third century (probably from the first half of that century) known as the *Didascalia Apostolorum* shows us the lodgment of the judicial function in the specialist hands of priests and bishops as an accomplished fact. 'It is now no longer "the Church", but in fact the bishop, God's office-bearer, who has to make the decisions. He is the head of the community and must not take his direction from the . . . tail.' He has 'the power of life and death'. But this does not mean that he can act as an autocrat. He is and remains the voice of the congregation and must pronounce his findings in accordance with the congregation's mind. 'It is true, a layman should not try to control a bishop; but the latter himself is not for this reason any the more free. He is subject to a law which is all the stronger. Woe unto him when, in his capacity as judge, he is vindictive or violent, when he allows himself to be influenced, when he does not find the courage to pursue, as a faithful shepherd and healer, the straight road of the Word of God both in punishment and in mercy.'[1]

The juxtaposition, in this sentence, of punishment and mercy reminds us that ecclesiastical discipline, just like secular government, has two aims: to protect society (in the ecclesiastical context: to keep it clean in the eyes of God) and to reclaim the criminal (in the ecclesiastical context: to return the sinner to a state of grace). The ouster of the community by a single judge was not the only shift that took place as Christianity matured: the replacement of an initial emphasis on the penal aspect by a later emphasis on forgiveness runs parallel to, and was connected with, it. Its final result was the emergence of auricular confession. Campenhausen sees the First Epistle of St. John as crucial in this context. It mirrors a consciousness of temptation and a fear of defilement and a wish for release from both which together are the firm foundations of the confessional practice in Catholicism. 'The wording itself nowhere forces us to think of a definite practice of confession . . . and absolution. But when we notice on the other side how much weight is laid on the close and intensive realization

[1] Ibid., pp. 267–9. Cf. also p. 264.

260

of a fraternal community, it is difficult to imagine that there were no spiritual encounters to correspond to the spiritual experiences [of the awakened brethren, the stirrings in them of a sense of guilt], no cure of souls, as it appears later on, for example, in early monasticism.' No, Christians must have tried to lift the clouds which, from time to time, overshadowed them as sinners. For centuries yet, they had the right to open their hearts to any fellow-Christian, even with the assurance of quasi-sacramental forgiveness.[1] But is it any wonder that it became their settled custom to confess to the priest?[2] This, too, was simply part and parcel of the process which the sociologist, in his soberness, labels specialization, or calls an unfolding of the principle of the division of labour.

The Gospel according to St. John, just like the Gospel according to St. Matthew, speaks of the power of the keys,[3] but there is a significant difference which has not escaped, and failed to impress, Campenhausen. 'With Matthew, in both versions, "to bind" stands before "to loose" from sin. The stress lies on the disciplinary character of the ecclesiastical power, the defence against and attainment of the sinner. John on the other hand has given pride of place to the right of forgiveness, and it is only as its reverse side that the retaining of sins remains in undiminished force.'[4] John, as we can see, was truly the Apostle of Love. His gentleness generated a developmental trend which gave to Christianity a new penal policy and practice.

What this trend brought about was that prophylaxis increasingly took the place of punishment. Only in cases which were notorious, i.e. where the facts were known anyway and a deterrent effect was particularly desirable, did publicity remain the rule – even publicity of confession (otherwise always confidential), and not only of sentence and satisfaction. (One thinks of St. Ambrose's handling of the Emperor Theodosius.)[5] Out of these special cases there arose later the Bishops' Courts or 'Courts Christian', with which, however, the ordinary man had little to do. His shame was never publicly paraded. Indeed, the secrecy around the confessional box became an ever more assured, because it became an ever more sacred, principle, the principle of the 'confessional seal'.

Of course, public penances would have disappeared in any case,

---

[1] Cf. our vol. III, p. 332.   [2] Campenhausen, loc. cit., p. 151.   [3] XX, 23.
[4] Campenhausen, loc. cit., p. 152.   [5] Cf. our vol. III, p. 260.

as the whole drift of cultural evolution has been against them. The revival of them in the Protestant fold has been short-lived. But it was not because of changes around her that the Church advanced from dealing with the sinner *coram publico* to dealing with him *in camera caritatis*: the true springs of this consummation were within her. When it became customary to go regularly to confession even if no mortal sins had been committed, and when it became obligatory to go at least once a year, whatever the condition of the penitent's soul, the priest's disciplinary work assumed for ever a new face. His was now an all-round cure of souls, not only an express duty to pillory and punish. It makes little difference that the remedies by which that cure is to be achieved are still administered within the framework of a tribunal rather than in a physician's, or rather a psychiatrist's, office: indeed, it is appropriate that this should be and remain so. For the ill from which the errant human is to be freed is in all typical cases moral, not physical; the *disciplinandus* is guilty, and knows himself to be guilty, not sick. The wound which is to be healed is sin, and in the last analysis original sin, our whole race's whole waywardness. Those denominations which have pushed their clergy to become analysts *à la* Adler or Freud or Jung or Moreno have in truth diverted them from the classical priestly function which is to repress human weaknesses, not to indulge them.

The mentioning of accidental and marginal tasks on the part of the ecclesiastical personnel, such as an occasional taking of the place properly reserved in the scheme of things for the psychiatrist, brings us to the last point which we have to consider in this section. In the course of the centuries, many extraneous labours have been heaped upon the shoulders of priests and of their pendants in all denominations. If an empirical study were made today as to how they spend their time, it would be found that the functions which we have asserted to be essential and to be the proper work for them, occupy them only during a fraction, often small, of their working week: many more hours are devoted to the administration of buildings, even the repair of plumbing, to the collection of funds, even the organization of drives and dances, and more of this kind. A statistically-descriptive picture would therefore look different from the one which we have presented. But the reader must remember that this is an analytical and typological study, not an attempt to produce a superficial replica of reality, a photograph of it, as it were, on paper: we ask what is the *essence* of the priestly calling, not what are its surface accompaniments. An ability to look after property or collect gifts does not make a priest into a priest; indeed, it hinders him from being one. We are saying this not in the spirit of moral indignation, but rather for the sake of analytical and definitional clarity. The extraneous jobs which we have mentioned do not constitute a priest, though they may occupy him. Making him more like an estate agent or like an advertising manager, they blur his picture: they certainly do not define it. What the empirical investigation of the priest's working week would in effect show more than anything else is the failure of the laity to give a helping hand in the Church's life, or rather, with the chores unavoidably connected with it: church buildings and church finances might be administered for the priesthood rather than by the priesthood, and if this could be arranged, it would be easier for the priests to be in practice what they are designed to be in principle. There is, in the contemporary world, a vast amount of what, rather soberly, might be described as a waste of sacerdotal manpower. This is not the context in which to suggest reforms, but a comparison between accidental fact and essential function suggests reforms as of itself. Indeed, we must go still further, in delineating the core-character of the priestly role, than we have yet done: all through history, the development of theology has been in priestly hands. It is understandable that this should have been so, just as it is no surprise that clerics run the buildings in which they live and operate or collect the cash for the needs of the parishes and their own. But even the development of theology is not an exclusively clerical function as is the preaching and teaching of the (theologically formed and informed) Christian doctrine. In receiving his holy orders, a priest receives sacerdotal powers and assignments, not intellectual ones, and it is these sacerdotal powers and assignments – their true number and nature – which we have tried to identify in the foregoing pages.

THE HIGHER ORDERS

In the last section, we have discussed the function of the clergy without making any distinction between the different levels of the hierarchy, and especially between the bishops and the diocesan priests subordinate to them. This was done deliberately. Our procedure can be justified – though only, as we well know, in a preliminary way – by two considerations, one logical, the other historical. Logically, the different levels may, for part of the way, be treated like one because, in a very important respect, they are one. Not every priest is a bishop, but every bishop is a priest. The two must therefore have assignable traits in common; the differentiation can be but partial – indeed, in a sense, but secondary, outer appearances notwithstanding. Historically, we find that in the earliest days of the Church the terms *presbyteroi* and *episkopoi* were used interchangeably, a habit still maintained by the Presbyterian churches who consciously base their rejection of an inner hierarchical structuring of the class of ministers on those very early days and their yet unsettled conditions. The splitting of the Catholic clergy into super- and sub-ordinated ranks was an aspect as well as an end-effect of the process by which the Church settled down into abiding forms. Its analysis can teach us why we have today the forms which we do have. A genetic investigation will reveal the hidden factors which have made for functional differentiation.

If, as we have insisted all along, the Catholic priest is above all, and indeed essentially, the man set aside for, and ordained to, the administration of the sacraments, it would seem appropriate to look within the sacramental system for the factor of differentiation between the episcopal and the simply sacerdotal office. And we do find in it an apparently important dividing line: of the seven sacraments, two, namely confirmation and ordination, are reserved for the bishops; only the remaining five are common. It must be emphasized at once, however, that this distinction is in fact not absolute. With his bishop's – his 'ordinary's' – permission, any priest can validly confirm; with the pope's permission, any priest can validly ordain; and in either case the basic priestly orders are sacramentally sufficient for the task. True, the non-episcopal priest may officiate in these two rites only while his temporary commission lasts; having confirmed or ordained as bidden, he returns to the ranks, so to speak, and must not confirm or ordain again, until once more expressly asked by his superiors to do so. Yet, with all this, it is not the division of the sacraments into common and specifically episcopal ones that finally contrasts the levels. Quite apart from the fact which we have mentioned, namely that a priest may, without change in his status, on occasion bestow the two reserved sacraments, there is above all the further fact that so far as the decisive sacrament, that of the altar, is concerned – in other words, the power to celebrate mass and to effect transubstantiation, a power which is definitely rated higher than the power to ordain to the priesthood – there is no difference whatever between priest and bishop, or even between priest and pope. For this reason it has been said that there is only one *ordo* in the Catholic Church.

This is, however, going too far. The situation, as it has historically developed, is unavoidably complex. On the one hand, so far especially as the Eucharist is concerned, there is only one *ordo*; on the other hand, so far especially as ordination to the priesthood is concerned, there are, if not two *ordines*, at least two *gradus* of the one *ordo*, and the distinction involved in the latter case is more than merely legal; it has, to say the least, sacramental-metaphysical connotations. Simply expressed: a bishop is no more than a priest for both can celebrate mass; and still he is more because ordinarily only he can make a layman into a cleric. Sociologically speaking, what we have before us is the formation of a higher class which has not been carried to its conclusion. In the Middle Ages, Peter Lombard was inclined to the view that the episcopate was not an order and hence that consecration to the office did not involve a separate sacrament; yet according to Duns Scotus, for instance, the consecration of an *episcopus* did involve a separate sacrament. Recent writers show the same division of mind;[1] indeed, they are divided against themselves. Bouessé, for instance, asserts that 'the episcopal office is merely an extension (*complément*) of the presbyter's priesthood', yet in a footnote to the very same passage he can say: 'The sacrament of the presbyterial priesthood appears as an integral part of that all-comprehensive priesthood which is the episcopal sacrament,' meaning by this formulation that it is merely derived from the latter. The one passage brings the bishop down, or nearly so, to the parish priest's level, the other exalts him above it. St. Thomas Aquinas, caught in the cross-fire, saves himself, as he always does, in a characteristically scholastic fashion, by making distinctions. Bishops do not constitute a special *ordo*, but they have received a special *ordinatio*; their consecration does not

[1] Cf. Bouessé, loc. cit., pp. 193 and 194 (note 17) for some of the relevant literature.

give them another 'character', but it does give them additional, i.e. episcopal, i.e. more-than-priestly, 'grace'. Thus the divergence of concepts seems to be overcome. Present opinion would appear to follow, by and large, the Aquinate's lead. Yet if there is a tendency to go beyond him – and the *Codex Iuris Canonici* seems, however carefully, inclined to do so – it is towards a fuller discrimination between the two *gradus*. Bouessé's second formulation to the effect that the *fullness* of holy orders inheres in the bishop and that the priests participate in it in a somewhat restricted manner, is fairly typical of the now accepted position. It is not really surprising that the general drift should be in this direction, for a trend of development, once established, has, in any society, a tendency to persist by its own momentum.[1]

If the consideration of the sacramental system and its implications remains somewhat inconclusive, a study of the other two aspects of the *sacerdotium*, and especially of the area of discipline, leads to much more determined results. Indeed, it is here that – for the sociologist at any rate – the true differentiation between bishop and priest resides. The bishop has greater powers of control than the priest. We are at this point wise in giving the word to a canon lawyer for it is in his field that the salient definitions, and hence distinctions, root. This is what Elizabeth Lynskey writes in her study, *The Government of the Catholic Church*:[2] 'The power of the Church is twofold, consisting of the power of *order* and the power of *jurisdiction*. The power of order is "the power to sanctify the faithful by sacred rites". The power of jurisdiction is the power "to govern the faithful for the attainment of the supernatural end for which the Church is established". (The teaching authority of the Church pertains in a general way to the power of jurisdiction . . .) This means . . . that the Church recognizes two hierarchies: the hierarchy of order and the hierarchy of jurisdiction. In the hierarchy of order are bishops, priests, and ministers or deacons. In the hierarchy of jurisdiction are the Supreme Pontiff and the subordinate episcopate.' Here, surely, we have total clarity. Bishops are, and priests are not, members of the hierarchy of jurisdiction, and this is what, in the last resort, distinguishes them from each other. 'Within their home dioceses,' Lynskey writes

---

[1] Cf. ibid., pp. 121, 122, 134, 140, 195, 196, 197; Lecuyer, loc. cit., pp. 31, 32, 34–6; Lowrie, loc. cit., pp. 9, 21, 22.
[2] New York, 1952.

later on, 'bishops have what political theorists call unitary power; authority flows from them to their delegates or subordinates.'[1] By jurisdiction is meant, of course, what canon lawyers call the *forum externum*, the outer or public forum, for instance adjudication in matrimonial causes, not the *forum internum*, the confessional. The latter leads to a sacrament, that of forgiveness, and belongs therefore more to the power of order than to that of jurisdiction, though, in a definite sense, which does not concern us here, it belongs to the power of jurisdiction also.

It is not, however, in the direct control of the faithful that the authority of the bishop has its chief allotted place, it is rather in the direct control of the clergy. Brutally speaking, he is their boss. He makes them when, in the ordination ceremony – of which he is the centre because he brings the required sacramental grace – he lays his hands on them; and he 'oversees' them for the same reason, in accordance with the legal principle that he who institutes a man in his office is also his natural judge.[2] In the Catholic Church, discipline is characteristically deployed from the top downward, in diametrical opposition to the religious groupings which have issued from the Radical Reformation where such discipline of the office-bearers as exists (in so far as there are any office-bearers at all) is from the bottom upward. This is the basic contrast of which we have spoken before, with the Moderate Reformation of Luther and Calvin once again somewhere on the continuum between the two extremities or poles – the hierarchical Church and the unstructured congregation.

For Catholicism, the descent of the right of governance from the heights to the depths is, first of all, a religious principle. 'Since the Church would be nought else but the Body of Christ . . . the glorified Christ is the proper source of her power . . . The whole constitution of the Church is completely aristocratic and not democratic, her authority coming from above, from Christ, and not from below, from the community', writes Karl Adam. Christ gave the grace to rule the faithful to the apostles, the apostles to

---

[1] Loc. cit., pp. 17, 18, 30. Brackets interpolated.
[2] Let us note that the bishop is the priest's overseer only so far as the latter's external actions are concerned. 'In the recent Codex of Canon Law the emphasis is strongly put on the . . . idea that the superior is not the natural or ordinary confessor of his subjects' (Butler, *Benedictine Monachism*, as quoted, p. 191).

their chosen 'firstlings' in the congregations which they founded, and they in turn handed it on to their successors, the bishops and priests of post-apostolic days. 'The power was exclusively an apostolic power, a thing reserved to the bishops who derived from the apostles.' This is the celebrated principle of apostolic succession which looms so large in the history, even the recent history, of Christendom. 'We may assert,' so Adam concludes the passage concerned, 'that the whole literature of early Christianity attests this conception. It is developed with classic lucidity in one of the earliest of Christian writings, the First Epistle of St. Clement (*Ad Corinthios*, XLIV, 3).'[1]

While this is purely religious language, there is connected with it a definite sociological principle. Indeed, the sociologist of knowledge would be inclined to argue that the sociological principle is underneath – forms the 'substructure' of – the religious conceptions involved. In a community in the sense of Tönnies, where the value-accent lies on the integral whole and not on the individual parts, prestige and therefore power will tend to drift into the hands of those who represent – better still: who incarnate in themselves – the social, here socio-sacred, system. Differently expressed: it will drift into the hands of those who show forth, and guarantee, the unity of the group. But this is precisely what the bishops do; and this is, as we may say in anticipation, what above all the chief bishop does, the Bishop of Rome, the Pope. Goodykoontz, though his background is both anti-papal and anti-episcopal, yet sees the final causes for the formation of the episcopate in exactly the same light as we do. 'The time came,' he writes,[2] 'when there was one bishop for each city, with a presbyter (now rapidly becoming a priest in the current Roman Catholic sense) in charge of each particular congregation. This development . . . was a natural unfolding of the concept of the bishop as *the man who was to unify the Church*.' It could not be otherwise, for contemporary society was, by its inmost principle, by its very ontology, we might say, bent on unity. The informing idea of community is concentration.

We are now standing at the borderline where the logico-definitional discussion meets with, and merges into, a historico-descriptive investigation. To be nodal points in a network that spans the world is not only the systematic function of the higher

[1] Adam, pp. 22–4.　　　　　[2] Goodykoontz, p. 43. Our emphasis.

orders in the hierarchy, it is also the genetic reason for the sake of which they were brought into being. The Founder of Christianity loved *all* men; He saw the globe as one sheep-fold under one shepherd. The second founders, therefore, Peter and Paul, as His disciples, thought in terms of a *securus orbis terrarum*, an integrated and unified humanity, and in order to achieve it, they imparted to their successors a movement which forced up, so to speak, from the masses of the faithful, and even from the more select circle of the presbyters, superior officers, i.e. the bishops, who would integrate and unify a wider area, the diocese, and be in turn integrated and unified in an all-comprehensive, i.e. catholic, world church. The chief contrast between Catholicism and Quakerdom consists in this that Catholicism formed in, and reflects, an age which strove for, and drove towards, an *oikumene*, a fusion of all men in one body, while Quakerdom formed in, and reflects, an age which strove for, and drove towards, the opposite – the freedom of the individual.

In principle, the incipient Church might have remained congregational or become presbyterian, or she might have stopped at being episcopalian; in practice she could not do either because there was in her an all-powerful *élan vital* which carried her forward and upward towards universality: she became, because she had to become, Roman, catholic and apostolic. We do not know too much about the earliest days to be sure of the detail. But we do know enough to understand the crucial choices that were presented and effected in the second half of the first century.

Originally, it would seem, every local congregation, every city, had just one presiding church officer, called either *episcopus* or *presbyter*, it did not matter which. Then when the Church spread, and there were too many adherents to be accommodated under one roof, a splintering into many small groupings was a distinct possibility. Parishes might have formed, each with its own priest independent of all others. But this precisely did not happen. Not the fissiparous but an integrational tendency won the upper hand. When a parent church had to hive off, so to speak, daughter churches, the presiding priest of the former remained in charge of the latter also, for that is what the community, bent on unity, wished for and worked for. The parent church became the cathedral with a bishop to say mass there; the daughter churches became parishes with priests to officiate in them. The city of Rome was soon dotted with places of worship, large and small. But a curious custom sprang up which demonstrated the abiding, nay increasing, unity of the whole. 'The priests of the various charges celebrated the Eucharist in their respective churches, but the Pope sent them a particle of bread which he himself had consecrated, and each one of them placed this particle, called *fermentum*, into the chalice wherever he celebrated; this rite signified, according to the explanation of Pope Innocent I to the Bishop of Gubbio, the very close bond which obtains between the bishop and his priests, and it was not restricted to the city of Rome and to Gubbio, but was in vogue in other dioceses also, as we learn from the *Liber Pontificalis*.'[1] Under this dispensation, the priests appear as the bishop's lieutenants; the title their ordinaries have often given them – *co-operatores ordinis nostri*, helpers with our office[2] – is therefore understandable. In any event, the cords between the centre and the circumference were never cut, and the result was the emergence of the diocesan organization such as the second century developed and the future inherited, and such as we possess, in essentials, to the present day.

While the description of the process which we have just given is but summary and schematic and therefore insufficient – details simply cannot be accommodated in our restricted framework – it yet conveys the gist of the matter in a realistic fashion. From the sociological point of view, the evolution of an episcopal upper class of priests is essentially a further step in the development of the division of labour. Herbert Spencer might have called it a secondary fission, the first being the split between the laity at large and the religious specialists at large, and the second the separation between a lower stratum of merely sacramental powers and a higher stratum of powers both sacramental and jurisdictional. Both changes must necessarily appear invidious in an age like ours, which is not merely post-Rousseauan and post-revolutionary, but even a period of permanent revolutionism; why, so we are inclined to ask, should the bishops become priests *plus* and the priests bishops *minus*? What has the bishop got which the priest has not? Such questioning is characteristic of, and inherent in, our associational society, and it started as soon as associational society itself started, in the days of Martin Luther. But no such rhetorical questions were asked in the post-apostolic age. All that

[1] Lecuyer, loc. cit., p. 40.   [2] Ibid., p. 43.

the men of those community-type societies wanted to know was what was required *in aedificationem Corporis Christi* – for the building up of the Church. We are giving these words (which go back to Ephesians IV, 12) deliberately in their Latin form because this form is classical and represents a kind of standing phrase used, again and again, in the early congregations. For the building up of the Church, you needed an upper level in your house, so to speak, in addition to the lower one, an episcopate as well as a parish priesthood, and that is why it developed and became established. It was as simple as that.

A negative point is difficult to prove, even though the silence of the sources seems to bespeak an absence of protest against the clerical class division which sprang up. But one small trait may be mentioned for what it is worth. Origenes has his complaints about the clergy and voices them in no uncertain manner. But there is no word against the fact that bishops exist and bear rule. The religiously more mature spirits, he urges, must give the less mature ones their loving guidance: hence the priest must help the layman and the bishop must help the priest. They must instruct them and even take their burdens and their failures upon themselves. The Jewish Church was hierarchical; so are the choirs of the angels above; what else then should the Church of Christ be? Origenes, it is true, was not a canon lawyer; his thinking is not jusridictional.[1] But he was deeply Christian, and the canonistic-jurisdictional consequences which more ordinary men drew were germinally contained in his extraordinarily intense Christian consciousness.

We are saying here once again what we have said before, namely that the Catholic Church has developed the forms she has in fact developed because she let the spontaneous tendencies towards a division of labour inherent in her, as in any society, freely unfold. What happened was so to speak 'natural'. But there was yet another factor in operation, and it was more strictly natural still. Behind the division between a ruling episcopate and a ruled presbyterate there lurks the division between old and young. It is understandable – 'natural' – in essentially static societies to give to the men well on in life more prestige and power than to those who are merely starting out. What matters is experience, and experience comes with grey hair or bald heads.

[1] Campenhausen, loc. cit., pp. 280–2.

Our contemporaries have challenged this form of life and thought along with so many other traditions, and this is not surprising, for in a dynamical society like capitalism adaptability matters more than experience and youth is at a premium. It is doubtful to what extent the low valuation of the older age-groups can reasonably be extended beyond the borderlines of science and technology; after all, staggering new insights in philosophy and religion appear to be rare and progress can hardly be said to be the hallmark of historical piety; but be that as it may, the early Christians did spontaneously give the primacy of jurisdiction to the ageing among their clergy, and that is why *episkopoi* and *presbyteroi* parted ways to the extent that they did. The First Epistle of Saint Peter, very ancient by any standard, whatever its exact date, and indeed whatever its authorship, clearly identifies superiority in ecclesiastical authority with superiority in years: 'The ancients that are among you I beseech . . . Feed the flock of God . . . Ye young men, be subject to the ancients . . .' (I Peter V, 1, 2, 5). The Pastoral Epistles of Paul (Timothy and Titus) carry the same message.[1] Towards the end of the first century, there is indeed a local and temporary crisis of which we know: at Corinth, still an important congregation, the younger men protest against the domination of the older men and demand elections. Eduard Meyer surmises that the local collective *presbyterium* had become 'rather senile'. Pope Clement intervenes in the year 96: he urges unity and lays it down as a principle that offices must go to 'proven men'. 'It appears that this intervention was crowned with full success.' Yet incidents like this did not pass without leaving a permanent effect. Meyer sees them as one of the factors which made for a definite monepiscopate, i.e. the appointment of *one* diocesan bishop who would be able to carry the charge and who, while as a rule not young, would not as a rule be in his dotage either. Asia Minor seems to have led the way towards this consummation which virtually coincides with the Church's modern condition. The Epistle of St. Ignatius of Antioch to the Smyrniotes – A.D. 112 – shows the monepiscopate fully unfolded, with the one bishop being a mature man, or at any rate being accepted as mature, whatever his physical age. Typological thinking (as we may explain in a sociological aside) aided this consummation. Just as a young widow was regarded, in the contemporary world, as an old woman

[1] Cf. especially I Timothy V, 1, 2, and Titus II, 2–6.

because normally widows were old, so even a young bishop was regarded as an older man because normally bishops were old. The bishop is a representative of fatherhood – 'the image of the father' – Ignatius tells his readers,[1] and he thereby strikes an important note, the ground bass, as it were, which is apt to underlie all development of structures of authority in stable, or at least non-dynamic, societies.

The fact which we have just encountered, namely that the Bishop of Rome could, as early as the year 96, intervene in the affairs of the Diocese of Corinth, and do it with authority and effect, proves *how* strong was the drive, inherent from the beginning in Christianity and Christendom, towards world-wide integration. The same process which forced up presbyters from the ranks of the faithful and bishops from the ranks of the presbyters, also singled out *one* bishop from the rest and established him above the whole hierarchy. It is to a study of this commanding figure that we now turn, and in doing so we can use once again the words with the help of which we have ushered in the study of the episcopate. In discussing the case of the bishops we have already spoken implicitly of the pope, for though not every bishop is pope, every pope is a bishop. But things are much simpler here than we found them before: whereas the bishop is both sacramentally and jurisdictionally superior to the simple priest (however small his superiority *quoad sacramenta* may be), the pope is only jurisdictionally, but not sacramentally, superior to the ordinary bishop. 'In the hierarchy of order the Pope, as bishop of Rome, possesses no more sacramental power than any other bishop,' writes Elizabeth Lynskey.[2] 'In the hierarchy of jurisdiction, however, he is set above other bishops, singly and collectively considered, by virtue of the doctrine of the primacy of the See of Peter, accepted by all the faithful, and by the doctrine of papal infallibility, which declares his definition of dogma to be infallible, on those rare occasions when he speaks *ex cathedra* as Vicar of Christ . . . In the hierarchy of order the bishops constitute the top of the pyramid, with the bishop of Rome one of their number,' Lynskey writes elsewhere,[3] giving pictorial expression to the same facts. 'In the hierarchy of jurisdiction, resident bishops constitute the base of the pyramid, the Pope its crown.'

[1] Meyer, loc. cit., vol. III, pp. 580 and 581.
[2] Op. cit., p. 19.　　　　　　　　　[3] Ibid., p. 31.

These words are not only remarkably clear, they also help us because they indicate, by implication, the three sociologico-political problems which are connected with the papacy: 1. the primacy of the See of Peter is indeed accepted by all the Catholic faithful (though even here degrees of acceptance are to be discerned), but it is not accepted by all Christians; 2. the same applies, point for point, to the dogma of papal infallibility; and 3. the question arises as to whether the pope is indeed collectively, as well as singly considered, superior to the diocesan bishops. The formula traditionally applied to Spanish kingship springs to mind here: *major singulis, universis minor* – 'above each, but beneath all'.[1] Does this maxim cover the case of the pope also, and, if so, in what way? Lynskey suggests that it does not, but the matter is not that simple; it presents an intricate problem. The so-called Conciliarist movement raised it in an insistent fashion.

As for the first problem, the fact that the primacy of the See of Peter has become a bone of contention in the Christian world, the sociological answer must surely be obvious to anyone who has read this volume (and even more to anyone who has read the preceding three volumes also). The drawing together of all authority into one focus can only be natural in a society, ecclesiastical or otherwise, which is of the community type in Tönnies' dichotomy. As soon as a step is taken in the direction of association, in other words, as soon as multiplicity is emphasized as against the unity of the body social, the ground is cut from under an institution such as the papacy. Speaking seriously, and not at all facetiously, we can say with entire justification that every Quaker is a pope unto himself, for this is precisely what the phrase 'supremacy of private judgment', characteristic of the Radical Reformation, means. We have the two end points of our basic dichotomy once more before our eyes. Luther soon got caught by the powerful forces of nationalism which welled up in his day, and which are even more punchingly displayed in sixteenth century England than in contemporary Germany. When he placed himself under the protection of the princes, the primacy of Peter became an impossible proposition for him. Calvin, too, did not believe in the primacy of Peter in the sense of the primacy of the Pope, but he believed in unity to a much greater extent than all the other Reformers, radical or moderate, together. It

[1] Cf. our vol. III, p. 139.

was his wish that Geneva should become in the future what Rome had been in the past. But as development in this direction was arrested before it had gone very far, the integration of the Reformed *Oikumene* in one centre did not succeed: its forces were not in the end drawn into one focus. Yet Calvinism certainly desired what Catholicism, under different social and historical presuppositions – to be quite fair, under far easier preconditions – had achieved: the building of a pyramid with one apex, even if this apex was envisaged by the Calvinists as a supreme church court rather than as one supreme world judge.

Inter-confessional polemics around the question of papal primacy and power have from the beginning centred around one crucial Gospel passage – Matthew XVI, 18: 'Thou art Peter, and upon this rock I will build my church.' Protestants have asserted that these words are not genuine, but rather a later interpolation, and they have pointed to the fact that there are no parallels in Mark, Luke and John. Yet precisely this passage exhibits particularly striking marks of authenticity. It does not sound convincing in its Greek guise: 'Thou art *Petros*, and upon this *petra* I will build my church.' But the Greek is, of course, if the passage is indeed genuine and reports an actual saying, only a translation from the Aramaic which was the language of Jesus Christ. In Aramaic, however, the discrepancy between the male *Petros* and the female *petra* which robs the logion of its point, at least its linguistic point, is absent: 'Thou art *Kepha*, and upon this *kepha* I will build my church.' The sentence is perfect in this form: the Aramaic original is visible at this point, as at no other, behind the Greek translation. Leading Protestant bible scholars, notably Oscar Cullmann,[1] have therefore conceded the originality of the line. They have, in consequence, shifted the emphasis to another aspect which is far more interesting for the sociologist. They have argued that Peter was indeed singled out for particular honour, but that this honour was only personally his and did not transfer to his successors. Peter may indeed have been called to the headship of the Church, but Linus, his successor, need not have been, for Peter was one man, and Linus quite another.

George Salmon has, in his much discussed book, *The Infallibility of the Church*, given strong expression to this opinion: 'Peter was honoured by being the foremost among the human agents by

[1] Cf. his *Petrus*, as quoted, pp. 215 et seq.

which the Church was founded,' he says. 'But . . . this was an honour in which it was impossible he could have a successor. We might just as well speak of Adam's having a successor in the honour of being the first man.'[1] Little does Salmon know that by writing these words he is steering the discussion in a direction which must be fatal to his argument.

For if it is true that Adam had no successor in the honour of being the first man, it is also true that he did have successors in the dishonour of being the first man to err and to fall. Christianity in all its classical forms has been based on the conviction that the guilt of our first forefather immediately involved all his offspring (the doctrine of original sin), in other words, that these offspring are solidary, are *one*, with him, that we all *are* Adam, in a sense. No variant of Christianity has more strongly insisted on this than Calvinism, the tradition from which George Salmon himself has sprung, and if he had given it up (which he would not, of course, have dreamt of doing), his own religious world would have collapsed as quickly as that of the papacy and of Rome. The New Testament, just like the Old, has, in decisive contexts, insisted upon the coincidence of successive historical person-alities. We have encountered this collective mode of thinking, highly characteristic of community-type societies, in our dis-cussion of the Apocalypse:[2] there, Domitian is equated with Nero, Nero with Caligula, Caligula with Antiochus Epiphanes, and he in turn with Nabuchodonosor; all enemies of good and God are simply one mind, one body, one hand. But what is true of these fiends, is true of God's friends as well: Petrus is Linus, and Linus is Anacletus, the third pope, and so on into the future, down to the present day, to John XXIII and to Paul VI and be-yond. *Dignitas non moritur*, said ancient and medieval man: a dignity does not die. Nor indeed does a burden. It was not an honour, as Salmon assumes, which Christ gave to Peter on the road to Cesarea Philippi, it was essentially a duty. This duty is perhaps more clearly enunciated in other words spoken to Kepha: 'Feed my lambs . . . Feed my sheep' (John XXI, 16 and 17). To any but modern, individualistic man, this is a charge laid of neces-sity not on one Peter, but on all Peters, present and to come. Catholics have simply held to these mental modes which pre-

[1] Op cit., abridged by Woodhouse, H. F., London 1952, p. 127.
[2] Cf. our vol. III, pp. 3 and 5.

vailed in earlier, more close-knit societies. When a newly elected pope enters the basilica for his coronation, the words which greet him are the great words of Cesarea Philippi: 'Thou art Peter . . .'. Englishmen at least ought not to be too surprised at this for when the Judge enters the local parish church for the Assize Sermon, the anthem intoned is 'God save the Queen'. In this tradition, too, we have the ancient conviction that one person can be identical with another. The judge on the bench *is* in a sense the Queen. So also is Giovanni Montini Simon Bar-Jona, or rather Peter the Rock. 'It is our belief,' writes Karl Adam with commendable directness, 'that we have in the bishop of Rome the Peter upon whom Christ at Cesarea Philippi established His Church.'[1]

Parallel to the argument which we have just discussed lies another to the effect that the Christian congregation at Rome was indeed the most respected of all congregations, but that this did not mean that its bishop was the most respected of all bishops, let alone that he was the bishop of bishops, the Universal Church's overall head. Thus Salmon makes much of the fact that Pope Victor I's intervention in the East's Easter controversy is formally conveyed, not in a personal letter, but in a letter of the Roman Church.[2] Harnack (though far more liberal and irenic than Salmon) asserts in the same spirit that Pope Calixtus I 'associated with his own personal position' a primacy which was possessed not by him, but rather by his church.[3] But this is merely the same line of approach which we have met before, and it leads to the same error – an undue modernization of the mentality which underlay the pre-Protestant, and still underlies the Catholic, Church. For the Church is in the bishop, and not only the bishop in the Church, and the Universal Church is in the Universal Bishop, the Pope, and not only the Pope in the Universal Church. St. Cyprian's great formula is applicable even here. It is true that he himself did not so apply it.[4] He still thought in terms of the equal sovereignty of all bishops. But the principle which he enunciated demanded, by dint of its own inherent logic, application to the

[1] Adam, loc. cit., p. 107. [2] Salmon, loc. cit., p. 164.
[3] Harnack, A., *History of Dogma*, trans. Buchanan, N., vol. II, Boston 1897, p. 163.
[4] Cf. *Campenhausen*, loc. cit., p. 306; but see also Butler, *The Church and Infallibility*, as quoted, p. 150.

Christian *oikumene* as soon as that had become a tangible reality, and since then the Pope speaks with sovereign authority, not only *urbi* (to his own diocese, the city of Rome), but also *orbi* (the whole world).

The formal establishment of the bishop of Rome as the undoubted Sovereign Pontiff which was carried out at the first Vatican Council in 1870, was therefore merely the legalization of a condition which had in fact existed for a very long time. But that Council gave to the Pope not only the *primatus* and *principatus jurisdictionis*, it also ascribed to him infallibility in matters of faith and morals if and when he speaks *ex cathedra*, i.e. expressly as the Voice of Authority, and thereby hangs another problem which has to be carefully considered, if it is to be rightly understood.

George Salmon refers to the contemporary pope, Pius IX, as 'an Italian ecclesiastic, of no reputation for learning'.[1] By using this slighting form of words, he wishes to point up the whole absurdity of the doctrine of papal infallibility. But the absurdity of that doctrine would hardly be less if Pius IX had been another kind of ecclesiastic, or indeed another kind of person, with a great reputation for learning. Is any human being ever infallible? Catholics believe it no more than other people do. Surely, the doctrine of infallibility makes sense only if it is not interpreted individualistically, or, more positively expressed, if it is interpreted collectivistically – if, in other words, the voice of the pope is considered as the voice of one who enunciates the thought of all, the *consensus omnium*, beyond which nobody down here below can have an appeal, and which must therefore stand as the ultimate tribunal of truth. If the doctrine were indeed interpreted individualistically – if the pope were considered as personally inspired, as Max Weber, with his lack of pertinent knowledge, thought Catholics did consider him,[2] which is totally false – the whole conception would assuredly be difficult to accept. But this interpretation can only be propounded and given a deceptive semblance of justice by breaking Catholic thinking on the subject of the papacy out of its historico-sociological context. If it is left in there, as it must be, the dogma concerned appears in an entirely different light, and indeed as rational.

[1] Salmon, loc. cit., p. 19.
[2] Cf. *The Sociology of Religion*, ed. Fischoff, as quoted, p. 74.

We should notice, first of all, that the unique papal privilege of infallibility covers only one of the aspects which, as we have seen, make up the priestly, and even the high-priestly, office. It is concerned with preaching, but not with the sacraments or with discipline. Not the whole *sacerdotium*, but only the *magisterium* is involved. In a pamphlet written especially to explain the doctrine and preceded by an express approbation of Pius IX, a leading bishop pointed out that the Pontiff 'has the gift of infallibility, according to the manifest sense of the words of the definition, only as supreme teacher of truths necessary for salvation revealed by God, not as supreme priest, not as supreme legislator in matters of discipline, not as supreme judge in ecclesiastical questions, not in respect of another question over which his highest governing power in the Church may otherwise extend.'[1] This cuts the privilege down considerably, yet nobody will deny that much remains. How have we to conceive of the claim which does remain?

A quotation from John Meng's Introduction to Elizabeth Lynskey's book will speed us on the way to truth. 'The Pope, or an ecumenical council,' he writes, 'may define doctrine – they do not create it.'[2] The development of religious thinking and teaching goes back to the very beginnings – for the religious consciousness, to the sayings of the God-made-Man, the so-called deposit of faith, for the sociologist of knowledge to the total life-situation within which Christianity, body and mind, first formed. Since then, there has been a constant process of unfolding which has made explicit which was originally given implicitly, in germ, so to speak, and this process was collective. We may – indeed, we must – compare it to the formation of folkways which William Graham Sumner has so well analysed in his classical book. Thus doctrines have taken shape: individuals have contributed much – who would forget a Tertullian, an Augustine, an Aquinas, a Bellarmin, a Newman? Yet with all that the maturation of the religious mind was essentially, almost exclusively, the achievement of collective forces. We refrain from saying more at this point because the matter will be thoroughly investigated in its proper

[1] Fessler, J., *The True and the False Infallibility of the Pope*, ed. New York 1875, p. 56.
[2] Lynskey, loc. cit., p. 2. On what follows, cf. also Adam, loc. cit., pp. 42–6 and 153–8 (especially p. 155), and Moulin, loc. cit., pp. 28 and 29.

place – volume V, which will deal with 'Types of Religious Culture'. Here we can sum up by asserting that doctrines are grown, not made. Not even the Pope of Rome can make one. But when doctrines have grown, when they have gained a degree of definiteness, they need formulation, for at first they are only an idea afloat, not a set of crystallized and crystalline propositions. There must be a formulator, and that precisely is what the Pope is. We may compare him to a codifier of custom. Such a lawyer does not make custom, he does not even make customary law, and least of all does he make law. The pope, in like manner, only puts into words what he finds in effect to be the law, or rather matured dogma. His formulations are indeed regarded as infallible, but there is no appeal from the House of Lords or the U.S. Supreme Court either. For secular society, the finally binding voice is the voice of the highest officer on the judicial bench; for the religious community of Catholicism it is the voice of the man who occupies the most exalted pulpit, the *Cathedra Petri*. On the basic principle that the Church is the Body of Christ, the word which issues from there is the word of Christ. It is therefore divine. The doctrine has been regarded as shocking by many. Yet Lutheranism and Calvinism, too, have maintained and maintain that the word of their predicants is the Word of God if and in so far as it is in agreement with revelation (*Catholice*, with the deposit of faith). The difficulties which they have felt with the doctrine of infallibility are therefore likely to lie, not with the principle of the thing, but merely with its application.

Before elaborating on this last statement, let us quickly give proof that we are not misrepresenting the dogma. 'The Holy Spirit was not promised to the successors of St. Peter that by His revelation they might make known a new doctrine,' writes Bishop Fessler, 'but that by His assistance they might holily preserve and faithfully expound the revelation delivered to the Apostles, or in other words, the 'deposit of the faith' (*depositum fidei*) . . . The Pope, in his [ex-cathedratic] doctrinal utterances, *only speaks what he finds*, under the special divine assistance, to be already part of the truth revealed by God as necessary for salvation . . .'[1] And in another context[2] he compares the pontiff, as we have done, to the judge. A judge may err as a man, but he cannot err when, as an official, he enunciates the law. In the same way 'the Pope as a

[1] Fessler, loc. cit., pp. 49 and 67. Our emphasis.   [2] Ibid., pp. 90 and 91.

private individual, may err in matters of faith'. But 'he cannot err when . . . he solemnly defines a truth revealed by God', or rather, as the sociologist will prefer to say, when he pours into the explicit form of concrete words what is pre-formed, nay fully formed, in the collective tradition. Not an individual right is contained in the doctrine of infallibility but rather a social duty: to be *the speaker* for all Christendom.

But is the Pope the speaker for all Christendom? In one sense, he obviously is not, for Protestants have repudiated his power and position. Yet perhaps in another sense he is. What has divided the confessions, Catholicism on the one side, Protestantism on the other, has been above all the charge that Catholicism has made 'additions' to the Bible which to Protestants is the only actual, if not indeed the only possible, source of revelation. And these 'additions' were precisely the ones with which papal prestige has been involved: the Mariological (or, as Protestants would say, Mariolatric) doctrines of the Immaculate Conception, and of the Bodily Assumption of the Virgin, the former defined in 1854 (before papal infallibility was finally enunciated as a dogma), the latter (after it) in 1950. To outsiders these teachings appear as impositions foisted by an irresponsible authority on an uninvolved and unasked laity, irrationalities and irrelevancies to the Christian faith.

Yet from an inner point of view, things bear a different aspect. As no other authoritative – 'ex-cathedratic' – pronouncements have ever been made, everything depends on the proper understanding of the two credal points which we have indicated. The doctrines concerned are certainly not explicitly spelled out in the Scriptures, but they are as certainly contained, by implication, in Christianity as such. For if God was to be made man, the belief which is the core of all Christianity whatever its colour, He had to prepare for Himself a mother who would be suitable for His incarnational and redemptive design, which would mean that she would have to be free from original sin, for God and sin can never mix. This, and this alone, is the burden of the dogma of the Immaculate Conception. And if there was a body which bore God as any other woman bears her children, then that body would be for ever privileged and could not be thought to be subject to decay as ordinary flesh and blood is. This, and this alone, is the burden of the other dogma, that of the Assumption of the Virgin. We are

281

not, of course, attempting to vindicate these dogmas; that is, assuredly, not the sociologist's business, whatever his religious views. What we are attempting to do is to explain the operation of a specific mentality, that of the collectivity which goes by the name of Catholic. We have seen again and again that the Church of Rome has in every instance unhesitatingly followed the spontaneous tendencies in her towards a more elaborate division of labour. We see the same now: she has, in every instance, followed the spontaneous tendencies in her towards a more elaborate system of doctrine. She has, in particular, not resisted a certain growing irrationality. This has estranged her from the modern rationalistic world, but it also kept her faithful to her own fideist past.[1] Protestants have acted differently: as their official structure refused to structure itself further, so their accepted beliefs refused to move deeper into the (rationally) unbelievable. The gap with the modern rationalistic world therefore appears smaller.

But perhaps we have gone too far just now: in any case, the gap merely *appears* smaller; it is not really so from an objective point of view. For though Protestants do not accept the Mariological dogmas of Catholicism (while protesting that they are giving due honour to the Mother of God), they are in other ways as deeply wedded to irrationality as Rome is. So far as the New Testament miracles are concerned, there is no difference whatsoever. The distinction between the contrasting irrationalities of the confessions does not lie there. It lies in the all-important fact that Catholics believe that the community can develop new insights and then have them papally defined, whereas Protestants vigorously deny this. Yet if we think of Protestantism proper, not of its decaying forms, but of men like Luther and Calvin, we find that they have their own specific irrationalities to which they hold with entire devotion. What Mariolatry is to Catholicism, Bibliolatry is to Protestantism. The great Reformers had no doubt whatever that Josue made the sun and the moon stand still over Ajalon for the space of one day (Josue X, 13), and that Jonas was in the belly of a great fish three days and three nights and was then vomited out upon the dry land without apparent damage to his body (Jonas II, 1 and 11). Weber's theory of 'growing disenchantment' or diminish-

[1] Incidentally, it has also brought her much closer to Orthodoxy, a consequence whose bearing and meaning we cannot pursue here. Cf. Butler, *Infallibility*, p. 74 (note).

ing irrationality is not applicable here, for classical Protestantism actually *increased* the willingness to believe the (rationally) unbelievable. According to medieval and Catholic man, the stories of the Old Testament are to be interpreted, not literally, but symbolically. They are lessons, imaginatively presented, for man's deeper understanding. A reading of the earlier parts of St. Augustine's *City of God* can show how true this is. According to modern, or rather Protestant, man, the stories of the Old Testament are to be understood, not symbolically, but literally. For though not all Protestants are consistent fundamentalists, their leaders were in no difficulty and doubt about the divine inspiration of the Scriptures in their totality, Josue, Jonas and all. Some irrationality is unavoidably connected with *all* religious life; indeed, some irrationality is unavoidably connected with all life. Vilfredo Pareto has shown how many superstitions dominate the allegedly scientific mind of modern, religiously emancipated man.

The insight to which we must hold on, then, is the recognition that Catholicism is characterized by a trust in the capacity of the Christian people to draw from the original deposit of faith dogmas which had not been clearly stated, but only implicitly carried, before. And this is sociologically the salient point. The Church is to herself not only the (collective) Body of Christ, she is also the (collective) Mind of Christ. Therefore she feels she cannot be wrong. What the credibility of this belief is, does not concern the sociologist; what does concern him, and concerns him greatly, is its collectivistic character. And so the analysis of the seeming power of one man, the pope, leads us back to the real power of all men within the Catholic tradition and credal system. Pius IX may have enunciated one Mariological dogma and Pius XII another, but it was the piety of all pious Catholics which developed it in a process of gestation which spanned the centuries. To mistake the role of the pope for that of the community would be as wrong as to regard the midwife as the mother of the child.

The proof of what we are saying consists in the fact that dogmas have never been promulgated before they had engulfed and filled up the masses of the faithful. A far-flung investigation preceded the encyclical *Ineffabilis Deus* in which the doctrine of the Immaculate Conception was formulated. It showed above all one thing: Catholics all over the world were surprised to hear that this belief (as well as that of the Assumption) was not already an established dogma. Cardinal Newman could therefore write, with his incomparable flair for the *mot juste*: 'Catholics have not come to believe it because it is defined, but . . . it was defined because they believed it.'[1] Curiously enough, George Salmon, the great condemner of infallibility, bears him out on this. 'I think it admits of historical proof,' he writes, 'that the Church of Rome has shrunk with the greatest timidity from exercising this gift of infallibility on any question which has not already settled itself . . .'[2] Precisely; this is what we are saying. The voice of the people speaks first, wordlessly as it were; the pope then adds the words, in an operation which is service and not command.

Of course, full-fledged rationalists will continue to have difficulties. How *can* the masses, it will be said, ever have believed such propositions? Are they not beyond anybody and anything? They are quite right: the new dogmas are beyond anybody and anything rational, scientific, even common-sensical. So are the old dogmas, those shared by the Protestants. But then religion as a whole is not rational, scientific or even common-sensical. It is no more difficult to accept the papally defined 'additions' to – or, as Catholics must say, inferences from – the basic Christian belief that 'the Word was made flesh and dwelt among us' than to accept this belief itself. Once again, our plea to the non-believing – 'scientific' – student of religion must be the same as before: he must reconcile himself to the fact that the mentality which he meets in his research is not like his own, or is even repulsive to his own. But that is as it is. After all, social anthropologists try to do justice to primitive life even though they would not like to live for ever in the comfortless villages which they are investigating, and they succeed on the whole.

A special word must yet be said about the dogma of infallibility itself. Its acceptance at the first Vatican Council was not totally unanimous though it was virtually so. A small group of bishops – Cardinal Manning, a great realist, thought it was about a dozen – held to the historical Gallican position according to which each bishop is sovereign and the Church an aristocratic republic, not a monarchy. The process known in American political jargon as 'arm-twisting' is said to have gone on behind the scenes to make them fall into line, for a unanimous vote was understandably

[1] *Apologia pro Vita Sua*, as quoted, p. 255.
[2] Salmon, loc. cit., p. 67. Cf. also p. 211.

desired by those who wanted to see the dogma promulgated.[1] The historian may regret that this course was taken, for a small minority vote *contra* would hardly have made much difference. The true test could not be avoided anyway. The arms of the laypeople could not be twisted: they could leave if they did not like what transpired. Some did leave: the 'Old-Catholic Church' formed in protest against the Vaticanum. At the time when this schismatic movement reached its widest extension, it numbered about 150,000 adherents. This means that one Catholic in about 2,000 violently disagreed.[2] The majority *pro* was therefore very close to 100 per cent.

Some indeed accepted the dogma in its substance, but doubted the necessity of its formulation, or even the wisdom of its formulation in the given circumstances. We are not concerned with the politic nature, or otherwise, of the move, but with its agreement, or otherwise, with basic socio-political trends, and such agreement can be asserted, nay, is obvious. For we have seen that the drive towards unity was inherent in the Church from the moment of her birth. Feudal society threatened ever anew to kill that unity for with its localism it tended to root the diocesan hierarchy in its domestic soil: Gallicanism, not to speak of Anglicanism, was its product. But modern society threatened such unity as existed even more. The years of the Vaticanum were the years which saw nationalism rise to a climax. It was the day of Garibaldi, Bismarck and Napoleon III. A counterblow from the forces of internationalism was due and it was struck by exalting the figure which symbolized the solidarity of Catholics across national border lines. True, the perfection of the monarchical constitution of the Church – for that is what the declaration of infallibility meant, politically considered – might have been postponed, just as it might have been anticipated. But it was judged that the time was ready and ripe for a fighting gesture. And so there was not only the ever present reason for giving the pope his sovereignty – the reason aptly worded by Basil Christopher Butler when he said: 'Society needs an instrument for the formulation and expression of its corporate

[1] Cf. MacGregor, G., *The Vatican Revolution*, Boston 1957.
[2] Cf. Butler, *The Church and Infallibility*, as quoted, p. 118. Cf. also the sources given there and p. 68. Quite a few Old Catholics left, not because they refused to accept the dogma of papal infallibility, but because they rejected internationalism in all its forms. Those were the days of the *Los-von-Rom* slogan of which we have spoken in vol. III (cf. p. 206). In the Latin countries, Old Catholicism had no popular following at all.

thinking'[1] – there was also a new and more pressing reason for formulating the dogma asserting that sovereignty – the need to defend the unity of all God's children, for the sake of which not only the papacy but even the episcopate was called into being.

We can sum up our discussion of infallibility by using lawyers' language and saying that the power it bestows on the pope is declaratory, not constitutive. This links fully with some fundamental observations we have made before.[2] The formula which St. John Chrysostom coined, to the effect that 'Peter acted as an expositor, not a preceptor',[3] holds as fully in the twentieth century as it did in the fourth.

One final remark is necessary. By saying that the pope's power is merely declaratory, and that what he has to declare depends on what the whole Church has resolved upon, we do not, and we must not, give the impression that papal rule is, overtly or covertly, democratic in the sense in which the term is taken in the world's democracies. Matters have recently come to a head in connection with the discussion of two encyclicals, *Sacerdotalis Celibatus* and *Humanae Vitae*, one of which reasserted the traditional principle of priestly celibacy, the other the equally traditional ban on artificial contraceptives within Christian marriage. It was asserted that the Pope was out of touch with modern thinking on these points, that he should poll at least the bishops, if not indeed the masses of the faithful for their opinion, and that he should then act in accordance with the opinions thus elicited. The *quaestio facti*, whether the pope now reigning is indeed in disagreement with a majority of his subjects, is nothing to our purpose: we are concerned with principle. But the principle is different from that prevailing in a democracy. A democracy lives in time, but the Church does not. A shift in opinion cannot set aside the whole *traditio patrum* for their voices must for ever count as much as the voices of contemporaries. To extinguish them, it would be necessary totally to overwhelm them, and of that there is no evidence at present. A democracy lives, and can live, by majority decisions, the Church needs virtual unanimity. The discussion must be kept going until an agreed solution emerges. This may be long and this must be painful; but this is the way in which matters have always been

---

[1] Ibid., p. 211. [2] Cf. above, pp. 141 and 206.
[3] *Commentary on Acts* III, 23; *Patrologia Graeca*, ed. Migne, J. P., vol. LX, Paris 1862, col. 36.

handled, as for instance Cardinal Newman has shown,[1] and as we, too, hope to show in our fifth volume. The dogmatic declarations of 1854, 1870 and 1950 were carried by the anonymous forces of Catholic Christendom, and that is why they could be made. It can hardly be different with minor matters – relatively minor matters, as we should rather say in this context. The duty of authority in such a protracted process of gestation can only be to resist change until the search for a way out of the impasse has succeeded and a compromise, or rather a synthesis, is reached which is acceptable to all.[2] The reader must remember here that the pope is the apex of the priesthood, and that the priesthood is, as we have shown,[3] by its whole nature the agent of persistence and not the protagonist of change.

Within persistence, however, what has to be preserved above all else is not this feature or that, be it dogma or institution, but unanimity – the principle of unity itself. In Salmon's attack on infallibility, there is one passage which shows the whole world-wide contrast between Catholicism and non-Catholic Christianity in this respect. 'Let us liberally grant,' Salmon says, 'that an ecclesiastical monarchy was the form of government best adapted to the needs of the Church at the time when, in temporal matters, the whole civilized word was governed by a single ruler; and yet it might be utterly unfit for her requirements in subsequent times when Europe

[1] Stark, *Social Theory and Christian Thought*, as quoted, pp. 112 et seq.
[2] Outlines of such compromises or concordances are perhaps already visible: the introduction of a life-long married diaconate which would leave the full priesthood (which alone would have the privilege of the altar) celibate, and the development of a mild pastoral practice (differently expressed: greater concessions to human weaknesses) with regard to marital conduct, which would leave the Christian ideal of self-control in principle inviolate. The papal resistance is all the more understandable, not to say, inescapable, as the changes clamoured for betoken a declining preparedness to accept personal limitations, morally a very serious matter. Martin Luther left the cloister and encouraged others to do so, but he warned them that this was only legitimate if the step was not prompted by the desire 'to free the flesh'. There is a rogue in all of us, he said – was he not looking out? The Old Adam was raising himself up – would he not demand the whole hand after he had been offered a finger? 'If you leave your station on this account . . . you have not followed me and I have not counselled you. That you must know! . . . You may be able to deceive people, but you will not deceive God.' Cf. Wingren, G., *Luther on Vocation*, Transl. Rasmussen, C. C., Philadelphia 1957, p. 97, and *D. Martin Luthers Werke*, as quoted, vol. X/1, 1, Weimar 1910, p. 494.
[3] Cf. above, pp. 178 et seq.

has been broken up into independent kingdoms; and we might be as right now in disowning papal authority as our ancestors were in submitting to it.'[1] Catholics have felt the other way round. The more the world has broken up into independent kingdoms, the more internationalism has waned and nationalism has waxed strong in the secular sphere, the more the Church of Rome has emphasized and elaborated her own oneness and coherence. The proclamation of the dogma of papal infallibility (which, as we have indicated, coincided with the climax of nationalistic feeling in Europe at large) was merely the last logical step in a series of adjustments all of which had the aim of securing for ever the unity of the Body of Christ. Nationalism began to raise its head in the second half of the fifteenth century, and immediately the Jesuit Order arose to counter and conquer it. It countered and conquered it not only in the court of princes, though that was the place where it struggled hardest to succeed, it countered and conquered it also in the Church herself where the forces of Gallicanism, inside of France and outside of it, were putting up a fairly stiff, if ultimately unavailing, resistance.

Since Ignatius Loyola, therefore, papal supremacy, as the symbol as well as the core of catholicity, has been a virtually impregnable principle, the citadel within the castle walls. But that the Church *has* gone in the direction of a monolithic monarchy, does not mean that she *had* to go in that direction. Might she not have taken another turning? Might she not have been a United Nations instead of One Nation under God, a fraternal republic of dioceses rather than an integrated *orbis terrarum*? Above all, might not a collectivity have become her head rather than a personality, the Council rather than the Pope? The appearance of a strong Conciliarist movement in the first half of the fifteenth century seems to indicate that things might well have shaped in this way. During the Council of Constance (1414–1417) it looked as if matters were in a state of balance. When that assembly declared that 'a General Council, as representing the Universal Church, held its power immediately from Jesus Christ . . . that every one, even the Pope, was bound to obey the Council in matters concerning faith . . . that the Council had authority over the Pope as well as over all Christians', and when the pope of the day approved of the Council's acts 'saving the rights, dignity, and pre-eminence of the Apostolic See',[2] all outer appear-

[1] Salmon, loc. cit., p. 153.
[2] Cf. Butler, *The Church and Infallibility*, as quoted, pp. 89 and 90.

ances indicated a stalemate, a state from which a multiplicity-in-unity might as easily develop as a unity-in-multiplicity and an ultimate unity. But outer appearances are deceptive rather than decisive; decisive are the inner forces, those stemming from the very essence of the Church herself. And those were – even during the Council of Constance, when Conciliarism reached its acme – firmly directed towards a monarchical constitution.

Although the fact is not very well known, Conciliarism (in the sense of an anti-papal attitude) has had a long history, even if that history is somewhat discontinuous and in part obscure. One of its earlier representatives was Facundus of Hermiane, an African bishop of the sixth century. He was unhappy about his contemporary popes, Vigilius I and Pelagius I, and would have been happier with a conciliar pre-eminence. But why? Because he wanted a weaker pope? By no means; quite the contrary; because he wanted a stronger lead. His opposition was directed against the emperor Justinian I, with his (to Facundus) objectionable habit of interference in Church affairs. The popes should, in the Bishop's opinion, have resisted the Emperor; they did not do so with sufficient energy. Therefore Facundus was tempted to think that an episcopal synod was needed to speak for the Church and to tell the secular power in no uncertain fashion to mind its own business.[1]

Eight hundred and fifty years later, when the classical period of Conciliarism started, the situation was structurally rather similar. As Vigilius and Pelagius had been too yielding in their relations with the emperor of Byzantium, so Urban IV and Clement V were too subservient in their relations with the king of France. The last-named pontiff moved the curia to Avignon and thereby started the so-called 'Babylonian Captivity of the Popes' which lasted from 1309 to 1378. Yet when Gregory IX, urged by St. Catherine of Siena, returned in the latter year to the Holy City, worse events befell the Church: the 'Great Schism' sprang up, and henceforth there were two pontiffs, one in Avignon and one in Rome. It was not until 1417 that Catholic Christendom had, once again, a single head. The very institution therefore which was created to safeguard the essential unity of the Church, was, for over a hundred years, hamstrung, and for nearly forty years divided against itself, a

---

[1] Campenhausen, loc. cit., p. 307. For the background, cf. the excellent exposition in Dawson, op. cit., pp. 252–4.

caricature, a mockery, a far-reaching failure. No wonder that concerned men everywhere sought a possible substitute, an institution which would provide the iron band and bond, lost under pope and anti-pope, that would keep the community together. No wonder either that they pinned their hopes on a grand assembly of bishops, a General Council, which would, they expected, be able to speak with a clear and unfaltering voice. The Council of Constance covers the last three years of the schism-ridden and schism-riven period. A century and more of frustration with the papacy dictated its utterances. And yet they were spoken at a time when the substitute unity provided by a Council was no longer really needed, and the traditional unity provided by the Pope was again available, for with the election of Martin V (November 11, 1417) the painful split was at long last healed.

Still, the troubles were not yet quite over. The Council of Basle (1431–1449) thought of itself as a prolongation of that of Constance, and in 1439 a new schism broke out, which was only laid to rest with the election of Nicholas V (April 25, 1449). This, however, finally meant the end of division and brought the dissolution of the Council. It also meant to all intents and purposes the end and the dissolution of Conciliarism. For the sovereign of the Tridentinum and of either Vaticanum was the pope-in-council, and not the council-above-the-pope. The historical accident and incident of conciliar (near-) supremacy was closed.

Conciliarism produced a copious literature, and this literature provides us with a mirror in which it is easy to perceive the nature of the whole phenomenon. Perhaps the most classical of its writings was Nicholas of Cusa's[1] *De Concordantia Catholica*, presented to the Council of Basle in 1433. This book has been called 'the Catechism of the friends of reform at Basle'.[2] Cusanus had been a disciple of Francesco Zabarella in Padua, and Zabarella in his lectures and publications had made much of the democratic idea of representation. A Council, for instance, represented for him ideally all the Christian people: it might therefore be good to have it elected by them. The College of Cardinals could well become a permanent representative of the faithful at large; and so on. But above all

---

[1] This form of his name has become customary in English books, though the great Cardinal's birthplace was really called Kues. It is the present-day Bernkastel-Kues on the Moselle, near Treves (Trier).

[2] Stumpf, Th., *Die politischen Ideen des Nicolaus von Cues*, Köln 1865, p. 17.

Zabarella introduced, and insisted on, a principle on which Cusanus, too, laid much stress: domination, he said, becomes legitimate through the consent of those subject to it.[1] *De Concordantia Catholica* starts in apparently modern fashion from a basic double assertion: all men are born free and all men are by nature equal, and it concludes, again in apparently modern fashion, that only agreement (*concordantia*) can create binding norms, and that only election can call guardians of these norms into office. Even God, says Nicholas of Cusa, asked Mary for her consent before He bestowed on her the dignity and inflicted on her the duty of becoming the mother of His Son.[2]

This sounds uncommonly like an early form of Rousseauism, but on closer inspection it will be seen that what we really have before us is a late form of Medievalism. While God has created all men in a manner equal, Nicholas maintains, he has at the same time so contrived their minds that the simple find it easy to accept (to consent to) the rule of the sophisticated and wise. One is reminded of Pareto here, especially of his asserted *sentiment de subjection* in the masses, but one is reminded even more of Aristotle and his emphasis on the superior claims of reason to rulership. In any event, the democratic principle turns under the hands of Cusanus, into a hierarchical one. Yet this is less decisive than another implication. According to Rousseau, according to democracy properly so called, consensus is built up from below: it grows out of diversity of opinion, and for the sake of it a good deal of general discussion and indeed disunity is accepted. This is not at all our Cardinal's conception. Consensus comes from above, in the last analysis from the Godhead; it is where the Holy Spirit is; from Him it flows down into the veins of the Body of Christ; and unity therefore is a primordial fact given as soon as society itself is given. Rousseauism and democracy generally presuppose a mechanistic philosophy, according to which political action is the resultant of individual strivings. Cusanus, however, was an organicist. The body politic is one, life is one, and consensus inheres in the members, if, and so long as, they are hale. This all-informing conviction gives an entirely different complexion to *De Concordantia Catholica*. What seems at first sight to be democratic thought is really organismic

[1] Cf. Meuthen, E., *Nikolaus von Kues*, Münster 1964, pp. 15 and 16.
[2] Cf. Watanabe, M., *The Political Ideas of Nicholas of Cusa*, Geneva 1963, pp. 38, 39, 45, 49, 57.

thought and as such has close affinities with conservatism. 'He never saw the laity as a democratic nation of voters,' writes one who knows Nicholas well, 'he saw it always as corporatively structured in a hierarchy of estates.'[1] Such organic hierarchies, however, are held together above all by their heads, the emperor in the state, the pope in the Church. And so Cusanus was from the beginning basically attuned to a far-reaching papalism. The trouble was merely that in his day this institution did not function as it should have done.

What really determined the theory and practice of Nicholas Cusanus was not his interest in the rights of individual men or of subordinate and partial institutions, but his devotion to the ideal of all-comprehensive ecclesiastical unity. Everything turned for him around this knob of things. In the last analysis his salient question was a practical one: who would secure unity – the Pope or the Council? Up to about 1439 he thought the Council would do it rather than the Pope; from then onward he was increasingly convinced that the Pope would do it rather than the Council. Indeed, he arrived at the conviction, or rather he was driven to it, that One Man had to be the Head of the Body of Christ, if organic coherence was to be possible at all. In 1433, he had expressed the opinion that the Pope did indeed signify the Universal Church, but only *confusissime* – in a very confused manner. He would not have said the same in 1443, let alone in 1463. As might be expected, Nicholas has been called a turncoat; people are quick with such sobriquets; but a more dispassionate study of the facts proves that he was entirely consistent. As a mature man, the Cardinal from Kues taught that *two* principles dominate the world: *differentia* and *concordantia*, diversity and unity. The organ of unity must not enslave the multiplicity subject to him; but the men who form the multiplicity must not dissolve the unity which they constitute into a mere plurality.[2]

Cusanus was both a highly refined philosopher and a highly successful statesman, a brilliant Platonist and a brilliant papalist. We can follow neither the one arm of his career nor yet the other, for to us the salient point is merely the sociological question as to

---

[1] Meuthen, loc. cit., pp. 33 and 34. Cf. also Watanabe, loc. cit., pp. 45, 46, 48, 49, 60, 70, 71.
[2] Cf. Meuthen, loc. cit., pp. 36 and 52, and for the intellectual implications, pp. 42–4 and 62. Also Watanabe, pp. 92, 93, 97–110, *passim*.

why he, and with him the great majority of Conciliarists, abandoned Conciliarism, and did it so thoroughly that the road was clear which would, in the fullness of time, lead to that total supremacy on the part of the pope which was finally sealed at the Vatican in 1870. The answer is simple: the split of the papacy into two warring pontiffs engendered, as a counter-stroke, the Conciliarist movement; but the split of the Councils into many warring factions engendered – who could be surprised at it?! – the counter-counter-stroke of flooding papalism. How much easier, it was now seen, was it to abolish the temporary schism between Eugenius IV and Felix V than to bring all the Council fathers, each one taken from one of the world's contending nationalities, under one hat![1] The election of Nicholas V clinched the matter. Conciliarism was no good. It left a bitter aftertaste. This is what an authoritative historian writes of Constance: 'The fathers of the Council were drawn from different lands, unsympathetic and often hostile to one another . . . It had held together' only 'under great difficulties.' And of Basle: 'National animosities rent the Council . . .'[2] The very fact that England and France were at war with each other while the assembly was in session proved to Cusanus, and proved to the world, that Conciliarism could not guarantee that unity which all knew to be the hallmark – the very being – of Catholic Christianity. To the man from Kues, these councils were not really councils at all. 'It is clear,' he had written in De Concordantia Catholica (II, 9), 'that – as a council is constituted by consensus – there is no council where dissension prevails'[3] – very clear and forthright words. He used consensus as the touchstone later on, to test, and reluctantly to condemn, the experiments of Constance and Basle. For him, the proof of the pudding was in the eating: but he saw that before it could even be eaten, it fell to bits on the plate. There is deep historical meaning to the fact that Cusanus, once the leader of the Conciliarist forces, had a slab mounted on his tombstone in San Pietro in Vincoli which shows him kneeling at the

[1] Even the Council of Trent, though it took place within a much more united Church, was still deeply disturbed by nationalistic rivalries, a fact which the composer Hans Pfitzner has made one of the main themes of his great opera Palestrina (1917).

[2] Prévité-Orton, C. W., The Shorter Cambridge Medieval History, Cambridge 1952, pp. 962 and 972.

[3] Cf. De Concordantia Catholica, Part II, so-called Heidelberg ed., Leipzig 1941, p. 135. Our translation.

feet of the Fisherman, *alter ego* of any pope. 'That he had served the Cathedra Petri – that is what he wished posterity to know about him.'[1]

It should not be thought, however, that Conciliarism was merely a passing phenomenon with no message for the future. On the contrary; it incorporated and elaborated an essential insight which must be remembered. The mental image which was before the Cardinal's eye when he preached his doctrine of consent was the symbolic marriage of Christ with His Church.[2] As a German, and a lawyer to boot, he knew the legal principle deep-rooted in Germanic law and lore: 'Husband and wife, one body, one life.' One body and one life can only continue to exist if they are also one mind and one will. This is what Nicholas was to preach to the end of his days. And this is what already St. Bernard had preached three hundred years before. When a fellow-Cistercian was elected pope as Eugenius III, he sent him a famous letter setting out the Saint's conception of the papal office. Remember the words of God to Abraham, Bernard wrote: 'Thy wife thou shalt not call Sarai, but Sara ' (Genesis XVII, 15). Sarai means *my* lady, but Sara means lady – a significant difference.[3] A wife is not a husband's possession: she is himself, the other part of himself. So also is the proper relation of Christ's pontiff and Christ's people.

This leads us to a final characterization of the Catholic concept of ecclesiastical rulership, or rather of the ideal content of it, for the never-ending insufficiency of men has left it very much in the realm of day-dreams. According to the system of ideas which we have been exposing all along, the community exists in two forms (which are, however, ontologically identical): one dispersed and individualized, the other concentrated and incarnate – multiplicity and unity, the innumerable faithful and the one pontiff. Rule means, in this context, the governance of all who are one by the one who is all. It is a vision of self-government that Catholicism has pursued, true self-government, though conceived very differently from the corresponding and contrasting concept of democracy. The concept characteristic of democracy is couched in terms of association and of a mechanistic sociology, that characteristic of Catholicism in terms of community and organicism. All therefore is of one piece

[1] Meuthen, loc. cit., p. 132.   [2] Ibid., p. 44.
[3] Luddy, loc. cit., p. 495.

within Catholic ecclesiology, and we can clearly see the strain of consistency which runs through this, as through all, life.

We are now ready to close our study of the microsociology of Catholicism as an ecclesiastical system, but before we do so we ought to emphasize that we have only considered the operative levels of the hierarchy and not all levels which exist. The pope, for instance, has attributes both high and humble which we have not mentioned. In addition to Bishop of Rome, he is also Primas of Italy and Patriarch of the West, two very honorific titles; in addition to priest and bishop, he is also doorkeeper, reader, acolyte and exorcist, as well as subdiacon and diacon, six rather unimportant, purely transitional degrees. These are deposits of the past, antiquated, almost fictional positions swallowed up by the presbyterate to which they normally lead. At one time, indeed, the diaconate and the subdiaconate loomed fairly large. Formally mainly the servants of the bishop around the Eucharistic table and in the administration of the Church's alms, the deacons were often enough in fact the bishop's right hand and occasionally felt rather superior to the parish priests. Yet a thorough involution has taken place, for reasons which today cannot interest anybody but the technical historian. What has remained is merely the opinion that subdiaconate and diaconate are still 'major' orders, while the remaining four are 'minor'.[1] Yet even they have never been quite dead. As recently as 1865, a great personality, unique in his combination of sinfulness and sanctity, received the four lowest orders (up to and excluding the subdiaconate): Franz Liszt, the inspired composer,[2] singer of the glory of God and of God's saints. It is not impossible that the sub-sacerdotal or sub-presbyterial degrees may play a greater part in the near future than they have done in the recent past. If the number of men who are willing or able to bear the burdens of the priesthood, especially celibacy, should further decline, the appointment (under any suitable name) of ministers without such duty might be an acceptable, though certainly not an ideal, resource, to make good the deficiency. This would bring part at least of the Catholic Church-servants closer to the Protestant clergy which is our next object of consideration.

---

[1] On all this, cf. Lecuyer, loc. cit., pp. 47, 53–5, 57, 58, 60–3, 65, 67, 68, 79.
[2] Cf. Seroff, V., *Franz Liszt*, New York 1966, especially p. 118.

THE OFFICE OF PREDICANT

In the opening pages of this volume, where we sketched the general framework within which our analysis was meant to move, we pointed out that there is a continuum which has at the one pole Catholicism, the totally structured community with a maximally developed division of labour, and at the other pole the consistently unstructured association with a minimally developed division of labour, such as we find it historically exemplified, for instance, among the Quakers. The classical forms of Protestantism, namely Lutheranism and Calvinism, we said, are somewhere along the line. This fact makes it rather difficult to discuss them. For though they have long since settled down into determinate patterns, they were originally further to the left than they are now and have only gradually drifted to the right, i.e. back towards 'Romanism'. One example will show what we mean. As a young man, Luther made much of I Corinthians XIV, 40: 'Let all things be done decently and according to order.' Organization is necessary, he preached, but at that stage it was to him no more than a human necessity, a prudential arrangement, a utilitarian thing without reference to the will of God. Later, however, the underlying conception changed. Organization is necessary, the Reformer began to teach, not only because it is convenient, but also because it is commanded – commanded by God Himself. The ecclesiastical pattern which was in the making thus became more tight and taut; but above all it became underlaid by metaphysical considerations and convictions. A preacher, for instance, was no longer simply any man who felt it incumbent on him to address his fellow believers (the Quaker idea), he was no longer simply any baptized man who in and through his baptism had been introduced into the 'universal priesthood' (Young Luther's conception), he was one who had been called to the office of preaching by competent authority and who had been properly ordained for it. Ordination, it is true, was not considered a sacrament; the Lutheran pastor does not become, like the Catholic priest, a *sacerdos in aeternum*. Yet, characteristically, Lutheran ordination gives a *permanent* character at least down here below: it is not repeated, it is not allowed to be repeated, on entry into a second or later charge. It takes place, once and for all, when the first pastorate is taken up. There is thus a significant difference from the complete informality of the simply sectarian products of the Reformation. 'Quaker minister' is almost a contradiction in terms. In any case, if there is such a person, he is merely a Quaker and no more. But a Lutheran or Calvinist predicant is very definitely a man set apart for the service of God and the Church.

This shift, first away from the old Church and then back again towards her, has blurred the outlines. In the nineteenth century, when the outer forms had become hard and fast, not to say ossified, the inner meaning of the ministry was still in contention. Julius Stahl maintained[1] that the pastoral office is of divine foundation; it does not come to a man from the congregation, it comes to him from the church which is not, like the congregation, merely an assemblage of human beings, but a divine institution; and there are not only individual pastors, there is also a clerical estate, a *status ecclesiasticus*. Johann Wilhelm Friedrich Höfling's opinions were very different.[2] He developed what is technically known as the 'transfer theory' (*Übertragungstheorie*) of the preaching function. This function belongs basically not to any mystically conceived church, but to the soberly observable concrete congregation, and from it or by it it is transferred to an individual office-holder. There are only such individual office-holders; there is no clerical estate, nor can there be one in Lutheranism for (Höfling insists) a Lutheran must think in individualistic terms. The contrast is clear: to Stahl the power to preach descends from above; to Höfling it rises up from below; and 'power' means something very different in the mouth of the one man from what it means in the mouth of the other. Stahl presents a Romanizing, Höfling a Quakerizing (dear reader, forgive the word!) version of Lutheranism. Matters were not much mended when A. W. Dieckhoff later asserted, or rather proved, that elements of both theories are contained in Luther himself.[3]

In the circumstances, all that we can do is to attempt an overall picture which does justice, both to the agreed middle ground which

[1] Stahl, J., *Die Kirchenverfassung nach Lehre und Recht der Protestanten*, Erlangen 1840.
[2] Höfling, J. W. F., *Grundsätze evangelisch-lutherischer Kirchenverfassung*, Erlangen 1850.
[3] Dieckhoff, A. W., *Luthers Lehre von der kirchlichen Gewalt*, Berlin 1865. On all this, cf. the summaries offered in Brunotte, W., *Das geistliche Amt bei Luther*, Berlin 1959, pp. 9–32.

has emerged, and to the polarizing tendencies which are still at work. We begin by casting a glance at the quasi-Catholic or crypto-Catholic conceptions which can be identified.

While Luther enunciated, and even kept to, the doctrine of the universal priesthood, according to which all the grace that a man needs in order to serve God in the pulpit or anywhere else is conferred in baptism, he could, as early as 1520, write as follows: 'Those who have emerged from baptism[1] might boast that they are already consecrated priest, bishop and pope; it does not, however, befit just anybody to exercise such an office. For while we are equally priests, nobody must put himself forward and undertake[2] to do without permission and election what we are all equally empowered to do.'[3] The legitimate predicant needs an express commission which can come from a congregation or else (here is the great ambiguity) from a bishop. While there is thus no need of a sacramental consecration, there is need of an authoritative call, and this, too, places a dividing line between those not entitled, and those entitled, to the pastoral office, the laity and the clerical class.

A call or a commission is, however, but a sober and a secular thing, and by itself it would not have put the Protestant pastor and the Protestant people into a sharp, specifically religious contrast. Yet there was more. According to Luther's settled opinion, an office did not come to a man, but a man was placed into an office. His thinking is institutional rather than individualistic in this particular, which is another way of saying that it is closer to Catholicism than to Quakerism. We have seen above[4] that Dante distinguishes the Holy See and him 'who is seated on it'. Luther does the same. 'The offices, both of rulers and officials, are godly and right,' he writes in his *Exposition of Psalm CI*. 'But those who occupy and practise them are usually of the devil.' In the same vein we read in *Whether Soldiers Too Can be Saved*: 'Although some of them abuse this office, destroy and slay without necessity, in sheer

[1] '*Aus der Tauf [ge]krochen*' – literally, 'crawled out' of the baptismal font, a somewhat crude mode of expression.

[2] '*unterwinden*' – this means almost 'arrogantly undertake', 'arrogate to himself'.

[3] *D. Martin Luthers Werke*, as quoted, vol. VI, Weimar 1888, p. 408. (This and the following quotations are given – unless otherwise stated – in our own translation.)

[4] Cf. p. 178.

wantonness, that is not the fault of the office, but of the person.'[1] These are weighty words which show that a Protestant clergyman is not simply a 'universal priest' as every baptized person is, but a universal priest *plus* something else, an objective office which is joined to him as a subject. But there is yet more. The Catholic priest's distinguishing privilege is, as we have seen, his exclusive power to offer up the sacrifice of the mass, and generally to administer the sacraments. Had Luther been consistent, he would have placed this power, too – this essential power – into the hands of all, of the whole 'universal priesthood'. But he did not. When it came to the point, he could not bring himself radically to abandon the principle of a sacramental class of priests. The Utraquists of Bohemia asked Luther how they could provide themselves with a clergy now that they had forsaken the Church of Rome, and in reply to their queries the Reformer sent them, in 1523, his treatise *De Instituendis Ministris Ecclesiae*. In it, he told them that they could easily appoint preachers who would expound to them the Holy Scriptures, but he told them in the same breath – and this is decisive in our context – that they would have to forgo the joy of the Lord's Table for the time being. For to handle the sacrament of the altar (which Luther retained), you have to be more than merely a 'universal priest'. This, however, puts, in principle at least, the same barrier between the Lutheran clergy and the Lutheran laity as the one which divides the Roman 'sacrificuli' (as Luther called them) from their flocks.[2] The salient point on which we insist is that the pastor's reserved privilege is, according to this expert opinion rendered by Luther to the Bohemian non-conformists, clearly sacramental.

If, however, a pastor has the exclusive power of ministrations which are metaphysical in meaning and effect – and the Lutheran Eucharist is, according to the doctrine of consubstantiation, of this character – then, it would seem, he also needs, to fulfil the task, an ordination which is metaphysical, which bestows a distinctive and distinguishing grace. Luther never drew this conclusion, nor did the Lutherans after him. Yet he and they introduced – or should

---

[1] Wingren, loc. cit., pp. 85 and 86. Cf. also p. 134. Cf. further *D. Martin Luthers Werke*, vol. LI, Weimar 1914, p. 254, and vol. XIX, Weimar 1897, p. 627.
[2] Cf. Brunotte, loc. cit., pp. 76–95, especially pp. 79, 80, 85, 88; also 167 (especially note 73 and the passages referred to there).

we say: retained – an ordination *ritus* rather kindred to the Catholic. Like the Roman priest, the Protestant preacher is ordained by the laying on of hands. It might be said that the similarity is formal, not real, that the Roman priest receives a new quality, a *character indelebilis*, whereas the Protestant preacher does not and remains what he had been before. But does he really not receive a new character? and indeed a new character which remains? Discussing this question, Wilhelm Brunotte (who is a good Lutheran, and who belongs to the church party which regards the office of predicant as divinely instituted) draws attention to two critical points: a young minister may preach once he has passed his theological exam, but he may not administer the Eucharist until he is ordained; and an old minister may still administer the Eucharist to his dying day, even though he is no longer in office.[1] This looks to Brunotte very much like rank Romanism: call to office and commission do not suffice, it appears, ordination has to be added, and ordination gives something which is different from, and in superaddition to, the bestowal of or introduction to an office; it gives a right, a privilege, a power; but if this is so, then we have a half-sacrament and a half-sacramental clerus. To obviate these (to Brunotte) un-Lutheran, un-Protestant implications, he suggests that the laying on of hands be abolished in the Lutheran communion. If this were done, the sacredness of the charge would remain, but it could not be said that a person was being sacred for it. But what this would-be reformer thus wishes to see abandoned, has become part and parcel of his church's historical tradition.

His church's historical tradition, but not only of his church's historical tradition: the development of Calvinist ecclesiology is none too different from that of Lutheran doctrine. The Reformed Churches, just like Martin Luther in his later days, would have nothing to do with the Radical Reformation's doctrine that ministers are delegates of the people, creatures of their making and always on sufferance only. Already in 1654, the English Presbyterians asserted that 'ministers ... are for the people, but not of the people', and in 1698, the General Assembly of the Church of Scotland coined and pronounced the curiously parallel and quite unambiguous statement that 'ministers are sent to the people, not by the people'. Since then, the conviction concerned has become ever stronger and ever more firmly held. How Romanist the position

[1] Brunotte, loc. cit., pp. 201 and 202.

now is can be gathered from the following words: 'There is but one essential ministry, that of Jesus Christ, the risen, ever-present Lord. He who in Galilee and in Judea was carrying out the Messianic ministry of the Suffering Servant continues that ministry in and through His church, which is His Body. As the body of which Christ is the Head, the church is manifestly more than just another human institution ... Despite its frailty and sinfulness, the church is the Body of Christ, and in and through it Christ is carrying on His mission to the world.' The sentences come from an American Presbyterian's pen; they might as well have been written in the inner chambers of the Vatican palace. Later in his book, the author, Harry G. Goodykoontz, quotes in support of his view so authoritative a member of his communion as T. W. Manson[1].

It is, however, incumbent on us expressly to show the presence of a semi- or quasi-sacramental element in these conceptions, otherwise our claim that Calvinism travelled back towards the medieval position is not substantiated. Happily, the sources are clear. A classical publication of the mid-seventeenth century, entitled *Jus Divinum Ministerii Evangelici* stated that nobody can become a minister without a call, and nobody can become a minister without ordination. At the General Assembly of the Church of Scotland in 1640, several leading worthies argued that ordination was not required. Thus Samuel Rutherford: 'Ordination of pastors is not that of absolute necessity but in an exigence the election of the people ... may supply the want of it.' This is a near-Quaker attitude. But the majority seems to have taken a near-Romanist position: 'Ordination is necessary and essential to the calling of a minister.' He cannot act 'without power, authority and commission'.

In this form of words, authority and commission may well be understood soberly and secularly, yet 'power' is in a different case. It must mean divinely bestowed power, power infused from above. But we need not infer what is meant, we have direct testimony. As among Lutherans, so among Calvinists, the administration of the sacraments is reserved for men on whom hands have been laid. 'The shortage of ministers meant that for years certain communities had to do without the Lord's Supper,' Goodykoontz reports about Colonial America. 'The Pilgrims landed in 1620 without an

[1] Goodykoontz, loc. cit., pp. 115, 96, 19, 20, 21, 52, 29, 150.

ordained minister. Elder Brewster gave spiritual leadership, but did not administer the sacraments. The colonists were without the sacraments for four years before their first minister, John Lyford, came . . . Manifestly the colonists believed that the sacraments were to be administered by ordained men.' Manifestly they did. No wonder, then, that ultimately something like a sacramental conception of the Presbyterian clergy emerged. It is reflected in such statements as the following from Goodykoontz: 'In the Reformed tradition, ordination is not a mere bit of symbolism . . . It is a deeply meaningful experience in which the promise of God is claimed and is acted upon by the Holy Spirit . . . If anything real happens to the ordained, it is because Jesus Christ through His Spirit acts in and upon him.' The words are cautious, almost non-committal. 'If anything real happens . . .' But, surely, we cannot assume that according to Presbyterians *nothing* real happens; else why would they preserve the rite so carefully and carry it out so devotedly? Thomas Torrance at any rate is clear: 'In the Church of Scotland,' he writes, 'we ordain a man to the ministry of the Word and Sacraments in the Church of God because we believe it is Christ Himself who ordains.'[1]

In spite of all this, Calvinists of all periods have protested that a difference or differences with Rome remain. Certainly; the detail of the official structure is different and so is the general philosophy into which it is fitted. But on the one point which occupies us here, namely the character of the rite called ordination, the dividing wall is paper-thin. Goodykoontz's exclamation: 'This is no mere form! God is at work in ordination!'[2] proves that present-day Presbyterianism, heir to the great Calvinist tradition, is far from the democratic end of the spectrum stretching from Catholicism to Quakerdom. The very words which he uses of ordination – a symbolism which is more than a symbolism; a form within which God is at work – are potential, if not actual, Catholic definitions of what is essentially sacramental.

However the relevant facts and statements are interpreted – and their interpretation varies not only from Lutheran and Calvinist to Catholic, but from Lutheran and Calvinist to Lutheran and Cal-

[1] Ibid., pp. 68, 69, 79, 116, 138. Cf. also 72, 71, 114–18, 120, 124, and Torrance, Th. F., *Conflict and Agreement in the Church*, vol. II, *The Ministry and the Sacraments of the Gospel*, London 1960, p. 49.
[2] Loc. cit., p. 121.

vinist also – they prove at the very least one thing: namely that there was and is a *tendency* operative in these particular folds, to force the minister up above the level of those to whom he ministers, the concept of universal priesthood notwithstanding. Only its strength and the length to which it has gone or succeeded can be in doubt, the existence of it cannot. But there is also a counter-tendency, an inhibitor of the drive towards a sacramental priest-hood in the proper or full sense of the word, and we can perceive it in the Lutheran doctrine of the *calling*. A predicant is called to his office, true, but so are all other people to theirs – street-cleaners, stable-hands, even soldiers and hangmen, though they bring death rather than life. Many are the passages in which Luther develops this conception, and most of them are rather picturesque. 'God works everything through you,' he says, for instance, in his Lec-tures on I Moses XXXI, 3–9. 'He will even milk a cow through you!' And in his treatise *Of the Married Life*, he writes: 'If a man went and washed the diapers or did some other despised job about the child and everybody derided him and considered him a monkey (*Maulaffe*) and a women's slave . . . God with all His angels and creatures would laugh,' laugh with a pleasure born of cordial approbation, for this, too, is doing God's work.[1] There is much more in the same style throughout Luther's writings. What the Bible is to a preacher, he says in one of his sermons, that a thimble or even a beer vat is to a tailor or a brewer: they remind him of God's Word and God's work.[2] For this reason, only one formulation is true of, and fair to, Luther, namely to say that he readjusts the traditional relation of clergy and people less by taking the clergy-man down a few pegs than by raising the people up. The whole society appears to Luther as a network of relations energized, as it were, by the will of God – a network within which, and through which, all serve God by doing precisely what they are doing. While medievalism had basically a very similar conception, it was much more shadowy; or perhaps we should rather say, the observable pattern of occupations reflected, according to medieval concep-tions, God's will only in its general outline, while the detail was due to human decisions. Luther executed a turn of mind which tended towards determinism in philosophy and conservatism in

---

[1] *D. Martin Luthers Werke*, as quoted, vol. XLIV, Weimar 1915, p. 6, and vol. X/2, Weimar 1907, p. 296.
[2] Ibid., vol. XXXII, Weimar 1906, p. 495.

politics. One of its effects – the one in which we are interested here – was to move the clerical office, so far as Weber's 'estimation of honour' was concerned, closer to all other lines of human activity.[1]

The Scripture passage which to Luther appeared of decisive importance in the matter of a man's life-work, was I Corinthians VII, 20: 'Let every man abide in the same calling in which he was called.' Ecclesiastes III, 22, also was close to his heart: 'I have found that nothing is better than for a man to rejoice in his work, and that this is his portion.' Briefly, his theory was that what comes to us from other people, comes to us from God: if they inflict pain on us, they are the messengers, the mediators, of God's wrath; if they bestow good on us, they are the messengers, the mediators, of God's love. He has a very plastic phrase which makes his idea perfectly clear: men, he says, are to each other 'masks' (*Larven*) of God, for God is hidden behind them. Other, similar phrases are also used; for instance, the Christian is called a 'conduit' or 'channel' through which God reaches men, or it is said that he is 'God's hand'.[2] In the Catholic order of ideas, these similes might well be applied to the priest and have in effect been applied to him by saying, for instance, that he is 'another Christ'. But it would hardly have been extended to other, purely secular avocations. If soldiers kill, *they* kill, rather than execute a divine behest. It is true, Catholics also believe that *in the last resort* all that happens is somehow divinely sanctioned, or at least permitted, but they are not in the habit of ascribing to His *direct* fiat all that befalls. The difference may not be absolute, but it is significant. For Luther, everybody is all the time bodying forth the will of God, and so the distinction between priestly action and all other enterprises dwindles and wastes away.

But can it waste away and vanish completely? Does it not remain true that the cleric brings to his fellow men the Word of God, a message more direct than any other, more clear, more wholesome,

---

[1] Cf. ibid., e.g. vol. VI, Weimar 1888, p. 541.

[2] Cf. Wingren, loc. cit., pp. 18, 19, 125–7, 137, 138, 140, 211, 224. Cf. also *D. Martin Luthers Werke*, as quoted, vol. XXX/1, Weimar 1910, p. 136, vol. XXXI/1, Weimar 1913, p. 436 and repeatedly. All men are God's masks, but the Christian knows it and willingly plays his role, while the unbeliever does not. He has merely *Berufseros*, the Christian *Berufsagape*. Cf. Wingren, pp. 72, 76, 77.

more saving? Luther is sometimes on the brink of saying just that,[1] but there remains a barrier through which he does not, apparently, like to break. We can guess at the reason. Church and state tended to become one in his time, and they tended to fuse in his mind also. If the preacher could not be granted a privilege in relation to ordinary men, he could even less be granted a privilege in relation to rulers. Of the Bible passages which loomed large in Luther's thought, a lapidary sentence from Proverbs loomed especially large: 'By *me* kings reign' (VIII, 15).[2] Gustaf Wingren, one of Sweden's foremost Luther experts, has observed that in the Reformer's later writings the magistrate progressively replaces the confessor and the abbot at least so far as discipline is concerned.[3] There could therefore be no question of exalting the bearer of the Bible above the carrier of the Criminal Code. Indeed, their relationship in Luther's doctrine appears to be one of co-ordination. 'With persons as His "hands" or "co-workers", God gives His gifts through the earthly vocations . . . Thus love [and wrath] comes from God, flowing down to human beings . . . through both spiritual and earthly governments. This can also be a connection between the two governments from man's point of view . . . He receives the good gifts of God's love [as well as correction] through both prince and preacher . . . Luther often emphasizes the simultaneity of these two governments over one and the same person.'[4] To one who is not a caesaropapist, some of Luther's pronouncements must be rather shocking. For instance: 'He who is in the seat of authority, is, as it were, an incarnate God.'[5] This sounds very much like Thomas Hobbes. In fairness to Luther, it must, however, be remembered, when such passages are considered, that God is, if not in, then at least behind *all* men who work with and on us. Yet the fact remains that the preacher is, in principle, at most on a par with the magistrate, and in practice below rather than above him.

[1] Cf. Wingren, loc. cit., pp. 150, 24, 25. 'The office of preaching', says this interpreter, 'as an office is clearly an office among others . . . Nevertheless through this particular vocation God carries out something distinctive and totally different from all other vocations' (p. 25, note 48).

[2] Cf. e.g. *D. Martin Luthers Werke*, as quoted, vol. XL/3, p. 210.

[3] Cf. loc. cit., p. 56, note 7.

[4] Wingren, loc. cit., pp. 27, 28, 26; cf. also pp. 69, 136, 193.

[5] Ibid., p. 127. Cf. *D. Martin Luthers Werke*, as quoted, vol. XLIII, Weimar 1912, p. 514.

One aspect of this tendency to level the man of God down to the plane of all God's men which must be mentioned, however briefly, is Luther's downright rejection of imitation in professional and religious life. To copy the saints, seemed to him a Catholic vice, not a Catholic virtue. We must do our own work, he urges, not that of others; we must look ahead of us, not back over our shoulder. This condemnation of imitation extended even to the imitation of Christ – not, of course, to the imitation of His ways, but certainly to the imitation of His work. It is best at this point to give Luther's precise words: 'Christ carried on His own office and station, but He has not for that reason rejected anyone else's office . . . If a station or office were not good for the reason that Christ did not carry it on, what would become of all stations and offices except the office of preaching which is the only one He practised? . . . Everyone must tend his own vocation and work.'[1] The passage is, of course, in the first place commonsensical: we cannot all preach, for if we did, we should all starve to death. But it has a message which goes well beyond that: if we preach, we are no more doing God's special work in the world than if we do anything else, and more especially if we rule. In this particular, Calvin was not to see eye to eye with his German predecessor, as we shall soon discover.

Having established the sociologically-typologically all-important fact that Moderate Protestantism introduced into church life a measure of democracy, though only a very limited one, while Catholicism continued to adhere to a church constitution distinguishing several super- and sub-ordinated layers and gradations, we can now turn to a consideration of the detail. In looking at it, we find exactly the same as before: there are significant differences between Catholic and Protestant ideas and institutions, but little that would readily be described as diametrical opposition.

The duties of the clergy are once again subsumable under our three headings – the administration of the sacraments, preaching and discipline. Luther, for instance, calls the new type of presbyter 'Christ's preacher' and says that he is a householder in the house of faith, who must provide the inmates with nourishment and rule

---

[1] We are quoting C. C. Rasmussen's translation as given in Wingren, op. cit., pp. 172 and 173. For the original wording, cf. *D. Martin Luthers Werke*, as quoted, vol. XI, Weimar 1900, p. 258.

the subject people (*Gesinde*).[1] The nourishment referred to is, of course, the nourishment of men's souls, in other words, the sacrament of bread and wine. Sometimes indeed Luther makes more words, but even when he does so,[2] the ternary pattern with which we have worked in analysing the functions of the Catholic priesthood can still be discerned and seen to be applicable. On the Calvinist side, the *Scots Confession of Faith* of 1560 speaks 'of the notes by which the true Kirk is discerned from the false' and says: 'First, there is the true preaching of the Word of God; secondly, the right administration of the sacraments of Christ Jesus; last, ecclesiastical discipline . . . whereby vice is repressed and virtue nourished.'[3]

It is not, therefore, the catalogue of essential clerical duties which distinguishes Protestant and Catholic, it is merely the different arrangement of the three items which they have in common. The Catholic priest is first of all an administrator of the sacraments; then, in the second place, he is a teacher and preacher; and his work in the confessional follows closely as a third assignment. The Protestant predicant is first of all a teacher and preacher; he is an administrator of the sacraments merely in the second place; and his task as a moral taskmaster forms today a third duty limping somewhat behind the others. But that was not always so. Even if one keeps to the ranging and ranking of the three salient elements of the ministerial office which we have just given – and one should perhaps keep to it, as Protestant literature regularly carries it in this form – one is sorely tempted to put discipline, at least for the heroic period of Calvinism, into a higher slot. It certainly played a prominent part, and was for a while second only to the thunder from the pulpit.

We have called this whole section 'The Office of Predicant' because the latter term seems to us to characterize the very gist of the

---

[1] *D. Martin Luthers Werke*, as quoted, vol. X/1, 2, Weimar 1925, pp. 123 and 126.

[2] Cf. *De Instituendis Ministris Ecclesiae*, II, 2, Brunotte, p. 83. The following tasks are enumerated: to teach, to preach, to announce the word of God, to baptize, to consecrate or administer the Eucharist, to bind and loose sins, to pray for others, to offer sacrifice, to judge people's doctrine and spirit. Cf. also Brunotte, pp. 157–9.

[3] Cit. Clark, I. MacN., *A History of Church Discipline in Scotland*, Aberdeen 1929, p. 65. (Spelling modernized.) Cf. also Goodykoontz, loc. cit., pp. 52 and 121, for the parallel conceptions of Calvin himself and of present-day Calvinists. Cf. further ibid., pp. 130–2.

Protestant ministry more strikingly than any other. The correctness of the label can hardly be in doubt. 'For Luther,' says Brunotte, after an exhaustive study of the source material, 'the function of preaching occupies so prominent a place that he mentions it most frequently in connection with the [pastoral] office, puts it high above other functions and describes the spiritual calling often as "preaching office" [*predig ampt*].' Luther's preferred Latin terms are *concionator*, *praedicator* and *assertor*.[1] There are passages of a polemical nature which show with all desirable clarity that the Reformer regarded the promotion of preaching to the first rank as the distinguishing mark, and indeed as the distinguishing excellence, of the new church which he was developing. 'Instead of ministers of the Word,' he says, for instance, voicing one of his main grudges against Rome, 'they ordain priestlings [*sacrificulos* – literally, little sacrifice-offerers] who offer up masses and hear confessions.'[2] Obviously, the latter two tasks were not quite so important to him as the first-named, *evangelisare*. In one context he even goes so far as to call a place of religious assembly a *Mundhaus* ('mouth house' – a house for the voice to be heard).[3]

Luther's associates were of the same opinion. Of Bugenhagen, valiant champion of the Reform to the north, it is reported that he once preached for seven hours. Bullinger, theologically somewhat further to the left, gave it as his opinion that 'ministers are chosen chiefly to teach'.[4] But most important, needless to say, is Jehan Calvin, in this context as in any other. To him it appeared that preaching was the very *quâ non* of an *ecclesia*. 'Where the preaching of the Gospel is reverently heard and the sacraments are not neglected,' he writes in his *Institutes* (IV, 1, 10), 'there . . . the Church is seen.'[5] The formulation is revealing: the sacraments must indeed not be neglected (a negative statement), but the Scriptures must be reverentially taught and received (a positive one). Coming from the Calvinist tradition, Goodykoontz says in the same spirit: 'The minister has no greater power, no higher responsibility, no more

---

[1] Brunotte, loc. cit., p. 169. Cf. also pp. 52 and 170.

[2] *D. Martin Luthers Werke*, as quoted, vol. XII, Weimar 1891, p. 173.

[3] Ibid., vol. X/1, 2, Weimar 1925, p. 48.

[4] Cf. Pauck, W., 'The Ministry in the Time of the Continental Reformation', in Niebuhr, H. R., and Williams, D. D., *The Ministry in Historical Perspectives*, New York, Evanston and London 1956, p. 134, and Goodykoontz, loc. cit., p. 54.

[5] *Institutes of the Christian Religion*, as quoted, p. 1024 (cf. above, p. 27).

vital function, than to proclaim, by teaching and preaching, the Word.'[1] So great is the Protestant emphasis on preaching that one observer at least has found in it the root of a specific Protestant clericalism. 'The preachers tend to be the spokesmen and the representatives of the church, and the church is often a preachers' church,' i.e. a church dominated by preachers, writes Wilhelm Pauck.[2] 'Whenever and wherever, in the course of the Reformation and later, such domination became a fact, it was caused chiefly by the prominence attributed by Protestants to the preaching office.'

In view of all this, it is not surprising to find the difference between Catholic priest and Protestant predicant elaborated along corresponding lines, i.e. following Luther's personal lead as given in the passage about the *sacrificuli* which we have just quoted. Gösta Hök, for instance, writes: 'The Roman Catholic ministry is that of the sacrificing priesthood and Roman Catholic priests are ordained to administer the sacraments . . . The Lutheran ministry, on the other hand, is a ministry of the Word . . . The Lutheran minister . . . dispenses the mysteries of God in preaching.'[3] There is nothing in these sentences to which one could take exception, and yet they are apt to mislead. The contrast of which they are speaking is real, but it is in reality less than it appears. We have touched upon this matter already;[4] we must return to it now, for here is the appropriate place to deal with it conclusively.

While the Catholic priest is undoubtedly a minister of the sacraments, and the Protestant predicant appears to be less so because he officiates from the pulpit rather than from the altar, even the office of the Protestant predicant has a sacramental side to it – not only because, he, too, as a secondary duty, dispenses the sacraments, but also because of his primary duty, preaching, too, being, in a very definite sense, a sacrament. What is a sacrament? It is a channel through which divine influences stream into human life. Preaching is such a channel. Protestants of the classical variety have never regarded the word spoken from the pulpit as only appeal and

---

[1] Loc. cit., p. 135. Cf. also, p. 133 and pp. 99–100, where several supporting authorities are quoted.
[2] Loc. cit., p. 114.
[3] 'Luther's Doctrine of the Ministry', in *Scottish Journal of Theology*, vol. VII (1954), pp. 16 and 17.
[4] Cf. above, p. 254.

argument; it is much rather the conveyor of good and grace. And so far as this conception is concerned, the Reformers spoke out of a tradition and fund of ideas which was not only deeply religious but also deeply Catholic. The breach between the older and the newer forms of Christianity appears, at this point at any rate, greater than it really is.

If one wants to understand the basic conceptions out of which there flowed the veneration of both Luther and Calvin for the Word of God, one could hardly do better than to turn to so typical a medieval figure as St. Bernard of Clairvaux. This is what he writes in the little treatise usually quoted as the *Treatise on Conversion*: '"Be converted, O ye sons of men." Observe that the Psalmist tells us deliberately that these words were spoken by God . . . Who would have the boldness to compare the words of God with any speech of men? For the words of God are "living and effectual" (Heb. IV, 12); His "voice is in power and magnificence" (Ps. XXVIII, 4). And we have the proof in these other testimonies: "He spoke and they were made, He commanded and they were created" (Ps. CXLVIII, 5). "He said: Be light made, and light was made" (Gen. I, 3). With equal power He can say to sinners: "Be converted, O ye sons of men," and they shall be converted . . . Simon, the son of John, although called by Christ and appointed by Him a fisher of men (Matt. IV, 19), yet laboured all night without taking anything; but when he let down his net at the word of the Lord, he "enclosed a very great multitude of fishes" (Luke V, 5–6). God grant that I too may let down my net today "at the word of the Lord", and so may experience the truth of what is written: "Behold, He will give to His word the voice of power" (Ps. LXVII, 34) . . . For His is the voice of magnificence and power that "shaketh the desert" (Ps. XXVIII, 8), that discloses secrets and awakens souls from the slumber of sin.'[1] Any rationalistic interpretation of the emphasis, the deep and devotional emphasis, of Luther and Calvin on the Word of God would be wrong. The mystical element which informs all true religiosity is alive in their system, and more especially in their conception of the preaching function within their system, and in that respect they are much closer to the religious world which preceded them than to the rationalistic world by which they were succeeded.

[1] Luddy, op. cit., pp. 386 and 387. Cf. also *Patrologia Latina*, as quoted, vol. CLXXXII, Paris 1854, col. 835.

What we have just said might also be expressed by suggesting that preaching, as conceived by Luther and Calvin, was a sacerdotal function. And as they thought of it in this way, as they thought, at least to some extent, in sacerdotal terms, it is not so surprising as might be imagined, in view of their sometimes violent insistence on their difference from Rome, that they reserved the administration of the two sacraments which they retained, Baptism and The Lord's Supper, to ordained men. Yet as we go over to the discussion of this second strand in the three-ply function of the clerical class, we do find a certain contrast to Rome. Both Lutherans and Calvinists, if they are what they are supposed to be, approach the sacraments, and especially The Lord's Supper, with deep devotion, more precisely expressed, with a devotion which carries in it a mystical element. This is especially true of Lutherans who, in accordance with their dogma of consubstantiation, believe in a real presence; it is, however, hardly less true of devout Calvinists even though their theology makes the rite merely a memorial meal, for around that memorial there hangs yet a sacredness which is, even to them, of inexhaustible depth and meaning. It is the same with Baptism. For Luther who did, indeed, have a leaning towards determinism, but never went as far as predestination, baptism is clearly a sacrament in the fullest sense of the word: it effects the entry of the child into the communion of the saved. Calvin's basic philosophical stance created difficulties for him: if we are predestined from all eternity either to damnation or to salvation, we are, in the latter case, members of the Body of Christ already before we are born. Why, then, must we be baptized? And what can baptism still add to our blessedness? It is not for us to discuss the arguments which the Reformer puts forward in order to get out of the impasse. But we must emphasize that baptism remains for him a necessity. Indeed, it was his conviction that 'baptism is no mere symbol without effect; it does effect what it signifies'. These words, in which Bohatec sums up the Genevan's doctrine, are to all intents and purposes identical with the Catholic definition of a sacrament.[1] Sacraments – genuine sacraments – are therefore basic to classical Protestant religiosity. Their reservation to ordained ministers was

[1] On all this, cf. Bohatec, op. cit., pp. 372, 373, 352, 353, and the passages from Calvin quoted and enumerated there. For the most important of them, cf. *Corpus Reformatorum*, vol. XXXX, Braunschweig 1874 (*Calvini Opera*, vol. XII), col. 482.

one of the mainstays of the prestige and power which the ministerial class enjoyed.

Nevertheless, the sacraments are, in Protestantism, and in the Protestant minister's work, secondary at least in the sense that they are hemmed-in – indeed, if the word be allowed, squeezed – by the other two ministerial types of action, preaching and correction. Wilhelm Pauck brings this out very well, and we therefore give the word to him. 'The administration of the sacraments,' he writes, 'was always accompanied by some kind of instruction. In Lutheran churches, young people were not admitted to the first communion service without having been [catechized and] examined by the minister on their faith . . . Services of confession and penitence . . . practically everywhere preceded the celebration of the Lord's Supper . . . People who intended to take the sacrament had to inform the minister beforehand, and he was not allowed to admit them without having held with them a service [of purgation] . . . In Geneva, the Lord's Supper was regarded as a service of the whole congregation that everyone had to attend . . . Here, too, a confessional service was held preceding the celebration of the sacrament. Meeting as the congregation of God, all were individually confronted with their responsibility worthily to approach the Lord's table. The ministers did not admit anyone who was not in good standing in the church. The communion service was thus placed in the context of church discipline. . . . None of those who had been cited to appear before the Consistory because of irregularities in faith or morals was permitted to take communion, unless evidence was given of his having corrected the faults.'[1] In Scotland, matters were substantially the same as in Geneva. Here 'the Reformers . . . not only required the young to undergo and pass an examination on the chief heads of religion, but they required all the members of the congregation, whether old or young, and whether communicating for the first or fiftieth time, to undergo examination before each celebration of the ordinance.'[2] A 'token' was necessary to approach 'the Lord's table', and tokens were only for those who, in the view of the minister and elders, were blameless – again the 'context of discipline'. Catholic children, it is true, also have to take instruction before their first communion; Catholic adults, too, are

[1] Pauck, loc. cit., pp. 135 and 136.
[2] Edgar, A., 'The Discipline of the Church', in Story, R. H. (ed.), *The Church of Scotland, Past and Present*, London n.d., p. 456.

expected to go to confession, do their penance and receive absolution, before communicating. But instruction and correction in the Catholic system clearly subserve the supreme sacrament. In the Protestant tradition, the sacrament has as at least one of its functions to foster instruction and ensure correction. It is to that extent secondary whatever is thought or felt about it otherwise.

The time has come, however, to speak less of the differences between Catholicism and Protestantism than of the differences between the Protestant churches themselves, for it is in this area, the area of discipline, which we shall now study, that deep and decisive dissimilarities obtain between Lutheranism and Calvinism. For Luther and the Lutherans, discipline – the power to loose from sin, the power of the keys – is merely an appendix to the preaching function, hardly to be distinguished from its normal instructional office. For Calvin and the Calvinists, on the other hand, it was at first a central concern, certainly the one through which the church impinged most forcefully on the lives of the faithful, and it was only through a long process of decay, through a protracted and ultimately *in toto* effective loss of power on the part of the church, that a condition was reached which reduced church discipline to one single means and method – the pulpit word, as in Lutheranism.[1]

Luther sometimes calls the preacher 'a shepherd' (*Hirte*) and his office 'pasturing' (*Weiden*); these words certainly suggest control from above, for the shepherd is the appointed ruler of those whom he pastures, the sheep. Yet preaching and shepherding are not really kept apart in Luther's mind. They are one office; more: when the one task is fulfilled, the other is fulfilled also. 'Luther shows, for instance in his commentary of 1523 on the First Epistle of Peter, that he means by the office of the shepherd or by the function of pasturing objectively the same as by the preaching office' or the preaching function, writes Brunotte, with his great knowledge of Luther behind him. 'Luther emphasizes very specially that the "pastoral" or shepherding office does not have the right to claim any power of rulership of its own, but that it is merely meant publicly to assert the Word of God . . . To that extent it is a spiritual office which . . . is to work merely with spiritual means, that is to say, exclusively with the Word of God.'[2]

[1] Cf. Clark, loc. cit., pp. 185, 186, 202, 211 et seq.
[2] Brunotte, loc. cit., p. 170. Cf. also p. 97.

Sometimes, indeed, Luther speaks of punishment, but even then he means no more than verbal reprobation. 'Tell me,' he writes, 'is it not a strict command of the Majesty on High that a preacher is in duty bound, by his soul's salvation, to punish the godless? For He speaks of public punishment when he lays on him the office to preach His word . . . But he says more particularly: the Word of God must be heard . . . But we have no word but the Scriptures; therefore it is by means of them that the godless are to be punished.' Elsewhere Luther writes – and we italicize one term in order to show what he means: 'God placed the ministry of the Word in this world, not that the ministers should keep silent, but that they should plead, instruct, console, *frighten* [*ut . . . terrerent*], and in this way save all that they can.'[1] The miscreant in the grip of the Lutheran communion was to be lashed – but he was not to be lashed to a pillory, as Hester Prynne was at Boston under the Puritanical discipline of the Puritans,[2] he was only to be lashed by the pastor's tongue. And even that lashing was as a rule rather demure for it was not in this field that the Lutheran clergy has ever tried to win its laurels.

At this point, our analysis of the microsociology of religion and especially of the clergy and its functions, must merge with the insights which we have gained in the earlier three volumes of our work. We established there two contrasting types of church, the caesaropapist type under which church and state are fused, and the anti-caesaropapist type under which church and state remain separate. Speaking more concretely, we elaborated on the opposition between Anglicanism on the one side and Catholicism on the other. The Reformation, almost as soon as it was launched, saw itself confronted with the necessity of choosing between these alternatives. Lutheranism went one way, Calvinism the other. And nowhere is their ultimate dissimilarity more obvious than in the area of ecclesiastical discipline.

Looking at things from the Calvinist–Presbyterian point of view, but judging fairly and correctly, I. M. Clark asserts that 'apparently Luther was willing to yield up a good deal of discipline to the civil magistrate', indeed that under Lutheranism 'matters of discipline [were] being left largely to the civil ruler'. 'Punishment by the civil

[1] *D. Martin Luthers Werke*, as quoted, vol. X/2, Weimar 1907, p. 108, and vol. XLIII, Weimar 1912, p. 46.
[2] We are referring, of course, to Nathaniel Hawthorne's novel, *The Scarlet Letter*.

magistrate was regarded as "satisfaction" by the church, and . . . absolution automatically followed or was pronounced.' This state of affairs is considered, by the author, as characteristic of all Caesaropapism, and we are inclined to agree with him. 'Erastianism . . . claims only the right to teach and exhort, to instruct and persuade, while disavowing all right to rule or censure, as being the province of the civil magistrate, a right that can only be conferred on the church by the civil authority.'[1]

'That view is not to be held!' exclaims Dr Clark[2] and thereby voices a deep Calvinistic conviction. 'Calvin had had to fight for the right of the church to excommunicate without consulting the civil powers, a right of spiritual independence which at last the state admitted. The Calvinistic churches, though acknowledging the state was also instituted by God for the ordering of temporal things, admitted no subservience to civil power – a note which, though marked [already] in the earliest stages of the Reformation in Scotland, grew even more pronounced in its expression as stated in the *Second Book of Discipline*.'[3]

The Calvinistic Reformation, just like the Lutheran, has often presented itself as a return to the primitive Church, but in this particular a great difference between old and new is obvious. True, penances in Geneva under Calvin, or in Scotland after 1560, or in the New England colonies, were public as they once had been, *but* whereas the primitive Church had not insisted on a public *confession* of the penitent, the Calvinist communities did. In other words, in the Rome of A.D. 400, you knew a brother had fallen, but you did not know *what* he had done. The nature of the sin was only disclosed to the priest, in fact whispered into his ears. Not so among the Puritans of all descriptions: the sin was blurted out, indeed, cried from the roof-tops. Thus the discipline of the predicants became a heavy burden, always involving personal exposure and shame. When, around the year 450, it was discovered that some districts (Campania and Samnium) practised not only public penance, but also public confession, the contemporary pope, St. Leo, intervened. This was not to be.[4] A mantle was wrapped around the sinner which the Reformation decided to tear off. We have here straight away one of the reasons why discipline decayed and disappeared in the end. Calvinism was attempting to build a totally sanctified

[1] Clark, as quoted, pp. 59, 60, 214.   [2] p. 214.
[3] Ibid., p. 65.   [4] Ibid., pp. 15, 16, 159, 160, 169.

society, but that is more than flesh and blood can bear, and so, by a spontaneous reaction, overly strict control led to overly lax half-control, indeed, to a fateful weakening of social pressures with whose consequences the world is still struggling today.

To come to the historical detail, and to use Scotland as our example, no sooner had the Reformation got into the saddle than it started to create a *forum externum*, or public court, to replace the confessional or *forum internum* of the old Church. That tribunal was (apart from cases involving the greater, or total, excommunication, which were handled by the regional Presbytery) the local Kirk Session, consisting of the minister or 'preaching elder' together with 'ruling elders' appointed for the task. These supervisors of the people were not supposed to wait until information about misdeeds reached them; they were invited to go out and get it. In technical language, not the accusatorial, but the inquisitorial mode of procedure was used. An enactment of the General Assembly of the Church of Scotland passed in 1646 declares: 'Let every elder have bounds assigned to him, that he may visit the same every month at least and report what scandals and abuses [are to be found] therein – also for keeping [the] sabbath.'[1] A most ambitious programme of moral guidance was thus initiated.

How it worked, could be illustrated by a truly overwhelming wealth of detail, but here just one example must suffice. The Presbytery Book of Strathbogie has the following entry under July 8, 1646, which we reproduce, for quaintness' sake, just as it stands: 'Compeired John Paterson, being summondit by ane reference from the Sessioun of Dumbennand, and accused of incest with Bessie Geddies, his wife's sister, confessed the same. The said John ordained to pay forty libs [in cash], and stand bear-footed in sack-cloth twenty-five saboths; and the said Bessie to satisfy in brankis and joggs to the contentment of the parochin.'[2] The very description of this misdemeanour as incest shows how fierce the persecution of sin was. An affair with a sister-in-law would hardly be given this terrible name today.

The *First Book of Discipline* (1560), the *Second Book of Discipline* (1578), the *Form and Order of Excommunication and of Public Repentance* published in the interval (1567), and the *Form of Process*

---

[1] Ibid., pp. 61, 118, 119. Cf. also pp. 64 and 119; Edgar, loc. cit., pp. 501, 502, 506.
[2] Clark, loc. cit., pp. 154 and 155. Brankis = halter; joggs = pillory; parochin = parish.

(1707),[1] the latter almost amounting to a third Book of Discipline,[2] are the main historical sources, and they are greatly revealing. We cannot even scratch their surface here. Various stages are laid down in pursuit of which individual cases are investigated, the sinner censured and increasingly pressured up to the possible climax of excommunication, and then, in reverse order, taken back into the church, if he gives 'satisfaction' and is given absolution.[3] The core of the procedure, needless to say, is the penance inflicted and incurred. A whole code tended to develop. In 1648, for instance, there were 'remedies propounded by the Assembly for the grievous and common sins of the land', and they stipulate: 'Let those who have fallen in fornication make public confession of repentance three several sabbaths; who is guilty in relapse in fornication, six sabbaths; who is guilty of trelapse in fornication or has once fallen in adultery, twenty-six sabbaths; and these sins to be confessed both in one habit, viz. in sackcloth . . .'[4] It was under such statutes that the poet Robert Burns was constrained, on July 9, July 30, and August 6, 1786, to stand up in church for 'admonition' as having been responsible for the pregnancy of Jean Armour.[5]

In Luther's 'Table Talk' there is a passage which applied to him and to the Lutheran clergy far less than it did to Calvin and the Calvinist ministry. 'The untamed masses,' he is reported as saying,[6]

[1] The official title of this enactment is as follows: 'Act approving a form of process in the judicatories of the Church, with relation to scandals and censures', but it is invariably quoted in the abbreviated form given above.

[2] The *Books of Discipline* are not only concerned with the repression of sin, but deal with the whole constitution of the church. It is, nevertheless, significant that they bear the name which they are bearing.

[3] Absolution, incidentally, was conceived in near-sacramental, if not fully sacramental, terms, in the sense that the formula physically pronounced was asserted to be metaphysically effective. 'If you unfeignedly repent your former iniquity and believe in the Lord Jesus, then I, in His name, pronounce and affirm that your sins are forgiven, not only on earth, but also in heaven, according to the promises annexed with the preaching of His Word and to the power put in the ministry of His Church' (spelling and word-forms modernized). Clark, loc. cit., p. 77. Clark adds: 'This is virtually claiming for the minister the commission given to the Apostles, for ministry here seems to means [the ordained] minister', not the elders or deacons who have more lay status. Cf. also pp. 123, 124, 160.

[4] Clark, loc. cit., p. 125. Cf. also p. 74.

[5] Cf. Carswell, C., *The Life of Robert Burns*, London 1930, pp. 187 and 192.

[6] Transl. by Tappert, Th. G., and printed in *Luther: Letters of Spiritual Counsel*, ed. Tappert, *The Library of Christian Classics*, vol. XVIII, London 1955, p. 304.

'are unwilling to be corrected and it is the duty of preachers to reprove them . . . And on this account laymen . . . try to find some fault in them, and if they discover a grievous offence, even if it be in the clergymen's wives or children, they are delighted to have their revenge on them. Except that they surpass other people in power, princes harass clergymen with a like hatred . . . Enmity towards clergymen will remain. As the old saying puts it, "Not until the sea dries up and the devil is taken up into heaven, will the layman be a true friend of the clergyman."' Perhaps Luther was a little too gloomy in this respect. In Scotland at any rate, the people tended to respect their minister, even if they feared him at the same time. The attitude of the parishioners to their presbyter was a little like the attitude of children to a strict and stern father. The rod is not nice, but those for whose back it is meant may well recognize that they need it. And one thing helped to sustain the prestige of Scots discipline, and of those who administered it: the infliction of censure on all, high and low alike.[1] Even today, criticism of the Queen and the royal family can only be heard from Scottish, not English, pulpits.

One thing, however, is true. The shadow of godliness as calvinistically understood lay heavily on the land. This is what a faithful son of the Kirk has to say about the matter, speaking more particularly of the time after the so-called Second Reformation in 1638, 'when the discipline of the church had reached its full development': 'Scouts were every night sent through all the ale-houses in every town and village, to see if any person was either drinking or selling drinks after "elders' hours". Scouts were, in like manner, sent through every village every Sunday during divine service to see if any that should have been in church were drinking in taverns . . . At every fair or race there were elders told off to perambulate the market-place or the race-course . . . and report every immorality they saw or heard. Not a wedding or a merry-making could be held without ecclesiastical detectives being set to inquire into all that happened thereat, and inform the kirk session of the numbers present and the nature of the entertainment.'[2]

It is, surely, not surprising that the Scottish people tried to escape from this condition, and they did so by simple non-cooperation. Where charges were brought, e.g. in case of insult or

[1] Cf. our vol. III, p. 115, and Clark, loc. cit., p. 80. But cf. below, p. 319, note 4.   [2] Edgar, A., loc. cit., p. 478.

libel, as when one Jonet at St. Andrews complained of John Scott that his 'tongue' had been 'false', i.e. that he had spread a lie,[1] it was easy to operate the system. But when hidden faults were at stake, i.e. in the very cases for which the inquisitorial method was devised and introduced, it was increasingly difficult to gather evidence and hence to convict. Strange methods had to be tried. Dr. Edgar reports a case from the past of the very parish in which he served as minister which shows how a suspect (a female with a *fama* for loose morals) might be treated: 'The midwife, Margret Wat, being with her in her greatest pains, did challenge her if ever she had ado with any other man and threatened that she would leave her to die in her pains, if she would not tell the truth, and she cried out and [said she] wished that she might never be better, if any man was the father of that child but J. W.'[2] But even this case was easy, for there was already a visible *corpus delicti*, namely a half-born baby of an unmarried mother. Truly hidden sins simply escaped. In the eighteenth century, Scots discipline had perforce to retire to the one area of 'fornication', and go by the one evidence that was available, an illegitimate offspring.[3] It was thus that they got Robert Burns. Allan Ramsay, another poet, characterized the situation very well in the following lines:

> Had Eppy's apron bidden down
> The kirk had ne'er a kend it,
> But when the word's gane thro' the town,
> Alake! how can she mend it.
> Now Tam maun face the minister,
> And she maun mount the pillar,
> And that's the way that they maun gae,
> For poor folk has nae siller.[4]

---

[1] Cf. Clark, loc. cit., p. 83.

[2] Edgar, loc. cit., p. 477. The quotation is from the records of the Mauchline Kirk Session (modernized).

[3] Clark, loc. cit., p. 179.

[4] a kend = known; maun = must; nae siller = no money. Cf. *The Works of Allan Ramsay*, edd. Kinghorn, A. M., and Law, A., vol. III, Edinburgh and London 1961, p. 53. Whether rich people could in fact buy themselves free, as the last two lines suggest, must remain an open question. Perhaps it was possible in the eighteenth century, when some localities did commute older penalties into monetary fines to be applied *ad pios usus*. In the seventeenth it was not. Cf. Edgar, loc. cit., pp. 533, 539, 540; 538, 541.

Often enough, the girl would refuse to give the name of her partner (as Hester Prynne did in *The Scarlet Letter*) and so there would be only one accused, not two, as there should have been.

Today it might still happen that an elder would bring a charge against a parishioner, but all that would follow would be for the minister to go to the culprit and remonstrate with him. Surveying the whole 'History of Church Discipline in Scotland', its rise and its decay, and drawing some pastoral conclusions from the experiment and experience, Ivo Macnaughton Clark comes to the conclusion that it would be best, even for Presbyterians, to encourage private confessions, i.e. to conform in this field to Roman Catholic practice.[1] Still, the Calvinist effort to produce a sanctified society, or at least a society in which sin was securely under control, remains one of mankind's most heroic efforts to be less despicable than they need be, and an account of it should not end on a completely negative note. In Scotland, for instance, it has produced a culture which is both imbued with high moral principles and with a passionate love of personal independence; and it has even stimulated a peculiar sense of humour. We can see it reflected in the dedication of P. G. Wodehouse's *The Clicking of Cuthbert*, a book on the glories of golfing: 'To the immortal memory of John Henrie and Pat Rogie who at Edinburgh in the year 1593 were imprisoned for playing of the gowff on the links of Leith every sabbath the time of the sermonses.'

In conclusion, a word must still be said about the disciplining of clergymen. Who took the place, in the Protestant dispensation, of the Catholic bishop? Lutheranism and Calvinism again characteristically diverged. Lutheranism developed in most of its area an office like that of Superintendent or a governing *gremium* like a Consistory, both – as is often emphasized – established merely *jure humano*, as purely human institutions. But Luther took the truly decisive step when he declared the prince to be *Notbischof* (emergency bishop) until such time as ecclesiastical conditions would totally change, a consummation which has never happened. Superintendents and consistories would therefore as a rule be securely under the king's or duke's thumb, like all his other appointees – a thoroughly caesaropapist set-up.[2]

---

[1] Clark, loc. cit., pp. 219 et seq. Cf. also p. 148.
[2] Cf. Pauck, loc. cit., pp. 122–4 and 142; concerning Luther's acceptance of the office of superintendent, cf. Hök, as quoted, p. 35; also Brunotte, pp. 172 and 173.

In the Calvinist areas, things shaped differently. Domination of the world by the church was attempted, and at least freedom of the church from the world was achieved. The *First Book of Discipline*, published in the year the Reformation was victorious in Scotland (1560), provided for superintendents who still recalled in some respects the bishops whom they were meant to replace. But by 1578, when the *Second Book of Discipline* appeared, the Kirk had found her proper form. That form was presbyterian, with equality of all presbyters as the firm basis. There was little inclination on the part of the Calvinist churches to follow the example of their Hungarian brethren who settled for bishop-superintendents. Scotland's *Second Book of Discipline* went the other way and introduced the system of courts which still exists. It laid down the principle 'that the office of bishop [coinciding, as in Apostolic times, with that of presbyter] is held by him who is minister to a congregation, and that he is to be superintended by the body of ministers, assisted by elders, of his own Presbytery; that the Synod has a superintending and reviewing power over all the presbyteries within its bounds, and the General Assembly over all the synods and the whole church.'[1] There is thus a relatively democratic organization. But we are using the word 'relatively' advisedly. An errant minister is not, like a simple parishioner, under the Kirk Session, but he is under the next higher court, the Presbytery, composed of the neighbouring ministers with whom selected elders sit in judgment. This means in practice that the clergy cannot be disciplined by their own people. Sociologically, this is extremely important. Unlike a Quaker 'minister', a Scots minister is still a man with a difference, a soul 'set apart'. And this confirms the whole estimate of the nature and of the effects of the Reformation, so far as the microsociology of religion is concerned, which we have tried to elaborate and to present in the foregoing pages.

Our survey has, of necessity, been a limited one. We have not spoken, for instance, of Baptists or Methodists, nor of the Church of England or of the Orthodox traditions. Nevertheless, we have fulfilled our set task which was, as ever, typological. Every concrete church body has its place somewhere along our continuum from Catholicism to Quakerism, and only a detailed investigation

---

[1] Clark, loc. cit., p. 114. Cf. also pp. 68–70, 111, 119, 120.

can show where exactly it is located. It is obvious, for instance, that Anglicanism and Orthodoxy are relatively close to Catholicism, and Baptism relatively close to the Society of Friends, with Methodism still close to, and yet a little further removed from, the latter pole. In this manner, the great variety of life can be realistically reduced to the relative simplicity of a scholarly scheme.

THE LAITY AND THE LAYMAN

Our last section was descriptive rather than analytical. We have shown that Catholic and Protestant clergy essentially differ in this that the work of the former is centred on the sacraments, whereas the work of the latter is centred on preaching. We have now to add, why this should be so, and in attempting to do this, we shall be led to the threshold of a new subject.

The Protestant emphasis on the pulpit (and, in the case of Calvinism, on the stocks) is in the final analysis a consequence of the comparatively individualistic stance which the Reformers took up both in life and in philosophy. Men do not rise up towards, or recede from, heaven collectively, together, they make their way towards salvation severally and singly. Christ is their helper, but other men cannot help them much. Souls in jeopardy cannot, for instance, draw on the merits of the saints to make up for their demerits as sinners. They must stand and fall by their own account. It was one of Luther's firmest convictions that only Christ can offer vicarious satisfaction to God; the Christian cannot do so. Indeed, there was an inclination on his part (we do not put it more strongly) to think that prayers for our neighbours do more good to ourselves than to them. The Calvinist attitude was similar. 'The Church,' writes Goodykoontz, 'is not co-savior with its Lord.' Calvinism, as it developed in the Anglo-Saxon countries, brought out its inherent individualism in sharp relief. There were, so its divines taught, three phases to the Devil's activity in the world. The first act of the drama was the temptation and the defeat of Adam in the garden. The second was the temptation and the victory of Christ in the wilderness. The third, for which the stage is set only now, is the combat between Good and Evil in each individual breast. Will man be weak like Adam or strong like Christ? Will he fall distressed and humiliated like the one, or rise triumphant like the other? That was the question, and it was one which each had to answer for himself. The struggle between sin and salvation was, according to John Downame, a civil war in our own bowels.[1]

Because this was so, because man had to stand alone while his lower self lured by Satan and his higher self led by Christ fought it out in his members, all that others could do for him was to strengthen the New Adam within his soul and to weaken the Old Adam there who was not willing to die. And this could be done mainly, if not only, by admonition and discipline. The latter tried to hold his wickedness down; the former attempted to lift his spirit up. Hence ministerial action – the word receives here a new and very pregnant meaning – is concerned by preference with these two things. The minister ministers above all to the individual believer's personal self.

Catholicism, as we have seen all along, was much more attuned to collectivistic life and thought. True, even according to this system of ideas, the individual had to seek good and shun evil, otherwise he would not be in a 'state of grace'; and being in a state of grace was, even according to this system of ideas, easiest, if one listened to the Church's doctrine and submitted to the Church's direction. But the root conviction was different. The individual did not have to make up his own mind; he had only to allow himself to be carried by the great stream of redemptive love which was the Church, the mother of all ransomed souls; he had only to allow her life to flow into his; then sin would be washed away and grace take its place. But the life of the Church, the Christ-life of grace, was above all in the sacraments; it was through them (provided they were received with true devotion) that it came to salvation-seeking humanity. 'The Church,' says St. Peter Damian, 'is so knitted together that she is one in many, and that she is wholly contained in each . . . Through the mystery of the sacrament she is believed to be filled by one soul . . . As man is called a microcosm in Greek rhetoric, that is to say, a world in miniature . . . so each of the faithful appears, so to speak, as the Church in miniature when, in the mystery of the hidden unity, he receives all the sacraments of human redemption which are divinely entrusted to the universal Church.' It is the Holy Spirit, the life-giver, who, both uniform and multiform, 'dwells in each and fills out all'; He it is who gives

[1] Cf. Brunotte, loc. cit., pp. 150, 153, 154; Goodykoontz, loc. cit., p. 21; Haller, W., *The Rise of Puritanism*, New York 1938, ed. 1957, pp. 150 et seq. For the quotation, cf. pp. 156 and 388.

one soul and one life to the world-wide society of the redeemed.[1] Not by accident does one word – the word 'life' – constantly push into our pen and try to get on to the paper here; for to the believer the sacraments are life, and unavoidably mysterious precisely because they are life. They are the depth-dimension of the Christian religion, and for this reason Luther and Calvin held on to them, and even to a largely sacramental clerical class. In Catholicism they are the very being of the Church, both individually and collectively considered, both so far as the cell and so far as the body is concerned. The scholar and the scientist can follow them down to the level of the collective subconscious from which they come; the eye of faith may discern beneath that an even deeper depth, an even more fundamental foundation, and that is the very ground of being, Divine Reality Itself.

From this point of view, Catholicism and Protestantism appear as two cultures, kindred and yet differing, which would fain enter into, and take possession of, individual men. As cultures, they have their basic problem in common – the problem which all cultural traditions of history and of the wide world must face, namely how to impose themselves on human nature and contain or control it; in St. Paul's simile, how to purge out the old leaven so that there may be a new paste (I Corinthians V, 7). This endeavour can, in the nature of things, never be more than partially successful. Not only has Christianity failed to engulf the whole world, in spite of St. Augustine's great word that there can be no true Church unless she is spread over all countries and extends herself to the ends of the earth;[2] what is worse, even the conversion of the converted is as yet an unfinished task. There are those whom the same saint, the saintly Bishop of Hippo, calls the *infirmi* and *mortui*, the sick or dead particles in the Body of Christ, whom the life of the whole reaches with diminished force or has failed to carry along.[3] They will always be with us. There are, for instance, the many – only God knows, how many! – who allow a spiritual religion to degenerate into a materialistic superstition, who turn prayer into magic formulae and sacraments into fetishistic objects. While inside the churches, they

---

[1] *Patrologia Latina*, as quoted, vol. CXLV, Paris 1867, cols. 235, 239, 236. Our translation.

[2] *Patrologia Latina*, as quoted, vol. XLIII, Paris 1865, col. 112. Our translation.

[3] Cf. Stark, *Social Theory and Christian Thought*, as quoted, p. 13.

are yet out of them; they are, in a manner, lost. Lost, too, are those who formally and finally leave, who close the doors behind them, who give themselves to a materialism not superstitious but flatly materialistic and will not consider the last things with which religion is concerned. From the point of view of the churches, each such soul is an even greater tragedy than each soul not yet gained. Both, however, are the crucial challenge, the essential mission, of the Christian. This fact is, of course, religious rather than sociological; but it must be emphasized even in a 'Sociology of Religion', if for no other reason, than to show that in the end it is for all religious communities the individual who is at the hub and centre of things, the individual to be won – won and finally kept – for God.

This said, we can quietly turn back to our sociological analysis. For what do we mean when we say, a soul is won for God? We mean that his mind, and his very self, is penetrated by the culture of Christianity, be it the older, strongly collectivistic variant of it which we call Catholicism, be it the newer, comparatively individualistic variant, Protestantism. And what do we mean when we say, a soul is lost to God? We mean that his mind, and his very self, ejects the culture of Christianity and replaces it by another set of assumptions and values, by another mode of experiencing, and reacting to, reality. Culture, however, is a social phenomenon, for it comes to the individual from society, to the enveloped one from the enveloping many. This simple fact gives us a further task. In the present volume we have considered the men who have embraced the Christian religion; in the next we must consider the Christian religion which they have embraced. Our concluding effort, guided by the sociology of knowledge, will be devoted to a study of the types of religious culture.

Index

The International Library of

Sociology

and Social Reconstruction

Edited by W. J. H. SPROTT

Founded by KARL MANNHEIM

ROUTLEDGE & KEGAN PAUL

BROADWAY HOUSE, CARTER LANE, LONDON, E.C.4

CONTENTS

PRINTED IN GREAT BRITAIN BY HEADLEY BROTHERS LTD
109 KINGSWAY LONDON WC2 AND ASHFORD KENT

GENERAL SOCIOLOGY

Brown, Robert. Explanation in Social Science. *208 pp. 1963. (2nd Impression 1964.) 25s.*

Gibson, Quentin. The Logic of Social Enquiry. *240 pp. 1960. (3rd Impression 1968.) 24s.*

Homans, George C. Sentiments and Activities: Essays in Social Science. *336 pp. 1962. 32s.*

Isajiw, Wsevelod W. Causation and Functionalism in Sociology. *165 pp. 1968. 25s.*

Johnson, Harry M. Sociology: a Systematic Introduction. *Foreword by Robert K. Merton. 710 pp. 1961. (5th Impression 1968.) 42s.*

Mannheim, Karl. Essays on Sociology and Social Psychology. *Edited by Paul Keckskemeti. With Editorial Note by Adolph Lowe. 344 pp. 1953. (2nd Impression 1966.) 32s.*

Systematic Sociology: An Introduction to the Study of Society. *Edited by J. S. Erös and Professor W. A. C. Stewart. 220 pp. 1957. (3rd Impression 1967.) 24s.*

Martindale, Don. The Nature and Types of Sociological Theory. *292 pp. 1961. (3rd Impression 1967.) 35s.*

Maus, Heinz. A Short History of Sociology. *234 pp. 1962. (2nd Impression 1965.) 28s.*

Myrdal, Gunnar. Value in Social Theory: A Collection of Essays on Methodology. *Edited by Paul Streeten. 332 pp. 1958. (3rd Impression 1968.) 35s.*

Ogburn, William F., and **Nimkoff, Meyer F.** A Handbook of Sociology. *Preface by Karl Mannheim. 656 pp. 46 figures. 35 tables. 5th edition (revised) 1964. 45s.*

Parsons, Talcott, and **Smelser, Neil J.** Economy and Society: A Study in the Integration of Economic and Social Theory. *362 pp. 1956. (4th Impression 1967.) 35s.*

Rex, John. Key Problems of Sociological Theory. *220 pp. 1961. (4th Impression 1968.) 25s.*

Stark, Werner. The Fundamental Forms of Social Thought. *280 pp. 1962. 32s.*

FOREIGN CLASSICS OF SOCIOLOGY

Durkheim, Emile. Suicide. A Study in Sociology. *Edited and with an Introduction by George Simpson. 404 pp. 1952. (4th Impression 1968.) 35s.*

Professional Ethics and Civic Morals. *Translated by Cornelia Brookfield. 288 pp. 1957. 30s.*

Gerth, H. H., and **Mills, C. Wright.** From Max Weber: Essays in Sociology. *502 pp. 1948. (6th Impression 1967.) 35s.*

Tönnies, Ferdinand. Community and Association. *(Gemeinschaft und Gesellschaft.) Translated and Supplemented by Charles P. Loomis. Foreword by Pitirim A. Sorokin. 334 pp. 1955. 28s.*

SOCIAL STRUCTURE

Andreski, Stanislav. Military Organization and Society. *Foreword by Professor A. R. Radcliffe-Brown. 226 pp. 1 folder. 1954. Revised Edition 1968. 35s.*

Cole, G. D. H. Studies in Class Structure. *220 pp. 1955. (3rd Impression 1964.) 21s. Paper 10s. 6d.*

Coontz, Sydney H. Population Theories and the Economic Interpretation. *202 pp. 1957. (3rd Impression 1968.) 28s.*

Coser, Lewis. The Functions of Social Conflict. *204 pp. 1956. (3rd Impression 1968.) 25s.*

Dickie-Clark, H. F. Marginal Situation: A Sociological Study of a Coloured Group. *240 pp. 11 tables. 1966. 40s.*

Glass, D. V. (Ed.). Social Mobility in Britain. *Contributions by J. Berent, T. Bottomore, R. C. Chambers, J. Floud, D. V. Glass, J. R. Hall, H. T. Himmelweit, R. K. Kelsall, F. M. Martin, C. A. Moser, R. Mukherjee, and W. Ziegel. 420 pp. 1954. (4th Impression 1967.) 45s.*

Jones, Garth N. Planned Organizational Change: An Exploratory Study Using an Empirical Approach. *About 268 pp. 1969. 40s.*

Kelsall, R. K. Higher Civil Servants in Britain: From 1870 to the Present Day. *268 pp. 31 tables. 1955. (2nd Impression 1966.) 25s.*

König, René. The Community. *232 pp. Illustrated. 1968. 35s.*

Lawton, Denis. Social Class, Language and Education. *192 pp. 1968. (2nd Impression 1968.) 25s.*

McLeish, John. The Theory of Social Change: Four Views Considered. *About 128 pp. 1969. 21s.*

Marsh, David C. The Changing Social Structure in England and Wales, 1871-1961. *1958. 272 pp. 2nd edition (revised) 1966. (2nd Impression 1967.) 35s.*

Mouzelis, Nicos. Organization and Bureaucracy. An Analysis of Modern Theories. *240 pp. 1967. (2nd Impression 1968.) 28s.*

Ossowski, Stanislaw. Class Structure in the Social Consciousness. *210 pp. 1963. (2nd Impression 1967.) 25s.*

SOCIOLOGY AND POLITICS

Barbu, Zevedei. Democracy and Dictatorship: Their Psychology and Patterns of Life. *300 pp. 1956. 28s.*

Crick, Bernard. The American Science of Politics: Its Origins and Conditions. *284 pp. 1959. 32s.*

Hertz, Frederick. Nationality in History and Politics: A Psychology and Sociology of National Sentiment and Nationalism. *432 pp. 1944. (5th Impression 1966.) 42s.*

Kornhauser, William. The Politics of Mass Society. *272 pp. 20 tables. 1960. (3rd Impression 1968.) 28s.*

Laidler, Harry W. History of Socialism. Social-Economic Movements: An Historical and Comparative Survey of Socialism, Communism, Co-operation, Utopianism; and other Systems of Reform and Reconstruction. *New edition. 992 pp. 1968. 90s.*

Lasswell, Harold D. Analysis of Political Behaviour. An Empirical Approach. *324 pp. 1947. (4th Impression 1966.) 35s.*

Mannheim, Karl. Freedom, Power and Democratic Planning. *Edited by Hans Gerth and Ernest K. Bramstedt. 424 pp. 1951. (3rd Impression 1968.) 42s.*

Mansur, Fatma. Process of Independence. *Foreword by A. H. Hanson. 208 pp. 1962. 25s.*

Martin, David A. Pacificism: an Historical and Sociological Study. *262 pp. 1965. 30s.*

Myrdal, Gunnar. The Political Element in the Development of Economic Theory. *Translated from the German by Paul Streeten. 282 pp. 1953. (4th Impression 1965.) 25s.*

Polanyi, Michael. F.R.S. The Logic of Liberty: Reflections and Rejoinders. *228 pp. 1951. 18s.*

Verney, Douglas V. The Analysis of Political Systems. *264 pp. 1959. (3rd Impression 1966.) 28s.*

Wootton, Graham. The Politics of Influence: British Ex-Servicemen, Cabinet Decisions and Cultural Changes, 1917 to 1957. *316 pp. 1963. 30s.*
Workers, Unions and the State. *188 pp. 1966. (2nd Impression 1967.) 25s.*

FOREIGN AFFAIRS: THEIR SOCIAL, POLITICAL AND ECONOMIC FOUNDATIONS

Baer, Gabriel. Population and Society in the Arab East. *Translated by Hanna Szöke. 288 pp. 10 maps. 1964. 40s.*

Bonné, Alfred. State and Economics in the Middle East: A Society in Transition. *482 pp. 2nd (revised) edition 1955. (2nd Impression 1960.) 40s.*
Studies in Economic Development: with special reference to Conditions in the Under-developed Areas of Western Asia and India. *322 pp. 84 tables. 2nd edition 1960. 32s.*

Mayer, J. P. Political Thought in France from the Revolution to the Fifth Republic. *164 pp. 3rd edition (revised) 1961. 16s.*

CRIMINOLOGY

Ancel, Marc. Social Defence: A Modern Approach to Criminal Problems. *Foreword by Leon Radzinowicz. 240 pp. 1965. 32s.*

Cloward, Richard A., and **Ohlin, Lloyd E.** Delinquency and Opportunity: A Theory of Delinquent Gangs. *248 pp. 1961. 25s.*

Downes, David M. The Delinquent Solution. A Study in Subcultural Theory. *296 pp. 1966. 42s.*

Dunlop, A. B., and **McCabe, S.** Young Men in Detention Centres. *192 pp. 1965. 28s.*

Friedländer, Kate. The Psycho-Analytical Approach to Juvenile Delinquency: Theory, Case Studies, Treatment. *320 pp. 1947. (6th Impression 1967). 40s.*

Glueck, Sheldon and **Eleanor.** Family Environment and Delinquency. *With the statistical assistance of Rose W. Kneznek. 340 pp. 1962. (2nd Impression 1966.) 40s.*

Mannheim, Hermann. Comparative Criminology: a Text Book. *Two volumes. 442 pp. and 380 pp. 1965. (2nd Impression with corrections 1966.) 42s. a volume.*

Morris, Terence. The Criminal Area: A Study in Social Ecology. *Foreword by Hermann Mannheim. 232 pp. 25 tables. 4 maps. 1957. (2nd Impression 1966.) 28s.*

Morris, Terence and **Pauline,** assisted by **Barbara Barer.** Pentonville: A Sociological Study of an English Prison. *416 pp. 16 plates. 1963. 50s.*

Spencer, John C. Crime and the Services. *Foreword by Hermann Mannheim. 336 pp. 1954. 28s.*

Trasler, Gordon. The Explanation of Criminality. *144 pp. 1962. (2nd Impression 1967.) 20s.*

SOCIAL PSYCHOLOGY

Barbu, Zevedei. Problems of Historical Psychology. *248 pp. 1960. 25s.*

Blackburn, Julian. Psychology and the Social Pattern. *184 pp. 1945. (7th Impression 1964.) 16s.*

Fleming, C. M. Adolescence: Its Social Psychology: With an Introduction to recent findings from the fields of Anthropology, Physiology, Medicine, Psychometrics and Sociometry. *288 pp. 2nd edition (revised) 1963. (3rd Impression 1967.) 25s. Paper 12s. 6d.*

The Social Psychology of Education: An Introduction and Guide to Its Study. *136 pp. 2nd edition (revised) 1959. (4th Impression 1967.) 14s. Paper 7s. 6d.*

Homans, George C. The Human Group. *Foreword by Bernard DeVoto. Introduction by Robert K. Merton. 526 pp. 1951. (7th Impression 1968.) 35s.*

Social Behaviour: its Elementary Forms. *416 pp. 1961. (3rd Impression 1968.) 35s.*

Klein, Josephine. The Study of Groups. *226 pp. 31 figures. 5 tables. 1956. (5th Impression 1967.) 21s. Paper 9s. 6d.*

Linton, Ralph. The Cultural Background of Personality. *132 pp. 1947. (7th Impression 1968.) 18s.*

Mayo, Elton. The Social Problems of an Industrial Civilization. With an appendix on the Political Problem. *180 pp. 1949. (5th Impression 1966.) 25s.*

Ottaway, A. K. C. Learning Through Group Experience. *176 pp. 1966. (2nd Impression 1968.) 25s.*

Ridder, J. C. de. The Personality of the Urban African in South Africa. A Thematic Apperception Test Study. *196 pp. 12 plates. 1961. 25s.*

Rose, Arnold M. (Ed.). Human Behaviour and Social Processes: an Interactionist Approach. *Contributions by Arnold M. Rose, Ralph H. Turner, Anselm Strauss, Everett C. Hughes, E. Franklin Frazier, Howard S. Becker, et al. 696 pp. 1962. (2nd Impression 1968.) 70s.*

Smelser, Neil J. Theory of Collective Behaviour. *448 pp. 1962. (2nd Impression 1967.) 45s.*

Stephenson, Geoffrey M. The Development of Conscience. *128 pp. 1966. 25s.*

Young, Kimball. Handbook of Social Psychology. *658 pp. 16 figures. 10 tables. 2nd edition (revised) 1957. (3rd Impression 1963.) 40s.*

SOCIOLOGY OF THE FAMILY

Banks, J. A. Prosperity and Parenthood: A study of Family Planning among The Victorian Middle Classes. *262 pp. 1954. (3rd Impression 1968.) 28s.*

Bell, Colin R. Middle Class Families: Social and Geographical Mobility. *224 pp. 1969. 35s.*

Burton, Lindy. Vulnerable Children. *272 pp. 1968. 35s.*

Gavron, Hannah. The Captive Wife: Conflicts of Housebound Mothers. *190 pp. 1966. (2nd Impression 1966.) 25s.*

Klein, Josephine. Samples from English Cultures. *1965. (2nd Impression 1967.)*
1. Three Preliminary Studies and Aspects of Adult Life in England. *447 pp. 50s.*
2. Child-Rearing Practices and Index. *247 pp. 35s.*

Klein, Viola. Britain's Married Women Workers. *180 pp. 1965. (2nd Impression 1968.) 28s.*

McWhinnie, Alexina M. Adopted Children. How They Grow Up. *304 pp. 1967. (2nd Impression 1968.) 42s.*

Myrdal, Alva and **Klein, Viola.** Women's Two Roles: Home and Work. *238 pp. 27 tables. 1956. Revised Edition 1967. 30s. Paper 15s.*

Parsons, Talcott and **Bales, Robert F.** Family: Socialization and Interaction Process. *In collaboration with James Olds, Morris Zelditch and Philip E. Slater. 456 pp. 50 figures and tables. 1956. (3rd Impression 1968.) 45s.*

Schücking, L. L. The Puritan Family. *Translated from the German by Brian Battershaw. 212 pp. 1969. About 42s.*

7

THE SOCIAL SERVICES

Forder, R. A. (Ed.). Penelope Hall's Social Services of Modern England. *288 pp. 1969. 35s.*

George, Victor. Social Security: Beveridge and After. *258 pp. 1968. 35s.*

Goetschius, George W. Working with Community Groups. *256 pp. 1969. 35s.*

Goetschius, George W. and **Tash, Joan.** Working with Unattached Youth. *416 pp. 1967. (2nd Impression 1968.) 40s.*

Hall, M. P., and **Howes, I. V.** The Church in Social Work. A Study of Moral Welfare Work undertaken by the Church of England. *320 pp. 1965. 35s.*

Heywood, Jean S. Children in Care: the Development of the Service for the Deprived Child. *264 pp. 2nd edition (revised) 1965. (2nd Impression 1966.) 32s.*

An Introduction to Teaching Casework Skills. *190 pp. 1964. 28s.*

Jones, Kathleen. Lunacy, Law and Conscience, 1744-1845: the Social History of the Care of the Insane. *268 pp. 1955. 25s.*

Mental Health and Social Policy, 1845-1959. *264 pp. 1960. (2nd Impression 1967.) 32s.*

Jones, Kathleen and **Sidebotham, Roy.** Mental Hospitals at Work. *220 pp. 1962. 30s.*

Kastell, Jean. Casework in Child Care. *Foreword by M. Brooke Willis. 320 pp. 1962. 35s.*

Morris, Pauline. Put Away: A Sociological Study of Institutions for the Mentally Retarded. *Approx. 288 pp. 1969. About 50s.*

Nokes, P. L. The Professional Task in Welfare Practice. *152 pp. 1967. 28s.*

Rooff, Madeline. Voluntary Societies and Social Policy. *350 pp. 15 tables. 1957. 35s.*

Timms, Noel. Psychiatric Social Work in Great Britain (1939-1962). *280 pp. 1964. 32s.*

Social Casework: Principles and Practice. *256 pp. 1964. (2nd Impression 1966.) 25s. Paper 15s.*

Trasler, Gordon. In Place of Parents: A Study in Foster Care. *272 pp. 1960. (2nd Impression 1966.) 30s.*

Young, A. F., and **Ashton, E. T.** British Social Work in the Nineteenth Century. *288 pp. 1956. (2nd Impression 1963.) 28s.*

Young, A. F. Social Services in British Industry. *272 pp. 1968. 40s.*

SOCIOLOGY OF EDUCATION

Banks, Olive. Parity and Prestige in English Secondary Education: a Study in Educational Sociology. *272 pp. 1955. (2nd Impression 1963.) 32s.*

Bentwich, Joseph. Education in Israel. *224 pp. 8 pp. plates. 1965. 24s.*

Blyth, W. A. L. English Primary Education. A Sociological Description. *1965. Revised edition 1967.*
1. Schools. *232 pp. 30s. Paper 12s. 6d.*
2. Background. *168 pp. 25s. Paper 10s. 6d.*

Collier, K. G. The Social Purposes of Education: Personal and Social Values in Education. *268 pp. 1959. (3rd Impression 1965.) 21s.*

Dale, R. R., and **Griffith, S.** Down Stream: Failure in the Grammar School. *108 pp. 1965. 20s.*

Dore, R. P. Education in Tokugawa Japan. *356 pp. 9 pp. plates. 1965. 35s.*

Edmonds, E. L. The School Inspector. *Foreword by Sir William Alexander. 214 pp. 1962. 28s.*

Evans, K. M. Sociometry and Education. *158 pp. 1962. (2nd Impression 1966.) 18s.*

Foster, P. J. Education and Social Change in Ghana. *336 pp. 3 maps. 1965. (2nd Impression 1967.) 36s.*

Fraser, W. R. Education and Society in Modern France. *150 pp. 1963. (2nd Impression 1968.) 25s.*

Hans, Nicholas. New Trends in Education in the Eighteenth Century. *278 pp. 19 tables. 1951. (2nd Impression 1966.) 30s.*
Comparative Education: A Study of Educational Factors and Traditions. *360 pp. 3rd (revised) edition 1958. (4th Impression 1967.) 25s. Paper 12s. 6d.*

Hargreaves, David. Social Relations in a Secondary School. *240 pp. 1967. (2nd Impression 1968.) 32s.*

Holmes, Brian. Problems in Education. A Comparative Approach. *336 pp. 1965. (2nd Impression 1967.) 32s.*

Mannheim, Karl and **Stewart, W. A. C.** An Introduction to the Sociology of Education. *206 pp. 1962. (2nd Impression 1965.) 21s.*

Morris, Raymond N. The Sixth Form and College Entrance. *231 pp. 1969. 40s.*

Musgrove, F. Youth and the Social Order. *176 pp. 1964. (2nd Impression 1968.) 25s. Paper 12s.*

Ortega y Gasset, José. Mission of the University. *Translated with an Introduction by Howard Lee Nostrand. 86 pp. 1946. (3rd Impression 1963.) 15s.*

Ottaway, A. K. C. Education and Society: An Introduction to the Sociology of Education. *With an Introduction by W. O. Lester Smith. 212 pp. Second edition (revised). 1962. (5th Impression 1968.) 18s. Paper 10s. 6d.*

Peers, Robert. Adult Education: A Comparative Study. *398 pp. 2nd edition 1959. (2nd Impression 1966.) 42s.*

Pritchard, D. G. Education and the Handicapped: 1760 to 1960. *258 pp. 1963. (2nd Impression 1966.) 35s.*

Richardson, Helen. Adolescent Girls in Approved Schools. *Approx. 360 pp. 1969. About 42s.*

Simon, Brian and **Joan** (Eds.). Educational Psychology in the U.S.S.R. *Introduction by Brian and Joan Simon. Translation by Joan Simon. Papers by D. N. Bogoiavlenski and N. A. Menchinskaia, D. B. Elkonin, E. A. Fleshner, Z. I. Kalmykova, G. S. Kostiuk, V. A. Krutetski, A. N. Leontiev, A. R. Luria, E. A. Milerian, R. G. Natadze, B. M. Teplov, L. S. Vygotski, L. V. Zankov. 296 pp. 1963. 40s.*

SOCIOLOGY OF CULTURE

Eppel, E. M., and M. Adolescents and Morality: A Study of some Moral Values and Dilemmas of Working Adolescents in the Context of a changing Climate of Opinion. *Foreword by W. J. H. Sprott. 268 pp. 39 tables. 1966. 30s.*

Fromm, Erich. The Fear of Freedom. *286 pp. 1942. (8th Impression 1960.) 25s. Paper 10s.*

The Sane Society. *400 pp. 1956. (4th Impression 1968.) 28s. Paper 14s.*

Mannheim, Karl. Diagnosis of Our Time: Wartime Essays of a Sociologist. *208 pp. 1943. (8th Impression 1966.) 21s.*

Essays on the Sociology of Culture. *Edited by Ernst Mannheim in co-operation with Paul Kecskemeti. Editorial Note by Adolph Lowe. 280 pp. 1956. (3rd Impression 1967.) 28s.*

Weber, Alfred. Farewell to European History: or The Conquest of Nihilism. *Translated from the German by R. F. C. Hull. 224 pp. 1947. 18s.*

SOCIOLOGY OF RELIGION

Argyle, Michael. Religious Behaviour. *224 pp. 8 figures. 41 tables. 1958. (4th Impression 1968.) 25s.*

Nelson, G. K. Spiritualism and Society. *313 pp. 1969. 42s.*

Stark, Werner. The Sociology of Religion. A Study of Christendom.
Volume I. Established Religion. *248 pp. 1966. 35s.*
Volume II. Sectarian Religion. *368 pp. 1967. 40s.*
Volume III. The Universal Church. *464 pp. 1967. 45s.*

Watt, W. Montgomery. Islam and the Integration of Society. *320 pp. 1961. (3rd Impression 1966.) 35s.*

SOCIOLOGY OF ART AND LITERATURE

Beljame, Alexandre. Men of Letters and the English Public in the Eighteenth Century: 1660-1744, Dryden, Addison, Pope. *Edited with an Introduction and Notes by Bonamy Dobrée. Translated by E. O. Lorimer. 532 pp. 1948. 32s.*

Misch, Georg. A History of Autobiography in Antiquity. *Translated by E. W. Dickes. 2 Volumes. Vol. 1, 364 pp., Vol. 2, 372 pp. 1950. 45s. the set.*

Schücking, L. L. The Sociology of Literary Taste. *112 pp. 2nd (revised) edition 1966. 18s.*

Silbermann, Alphons. The Sociology of Music. *Translated from the German by Corbet Stewart. 222 pp. 1963. 32s.*

SOCIOLOGY OF KNOWLEDGE

Mannheim, Karl. Essays on the Sociology of Knowledge. *Edited by Paul Kecskemeti. Editorial note by Adolph Lowe. 352 pp. 1952. (4th Impression 1967.) 35s.*

Stark, W. America: Ideal and Reality. The United States of 1776 in Contemporary Philosophy. *136 pp. 1947. 12s.*
The Sociology of Knowledge: An Essay in Aid of a Deeper Understanding of the History of Ideas. *384 pp. 1958. (3rd Impression 1967.) 36s.*
Montesquieu: Pioneer of the Sociology of Knowledge. *244 pp. 1960. 25s.*

URBAN SOCIOLOGY

Anderson, Nels. The Urban Community: A World Perspective. *532 pp. 1960. 35s.*

Ashworth, William. The Genesis of Modern British Town Planning: A Study in Economic and Social History of the Nineteenth and Twentieth Centuries. *288 pp. 1954. (3rd Impression 1968.) 32s.*

Bracey, Howard. Neighbours: On New Estates and Subdivisions in England and U.S.A. *220 pp. 1964. 28s.*

Cullingworth, J. B. Housing Needs and Planning Policy: A Restatement of the Problems of Housing Need and "Overspill" in England and Wales. *232 pp. 44 tables. 8 maps. 1960. (2nd Impression 1966.) 28s.*

Dickinson, Robert E. City and Region: A Geographical Interpretation. *608 pp. 125 figures. 1964. (5th Impression 1967.) 60s.*
The West European City: A Geographical Interpretation. *600 pp. 129 maps. 29 plates. 2nd edition 1962. (3rd Impression 1968.) 55s.*
The City Region in Western Europe. *320 pp. Maps. 1967. 30s. Paper 14s.*

Jackson, Brian. Working Class Community: Some General Notions raised by a Series of Studies in Northern England. *192 pp. 1968. (2nd Impression 1968.) 25s.*

Jennings, Hilda. Societies in the Making: a Study of Development and Redevelopment within a County Borough. *Foreword by D. A. Clark. 286 pp. 1962. (2nd Impression 1967.) 32s.*

Kerr, Madeline. The People of Ship Street. *240 pp. 1958. 28s.*

Mann, P. H. An Approach to Urban Sociology. *240 pp. 1965. (2nd Impression 1968.) 30s.*

Morris, R. N., and Mogey, J. The Sociology of Housing. Studies at Berinsfield. *232 pp. 4 pp. plates. 1965. 42s.*

Rosser, C., and Harris, C. The Family and Social Change. A Study of Family and Kinship in a South Wales Town. *352 pp. 8 maps. 1965. (2nd Impression 1968.) 45s.*

RURAL SOCIOLOGY

Chambers, R. J. H. Settlement Schemes in Africa: A Selective Study. *Approx. 268 pp. 1969. About 50s.*

Haswell, M. R. The Economics of Development in Village India. *120 pp. 1967. 21s.*

Littlejohn, James. Westrigg: the Sociology of a Cheviot Parish. *172 pp. 5 figures. 1963. 25s.*

Williams, W. M. The Country Craftsman: A Study of Some Rural Crafts and the Rural Industries Organization in England. *248 pp. 9 figures. 1958. 25s. (Dartington Hall Studies in Rural Sociology.)*
The Sociology of an English Village: Gosforth. *272 pp. 12 figures. 13 tables. 1956. (3rd Impression 1964.) 25s.*

SOCIOLOGY OF MIGRATION

Humphreys, Alexander J. New Dubliners: Urbanization and the Irish Family. *Foreword by George C. Homans. 304 pp. 1966. 40s.*

SOCIOLOGY OF INDUSTRY AND DISTRIBUTION

Anderson, Nels. Work and Leisure. *280 pp. 1961. 28s.*

Blau, Peter M., and **Scott, W. Richard.** Formal Organizations: a Comparative approach. *Introduction and Additional Bibliography by J. H. Smith. 326 pp. 1963. (4th Impression 1969.) 35s. Paper 15s.*

Eldridge, J. E. T. Industrial Disputes. Essays in the Sociology of Industrial Relations. *288 pp. 1968. 40s.*

Hollowell, Peter G. The Lorry Driver. *272 pp. 1968. 42s.*

Jefferys, Margot, with the assistance of Winifred Moss. Mobility in the Labour Market: Employment Changes in Battersea and Dagenham. *Preface by Barbara Wootton. 186 pp. 51 tables. 1954. 15s.*

Levy, A. B. Private Corporations and Their Control. *Two Volumes. Vol. 1, 464 pp., Vol. 2, 432 pp. 1950. 80s. the set.*

Liepmann, Kate. Apprenticeship: An Enquiry into its Adequacy under Modern Conditions. *Foreword by H. D. Dickinson. 232 pp. 6 tables. 1960. (2nd Impression 1960.) 23s.*

Millerson, Geoffrey. The Qualifying Associations: a Study in Professionalization. *320 pp. 1964. 42s.*

Smelser, Neil J. Social Change in the Industrial Revolution: An Application of Theory to the Lancashire Cotton Industry, 1770-1840. *468 pp. 12 figures. 14 tables. 1959. (2nd Impression 1960.) 50s.*

Williams, Gertrude. Recruitment to Skilled Trades. *240 pp. 1957. 23s.*

Young, A. F. Industrial Injuries Insurance: an Examination of British Policy. *192 pp. 1964. 30s.*

ANTHROPOLOGY

Ammar, Hamed. Growing up in an Egyptian Village: Silwa, Province of Aswan. *336 pp. 1954. (2nd Impression 1966.) 35s.*

Crook, David and **Isabel.** Revolution in a Chinese Village: Ten Mile Inn. *230 pp. 8 plates. 1 map. 1959. (2nd Impression 1968.) 21s.*
The First Years of Yangyi Commune. *302 pp. 12 plates. 1966. 42s.*

Dickie-Clark, H. F. The Marginal Situation. A Sociological Study of a Coloured Group. *236 pp. 1966. 40s.*

Dube, S. C. Indian Village. *Foreword by Morris Edward Opler. 276 pp. 4 plates. 1955. (5th Impression 1965.) 25s.*
India's Changing Villages: Human Factors in Community Development. *260 pp. 8 plates. 1 map. 1958. (3rd Impression 1963.) 25s.*

Firth, Raymond. Malay Fishermen. Their Peasant Economy. *420 pp. 17 pp. plates. 2nd edition revised and enlarged 1966. (2nd Impression 1968.) 55s.*

Gulliver, P. H. The Family Herds. A Study of two Pastoral Tribes in East Africa, The Jie and Turkana. *304 pp. 4 plates. 19 figures. 1955. (2nd Impression with new preface and bibliography 1966.) 35s.*
Social Control in an African Society: a Study of the Arusha, Agricultural Masai of Northern Tanganyika. *320 pp. 8 plates. 10 figures. 1963. (2nd Impression 1968.) 42s.*

Ishwaran, K. Shivapur. A South Indian Village. *216 pp. 1968. 35s.*
Tradition and Economy in Village India: An Interactionist Approach. *Foreword by Conrad Arensburg. 176 pp. 1966. (2nd Impression 1968.) 25s.*

Jarvie, Ian C. The Revolution in Anthropology. *268 pp. 1964. (2nd Impression 1967.) 40s.*

Jarvie, Ian C. and **Agassi, Joseph.** Hong Kong. A Society in Transition. *396 pp. Illustrated with plates and maps. 1968. 56s.*

Little, Kenneth L. Mende of Sierra Leone. *308 pp. and folder. 1951. Revised edition 1967. 63s.*

Lowie, Professor Robert H. Social Organization. *494 pp. 1950. (4th Impression 1966.) 50s.*

Mayer, Adrian C. Caste and Kinship in Central India: A Village and its Region. *328 pp. 16 plates. 15 figures. 16 tables. 1960. (2nd Impression 1965.) 35s.*
Peasants in the Pacific: A Study of Fiji Indian Rural Society. *232 pp. 16 plates. 10 figures. 14 tables. 1961. 35s.*

Smith, Raymond T. The Negro Family in British Guiana: Family Structure and Social Status in the Villages. *With a Foreword by Meyer Fortes. 314 pp. 8 plates. 1 figure. 4 maps. 1956. (2nd Impression 1965.) 35s.*

DOCUMENTARY

Meek, Dorothea L. (Ed.). Soviet Youth: Some Achievements and Problems. *Excerpts from the Soviet Press, translated by the editor. 280 pp. 1957. 28s.*

Schlesinger, Rudolf (Ed.). Changing Attitudes in Soviet Russia.

2. The Nationalities Problem and Soviet Administration. Selected Readings on the Development of Soviet Nationalities Policies. *Introduced by the editor. Translated by W. W. Gottlieb. 324 pp. 1956. 30s.*

Reports of the Institute of Community Studies

(Demy 8vo.)

Cartwright, Ann. Human Relations and Hospital Care. *272 pp. 1964. 30s.*

Patients and their Doctors. A Study of General Practice. *304 pp. 1967. 40s.*

Jackson, Brian. Streaming: an Education System in Miniature. *168 pp. 1964. (2nd Impression 1966.) 21s. Paper 10s.*

Jackson, Brian and **Marsden, Dennis.** Education and the Working Class: Some General Themes raised by a Study of 88 Working-class Children in a Northern Industrial City. *268 pp. 2 folders. 1962. (4th Impression 1968.) 32s.*

Marris, Peter. Widows and their Families. *Foreword by Dr. John Bowlby. 184 pp. 18 tables. Statistical Summary. 1958. 18s.*

Family and Social Change in an African City. A Study of Rehousing in Lagos. *196 pp. 1 map. 4 plates. 53 tables. 1961. (2nd Impression 1966.) 30s.*

The Experience of Higher Education. *232 pp. 27 tables. 1964. 25s.*

Marris, Peter and **Rein, Martin.** Dilemmas of Social Reform. Poverty and Community Action in the United States. *256 pp. 1967. 35s.*

Mills, Enid. Living with Mental Illness: a Study in East London. *Foreword by Morris Carstairs. 196 pp. 1962. 28s.*

Runciman, W. G. Relative Deprivation and Social Justice. A Study of Attitudes to Social Inequality in Twentieth Century England. *352 pp. 1966. (2nd Impression 1967.) 40s.*

Townsend, Peter. The Family Life of Old People: An Inquiry in East London. *Foreword by J. H. Sheldon. 300 pp. 3 figures. 63 tables. 1957. (3rd Impression 1967.) 30s.*

Willmott, Peter. Adolescent Boys in East London. *230 pp. 1966. 30s.*

The Evolution of a Community: a study of Dagenham after forty years. *168 pp. 2 maps. 1963. 21s.*

Willmott, Peter and **Young, Michael.** Family and Class in a London Suburb. *202 pp. 47 tables. 1960. (4th Impression 1968.) 25s.*

Young, Michael. Innovation and Research in Education. *192 pp. 1965. 25s. Paper 12s. 6d.*

Young, Michael and **McGeeney, Patrick.** Learning Begins at Home. A Study of a Junior School and its Parents. *About 128 pp. 1968. 21s. Paper 14s.*

Young, Michael and **Willmott, Peter.** Family and Kinship in East London. *Foreword by Richard M. Titmuss. 252 pp. 39 tables. 1957. (3rd Impression 1965.) 28s.*

The British Journal of Sociology. *Edited by Terence P. Morris. Vol. 1, No. 1, March 1950 and Quarterly. Roy. 8vo., £3 annually, 15s. a number, post free. (Vols. 1-18, £8 each. Individual parts £2 10s.*

All prices are net and subject to alteration without notice

15

1268 H.B.